One God, Three Persons, Four Views

Studies in the Doctrine of God: Exploring Classical and Relational Theism

Studies in the Doctrine of God: Exploring Classical and Relational Theism is a series of books that explore the nature and attributes of God in the context of current debates over classical theism and relational models of God. This series includes volumes that advance the discussion of the doctrine of God, with particular focus on advancing the discussion of conceptions of God that affirm the Creator-creature distinction while also affirming that God is freely and genuinely related to the world in a way that makes a difference to God. Such conceptions of God are sometimes referred to as modified or moderate classical theism or neoclassical theism. These conceptions of God are classical in that they affirm some core tenets of classical theism (divine perfection, necessity, aseity, self-sufficiency, unity, eternity, immutability, omnipotence, omniscience with foreknowledge, and omnipresence). At the same time, such conceptions are also relational in that they affirm God is genuinely related to the world and depart from one or more attributes of (strict) classical theism such as divine timelessness, strict simplicity, strict immutability, and/or strict impassibility. Each volume in this series will address some aspect or aspects of the nature and attributes of God and the God-world relation in a way that advances the discussion of approaches that are both classical and relational in these respects.

SERIES EDITORS:
R. T. Mullins
John C. Peckham

EDITORIAL BOARD:
David Baggett
Daniel Castelo
Paul Copan
Jeanine Diller
Scott Harrower
William Hasker
Veli-Matti Kärkkäinen
Kevin Kinghorn
Andrew Loke
Roger Olson
Anastasia Scrutton
Jordan Wessling

One God, Three Persons, Four Views

A Biblical, Theological, and Philosophical Dialogue on the Doctrine of the Trinity

Edited by
C. A. MCINTOSH

ONE GOD, THREE PERSONS, FOUR VIEWS
A Biblical, Theological, and Philosophical Dialogue on the Doctrine of the Trinity.
Studies in the Doctrine of God

Studies in the Doctrine of God: Exploring Classical and Relational Theism

Copyright © 2024 C. A. McIntosh. All rights reserved. Except for brief quotations in critical publications or reviews, no part of this book may be reproduced in any manner without prior written permission from the publisher. Write: Permissions, Wipf and Stock Publishers, 199 W. 8th Ave., Suite 3, Eugene, OR 97401.

Cascade Books
An Imprint of Wipf and Stock Publishers
199 W. 8th Ave., Suite 3
Eugene, OR 97401

www.wipfandstock.com

PAPERBACK ISBN: 978-1-6667-1905-5
HARDCOVER ISBN: 978-1-6667-1906-2
EBOOK ISBN: 978-1-6667-1907-9

Cataloguing-in-Publication data:

Names: McIntosh, C. A. [editor] | Hasker, William, 1935– [author] | Craig, William Lane [author] | Tuggy, Dale [author] | Branson, Beau [author]

Title: One God, Three Persons, Four Views : a Biblical, Theological, and Philosophical Dialogue on the Doctrine of the Trinity / edited by C. A. McIntosh.

Description: Eugene, OR: Cascade Books, 2024 | Series: Studies in the Doctrine of God | Includes bibliographical references and index.

Identifiers: ISBN 978-1-6667-1905-5 (paperback) | ISBN 978-1-6667-1906-2 (hardcover) | ISBN 978-1-6667-1907-9 (ebook)

Subjects: LCSH: Trinity. | God (Christianity). | Philosophical theology. | Theology, Doctrinal.

Classification: BT111.3 M35 2024 (print) | BT111.3 (ebook)

To Stephen Wykstra, professor extraordinaire

Contents

Acknowledgements ix
Contributors xi
Introduction xiii

I. Main Essays
    Knowing God as Trinity, *William Hasker* | 3
    Tri-Personal Monotheism, *William Lane Craig* | 28
    God and His Word and His Spirit Are One God, *Beau Branson* | 55
    New Testament Theology Is Unitarian, *Dale Tuggy* | 86

II. *Ad* Hasker
    Shall We Proceed? *William Lane Craig* | 115
    One Movement of Three *Hypostases*, *Beau Branson* | 123
    The "Faith Once Delivered"?, *Dale Tuggy* | 133

III. *Ad* Craig
    We Do Need the Processions, *William Hasker* | 145
    Socialist Trinitarianism, *Beau Branson* | 147
    Changing the Subject, Cognitive Faculties, and "God," *Dale Tuggy* | 158

IV. *Ad* Branson
    The One God Is the Trinity, *William Hasker* | 169
    Why Complicate Things?, *William Lane Craig* | 175
    An Ancient, Triadic, Unitarian Theology, *Dale Tuggy* | 183

V. *Ad* Tuggy
    T vs. U? A Mis-Framed Debate, *William Hasker* | 195
    Is Socinianism Biblical?, *William Lane Craig* | 200
    The Icon of the Invisible God, *Beau Branson* | 210

VI. Final Replies
    God Ultimate and Triune, *William Hasker* | 225
    In Defense of Biblical Trinitarianism, *William Lane Craig* | 235
    A Defense of Creedal Trinitarianism, *Beau Branson* | 247
    Facts Are Facts, *Dale Tuggy* | 258

Bibliography | 267
General Index | 281
Scripture Index | 286

Acknowledgements

Besides the present contributors, I want to thank Philip Carey, James Anderson, and Scott Williams for at some point agreeing to contribute, but for one reason or another, it didn't work out. It would have been just as fine of a volume with any of them. Special thanks is owed to Dr. Anderson for giving me feedback on an earlier, much longer version of the introduction, which had to be scrapped. Finally, I want to thank Ryan Mullins for inviting me to revive my idea for a multi-views book on the Trinity, which I told him about years before he was editor of the present series. The fact that he offered me this opportunity over any number of more qualified people speaks volumes to his integrity and good nature.

CAM

Contributors

Beau Branson (PhD, University of Notre Dame) is associate professor of philosophy at Brescia University in Owensboro, Kentucky. His dissertation, "The Logical Problem of the Trinity," focused on the logic and metaphysics involved in St. Gregory of Nyssa's defense of the doctrine of the Trinity. Dr. Branson has published in leading journals, such as *American Catholic Philosophical Quarterly*, *Journal of Applied Logics*, and *TheoLogica*. For more about Dr. Branson's work, visit his website at beaubranson.com.

William Lane Craig (PhD, University of Birmingham; DTheol, Universität München) is visiting scholar of philosophy at Talbot School of Theology and professor of philosophy at Houston Christian University. In addition to authoring over a hundred scholarly articles in professional journals, Dr. Craig has authored or edited over thirty books on the existence and nature of God and the historical Jesus, including *God and Abstract Objects* (2017) and *Atonement and the Death of Christ* (2020). Dr. Craig has proposed a view of the Trinity in his book (co-authored with J. P. Moreland) *Philosophical Foundations for a Christian Worldview* (2003), which he has defended in leading philosophy of religion journals as well as in *Philosophical & Theological Essays on the Trinity* (eds. Thomas McCall and Michael C. Rea, 2009). For more about Dr. Craig's work, visit his website at reasonablefaith.org.

William Hasker (PhD, The University of Edinburgh) is distinguished professor emeritus of philosophy at Huntington University. Dr. Hasker has authored and edited over ten books in the areas of metaphysics, philosophy of mind, and philosophical theology, including *God, Time, and Knowledge* (1989), *The Emergent Self* (1999), *The Triumph of God over Evil* (2008), and *Providence, Evil, and the Openness of God* (2004). In addition to authoring over a dozen articles on the doctrine of the Trinity, Dr. Hasker's most recent book, *Metaphysics and the Tri-Personal God* (2013) is the only stand-alone monograph on the Trinity by a contemporary philosophical theologian, and as such has been widely interacted with since its publication.

Dale Tuggy (PhD, Brown University) was professor of philosophy at SUNY at Fredonia from 2000–2018. Dr. Tuggy has published over a dozen papers on the doctrine of the Trinity in leading journals such as *Faith and Philosophy* and *International Journal for Philosophy of Religion*, criticizing contemporary efforts by theologians and philosophers to defend the doctrine. Dr. Tuggy has recently co-authored (with Christopher Date) *Is Jesus Human and Not Divine?* (2020), and is the author of the *Stanford Encyclopedia of Philosophy* entry, "Trinity." Beginning in 2019, Dr. Tuggy has served as chair of the Board of the Unitarian Christian Alliance. For more about his work, visit his website at trinities.org.

Introduction

WHEN I PITCHED THE idea of doing an independent study on the doctrine of the Trinity to Kelly James Clark my senior year at Calvin College back 2012, he said he thought that was the hardest topic a Christian philosopher could work on. If it isn't the hardest topic, I discovered that it may be the richest: at its heart are metaphysical questions concerning personhood, the one and many, logic, identity, substances, properties, relations, and action; axiological questions concerning the nature of perfection, ultimacy, love and community; and epistemological questions concerning the authority of Scripture and tradition, and the rationality of belief in mystery and paradox. Whew!

But it is one thing to reflect philosophically on the doctrine of the Trinity; it is quite another to bring to those reflections the nuance of a biblical scholar and theologian. Too often we see scholars in their respective disciplines working separately, each producing his or her own lopsided picture. None of the four contributors to this volume can be justly criticized on such grounds. While this is a "four views" book, in that each author defends a distinct view, the contributors were not sought out as representatives of some main view already out there. Rather, they were sought because of the wholistic, interdisciplinary, and rigorous approach that characterizes their work.

One drawback to this editorial decision is that not every "major" view about the Trinity out there is represented. Most conspicuous by its absence is a "Latin" or Thomistic view. I'm sorry for the omission, but my efforts to secure someone (or even a team!) who could pen a robust biblical, theological, and philosophical defense of that view were unsuccessful. Despite this drawback, I'm proud of the volume in your hands, which is anything but a superficial introduction to the topic via a debate format. I believe this volume is a significant contribution to the literature on the doctrine of the Trinity.

Speaking of format: I have asked each contributor to address two questions in the course of presenting his view. First, why think it's true? That is, what justification is there for your view? I have called this the *probative component* of one's view. Second, how does it work? That is, how does your view coherently "hang together"? I have called the this the *model component* of one's view. It was hoped that by addressing both of these components, each contributor would present a reasonably full-orbed view that showcases the interdisciplinary competence spoken of above. The reader is invited to judge their success.

I. Main Essays

1

Knowing God as Trinity

William Hasker

THE CHRISTIAN CHURCH KNOWS God as the Holy Trinity of Father, Son, and Holy Spirit. The task of this essay is to enable an understanding of this doctrine that is as complete and accurate as possible. The task has two main parts: first, to see the reasons for holding the doctrine that God is the Trinity, and second, to arrive at an articulation of the doctrine that is clear and intelligible, and consistent with the scriptural basis for the doctrine and with the doctrinal tradition.

First, however, we need a brief, if overly simple, initial statement of what the doctrine of the Trinity is. The doctrine states that there is one and only one God, but somehow "in" that God there are three entities, traditionally called "Persons,"[1] namely the Father, the Son, and the Holy Spirit. Furthermore, one of these Persons, the Son, has in some way become, or has manifested itself in, a human being, namely Jesus of Nazareth. This statement is elaborated in the doctrine of the incarnation, but without that statement the doctrine of the Trinity would lose its point. And finally, in keeping with the reference to tradition, the mainstream thinking of the Christian churches has recognized an important classical statement of the doctrine in the "Nicene Creed," promulgated by the Council of Constantinople in 381 A.D.

---

1. I will employ the word "Person," with the capital "P" to designate the Trinitarian Three without commitment as to the nature and ontological status of the Persons. When used without the capital, "person" will express our ordinary concept of a person: roughly, a center of consciousness with the capacity for mental states, which may be cognitive, affective, or volitional, and with a capacity for relationships with other persons.

Why Should We Believe in the Trinity?[2]

Why, then, should we Christians believe that God is the Trinity? I say, "we Christians," because non-Christians will typically not have certain other beliefs that are requisite if one is to have a well-grounded belief in the Trinitarian God. To have grounding for belief in the Trinity one must believe that God has been revealed in the Scriptures of the Old and New Testaments, and in particular in the coming into the world of Jesus, and in his teachings, his life, his death, and his resurrection from the dead. These convictions are presupposed in Christian discourse about the Trinity, though of course there are diverse ways of understanding some of these points, ways we shall discuss when we have reached the appropriate stage in our discourse.

Without doubt, the doctrine of the Trinity has its foundation in the Old Testament (OT) doctrine of the one God, the God of Israel. This picture of God is initially set forth in the Pentateuch and is confirmed and amplified in the biblical prophets. God is the unique Creator, unlike the gods of the nations which, if they exist at all, are mere personifications of various natural forces. God, Yahweh, is the only true God, there is no other alongside of him. God is the Lord of history, the true King over all. He reveals himself in the history of Israel, witnessed to by Moses and the prophets. He is Israel's covenant partner, to be obeyed not out of fear but out of love, as towards a father. The OT as a whole provides an exceedingly rich portrayal of this God and of his relationship with his chosen people.

There is also, however, abundant evidence that the Israelites were recalcitrant in their reception of this understanding of God. There were periodic crises where the worship of strange deities became a burning issue, events such as the golden calf at Sinai and the worship of Baal in the northern kingdom under Ahab and Jezebel. But the inclination to supplement or replace the worship of Yahweh with that of other gods was a perennial threat, constantly subjected to prophetic denunciation. In the end, only the wrenching experience of exile was able to convince the Jewish people that their future and their hope lay in the worship of the one true God alone. This situation may provide part of the answer to the question, Why was God not revealed as the Trinity at an earlier stage? Such a revelation, if we can conceive of this as a possibility, would have readily been assimilated to the pantheons of ancient Semitic religions, of Greece and Rome, and the like, and would have made it even more difficult to drive home the uniqueness of the one and only God of Israel.

---

2. This section of the paper corresponds to the "probative component" identified by the editor in his introduction.

Without any doubt, the decisive turning point in this story came in the life and ministry of Jesus. He is portrayed in the Gospel records as having exerted a magnetic influence over crowds of ordinary Palestinian Jews. In part, this was due to his "signs and wonders"—healings and exorcisms—but his teaching also had compelling power; "he taught them as one having authority, and not as their scribes" (Matt 7:29). On numerous occasion he felt the need to tell persons he had healed not to spread word about him, and in particular not to say openly that he was the promised Messiah. This was likely due to his desire to forestall a reaction from the authorities if he were perceived as becoming powerful, and thereby a possible threat to those same authorities. Eventually, however, such a reaction inevitably occurred—in the first instance, from Jewish leaders who feared their own authority was being usurped, but then also from the Roman rulers who feared a possible Jewish uprising. As a result, Jesus was sentenced to death by crucifixion, which should have decisively ended the "Jesus movement." In fact, however, his followers were soon proclaiming that he had been raised from the dead, and, far from disappearing, the movement gained momentum and began to spread.

Our record of these events is found in the writings of the New Testament (NT), and it is in these writings, however they are to be interpreted, that we must look for the primary theological basis for the doctrine of the Trinity. The earliest of these writings are letters from the apostle Paul. The letters show clearly what Paul took the message concerning Jesus to be, and they also shed light on the very earliest years of the Jesus movement, at a time before Paul had come to play an important role in that movement.[3] These letters were probably written in the 50s but take us back to the time of his conversion, within a year or two of the crucifixion. Paul is emphatic in his scornful rejection of the pagan deities and the worship practices directed at them, and insists that his converts take no part in such practices ("You cannot drink the cup of the Lord and the cup of demons" [1 Cor 10:21]). Clearly, he thought of himself as continuing the Jewish insistence on the exclusive worship of the one God. At the same time, however, the place occupied by Jesus in his thought, and in the worship practices of the communities he established, was unprecedented in earlier Jewish experience. Jesus was "Christ," the Jewish Messiah. He was also "the Son of God." Perhaps most significantly, he was *ho Kyrios*, "the Lord." To be sure, *kyrios* was used in Greek as a respectful term of address, equivalent to "sir" or "master." But it was also a reverential term addressed to deities. More than this, however,

---

3. In what follows I shall make extensive use of Larry Hurtado, *Lord Jesus Christ*. Hurtado provides thorough justification for relying on Paul in this connection, though he also considers several additional sources.

it was the Greek word commonly used as the translation for the tetragrammaton, YHWH, which by that time was no longer pronounced by Jewish worshipers. Paul himself uses *Kyrios* to designate God, and it functions for him as a Greek substitute for God's name. Hurtado points out that "it is remarkable that, in other citations of OT passages which originally have to do with God, Paul applies the passages to Jesus, making him the *Kyrios*: Romans 10:13 (Joel 2:32), 1 Corinthians 1:31 (Jer 9:23–24), 1 Corinthians 10:26 (Ps 24:1), 2 Corinthians 10:17 (Jer 9:23–24)."[4]

There is also the amazing christological passage Philippians 2:5–11, which I quote in full:

> Let the same mind be in you that was in Christ Jesus
> who, though he was in the form of God,
> > did not regard equality with God
> > as something to be exploited,
> > but emptied himself,
> > taking the form of a slave,
> > being born in human likeness.
>
> And being found in human form,
> > he humbled himself
> > and became obedient to the point of death—
> > even death on a cross.
>
> Therefore God also highly exalted him
> > and gave him the name
> > that is above every name,
> > so that at the name of Jesus
> > every knee should bend,
> > in heaven and on earth and under the earth,
> > and every tongue should confess
> > that Jesus Christ is Lord,
> > to the glory of God the Father. (NRSV)

Here we have Jesus' pre-existence in an exalted state, describable as "in the form of God" (*en morphē theou*), and as "equality with God" (*to einai isa theō*). This is followed by his voluntary self-humbling, and the exaltation subsequently bestowed on him. The depiction of that exaltation makes reference to Isaiah 45:23, where God avows that "To me every knee shall bow, every tongue shall swear" (NRSV). The universal acknowledgment and obeisance that in Isaiah is directed to God, *is now to be given to Jesus*. Two additional points can be made concerning this passage. First, 2:6–11 is widely recognized as having been an early Christian hymn, one that

---

4. Hurtado, *Lord Jesus Christ*, 112.

likely originated much earlier than the epistle in which it is preserved. But secondly, it is noteworthy that Paul *feels no need to explain or justify* these christological affirmations, or the application of the Isaiah passage to Christ. Rather, they are taken for granted as matters that will be readily understood and accepted by his readers, and can thus be made the basis for an appeal to them to exhibit similar humility and self-sacrifice. The constellation of beliefs, about God and about Jesus, that are in evidence here (and in other early Christian writings) has been termed by several scholars "christological monotheism"—it is a monotheism in which *Jesus is honored and reverenced along with God* in a way that is unprecedented in pre-Christian Judaism.[5]

Hurtado goes on to point out features of the worship practices of the early Pauline Christians which show the remarkable place given to Jesus. There is prayer that is offered *through Jesus*—and at times, directly *to* Jesus. There are hymns about Jesus and to Jesus. There is the *invocation* of Jesus, memorably shown in 1 Corinthians 16:22, in the prayer *marana tha*, Aramaic for "Our Lord, come!" Apparently this Aramaic expression was so well known to Paul's gentile converts in Corinth that there was no need for translation or explanation; it must already have become a familiar part of their worship practice. Christians were to confess that "Jesus is Lord." They were baptized "in Jesus' name." There is the Lord's Supper, the "Christian cult meal where the Lord Jesus plays a role that is explicitly likened to that of the deities of the pagan cults and, even more astonishingly to the role of God!"[6] Hurtado concludes that "when this constellation of devotional actions is set in the general first-century religious context, it is properly understood as constituting the cultic worship of Jesus."[7] What we have here, in fact, is a pattern of "binitarian worship"—and one that originated surprisingly early in the newborn Christian movement. A striking portrayal of such binitarian worship can be found in the slightly later book of Revelation. The author is intent on discouraging his readers from any compromise with idolatry, in the form of the emperor cult; he pleads with them to "be faithful unto death" (2:10) if need be. He condemns the worship of "false and invalid objects

---

5. Richard Bauckham states, "The concern of early Christology was not to conform Jesus to some pre-existing model of an intermediary figure subordinate to God. The concern of early Christology, from its root in the exegesis of Psalm 110:1 and related texts, was to understand the identification of Jesus with God. Early Jewish monotheism provided little precedent for such a step, but it was so defined and so structured as to be open for such a development." See Bauckham, "Throne of God and the Worship of Jesus," 64.

6. Hurtado, *Lord Jesus Christ*, 146.

7. Hurtado, *Lord Jesus Christ*, 138.

of devotion (e.g., 9:2–21; 13:4; 14:9–11)."[8] And the exalted angels who are instructing the seer specifically forbid his offering worship to them (19:10; 22:8–9). Yet in 5:11–13 we find the heavenly host *worshiping the Lamb along with God*: "Worthy is the Lamb that was slaughtered to receive power and wealth and wisdom and might and honor and glory and blessing! . . . To the one seated on the throne *and to the Lamb* be blessing and honor and glory and might forever and ever!" Without doubt, this description of the heavenly worship provided a template for the worship that was to be offered, and that was in fact offered, in the churches for whom the book was written.

Paul's gentile churches were not, of course, the very first Christian groups, and many scholars have thought to find a divergence between them and the early Jewish circles of Christianity. Often, furthermore, the high Christology evident in Paul's letters has been seen as the result of a gradual development that was heavily dependent on the general religious environment, especially the mystery cults. The evidence, however, provides little support for these speculations. The sharp opposition to pagan religious practices among first-century Jews, including Paul, argues against any major borrowing from pagan sources. What we can learn about the early Jewish Christian groups, both from Paul's letters and from the accounts in Acts, shows a devotion to Christ that is very much in line with what we find in the Pauline churches. There is actually a rather powerful argument from silence here, based on what Paul does *not* say on this subject. Paul was hardly timid or reticent in expressing his views when the faith he was promulgating was challenged! Indeed, his rhetoric became almost violent at times, as seen especially in Galatians. His polemics were directed especially at the "Judaizers"—those who insisted that, in order to be fully accepted into the Christian movement, gentile converts must be circumcised and obey the Mosaic law. But there is in Paul almost a complete absence of controversy over his views concerning Jesus Christ. These matters are treated as well known and able to be taken for granted: "there is hardly any indication in Paul's letters that he knew of any controversy or serious variance about this exalted place of Jesus among the various other Christian circles with which he was acquainted."[9] Rather than showing evidence of a division between his own churches and the Jewish Christians of Judea, Paul's letters reveal that he was anxious to maintain fellowship between them, as shown especially in the collection for the Jerusalem Christians to which he devoted so much effort.

---

8. Hurtado, *Lord Jesus Christ*, 593.
9. Hurtado, *Lord Jesus Christ*, 135.

The early date at which these developments appear is also remarkable. Many scholars are eager to find an early group of "Jesus people" who reverenced Jesus as a wise teacher and leader, but did not subscribe to, and may have been unaware of, the high Christology that appeared later on. Such groups, however, seem not to have left any historical traces, if indeed they ever existed. Hurtado states, "In historical terms we may refer to a veritable 'big bang,' an explosively rapid and impressively substantial Christological development in the earliest stage of the Christian movement."[10] According to Martin Hengel, "The time between the death of Jesus and the fully developed Christology which we find in the earliest Christian documents, the letters of Paul, is so short that the development which takes place within it can only be called amazing."[11]

There is of course much, much more that could be said about all this. A full description of the NT witness to Christ would fill many volumes; indeed, entire libraries. Further discussion will be found in the essays by the other contributors, and we may need to return to some points in responding to criticism—especially, one may suppose, in the criticisms that will be raised by Dale Tuggy. By way of summary at this point, however, it may be helpful to list briefly several of the distinctive ways in which the NT writers express their exaltation of Jesus. This will be followed by an outline of the main ways in which later Christian authors have understood these affirmations.

New Testament Affirmations concerning Jesus

i. Jesus is the Christ (=Messiah)

ii. Jesus is the Son of God

iii. Jesus is the Lord (*Kyrios*, sometimes =Yahweh)

iv. Jesus is pre-existent

v. Jesus is Creator (John 1:3; Heb 1:2)

vi. Jesus is the Savior who died for our sins

vii. Jesus is the recipient, along with God, of "binitarian worship"

viii. Jesus is God (John 1:1, 18; 20:28; Rom 9:5; Titus 2:13; 2 Pet 1:1)[12]

---

10. Hurtado, *Lord Jesus Christ*, 135.

11. In Hengel, *Jesus and Paul*, 31, cited by Hurtado, *Lord Jesus Christ*, 135.

12. See the essay by William Craig for a discussion of these passages.

Responses to the Affirmations

Given this stunning constellation of affirmations, each person is faced with Jesus' challenge, "Who do you say that I am?" Clearly, there are many possible answers to that question. However, the answers that have been historically important fall into three main groups:

Unitarian Answers

Jesus is ontologically merely human, though a specially gifted and divinely empowered human. This answer, however, groups together two quite different classes of interpreters. *Classical Unitarians* believe their understanding of Jesus is consistent with what the NT says about Jesus, rightly understood. This means that the affirmations are to be understood, wherever possible, in ways that are not inconsistent with his ontological status as a human being and nothing more. For instance, it is pointed out that various entities other than God are said to be "worshipped," and it is entirely possible (though perhaps surprising) that God should command that a mere human being, Jesus, be worshipped alongside of God. In other cases, where what is said about Jesus clearly exceeds what could be true of any merely human person (for instance, that he is the pre-existent Creator), the real subject of the assertion is not Jesus the man but some divine aspect or attribute (such as the divine Wisdom) which is said to be embodied in him.

In contrast with this, *liberal Unitarians* do not claim to accept as literally true all that the NT affirms concerning Jesus. They adopt the stance referred to in the summary given above, whereby Jesus was originally a human teacher, leader, and example, who became the focus of a movement within Palestinian Judaism. The more extravagant claims later made about him cannot and should not be taken as literally true; indeed, they might have scandalized Jesus himself. These claims can be retained, if at all, only in a heavily "demythologized" version that expresses the importance of Jesus for his followers today, but not as literal truths about his divine or quasi-divine status.

Historically, Unitarians play a very small role in the history of the ancient Christian church; they barely earn a brief mention in the history of Christian thought. (One possible example is Paul of Samosota, c. 260, sometimes described as a "dynamic monarchian.") Classical Unitarians play a role in modern church history, but have failed to establish themselves as a major force in the church—very likely, one might think, because the actual contents of the NT make such a view very difficult to sustain. At present there is a rather small cohort of "biblical Unitarians," a group of which Dale Tuggy is a distinguished member. In contrast, liberal Unitarianism is central to the story of liberal Christianity, from Kant, Hegel, and Schleiermacher to Ritschl, Harnack, and on down to the present. This is so, whether or not the individuals in question wear the label "Unitarian." For Unitarians of both sorts, the doctrine of the Trinity is a mistake, which may be ignored, ridiculed, or subjected to scholarly criticism, depending on which stance seems more advantageous.

Subordinationist ("Arian") Answers

Jesus is a supremely great, supernatural being and can be called "God" in a secondary sense, but ontologically he is a creature, not God. All of the NT affirmations need to be understood with this proviso. Subordinationism in its various forms (typically called "Arianism") was a major issue in the ancient church; it was the struggle with Arianism that led to the formulation of the Nicene Creed, with its famous pronouncement that Christ is *homoousios* ("of the same substance") with the Father. Arianism made a reappearance in the early modern period (Isaac Newton and Samuel Clarke, among others, were Arians), but it failed to establish itself in the church, and it plays no role in the main Christian churches today. (The Jehovah's Witnesses, however, maintain an Arian presence on the current religious scene.)

Trinitarian (and Proto-Trinitarian) Answers

All of the items in the NT witness to Jesus are fully accepted; Jesus is "God" in precisely the same sense in which the Father is God. This is then extended to the Holy Spirit, so that all three are God in the same sense (*homoousios*). This conviction becomes the fundamental source of the doctrine of the Trinity. With regard to some early thinkers we may better speak of "proto-Trinitarianism," because while Jesus is in some way of the same nature as the Father, this is qualified or compromised in a way that is somewhat reminiscent of subordinationism. Thus, Tertullian held that the Son is formed *from a portion of* the Father's substance, and Origen held that the Son *participates in* the Father's divine nature. The issues here were not fully resolved until the fourth century, and in acknowledgement of this fact we may speak of "proto-Trinitarianism."

The position taken in this essay is that the Trinitarian answer to Jesus' question, "Who do you say that I am?" is the right one, and that further constructive thinking on these topics needs to proceed along these lines.

Indeed, this answer may be taken as the fulfillment of the promise given in John 16:13-14: "the Spirit of truth . . . will guide you into all the truth. . . . He will glorify me, because he will take what is mine and declare it to you." If this promise has been fulfilled, where better should we look for the fulfillment than in the doctrines of Trinity and Incarnation? These doctrines concern what is absolutely central to the Christian message, and to the Christian understanding of God. And here, more than anywhere else, there is genuine consensus among all the main Christian churches. The remainder of the essay is devoted to working out the implications of this fundamental conviction.

Constructing the Doctrine of the Trinity[13]

Once the doctrine of the Trinity has been formulated it should be possible to understand it as an organic, unified whole, not as a collection of bits carefully pieced together. While the doctrine is under construction, however, there is merit in building it up step by step in a series of distinct propositions. In this way the process of constructing the doctrine is made transparent; furthermore, if difficulties appear it should be easier to pick out the particular point at which they arise. There is no one best way in which this should be done; it is hoped that the series of steps indicated here will help the reader to grasp clearly what is going on.[14]

  1. *Jesus is the eternal divine Son.*

In Hebrews 1:2 we read, "in these last days [God] has spoken to us by a Son . . . through whom also he created the worlds." And in John 17:3, Jesus asks the Father to "glorify me in your own presence with the glory that I had in your presence before the world existed." This man, Jesus, is the *same identical person* who shared the Father's glory from all eternity and who participated, along with the Father, in the creation of the universe. This is of course an absolutely amazing, indeed astonishing, affirmation, but one that we must come to terms with if we are to embrace the witness of the NT to Jesus Christ. And it immediately presents to us a question: How is it possible that a human being, one who was born in ancient Palestine and lived there

---

13. This section of the paper corresponds to the "model component" identified by the editor.

14. A somewhat different series of steps is found in Hasker, *Metaphysics and the Tri-Personal* God, 177–258. The differences result in part from the fact that in that book the starting-point is taken in the Nicene doctrine of the Trinity, as seen in Gregory of Nyssa and Augustine, rather than building up from the NT writings, as is done here.

a human life, could be the *very same individual* that co-existed with the heavenly Father from all eternity? This, of course, is the central question of Christology—the issue that became the central item in the church's theological agenda once the Trinitarian issue had been settled by the Council of Constantinople. The accepted answer to this question was given by the council convened at Chalcedon in 451—but that answer goes beyond what can be discussed in this essay on the Trinity.

Over and above its inherently marvelous and astonishing content, this affirmation concerning Jesus has important epistemological implications. If Jesus is the eternal divine Son, then *the words and deeds of Jesus are the words and deeds of the Son.* And this in turn implies that *everything said about Jesus in the Gospels reveals the life of the eternal Son.* This means that much, much more is available to us than would be the case if we were to rely merely on the comparatively few—and some might think, comparatively obscure—direct references to the Son's pre-incarnate life and activity. Here we see the full force of the assertion that God "has spoken to us by a Son." *If God wishes to speak to us humans, this is likely to go far better if he speaks a language we have some ability to grasp*—the language of a human life.

2. *The Holy Spirit is a third, fully divine, Person along with the Father and the Son.*

The Holy Spirit is by no means absent or obscure in the pages of the NT. The Spirit came upon the virgin Mary in the conception of Jesus. He descended upon Jesus at his baptism in the form of a dove, and Jesus' followers were baptized with the Spirit. On the day of Pentecost he filled the disciples and enabled them to speak in many different languages. In the newly established church he conferred the charismatic gifts, such as healing and prophecy, and also produced in the disciples the fruits such as love, joy, peace, and the like.

All these references, however, are concerned mainly with the *activity* of the Spirit; they do not reveal a focused reflection on the *nature* of the Spirit, comparable to what we have seen in the case of Jesus. Many of these passages are compatible with an understanding of the Spirit as an impersonal force, or perhaps as simply an aspect or attribute of God. Unlike Jesus, the Spirit is not made the recipient of worship. Compared with the Son, less is available in answer to the question concerning the Spirit's nature.

However, indications along this line are not altogether lacking; there are indeed statements that point to a role and position for the Spirit comparable to that of the Father and the Son. The Spirit "sighs deeply," as he intercedes for believers (Rom 8:26-27), this surely represents the Spirit as a person with desires and emotions. The Spirit can be "lied to" (Acts 5:3) or "outraged" (Heb 10:29); both are sorts of actions that can only meaningfully be directed at persons. Especially telling is John 15:16–17: "I will ask the Father, and he will give you another Advocate, to be with you forever. This is the Spirit of truth." Another Advocate, replacing Jesus himself, must surely be another *person;* it would make little sense to say this of an impersonal force. And this Advocate is *equal in status and excellence to Jesus himself,* so that the coming of this Advocate is adequate compensation—indeed, *more* than adequate—for the loss of Jesus' own bodily presence with his disciples (16:7). Finally, there are a number of occurrences in the NT of three-fold formulas, such as the command to baptize disciples "in the name of the Father and of the Son and of the Holy Spirit" (Matt 28:19). These formulas would make little sense if the nature and status of the Spirit were conceived as radically different than that of the Father and the Son. Altogether, there is no reason to demur from the decision of the church to group together Father, Son, and Spirit as the Trinity of Persons in God.

> 3. *The Persons of the Trinity, the Father, the Son, and the Holy Spirit, are persons.*

That is to say, they are centers of consciousness with the capacity for cognitive, affective, and volitional mental states, as well as the capacity for relationships with other persons. And with this we have arrived at a conclusion with regard to one of the fraught questions in contemporary Trinitarian theorizing, the question of "social" vs. "psychological"—or, as some would prefer, "Latin"—Trinitarianism. But in spite of its contested character, this conclusion emerges almost without effort from the propositions already accepted. We have seen that, given standard assumptions concerning Trinitarian reasoning, the words and deeds of Jesus are the words and deeds of the eternal divine Son. From this it follows that the relationship between Jesus and his heavenly Father is correctly understood as a *relationship between Father and Son within the Trinity.* But who can doubt that this relationship, as it is portrayed in all four Gospels, is a *personal* relationship, the sort of relationship that could only exist *between persons,* as we are understanding the notion of a person? And the more limited evidence we have concerning the Holy Spirit, as noted above, also points in the direction of actions and attitudes that only make sense if attributed to a person.

Understanding the Trinitarian Persons as persons also resonates with the biblical description of God as love (1 John 4:8), and with Jesus' presentation of love as the fundamental demand God makes of us (Matt 22:36–40). If love is in this way fundamental to the structure of reality, it seems fitting, to say the least, to represent the inner life of God as one of loving relationships between the Father, the Son, and the Holy Spirit. If this is not present—if, as some would have it, God is and must be only a single person—then the only love possible for God in his aloneness is self-love. And while self-love is a right and proper thing, self-love by itself falls far short of the richness that is possible in love directed to persons other than oneself. Taking this line tends to push us in the direction of saying that God of necessity creates a world in order to have an appropriate object for his love. This, however, is a direction that mainstream Christian theology has been very reluctant to go.

Another point that bears mentioning here is that Trinitarian opponents of Social Trinitarianism have great difficulty in formulating a different account of divine Personhood that provides some sort of alternative understanding. One of the more popular alternatives is to say that the Persons are "modes of being" (Barth) or "modes of subsistence" (Rahner) of the one person, God. This translates the ancient Greek expression, *tropoi hyparxeos*. It does not, however, capture the meaning of that expression as used by the Greek fathers. Originally, the expression was not meant to tell us what a Person *is*, but rather to indicate the specific *way of existing* of the various Persons—for the Son, for instance, the way of being generated by the Father. Considered as a statement of what a Trinitarian Person *is*, the expression is remarkably uninformative. It signals that the Persons are objectively different from each other in some way other than by being different *persons*, but fails to give us any positive indication of what this difference amounts to.[15]

All this having been said, it must still be acknowledged that the representation of the divine Persons as persons remains intensely controversial. Given the space limitations of this essay, a full exploration of the issues and arguments at this point is impossible. Still, I will mention a few of the lines that have been taken in arguing against a social conception of the Trinity, and will indicate very briefly the responses that can be made to these arguments.

One point of some importance is that our modern, psychological conception of a person did not exist in ancient times, and that it is anachronistic to attribute this conception to early Christian authors. Up to a point, this is well taken; we do need to avoid reading modern conceptions of personhood into ancient sources. It can be argued, however, that the minimal conception of personhood I have appealed to is part of the basic conceptual equipment

---

15. Another attempt, which I have to admit I find amusing, is proffered by Sarah Coakley: Father, Son, and Spirit are "personal entities so subtly distinguishable qua inherent relations that one can at best talk of each attracting the possibility of verb-forms, and then only in mutual 'co-inherence' with each other." See Coakley, *God, Sexuality, and the Self*, 321.

of human beings as such. If we limit ourselves to this basic, limited, conception we need not be guilty of anachronism in our interpretations.

It has been argued, however, that in interpreting Gregory of Nyssa and Augustine, for example, as Social, or pro-Social, Trinitarians we are misinterpreting their writings. To this, my response is one of stout denial![16] It is significant that Gregory embraces the "three men" analogy for the Trinity, a move that decisively favors the social interpretation. With regard to Augustine, it is true that much of his *De Trinitate* is occupied with the elaboration of "psychological analogies" for the Trinity, most prominently memory, understanding, and will. But much of the fifteenth and last book is occupied with complaints that these analogies fail to accomplish what is needed. He concludes, "the three things of one person were quite unable to match those three persons . . . as we have been demonstrating in this fifteenth book."[17] We Social Trinitarians will agree!

Without doubt, the most important objection to Social Trinitarianism is that this view simply does not give us a strong enough affirmation of divine unity to count as monotheism. In the nature of the case, this objection does not admit of a neat, concise answer. Much of the remainder of this essay will be occupied with presenting the case for a Social Trinitarianism that is genuinely monotheistic. However, there is a concise argument that ought to make Christians hesitant to affirm that a three-self Trinity cannot be monotheistic:

(1) The beliefs and worship practices of the early Christian communities, as depicted in the writings of the NT constitute a valid and acceptable form of monotheism.

(2) The early Christians perceived God the Father and Jesus Christ as distinct persons—as distinct centers of knowledge, will, love, and action.

(3) The early Christians exhibit a pattern of "binitarian" belief and worship, in which Jesus is honored, praised, and worshiped along with God the Father.

(4) No non-divine person can properly be the recipient of divine worship. Therefore,

(5) There is a valid and acceptable version of monotheism in which there is more than one divine person.

---

16. For Gregory, see my *Metaphysics and the Tri-Personal God*, 26–39; and for Augustine, see 40–49.

17. Augustine, *On the Trinity* 15:435.

Moving on, then, to the fourth step in the process of constructing the doctrine:

> 4. *The Persons of the Trinity, the Father, the Son, and the Holy Spirit, are together the one God.*

In saying this, we for the first time go clearly beyond what is said in the NT. Yet, what is thus said is unavoidable and essential for a viable doctrine of the Trinity. Let me explain.

This proposition goes beyond the NT for a simple linguistic reason: There is not in the NT any word for "Trinity," nor is the word "God" ever used for the group of Father, Son, and Spirit. In the vast majority of cases, the individual designated by "God" is the Father. (As we have seen, there is a smaller number of very important instances in which the Son is said to be "God.") Nevertheless, it is essential to identify the entire Trinity as God if Trinitarianism is to be a form of monotheism. If we insist on the identification of the one God with the Father alone, and if we also assert that the Son and the Spirit are fully divine (as we must if we are to be Trinitarians), we will have, *in addition to God*, two other fully divine Persons. This, it seems, is no longer monotheism. Or if not that, then we must demote the Son and the Spirit to a sort of quasi-divine status—but that is to abandon Trinitarianism for subordinationism or Arianism. What shall we make of this perplexing situation?

At this point a bit of historical perspective is required. Recall the words from Hebrews: "God has spoken to us through a Son." The revelation that led to the doctrine of the Trinity did not consist in a prophet laying out a creed for believers to memorize and recite. That revelation consisted, in the first instance, in an *event*, the event of God's Son coming into the world. Prior to this event, for faithful Jews "God" could only designate Yahweh, the One God of Israel. During Jesus' lifetime this usage continued; he did not teach his disciples to pray to the Trinity, but rather to the Father in heaven. And this usage naturally extended beyond Jesus' lifetime, into the practice of the early church. Jesus was the "Son of God," where clearly, God = the Father. But as Jesus' own divine status was more and more clearly recognized, a linguistic shift was needed to match this major transition in the Christians' comprehension of the divine. This shift, however, did not take the form of simply abandoning the former usage: the Christians thought of themselves as continuing, not abandoning, the faith of Jewish monotheism. So "God" continued to be used primarily to refer to the Father, but with various other linguistic devices to indicate the exalted place now attributed to the Son. Sometimes the Son is initially referred to as "Lord," but is subsequently said explicitly to be "God," that is to say divine.[18] In other cases (for instance, in the baptismal formula given by Jesus), the first Person is called simply the Father, avoiding the appearance of inequality that results if only the first Person is termed "God." Eventually, however, the pressure of the situation led to the explicit identification of "God," in the most fundamental sense, with the Trinity as a whole. As Gregory of Nazianzen said, "When we say God, we mean Father, Son, and Holy Ghost."[19]

Finally, it must be acknowledged that there is even today a variety of Trinitarianism, called by its adherents "Monarchical" Trinitarianism, that still insists on using "God," in a nominative sense, as referring only to the Father. This in fact is the view to which Beau Branson subscribes; we shall need to learn from his essay how he proposes to resolve the problems that result from this usage.

> 5. *The divine Persons enjoy the closest possible communion and interpenetration.*

In saying this we continue the task of explaining the unique unity that enables the Trinity of Persons to be described as, and to be, one single God. This communion and interpenetration of the Persons is often expressed by the Greek word, *perichoresis*, sometimes translated as "co-inherence." This idea takes us quite a bit of the way towards a positive understanding of the unity of the Persons. C. F. J. Williams, citing a poem by Browning in which a lover achieves perfect spiritual union with his beloved, but only for a "good minute," writes

> The life of God is for all eternity, I suggest, what Browning's lover achieved only for a minute. Each of the Persons of the Trinity has knowledge and will of his own, but is entirely open to those of the other, so that each adopts those of the other, sees with his eyes, as it were.[20]

Here, however, a further problem raises its head. Some writers, citing patristic assertions about "one will" between the Persons of the Trinity, have concluded that there is literally only *one set of mental actions* for all three Persons. But this conflicts with the claim that the Persons are *persons*. That claim implies, as Augustine recognized, that each Person has *his own*, personal, will; it is not enough that they share a single, common will between them.

---

18. Both the Gloria and the Nicene Creed are instances of this.
19. Quoted by Wright, "On Whether or How Far We Can Know God," 115.
20. Williams, "Neither Confounding the Persons nor Dividing the Substance," 240. For a bit more on Williams' views, see my *Metaphysics and the Tri-Personal God*, 204–5.

The interpretation of the "one will" assumed in this objection is, however, mistaken. The one will shared by Father, Son, and Spirit is a *common purpose* between the Persons; it is impossible that one Person should be resisting, or indeed failing to fully cooperate with, something that another Person is working to achieve. This does not, however, preclude that the different Persons may be *doing different things* in order to achieve that common purpose. According to Gregory of Nyssa, "every activity which pervades from God to creation . . . *starts off* from the Father, *proceeds* through the Son, and *is completed* by the Holy Spirit."[21] Here the "activity" is the common objective—the common project, as we might say—and the different verbs represent the different things that may be done by the Persons in pursuit of that project. Gregory goes on to illustrate:

> For as when we learn concerning the God of the universe, from the words of Scripture, that He judges all the earth, we say that He is the Judge of all things through the Son: and again, when we hear that the Father judgeth no man, we do not think that the Scripture is at variance with itself,—(for He Who judges all the earth does this by His Son to Whom He has committed all judgment; and everything which is done by the Onlybegotten has its reference to the Father, so that He Himself is at once the Judge of all things and judges no man, by reason of His having, as we said, committed all judgment to the Son).[22]

Here the Son exercises his individual will by judging, and the Father exercises his own will, not by himself judging, but by delegating the task of judging to the Son. All is in harmony, but the Persons have their distinct personal wills, and exercise them in distinct ways.

> 6. *The Son is eternally generated from the Father; the Spirit eternally proceeds from the Father.*[23]

The communion of the Persons, though of great importance, is not in itself sufficient to allay all possible concerns concerning the unity of the Trinity. For it is conceivable, or at least imaginable, that the three Persons have diverse origins, and only subsequently enter into the intimate union expressed in the doctrine of *perichoresis*. That possibility is eliminated, however, by the

---

21. Gregory of Nyssa, "On Not Three Gods, to Ablabius," 334.

22. Gregory of Nyssa, "On Not Three Gods, to Ablabius," 334.

23. In the interest of brevity, we will not be discussing the issues concerning the famous *filioque* clause. The position taken here is that the essential questions concerning the Trinity can be engaged while leaving that question open.

doctrine of "processions in God," as stated above. The common source is the Father, who eternally causes the existence of both Son and Spirit.

The doctrine of the processions (as I shall term it) was an unchallenged component of Trinitarianism for many centuries, but recently it has been questioned by a number of conservative Protestant theologians and philosophers, including Wayne Grudem, Millard Ericson, Paul Helm, R. T. Mullins, and William Craig.[24] The principal objections against the processions are that the doctrine lacks biblical warrant, and also that it assigns to the Son an inferior role, thus imperiling the Son's full deity. We begin with the latter objection.

The claim that the Son cannot be fully divine if he is generated from the Father echoes the complaint of the most formidable ancient opponent of Trinitarianism, the subordinationist (or "Arian") Eunomius. According to Eunomius, it is the defining attribute of God to be "ingenerate." To this, the Nicenes replied that ingeneracy is the *personal property* of the Father, parallel to "being generated" for the Son and "proceeding" for the Spirit. But it is precisely the processsions that *guarantee* the full Godhood of the other two Persons, because the processions entail that each of them enjoys the fullness of the divine nature (= *homoousios*) and so is fully God. Among human beings, it may be noted, the generation of each person from their parents entails that the person generated shares with the parents the full human nature; it does not, however, imply any necessary inferiority on the part of the one generated. Unfortunately, relations between humans very often involve contention about superiority and inferiority, but it is misguided to insert these ideas into the relationships between Father, Son, and Spirit.[25]

Social Trinitarians, furthermore, are able to provide a positive theological rationale for the doctrine of processions. The Father, they say, was motivated in generating the Son and the Spirit by the incomparably great value of a situation in which each divine Person has another divine Person as a fully suitable and worthy object of love. And as Richard of St. Victor pointed out, the mutual love of two persons is greatly enhanced by their sharing in love for a third person.[26]

---

24. For a more extensive discussion of these objections, see Mullins, "Hasker on the Divine Processions" and Hasker, "God's 'Only Begotten Son'" in the same issue.

25. Thus, it is unfortunate when the doctrine of the Trinity becomes involved in the debates about patriarchalism vs. equalitarianism in the marriage relationship.

26. Richard Swinburne has devised an ingenious, and perhaps sound, argument for the conclusion that there must be exactly three divine persons. See his "Social Theory of the Trinity." We begin by accepting Richard of St. Victor's argument that there must be at least three divine persons: since it is all-things-considered best that this should be so, the Father will of necessity bring about the existence of a second and a third person. We then suppose that, since the existence of a divine person is a good thing, any world

Does the doctrine of processions enjoy biblical warrant? The answer is affirmative. Over and above the disputed term *monogenēs* (traditionally, "only-begotten," as in John 3:16, but this translation is now widely criticized), there are a number of other biblical expressions that convey the idea of a dependency of the Son on the Father. The very terms "Father" and "Son" already suggest such a dependency, especially when they are used in contexts where they cannot refer only to times subsequent to the incarnation (see Heb 1:2). In John 1:1-2, the *Logos* (Word, or Reason) is the Word or Reason *of God* (= the Father); see also Hebrews 1:3. Perhaps most striking of all is John 5:26: "just as the Father has life in himself, so he has granted the Son also to have life in himself." To *have life in oneself* has to be an essential divine attribute, and as such it can be given to the Son by the Father only in the act by which the Son is given existence by the Father. I submit that anyone wishing to contest the biblical warrant for the doctrine of processions will need a compelling alternative explanation for this passage.

7. *The three Persons have in common a single instance of the concrete divine nature.*

To say that the Persons are fully God is to say that they possess the entire divine nature. But is this a common *abstract* nature, as in the case of three trees, each of which exemplifies "treeness," or three human beings? A few Trinitarians have taken this route, but the mainstream position is the one that has been stated concisely by Thomas Aquinas: "Among creatures, the nature the one generated receives is not numerically identical with the nature the one generating has. . . . But God begotten receives numerically the same nature God begetting has."[27] This was evidently the view of Augustine, as well as that of Gregory of Nyssa and the subsequent Greek tradition. But should a contemporary Trinitarian adhere to this part of the tradition? I believe the answer is affirmative. To see why, we consider the implications if

---

with more divine persons is so far better than any world with fewer. This sets up an infinite series of better and better worlds, each with one more divine person than the previous world. Since the series has no end, there is no world that is overall the best. In such a situation a good person will choose one of the good options available to her; her goodness is not compromised by the fact that another choice would be still better, since this is logically unavoidable. Suppose then, the Father brings about a world in which there are n divine persons. Now, if $n \geq 4$, it will be the case that the demands of perfect divine goodness could have been satisfied with $n-1$ divine persons; it follows that bringing about the existence of the nth divine person was optional for the Father. If so, however, the existence of the nth divine person is contingent rather than necessary. This, however, is impossible: no being that exists only contingently can be divine. It follows that there must be exactly three divine persons.

27. Aquinas, *Summa Theologiae* Ia 39.5 and 2.245a.

we were to hold that the common nature of the Persons is merely an abstract nature—in essence, a set of properties. In exploring these implications, we need to consider again the question discussed in the previous section: shall we or shall we not affirm the doctrine of processions? If we deny the processions, then we have in principle no reason to reject the possibility that the Persons have diverse origins, and only subsequently enter into the intimate relationships we take to exist between them in the Trinity. This seems clearly unacceptable.

But suppose we do affirm the processions. In this case, an interesting case study is provided by Richard Swinburne. In an early writing concerning the Trinity, Swinburne wrote:

> If it is an overall best act that a solitary God share his essential almightiness, the only way in which this can be done is if he creates as a separate God what is God anyway, i.e., if he divides himself. The creation being everlasting, this is to be read as: he creates as a separate God what, but for his creative action, would be himself.[28]

But this has strange consequences. Since the processions are everlasting, there can never have been a time at which what was to be the nature of the Son and the nature of the Spirit was actually a part of the Father. We have, then, a view according to which the divine essence exists eternally partitioned into three parts, due to the Father's eternal will that this should be so, rather than the divine nature's belonging in its entirety to the Father alone. Later on, Swinburne came to reject this; he wrote, "I doubt that it makes any sense to talk of a non-physical being dividing itself—division only applies to extended and so physical substances."[29] But if not this, then what? The only apparent candidate is Swinburne's later conclusion that the Son and the Spirit are created *ex nihilo*[30] by the Father—and created as (supposedly) co-equal divine persons. But surely, this cannot be accepted. We see, then, that the stakes are high, when we ask whether the three Persons can share a single concrete divine nature. Indeed, the most reasonable conclusion would seem to be that an adequate conception of divine unity requires us to affirm *both* the eternal relations of origin within the Trinity, and the singular concrete divine nature.

---

28. Swinburne, "Could There Be More Than One God?," 232.

29. Private e-mail.

30. Swinburne chooses not to use this language. But the thought is there, even if the specific terminology is avoided. For discussion, see my *Metaphysics and the Tri-Personal God*, 147–54.

8. *The Three Persons are each constituted by the single divine nature.*

At this point, I go beyond anything that is clearly sanctioned by the Trinitarian tradition. The last section left us with a problem, one that demands a solution. How can it be, that there are three distinct individuals—three persons—that share a single concrete nature? There are serious Trinitarian thinkers who deny that this is possible.[31] I do not think there are conclusive arguments for this impossibility, but even so, we surely need to respond in some way that goes beyond bare assertion. In this section I consider one solution, widely advocated in the Trinitarian tradition, which I believe we cannot accept. I then mention two possible solutions.

The solution to our problem that has been historically most widely accepted appeals to the doctrine of divine simplicity. According to this doctrine, in its standard form, there is ultimately no complexity of any sort within the being of God. Augustine's application of this to the Trinity is neatly summarized by Lewis Ayres:

> The Father generates the Son who is light from light, wisdom from wisdom, and essence from essence. The Son is an essence in Himself, not just a relationship: to talk of the person of the Son is to talk of the Son's essence. And yet, because the Father's and the Son's essences are truly simple, they are of one essence. ... Thus, in using the grammar of simplicity to articulate a concept of Father, Son, and Spirit as each God, and as the one God, we find that the more we grasp the full reality of each person, the full depth of the being that they have from the Father, the more we are also forced to recognize the unity of their being.[32]

Without doubt we have here an elegant intellectual structure. Yet a problem remains, which Ayres seems not to have noticed—a problem that arises from the very concept of identity. Identity, as this notion is understood by logicians, is a relation that is symmetrical and transitive: if A is identical with B, and B with C, then A is identical with C. So if the Father is an essence in himself, and the Son also is an essence in himself, and yet their essences are identical, it follows inexorably that the Father is identical with the Son, a heretical conclusion that cannot possibly be accepted—and of course, Augustine does not accept it. Without further elaboration, I will simply say here that the same problem will arise with any attempt to apply the strong doctrine of divine simplicity to the Trinity. Whatever maneuvers

---

31. Including Keith Yandell and Richard Swinburne
32. Ayres, *Nicaea and Its Legacy*, 379-80.

may be attempted, in the end simplicity will annihilate the very differences between the Persons that the doctrine of the Trinity needs to preserve. We need a different solution.

One philosopher who has sought to provide such a solution is William Craig. As a first effort at conceptualizing the Trinity, Craig suggests Cerberus, the three-headed dog from Greek mythology. We may name the three heads Rover, Bowser, and Spike. Each of the three is "fully dog"—that is, is completely canine—in nature, but each is not *a dog*; rather, they are together *one* dog, but a dog with three heads. So far, perhaps, this is not too bad as an image for the Trinity. This image breaks down, however, if we think of the death of Cerberus: each of the three presumably has its own soul (Craig is a dualist), so after death, with the body removed, we have three distinct individuals, which won't work for the Trinity. However, the failure of this image suggests another:

> Now God is very much like an unembodied soul; indeed, as a mental substance God just seems to be a soul. We naturally equate a rational soul with a person, since the human souls with which we are acquainted are persons. But the reason human souls are individual persons is because each soul is equipped with one set of rational faculties sufficient for being a person. Suppose, then, that God is a soul which is endowed with three complete sets of rational . . . faculties, each sufficient for personhood. Then God, though one soul, would not be one person but three, for God would have three centers of self-consciousness, intentionality and volition, as social trinitarians maintain. . . . God would therefore be one being that supports three persons, just as our own individual beings each support one person. Such a model of Trinity monotheism seems to give a clear sense to the classical formula, "three persons in one substance."[33]

It seems to me that this image does indeed capture the sense of the classic formula, and indeed it gives a better understanding of that formula than any other proposal of which I am aware. Accordingly, I hereby adopt this model as a basis for further explorations.

However, one would like to have a more precise, or at least more philosophically developed, account of the relation between the three Persons and the one divine substance or nature. As a candidate for such an account, I propose the metaphysical notion of *constitution*.[34] Constitution has been

---

33. Moreland and Craig, *Philosophical Foundations*, 594. (Craig is primarily responsible for the material on the Trinity.)

34. The concept of constitution employed here is derived from the work of Lynne Rudder Baker, as seen in her book, *Metaphysics of Everyday Life*. I apply constitution

proposed as a relation that enables us to handle some otherwise perplexing situations in the metaphysics of material objects. Consider a golden statue, made of a single mass of gold. Our first thought will likely be that the statue is identical with the mass of gold. But this thought cannot be quite right, for an interesting reason. For an object x to be identical with an object y, it must be the case that x and y have all of their properties in common, but this is not the case here. The mass of gold, but not the statue, has the property of *being such that it would continue to exist if the gold were hammered into a different shape.* (The mass may also have existed before the statue, for instance in the form of a bar of gold.) So the mass and the statue are not identical, yet they clearly are very closely related. It is proposed that they are related by *constitution:* the gold *constitutes* the statue, but is not identical with it. Other examples of constitution are: a mass of water can constitute an ice cube, a piece of colored metal can constitute a stop sign, a piece of paper, when folded, can constitute a toy airplane, and so on and on. In each case, we can say that the constituting object "is" the constituted object, but the "is" here signifies constitution, not identity.

The proposal for the Trinity, then, is that the divine nature constitutes each of the Trinitarian Persons. As a formal analysis of the notion of constitution involved, we have the following:

x constitutes y at time t just in case x is of primary kind F, y is of primary kind G, and at t,
  i. x and y have all parts in common,
  ii. x is in G-favorable circumstances,
  iii. necessarily, if x of primary kind F is in G-favorable circumstances, an object of primary kind G shares all its parts with x, and
  iv. causal activity is required for there to be such a G, the form of activity depending on the natures of F and G.

In the case of the statue, kind F = masses of gold, kind G = statues. The G-favorable circumstance is that the mass has been formed into a statue-shape, and retains that shape. And this forming is the required causal activity, as specified in clause (iv). The application to the Trinity goes as follows: Kind F is the divine nature, kind G is the kind, Trinitarian Persons. Since both the nature and each of the Persons are mereologically simple—that is, not made up of separable parts—they have in common the one "improper" part

---

to the Trinity in *Metaphysics and the Tri-Personal God*, 238–45. However, the concept employed in this essay represents a modification and further development beyond the concept as given there. For the reasons for the modification, see my exchange with Brian Leftow in *Religious Studies*.

of both, namely the divine nature itself. The *G*-favorable circumstances in which the *F* constitutes a *G* is the circumstance in which the divine nature supports, e.g., the Son-life-stream. And the causal activity required for the Son to exist is that the Son-life-stream actually occurs.

Clearly, there are many further questions to be answered, both about the constitution relation itself and about its application to the Trinity. Limitations of space prevent our pursuing these matters at this point; interested readers are invited to consult the appropriate literature. Additionally, it must be acknowledged that some philosophers find the notion of constitution unpalatable, either in general or in its application to the Trinity. These philosophers, if they are Trinitarians, will need to find their own account of the relation between the divine Persons and the divine nature.

The Holy Trinity

God is Father, Son, and Holy Spirit because it is the nature of God to be Trinitarian. But we human beings are able to know God as the Trinity because the Son became incarnate in Jesus of Nazareth, and the Holy Spirit is manifested in the events of Pentecost and beyond. It was evident from the beginning that Jesus was a person distinct from the Father. But his existence as a distinct divine person was not limited to his earthly life: the Son was with the Father and shared his glory "before the world existed" (John 17:5). So the doctrine of the Trinity affirms that from all eternity there is a distinction within God of three persons, three subjects and centers of consciousness—Father, Son, and Holy Spirit—each of whom is fully and equally divine. But this community of persons cannot be liable to degenerate into individualism and conflict, as so often happens with human communities. The doctrine of *perichoresis*—of the mutual indwelling and interpenetration of the divine Persons—shows why this does not and cannot happen. The three Persons, while distinct in their actions (only the Son became man as Jesus of Nazareth), are necessarily united in their purposes and in their actions towards the world.

This affirmation of the personal union and communion of the Persons does not yet say everything that needs to be said about the divine unity. The doctrine of the Trinity affirms that the three Persons are together a *single concrete being*—that they share between them a single trope of deity, a single concrete instance of the divine nature. This claim can be modeled by the notion of a single mental substance, or soul, supporting simultaneously three distinct conscious lives, three distinct streams of experience. It can also be said that the divine nature or substance *constitutes* each of Father, Son, and

Holy Spirit, using the notion of constitution in a way closely analogous to its use in contemporary metaphysics. It is conceptually possible for the divine nature to exist without constituting (for instance) the Holy Spirit, but under the circumstances in which that nature supports the Spirit-life-stream (circumstances that do in fact obtain, and do so of metaphysical necessity) there exists the person of the Holy Spirit, a member of the divine Trinity.

The explanation for this threefold sharing of the divine nature is given in the doctrine of processions, which affirms that the Son is eternally begotten from the Father, and the Spirit eternally proceeds from the Father (through the Son). The doctrine asserts that, even as a human parent gives part of his or her being to become the being of an offspring, so the Father eternally makes it the case that the divine nature, which is originally the being of the Father alone, becomes in its entirety also the being of the Son and of the Holy Spirit, without thereby being divided or separated from the being of the Father. That this occurs is not a contingent choice on the Father's part, but rather is a necessary consequence of the perfection of the Father, a perfection that could not be perfectly fulfilled apart from the Father's eternal communion with the Son and the Holy Spirit.

For Christians, the full and final answer to the question, "What is God?" is and can only be, "God is the Holy Trinity of Father, Son, and Holy Spirit." The Trinity is not a single person, but the closest possible union and communion of the three divine Persons. Yet in virtue of the closeness of their union, the Trinity is at times referred to *as if* it were a single person. The Trinity is divine, exhibiting all the essential divine attributes—not by possessing knowledge, power, and so on distinct from those of the divine Persons, but rather in view of the fact that the Trinity consists precisely of those three persons and of nothing else. It is this Trinity which we are to worship, and obey, and love as our Lord and God.[35]

---

35. My thanks to Alan Padgett and to Charles Taliaferro, who provided helpful comments on an earlier version of this material.

2

Tri-Personal Monotheism

William Lane Craig

IN HIS INTRODUCTION TO this volume Chad McIntosh helpfully distinguishes between two components of a view of the Trinity: a probative component, which is concerned with what justification there is for the doctrine of the Trinity, and a model component, which is concerned with the doctrine's logical and metaphysical coherence. My focus is this essay is on the probative component, specifically with the biblical justification for the doctrine.[1]

Probative Component

At the heart of any biblical case for the doctrine of the Trinity will be justification for believing in the deity of Jesus Christ. If Christ as well as the Father is divine, then we have at least Binitarianism. From there it will be a short step to affirmation of a full Trinitarian doctrine of God. Various lines of biblical evidence support the conclusion that Jesus is divine.[2] Entire books have been written on this evidence, so in this essay I shall focus on just one point, namely biblical texts that straightforwardly call Jesus God. These texts are

---

1. For a fuller account see my forthcoming *Systematic Philosophical Theology*, vol. II, from which this essay is excerpted.

2. The New Testament (NT) authors expressed Christ's divine status in a dazzling variety of ways. He occupies exclusively divine roles such as being the Creator, Savior, and Judge; he possesses divine attributes such as pre-existence and eternity; he is ascribed the full range of divine honors such as power, majesty, and glory; he is the recipient of human and angelic worship and of prayer; he is the bearer of many titles and names used of God in the Old Testament (OT). For an outline of implicit and explicit christological claims in the NT see Harris, *Jesus as God*, Appendix II. These are discussed in a popular but thorough survey by Bowman and Komoszewski, *Putting Jesus in His Place*.

especially important, not only because they state directly that Jesus is God, but because they refute the claim of Unitarians that statements about the Fatherhood of God are to be taken as identity statements. Rather both the Father and Christ are said to be God.

God the Father

Although my focus will be on the deity of Christ, it will be helpful to say a word first about God the Father. The paternal metaphor of God as Father is rooted in the Old Testament (OT), which occasionally refers to the God of Israel as "Father." In Deut 32:6 the Pentateuchal author connects God's role as Father to his special covenantal relationship with Israel whereby Israel became Yahweh's children. Elsewhere, Yahweh is designated the Father of the Jewish king (1 Sam 7:14; Ps 89:26) and, accordingly, the king is designated God's son (Ps 2:7). Nonetheless, this paternal relation is not restricted to royalty but extends to all the people, even to the least (Ps 68:5; Mal 2:10). Among the prophets, Isaiah and Jeremiah find encouragement and comfort in the Fatherhood of God (Isa 63:16; cf. 64:6–8; Jer 3:19–20). In the apocryphal literature we find a few references to God as Father (Tob 13:3–4; Sir 23:4–5; Wis 14:3).

NT Christians obviously accepted the metaphor of "Father" in reference to God, as such language pervades the NT, being found in every book of the NT except 3 John. Jesus thought of God as his heavenly Father, and he taught his disciples to pray to God as their Father (Matt 6:9). It is uncontroversial, then, that NT Christians regarded God as their Father. This was the inherited tradition of Jewish Christians, so that when they spoke of God they naturally had reference to the Father. Gentile Christians would have quickly come to understand that in virtue their coming to faith in Christ, they, too, were now related to God as Father. Thus, the Greek word for God, *theos*, in Christian as well as Jewish usage was typically understood to refer to the Father. This fact is patent in expressions like "God the Father," "God our Father," "[our] God and Father," and "the God and Father of our Lord Jesus Christ." Given such widespread usage, the word *theos* was naturally understood to have reference to God the Father.

Jesus Christ

For Jews and Christians "God" and "the Father" were typically co-referring terms, that is to say, terms having the same referent, if not the same meaning, just as in a certain context of use "the President" and "Barack Obama" are co-referring terms.³ Given this fact, it would have been seriously misleading, no matter how exalted a view they held of Jesus, for early Christians to assert that Christ is (*ho*) *theos*, for such an assertion would have been understood to mean that Christ is God the Father, which is emphatically not what Christians believed. They did not believe that the Father had become incarnate and died on the cross. There was thus clearly a personal distinction between Jesus and the Father. Such a distinction might be marked by referring to Christ as "the Son of God," but even such a lofty title, while making the distinction clear, failed to convey fully what Christians wanted to claim about Christ's status.⁴ Some other way, more adequate to Christ's exalted status, had to be found for referring to Christ.

Christ as *Kyrios*

The early Christians' solution to this problem was startling and ingenious. They adopted the term *kyrios* ("Lord") as their principal means of referring to Christ (368 times in the NT). The christological significance of this term lies in the fact that while it, like the English word "lord," has a wide range of meaning, from a term of polite address ("sir") to divinity, *kyrios* is

---

3. We may draw upon Gottlob Frege's important distinction between the sense and reference of singular terms to say that "God" and "Father" may in certain contexts have the same referent even though they do not have the same sense. In many biblical passages we could not substitute "Father" for "God" without changing the meaning, e.g., the expressions cited in the text obviously do not mean "Father the Father," "Father our Father," "[our] Father and Father," etc. The point I am making seems to require that there be connotative proper names as well as non-connotative proper names. It seems to me that some names do, indeed, have senses, e.g., "Black Beauty," "Champ," "Mom," etc. "Father" seems like this. For that reason it cannot always be substituted for "God" without meaning change. This point would go double for cases where "God" is not a proper name but part of a definite description, e.g., "the only true God," which obviously does not mean "the only true Father." Similarly, when Jesus Christ is occasionally called *theos* in the NT, this should not be understood as the assertion that he is the Father. Drawing the distinction between sense and reference serves to expose the error of Tuggy when he says, "Never in the Bible does 'God' refer to some collective or group of divine persons, or to something like a 'soul' which underlies or supports three selves, or to something which isn't a self but which consists of or contains divine selves" (Tuggy, "Divine Deception and Monotheism," 200). Tuggy has no non-question begging way of knowing that just as "Phosphorus" ("the morning star") and "Hesperus" ("the evening star"), though different in sense, both referred to Venus even though the ancient Babylonian astrologers did not realize it, so "God" does not on occasion refer, not to the Father, but to the Trinitarian God, even though the NT authors did not realize it.

4. In a Jewish context, Christ's being God's Son may have conveyed merely his messianic status, which did not entail his divinity. In a gentile context, however, the designation may have carried such import.

the term Greek-speaking Jews substituted for God's proper name "Yahweh" in the OT! In reading aloud the Scriptures, Hebrew-speaking Jews would not pronounce the sacred name "Yahweh," but substituted for it the word *Adonai*, such usage being represented in our English translations as "Lord" with small capitals. Greek-speaking Jews in turn substituted *kyrios* for the Hebrew *Adonai*. It was this divine title that early Christians seized upon to express Jesus' exalted status.

The theological import of *kyrios* in reference to Jesus Christ is conveyed by the NT authors' unsettling practice of quoting OT prooftexts about Yahweh in application to Christ.[5] To give just three examples: in Romans 10:9 Paul affirms, "If you confess with your lips that Jesus is Lord and believe in your heart that God raised him from the dead, you will be saved." Paul assures his Roman readers that "there is no distinction between Jew and Greek; the same Lord is Lord of all and bestows his riches upon all who call upon him. For, 'Every one who calls upon the name of the Lord will be saved'" (Rom 10:11). The prooftext is Joel 2:32, speaking of Yahweh, "the Lord, your God" (v. 23).

Again, in Philippians 2:10-11, Paul writes, "at the name of Jesus every knee should bow, in heaven and on earth and under the earth, and every tongue confess that Jesus Christ is Lord, to the glory of God the Father." The confession here is drawn from LXX Isaiah 45:23, "to me every knee shall bow and every tongue shall confess to God," with reference to "the Lord, the God of Israel" (v. 3). That a text from so fiercely monotheistic a passage as Isaiah 45 should be applied to Jesus Christ displays dramatically the divine status ascribed to him by Christians.

Again, in Hebrews 1:6: "When he brings the first-born into the world, he says, 'Let all God's angels worship him,'" the prooftext is either LXX Deuteronomy 32:43 or Psalm 97:7, both of which have reference to Yahweh, to whom, as God, worship is solely due, notably, not only from human beings but from the highest angelic beings. Further, in Hebrews 1:10-11 the statements that are cited from Psalm 102:25-27 in application to Christ originally had reference to Yahweh.

---

5. See Capes, *Old Testament Yahweh Texts in Paul's Christology*. As Capes points out, the theological significance of this practice is that *kyrios* is employed as a christological title to "apply to Christ concepts and functions which Yahweh is expected to fulfill according to the Old Testament" (164). Not only Paul, but the Evangelists as well do the same, portraying the canonical Jesus as applying to himself concepts and texts which the OT applied to Yahweh (179-80).

Christ as *Theos*

The use of the divine title *kyrios* enabled NT Christians to regard the Father and the Son as equally divine while maintaining a personal distinction between them. At times, however, as if carried away by their exuberance for Christ, the NT authors seem to throw caution to the winds and come right out and affirm boldly that Christ is, indeed, *theos*. Not that they were completely unguarded in their assertions: in any context in which Christ is referred to as *theos* there is almost always some personal differentiation between the Father and Christ, lest Christ be confused with the Father. Their personal distinction remains inviolate. Nonetheless, on several occasions the NT does affirm that Jesus Christ is God.

The majority of NT scholars hold that *theos* is applied to Jesus no more than nine but no fewer than five times in the NT.[6] These remarkable texts have been meticulously examined and ranked by Murray Harris as follows: *theos* is applied to Jesus Christ certainly in John 1:1; 20:28; very probably in Romans 9:5, Titus 2:13, Hebrews 1:8, and 2 Peter 1:1; and probably in John 1:18.[7] I shall briefly examine these texts in what I consider to be an ascending order of confidence in their referring to Christ as (*ho*) *theos*, climaxing with the decisive texts of the Johannine corpus. Since some of our readers will presumably not read Greek, I shall present the NRSV translation before providing the Greek text.

ROMANS 9:5

> to them belong the patriarchs, and from them, according to the flesh, comes the Messiah, who is over all, God blessed forever. Amen.

> *hōn hoi pateres kai eks hōn ho Christos to kata sarka ho ōn epi pantōn theos eulogētos eis tous aiōnas, amēn.* (Rom 9:5)

The key interpretive question regarding this statement concerns its punctuation. Should there be a stop after *sarka*, or should the subsequent words

---

6. Harris provides a list of scholars in his *Jesus as God*, 274. Though Harris' list obviously needs updating, Komoszewski informs me that not much has changed since Harris wrote, though the case for a reference to Christ as *theos* in Titus 2:13 and 2 Peter 1:1 has been strengthened. The major change has been that "virtually every exegetical commentary since Harris has affirmed 1 John 5:20 as a reference to Jesus as *theos*" (private communication, March 23, 2022).

7. Harris also judges that *theos* is possibly but not probably applied to Christ in Acts 20:28, Hebrews 1:9, and 1 John 5:20. See previous note.

be taken to be a relative clause? Translations differ. In the first case, *theos* would presumably denote the Father, but in the latter case Christ. Grammatically, the articular participle *ho ōn* may be used either retrospectively to further describe a prior subject and so mean "who is" or prospectively to introduce a new subject and so mean "He who is."

The basic difficulty with taking *ho ōn* to begin a new sentence is that such an understanding separates *ho ōn* from its natural antecedent *ho Christos*. Given that *ho Christos* precedes and agrees with *ho ōn*, a change of subject is *prima facie* improbable. Inclusion of at least the phrase *epi pantōn* in the relative clause is appropriate to Christ, since he is *Kyrios* (Rom 10:12; 14:9; Phil 2:9-11; cf. Col 1:16-17; Eph 1:20-23), so that a reader would naturally assume that the same subject is involved. Harris judges that to promote a divorce of *ho ōn* from the grammatically consonant *ho Christos* "is unconscionable."[8]

Moreover, a major problem with the view that the doxology begins a new sentence is that whenever *eulogētos* occurs in an independent doxological clause, it always *precedes* God's name (2 Cor 1:3; Eph 1:3; 1 Pet 1:3). Normal biblical word order for independent doxologies would require here something like *eulogētos ho theos eis tous aiōnas, amēn*. By contrast in NT doxologies in a relative clause (e.g., Rom 1:25; 11:34-36) there is always an antecedent for the subject of the doxology in a prior phrase.[9] The available antecedent in v. 5a is *ho Christos*. Word order thus makes it quite improbable that Romans 9:5 contains an independent doxology to God the Father.

Harris reports that of the fifty-six principal commentators consulted for his study, only thirteen take *theos* to refer to God the Father, while thirty-six see a reference to Christ, a reading that is captured by the punctuation of the Greek text adopted in the 26th edition of the Nestle-Aland text and the third edition of the United Bible Society text, in a significant reversal of their previous positions.[10]

Accordingly, in Romans 9:5 Christ is very probably said to be God. The designation of Christ as God cannot plausibly be construed as some weak sense of divinity, not only because of what Paul says elsewhere about Christ's preeminent status (Phil 2:5-11), but also because Christ is said in this very passage to be "over all things." So in calling Christ *theos*, Paul is either identifying Christ with God the Father or ascribing to Christ the same

---

8. Harris, *Jesus as God*, 158.

9. For discussion see Carraway, *Christ Is God over All*, 51-56. Even in independent doxologies, the one blessed has usually been previously referred to. But in Romans 9:5 God has not been previously mentioned.

10. Harris, *Jesus as God*, 172. The revised punctuation is retained in the current NA[28] and UBS[5].

divine status held by the Father. Since Paul obviously distinguished between Christ and the Father, he must be placing Christ and the Father on the same ontological plane but without sacrificing his Jewish monotheism. The fact that *theos* is here anarthrous is consonant with its not being a proper name but a predication of deity. So here Christ is held to be God, just as the Father is God.

Hebrews 1:8

In the opening chapter of Hebrews we read that God says to the Son,

> Your throne, O God, is forever and ever
>
> *Ho thronos sou ho theos eis tōn aiōna tou aiōnos* (Heb 1:8)

The principal question to be settled here is whether *ho theos* should be understood as a vocative form of address ("Your throne, O God, is forever and ever") or as a nominative subject ("God is your throne forever and ever"). Since either is grammatically possible, considerations of background and context must guide our determination of meaning.

In terms of background, the author is citing LXX Psalm 44:7 (= Ps 45:7): "*Ho thronos sou, ho theos, eis ton aiōna tou aiōnos.*" The traditional interpretation of this verse in the original Hebrew is that *elohim* (God) is a vocative, so that either the king or God himself is addressed. The vocatival understanding of the verse is even more apparent in the LXX, which inserts the vocative *dynate* ("O Mighty One") from v. 4 into v. 6, increasing the probability that *ho theos* in v. 7 is used vocatively.[11] This traditional understanding is reflected in the punctuation of the verse in the LXX.

Considerations of context heavily favor the vocatival reading. In order to show the Son's superiority to any angelic being the Son is addressed in vv. 8, 10 as both "God" and "Lord," twin titles for deity:

> "Your throne, O God, is forever and ever." (v. 8)
>
> "In the beginning, Lord, you founded the earth." (v. 10)

The vocative *kyrie* in v. 10 supports reading the *ho theos* in v. 8 vocatively as well.[12] The whole point of the opening section of Hebrews is to show the Son's superiority to the angels. Calling Christ both "God" and "Lord"

---

11. In the Psalter of the LXX there are sixty-three such instances of *ho theos* as a vocative.

12. The articular nominative of address is an established NT usage.

in contrast to angels thus supports the theological point that the author is making. Harris therefore reports that in Hebrews 1:8 "the overwhelming majority of grammarians, commentators, authors of general studies, and English translations construe ὁ θεὸς as vocative."[13] Thus, Christ is here very probably called God.

There is no denying the christological import of this appellation. The parallelism of the Son's being addressed as both "God" and "Lord" and the exalted descriptions of him in his superiority to angelic beings make it clear that Christ is not addressed merely in the way that a Jewish king might be called *elohim*. God is said to have created the world through the Son and made him heir of all things (Heb 1:2). "He reflects the glory of God and bears the very stamp of his nature [*hypostasis*], upholding the universe by his word of power" (v. 3). Nothing of this sort could be said of any angelic being.

Harris points out that of the three main titles given to Jesus in Hebrews 1 "Son" is the title on which attention is focused (vv. 2, 5 *bis*, 8), so that "God" and "Lord" serve to explicate two aspects of his Sonship, namely, divinity and sovereignty.[14] Whereas "God" is a monadic predicate applied to the Son absolutely, "Lord" is a dyadic predicate applied to him relationally. The Son is God even in the absence of creatures, but in relation to creatures he is the sovereign Lord of all. This distinction between absolute and relational predicates sheds light on the heavy emphasis on the subordination and exaltation of the Son found in Hebrews and throughout the NT. Although from the very beginning of creation, Christ was Lord, having created both the heavens and the earth (1:10), nevertheless he was "for a little while made lower than the angels" (2:9), taking on flesh and blood "that by the grace of God he might taste death for every one" (2:9, 14). But God has raised him from death and "crowned [him] with glory and honor because of the suffering of death" (2:9).

This same theme of the abasement and exaltation of the Son to Lordship over all things is expressed by Paul in Philippians 2:5-10. Here Christ is elevated, not from being a creature to divinity, which would have been absurd and blasphemous in Jewish ears, but from voluntary self-abasement to Lordship, from a state of temporary humiliation to glory. Such self-abasement and elevation concern functional or economic, not ontological, subordination and exaltation.

So in Hebrews Christ is affirmed to be the perfect representation of God's glory and nature (1:3), to have existed in some sense "prior" to

---

13. Harris, *Jesus as God*, 217-18.
14. Harris, *Jesus as God*, 223.

creation (1:10), to be the subject of passages about Yahweh in the OT (1:6, 10–12; 3:7–11, 15), and to be the appropriate object of worship of both men and angels (1:6; 12:2). Ontologically he is God. At the same time he is subordinate to the Father in that the Father is responsible for the preparation of his body (10:5), for his introduction into the world (1:6), for his resurrection (13:20) and his exaltation to the Father's right hand (1:13), for his appointment to the office of high priest (3:2; 5:5, 10), and for his being designated heir of all things (1:2). These roles are clearly economic and thus compatible with his sharing full divinity with the Father.

Titus 2:13

The writer to Titus expresses our hope in Christ's eschatological appearing with the words,

> while we wait for the blessed hope and the manifestation of the glory of our great God and Savior, Jesus Christ.
>
> *prosdexomenoi tēn makarian elpida kai epiphanein tēs doxēs tou megalou theou kai sōtēros hēmōn Iēsou Christou.* (Titus 2:13)

The main interpretive question about this statement concerns its grammatical construction. Do *theou* and *sōtēros* designate one person ("our great God and Savior") or two ("the great God and our Savior")? Fortunately, there is a clear answer to this question. There is broad majority support for understanding the reference to be to a single person, for at least two reasons.

First, it is characteristic of Greek grammar, roughly speaking, that the construction <definite article + common noun + "and" + common noun> takes a single referent rather than two. Originally formulated by Granville Sharp, the principle may be more accurately—and, for our purposes, relevantly—formulated as follows:

> In native Greek constructions (i.e., not translation Greek), when a single article modifies two substantives connected by *kai* (thus, article-substantive-*kai*-substantive), when both substantives are
>
> i. singular (both grammatically and semantically),
> ii. personal, and
> iii. common nouns (not proper names or ordinals),
>
> they have the same referent.[15]

---

15. Wallace, *Sharp's Canon*, 132.

Daniel Wallace points out that none of the five classes of alleged exceptions to Sharp's Rule comprises, in fact, exceptions to this formulation of the principle; but even if they did, Titus 2:13 does not fall into any of those classes.[16] "Consequently, in Titus 2:13 . . . we are compelled to recognize that, on a *grammatical* level, a heavy burden of proof rests with the one who wishes to deny that 'God and Savior' refers to one person, Jesus Christ."[17]

Second, the expression *theos kai sōtēr* ("God and Savior") was a stereotyped formula common in first-century religious terminology, both in the classical authors and in the *koiné*. It was apparently used by both Palestinian and Diaspora Jews in reference to Yahweh. It invariably denoted one deity, not two. In usage contemporaneous with the NT the formula *theos kai sōtēr* never refers to two persons or deities. Wallace concludes that "regardless of the source of the expression, the use in Titus 2:13 and 2 Pet 1:1 of this idiom is almost certainly a reference to one person, confirming once again Sharp's assessment of the phrase."[18]

Harris reports that on the basis of such considerations almost all grammarians and lexicographers, many commentators, and many writers on New Testament theology or Christology are agreed in the verdict that in Titus 2:13 Jesus Christ is called "our great God and Savior."[19] More recently Gordon Fee observes that this view is "the currently 'reigning' point of view, adopted by almost everyone in the NT academy."[20]

2 Peter 1:1

The same grammatical question that attends Titus 2:13 also attends 2 Peter 1:1, which speaks of

> the righteousness of our God and Savior Jesus Christ
>
> *dikaiosynē tou theou hēmōn kai sōtēros Iēsou Christou.* (2 Pet 1:1)

---

16. Wallace, *Sharp's Canon*, 249–51. Wallace reports, "After perusing some three to four million words of Greek text, from classical Greek through the first millennium CE, I was amazed at how consistently valid this principle is. At the outset of this investigation, I fully expected to find several exceptions to the rule. . . . But after observing probably thousands of TSKS [article-substantive-*kai*-substantive] constructions, my own reticence to fully accept Sharp's rule as valid has been overturned" (281–82).

17. Wallace, *Sharp's Canon*, 284.

18. Wallace, *Sharp's Canon*, 248.

19. Harris, *Jesus as God*, 185, with appropriate documentation.

20. Fee, *Pauline Christology*, 441.

Is the reference to one person or two? The only difference in the construction is that here the possessive pronoun *hēmōn* is brought forward to follow *theos* rather than *sōtēr*. Accordingly, unless the position of *hēmōn* is a game-changer grammatically, Sharp's Rule and the use of the standardized formula *theos kai sōtēr* require here as well reference to one person.

But the difference in the position of *hēmōn* is trivial.[21] What is critical is that the two substantives are governed by a single definite article, in which case the personal pronoun applies to both substantives, whether it precedes both (e.g., 2 Pet 1:10) or follows either of them (e.g., Eph 3:5; 1 Thess 3:7). Revelation 1:9 provides an exact parallel to 2 Peter 1:1: *ho aelphos hēmōn kai sungkoinōnos* in reference to one person. Elsewhere in 2 Peter we have three instances of *tou kyriou hēmōn kai sōtēros Iēsou Christou* (1:11; 2:20; 3:18) where the single referent of *kyrios* and *sōtēr* is indisputable.

So Sharp's Rule and the use of the stereotypical formula *theos kai sōtēr* go to justify reading 2 Peter 1:1 as "the righteousness of our God and Savior, Jesus Christ." This reading is confirmed by the use of *sōtēr* throughout 2 Peter (1:1, 11; 2:20; 3:2, 18). The term always refers to Jesus Christ, is always anarthrous and conjoined by *kai* with a preceding articular noun, either *kyriou* or *theou*, and the phrase *ho kyrios hēmōn kai sōtēr* always refers to a single person. It would be unprecedented if *tou theou hēmōn kai sōtēros Iēsou Christou* in v. 1 did not also have a single referent.

Harris reports that the view that in 2 Peter 1:1 the title "our God and Savior" is applied to Jesus Christ is endorsed by the great majority of twentieth-century commentators, by most grammarians, and by authors of general works on Christology or 2 Peter. Titus 2:13 and 2 Peter 1:1 are thus mutually reinforcing, confirming the view that by the time these works were written Christ was being referred to as God.

Johannine Writings

Even highly skeptical critics overwhelmingly admit that by the time we get to the Johannine writings, the belief in the full deity of Christ had evolved and come to expression in the NT.[22] The christological bookends of the Gospel of John are the affirmation of Christ's deity in the Prologue (John

---

21. See discussion by Wallace, *Sharp's Canon*, 265–66.

22. Space permits just two examples: Rudolf Bultmann thought that John 20:28 is the one instance in the NT where Jesus Christ is "undoubtedly designated" as God (*Essays*, 276). Bart Ehrman thinks that in John's Gospel, "Jesus is decidedly God and is in fact equal with God the Father—before coming into the world, while in the world, and after he leaves the world" (*How Jesus Became God*, 271).

1:1) and Thomas' ringing confession in the narrative of Christ's resurrection appearance to Thomas and the Twelve (John 20:28).

John 1:1

The Prologue opens with a triadic formula:

> In the beginning was the Word,
> and the Word was with God,
> and the Word was God.

> *En arxē ēn ho logos,*
> *kai ho logos ēn pros ton theon,*
> *kai theos ēn ho logos.* (John 1:1)

The Prologue reflects the influence of the Logos doctrine of Middle Platonism.[23] So I shall speak henceforth of the Logos. According to v. 1a the Logos was "in the beginning," doubtless an echo of LXX Genesis 1:1, "In the beginning . . ." (*En arxē*). The statement thus endorses the traditional Logos doctrine that the Logos "pre-existed," in the sense that the Logos did not begin to exist at the moment of creation nor is a creature. As in Middle Platonism, the Logos is the instrumental cause of creation (John 1:3). This Logos is said in v. 1b to have existed with God and so to be in some sense differentiated from God. Nonetheless v. 1c states that the Logos was God, thus in some sense identifying them. As in Middle Platonism, then, the deity of the Logos is clearly affirmed, while an inner distinction within God is postulated.

So the crucial question is, whom are we talking about here? It is indisputable that John identifies the Logos with the pre-incarnate Christ (John 1:14, 17b). The Logos himself entered human history (John 1:10–11). The Prologue thus affirms the pre-existence of Jesus Christ, his uncreated being, and his deity. Although the opening formula involves a host of interpretive niceties, most of them are of no significance for the question in which we are interested, namely, the deity of Christ. For example, whether *ho theos* in v. 1b is identified with God the Father or with a generic God, that is, a Supreme Being, the Logos or Christ is affirmed in v. 1c to be God.

Again, whether we understand the anarthrous *theos* in v. 1c definitely to indicate grammatically the predicate position of a definite noun or qualitatively to indicate the nature of deity, the result is the same: Christ is ascribed deity. While John might have instead written *theios* (divine) or

---

23. See my *God over All*, chapter 2.

tou theou (of God) instead of *theos* to express the Logos' deity, the resulting statement would have been open to the interpretation that the Logos possessed a sort of diluted divinity or merely belonged to God. By choosing the substantive term *theos* John expresses strongly the equal divinity enjoyed by God the Father and the Son.

Although various translations and paraphrases have been offered to capture the sense of v. 1c, such as

> what God was, the Word was (NEB, REB)
> what God was, the Word also was (TEV)
> the nature of the Word was the same as the nature of God (Barclay)
> he was the same as God (GNB)
> the Word was the very same as God (Cassirer)
> the Word had the same nature as God (Harner),

nonetheless Harris advocates sticking with the customary translation "the Word was God" because of its succinctness and force; but he adds the proviso that it requires that the word "God" be carefully defined or qualified to avoid identifying the Logos with the Father.[24]

John 1:18

> No one has ever seen God. It is God the only Son, who is close to the Father's heart, who has made him known.
>
> *theon oudeis heōraken pōpote; monogenēs theos ho ōn eis ton kolpon tou patros ekeinos eksēgēsato.* (John 1:18)

After referring to Jesus as *monogenēs para patros* in v. 14, now John boldly calls him *monogenēs theos*. The presence of *monogenēs theos* in both 𝔓[66] and 𝔓[75] has convinced most textual critics that *monogenēs huios* is a later emendation of the text, so that we may proceed with confidence, if not certainty, that here Jesus Christ is called *theos*.[25] By means of the stunning appellation "the only-begotten God" John differentiates Christ the Son from God the Father while regarding both as God.

Although interesting and important interpretive questions arise concerning the meaning of *monogenēs*, once again their resolution is not germane to our interest in Christ's deity. For example, is *monogenēs* an adjective ("the only-begotten God") or a substantive ("the Only-Begotten, God")? For

---

24. Harris, *Jesus as God*, 70.
25. For a discussion of the textual variants see Harris, *Jesus as God*, 74–83.

our purposes it does not matter, since in either case Christ is referred to as "God." So, we may ask, what is the meaning of *monogenēs*, whether construed adjectivally or substantively? As a compound of *monos* (single) + *genos* (kind), it might be taken on etymological grounds to mean "unique" or "one of a kind." In that case *monogenēs theos* might be translated "God the one and only," which, though of dubious sense, nonetheless asserts the deity of Christ. In a familial context, however, which is the primary context of usage, *monogenēs* means "of sole descent," referring to the only child in a family.[26] In the Johannine writings the association of *monogenēs* with *huios* (John 3:6, 18; 1 John 4:9) indicates John's interest in Jesus as the sole Son of God. Accordingly, it would seem appropriate to take *monogenēs theos* to mean "only-begotten God" or "Only-Begotten, who is God," just as a man might refer to his only child as "my only-begotten." We may agree that John does not contemplate the eternal generation of the Son from the Father; but in ordinary language "only-begotten" just means "sole-born." The translation "the only-begotten God" is therefore unobjectionable, though perhaps, like the translation of John 1:1c, requiring some explanation. However that may be, the overriding point remains that all of the proposed translations of *monogenēs theos* refer to Jesus as "God."

Even if *theos* in John 1:18a is a reference to the Father (itself a moot point), it is obvious that in John 1:18b *theos* is a generic term for the Supreme Being, not a designation of the Father, for "only-begotten" itself implies a differentiation of the child from the parent, here the Son from the Father (cf. John 1:14: *monogenēs para patros*), and Christ is said to be "in the bosom of the Father," indicating an intimate personal relationship of Father to Son. It would make absolutely no sense to say that the only-begotten Father, who is in the bosom of the Father, has made him known. Nothing could indicate so powerfully both the shared deity of the Son and Father while at the same time emphasizing their personal distinction as this remarkable designation of Jesus Christ as *monogenēs theos*.

Equally startling as the expression *monogenēs theos* is John's claim, in connection with 1:18a "No one has ever seen God," that the vision of the Lord of hosts described in Isaiah 6:1 was in actuality a vision of the preincarnate Christ: "Isaiah said this because he saw his glory and spoke of him" (John 12:41)! The idea here seems to be that no one has ever seen God the Father, but God the Son has revealed him. Therefore, Isaiah's vision of the Lord upon his throne was a vision of God the Son! We have here not merely the application of an OT proof text about Yahweh to Jesus, but rather the actual retrojection of Christ into a prior historical circumstance. He is

---

26. See Harris, *Jesus as God*, 84, who notes that this meaning is attested in secular Greek literature, the LXX, and other Jewish literature, and the NT.

here clearly equated with God. John differentiates the Son from the Father, but he says that it is the only-begotten God that Isaiah saw.

John 20:28

We reach the christological climax of the Gospel of John in Thomas' confession to the risen Jesus:

> My Lord and my God!

> *Ho kyrios mou kai ho theos mou.* (John 20:28)

Here we confront no textual issues, no interpretive conundrums, no translation difficulties, just a blunt and straightforward confession. Bringing together the titles "Lord" and "God," Thomas' confession of who Jesus truly is constitutes a fitting climax to the entire Gospel. This pairing of *kyrios* and *theos* is abundantly attested in the LXX, the closest parallel being LXX Psalm 34:23 [35:23]: *ho theos mou kai ho kyrios mou*, addressed to Yahweh.[27] That Thomas' confession was not just ecstatic utterance is obvious not only from its OT background but also from the fact that Jesus blesses him for his confession, along with those who believe similarly (v. 29).

Kyrios and *theos* are both terms used of Yahweh in Judaism and should be given their due force here. That is not to say that Jesus is, in John's thinking, Yahweh, for John distinguishes throughout his Gospel between the Father and the Son. Rather *kyrios* and *theos* are here employed as titles, not proper names, as the use of the possessive pronoun "my" in each case shows. The claim is not that Jesus is the Father but that both the Father and the Son are equally God.

1 John 5:20

> we know that the Son of God has come and has given us understanding so that we may know him who is true; and we are in him who is true, in his Son Jesus Christ. He is the true God and eternal life.

> *oidamen de hoti ho huios tou theou ēkei, kai dedōken hēmin dianoian hina ginōskōmen ton alēthinon; kai esmen en tō alēthinō, en tō huiō autou Iēsou Christō. houtos estin ho alēthinos theos kai zōē aiōnios.* (1 John 5:20)

---

27. See list of citations in Harris, *Jesus as God*, 120–21.

The question, in Greek as in English, concerns the antecedent of the demonstrative pronoun *houtos* ("this" or "he"): is it *ton alēthinon* ("him who is true" or "the True One") or is it *Iēsou Christō* ("Jesus Christ")? Either is grammatically possible, and so considerations of context will have to guide our decision. We mentioned that although Harris esteemed both alternatives to be equally probable, the wide majority of scholars since he wrote have argued that *houtos* refers to Jesus Christ as God.[28]

Generally, *houtos* refers back to the most recently mentioned available antecedent, which in this case is *Iēsou Christō*. Nonetheless, *houtos* may take a more remote antecedent if it is uppermost in the author's mind. There are two notable instances in the Johannine epistles:

> Who is the liar but he who denies that Jesus is the Christ? This is the antichrist, he who denies the Father and the Son. (1 John 2:22)

> For many deceivers have gone out into the world, men who will not acknowledge the coming of Jesus Christ in the flesh; such a one is the deceiver and the antichrist. (2 John 1:7)

The antecedent in both cases is indisputably not Jesus Christ. In 1 John 5:20 it might be thought that what is uppermost in the author's mind is the True One, who is God the Father. This consideration is, however, not so persuasive as it may at first appear. For in the two noted instances there is absolutely no ambiguity about the antecedent, all the immediately preceding words being collected into a participial phrase that forms a definite description of the thing being referred to.[29] Verse 5:20e features no such description and belongs in a different category precisely because of its ambiguity. Referring to Jesus Christ accords with 1 John 5:5–6: "Who is it that overcomes the world but he who believes that Jesus is the Son of God? This is he who came by water and blood, Jesus Christ." Harris deems the parallel only verbal, since "this is" is here prospective, not retrospective, in contrast to 1 John 5:20. But *pace* Harris, surely *houtos* here does naturally refer back to Jesus, not merely forwards.[30]

"The True One" doubtless refers to God the Father, not only because we are said to be "in his Son," but also because God the Father is called

---

28. Komoszewski informs me that of the thirty-eight scholarly sources he has consulted on 1 John 5:20 since Harris' work in 1992, thirty-one think that the text calls Jesus *theos*; while only seven disagree (private communication, March 23, 2022).

29. See Griffith, *Keep Yourselves from Idols*, 76.

30. Harris' claim that when "Christ" is the antecedent, the pronoun is always *ekeinos*, not *houtos*, is counterbalanced by the fact that John never uses *houtos* in reference to the Father in his gospel or epistles.

"the only true God" (*ton monon alēthinon theon*) in John 17:3. But who is "eternal life"? When v. 20 is read within the wider context of the Johannine literature, the most probable referent is Jesus Christ. In John's first epistle we find statements like "the word of life—the life was made manifest, and we saw it, and testify to it, and proclaim to you the eternal life which was with the Father and was made manifest to us" (1:1–2), "God gave us eternal life, and this life is in his Son. He who has the Son has life; he who has not the Son of God has not life" (5:11–12), and "I write this to you who believe in the name of the Son of God, that you may know that you have eternal life" (5:13). In the Gospel not only is life found in the Son (John 1:4) but Jesus is said to be "the life" (11:25; 14:6). The only comparable statement in the Johannine literature concerning the Father is John 17:3, which, however, also mentions Christ. So reference to Jesus Christ as "eternal life" in v. 20e seems particularly apt.

One might wonder if *ton alēthinon* might refer to the Father and *zōē aiōnios* refer to the Son. But this interpretation runs afoul of Sharp's Canon, since *zōē aiōnios* is anarthrous, so that there is one and only one referent for the phrase *ho alēthinos theos kai zōē aiōnios*. The adjective *alēthinos* is applied to Jesus five times in the Johannine literature (John 1:9; 6:32; 15:1; 1 John 2:3, 8; Rev 3:14) and so is perfectly appropriate here.

Many commentators have observed that taking *houtos* to refer to "him that is true" makes the phrase into a tautology ("This True One is the true God") and functions poorly rhetorically at the letter's close.[31] But a description of Jesus Christ as the true God is a dramatic closing wholly consonant with Johannine theology and, in light of John 1:1, 18; 20:24, almost to be expected. Here at the close of John's epistle the expression forms a beautiful *inclusio* with the words of his opening in 1 John 1:1–3. Now at the close how suitable to say of Jesus Christ, the Son of him that is true, that this is the true God and eternal life!

One suspects that Harris' fundamental objection to taking "Jesus Christ" to be the referent of "this" is that 5:20e, *understood as an identity statement*, makes the Son personally identical with the Father, which is patently not what John believed. Leave aside for the moment the assumption that 5:20e is intended to be an identity statement. The objection presupposes that in v. 20e "the true God" connotes the Father. But this interpretation is dubious. In John 17:3, when Jesus describes the Father as "the only true God," that expression is plausibly not a definite description connoting the Father, lest Jesus' assertion be that the Father is the only true Father, which is not John's intent. Rather, "God" is plausibly used in 17:3 generically

---

31. E.g., Olsson, "*Deus Semper Maior?*," 149.

for the Supreme Being, to assert that the Father is the true Supreme Being. False gods, by contrast, are not false fathers but false claimants to the status of Supreme Being (cf. 1 John 5:21). Similarly, in 1 John 5:20e "the true God" plausibly connotes the Supreme Being, and Jesus is said to be that Supreme Being. John believed that just as the Father is God, so the Son is God.[32] Whether we can make sense of such a statement is a question for the philosophical, not the biblical, theologian.

Harris thinks that if we do not take 5:20e to assert the personal identity of the Son with the Father, "The only other option would seem to be identity of nature."[33] Harris' formulation of the option is confused. An assertion of the identity of the Son with the divine nature would seem to be an assertion of divine simplicity,[34] which is neither John's nor Harris' intent. Rather, the envisioned option is that the Son and the Father both share the divine nature. Never mind that 5:20e is not a statement about both the Father and the Son, that they share the same nature, but about the Son, that he is the true God. The more important point is that the statement that the Son has the divine nature is not an identity statement at all but a predication. According to this option John should not be understood as making an identity statement of any sort but a predication, predicating deity in its fullest sense to Christ.

Harris protests, "The Achilles' heel of such proposals is the presence of the article. . . . [I]n declaring *what* anyone is, the predicate must have no article; in declaring *who* anyone is the predicate must have the article."[35] This stipulation seems to contradict Harris' own statement that definiteness and qualitativeness are not mutually exclusive categories; a definite noun like *ho theos* could carry a qualitative sense like *deity*.[36] The principle that the article before a noun is omitted "when the writer would lay stress on the quality or character of the object"[37] is consistent with qualitative use of articular nouns.

Compare Thomas' confession in John 20:28. There Harris gives *theos* a qualitative interpretation but says that the article is required grammatically by the nominative of address. But analogously one can say that in 1 John 5:20 *theos* is used qualitatively but the article is required grammatically to bind together the complex expression *ho alēthinos theos kai zōē aiōnios* to

---

32. N.B. that John does not say in John 17:3 that only the Father is the true God (to the exclusion of the Son) but that the Father is the only true God (as is the Son).

33. Harris, *Jesus as God*, 250.

34. Strong simplicity theorists deny a distinction between God and his nature.

35. Harris, *Jesus as God*, 250.

36. Harris, *Jesus as God*, 62-63.

37. Harris, *Jesus as God*, 65; cf. 305.

pick out a single referent in line with Sharp's Canon. In short, we need not think that if *houtos* refers to Jesus Christ, 5:20e means to affirm the identity of Jesus Christ with the Father.

Most NT scholars, then, do not agree with Harris' judgment that in 1 John 5:20 it is equiprobable that *houtos* refers to God or to Jesus Christ. Indeed, many consider the reference to Jesus Christ to be more than merely probable. The preeminent Johannine commentators Raymond Brown and Rudolf Schnackenburg, for example, conclude respectively, "I think the arguments clearly favor *houtos* as a reference to Jesus Christ"[38] and "There is no longer any doubt . . . that the following *houtos* . . . refers to Jesus Christ."[39]

Together the passages we have examined combine to constitute a powerful case that Jesus Christ is presented as God in the pages of the NT. Christ is declared to be divine, just as the Father is divine. The specification of necessary and sufficient conditions for (full) divinity is thus somewhat beside the point. What matters is that Christ is divine in the same sense that the Father is divine, that they are equally divine.

It will not be enough for the Unitarian theologian to dispute the interpretation of just some of these passages; all must fall. The possibility that in every case the majority verdict is mistaken is highly improbable. This fact should give the Unitarian serious pause.[40] I have been wont to emphasize that in each case the wide majority of NT scholars have understood these passages to refer to Christ as God. The point is not that majority opinion serves as evidence for Christ's being called God. There is no substitute for arguments. Rather, majority opinion is evidence that the arguments offered in support of Christ's being called God are convincing. The large majority of those who are experts in the field find these arguments to be cogent. The Unitarian who finds these arguments unconvincing therefore finds himself confronted with powerful evidence that his failure to be convinced says more about his personal psychology than the weakness of the arguments. Thomas McCall speaks the sober truth: "To assume that the monotheism of Scripture prescribes belief in only one divine person while proscribing belief in multiple divine persons is painfully naïve, and in light of the work of contemporary biblical scholarship such an assumption looks misguided indeed."[41]

---

38. Brown, *Epistles of John*, 66.

39. Schnackenburg, *Johannine Epistles*, 262.

40. Wainwright rightly remarks that one "will not want to dismiss an example, which has six companions, as easily as one which stands alone" (*Trinity in the New Testament*, 66).

41. McCall, *Which Trinity?* 95.

The Holy Spirit

David Brown has observed that while debate over the Son has focused on his deity rather than his personal distinctness, in the case of the Holy Spirit "the divinity has never been in doubt; what has been challenged is his separate identity."[42] Although the biblical words *rūach* and *pneuma* are frequently used in various impersonal senses, they are also employed in a personal sense to designate intellectual substances, that is, immaterial personal agents or spirits, including human spirits, unembodied finite spirits, and preeminently the divine Spirit.[43] The expression "the Holy Spirit" is a designation uniquely used of the biblical God, employed hypostatically to refer to the divine Spirit as a personal agent.

In the Gospels the canonical Jesus—whatever one thinks about the historical Jesus[44]—was anointed and inspired throughout his ministry by the Holy Spirit. Luke is especially emphatic on the role of the Holy Spirit in Jesus' life and ministry. In the angel's annunciation to Mary of her virginal conception all three of the traditional Trinitarian persons are mentioned (1:32–34). At Jesus' baptism the Holy Spirit comes upon him to anoint him for his messianic ministry. Again we find all three of the Trinitarian persons involved in this pivotal event (3:21). When Jesus publicly announces his ministry in the synagogue at Nazareth, he quotes, as fulfilled, Isaiah's prophetic words: "The Spirit of the Lord is upon me, because he has anointed me to preach good news to the poor" (4:18; cf. Isa 61:1). Here once more we find all three Trinitarian persons mentioned.

In the book of Acts, Luke presents an explosion of activity inspired by the Holy Spirit. Following the outpouring of the Holy Spirit at Pentecost, the remainder of Acts describes the apostles' Spirit-inspired ministry. In story after story we see that the Holy Spirit is God himself and therefore manifestly personal. Not only did he speak via the OT prophets (1:16; 28:25), but he speaks to and directs the apostles (8:29; 10:19; 11:12). Especially interesting is Acts 13:2: "While they were worshiping the Lord and fasting, the Holy Spirit said, 'Set apart for me Barnabas and Saul for the work to which I have called them.'" The Holy Spirit here not only speaks but uses first-person

---

42. Brown, *Divine Trinity*, xvi.

43. See the thorough treatment by Kleinknecht et al., "πνευμα, πνευματικος," 332–451, esp. 338, 359.

44. For a historical case see Dunn, *Jesus and the Spirit*. Dunn argues that Jesus was a charismatic: "it is certain that Jesus believed himself to be empowered by the Spirit and thought of himself as God's son. . . . If we spell out Jesus' own religious experience, his experience of God, solely in terms of sonship, we misunderstand Jesus almost totally. Jesus' experience was also of God as Spirit" (63, 89).

indexicals, ruling out any interpretation of the Holy Spirit as an impersonal power. The Holy Spirit is described as having appointed the apostles to their ministry (20:28) and as guiding them in their ministry travels (13:4), deeming certain actions to be good (15:8) but forbidding other actions to them (16:6–7). The Holy Spirit testifies not only to the apostles (20:23) but also through them to others (5:32), who are sometimes said to resist the Holy Spirit (6:10; 7:51). The story of Ananias and Saphira's deception is especially interesting. To Ananias Peter says, "Why has Satan filled your heart to lie to the Holy Spirit?" (5:3) and to Saphira "How is it that you have agreed together to tempt the Spirit of the Lord?" (5:9), implying the Spirit's personhood. Peter expressly says, "You have not lied to men but to God" (5:4), thereby implying his full divinity.

In John's Gospel we have a great deal of teaching by the canonical Jesus concerning the person and work of the Holy Spirit. All three of the traditional Trinitarian persons feature prominently in these teachings. Jesus promises that since he is departing, "I will pray the Father, and he will give you another Counselor, to be with you for ever, even the Spirit of truth" (14:16–17; cf. 16:4–7). This Counselor is to be sent by the Father during the impending period of Jesus' absence and is therefore distinct from both. The notion of a Counselor or Advocate or Comforter (*paraklētos*) is inherently personal. That implication is underlined by Jesus' use of the adjective *allos* rather than *heteros* with respect to the Paraclete, indicating another counselor of the same nature, someone like Jesus. His personhood becomes evident in Jesus' description of his ministry: "The Counselor, the Holy Spirit, whom the Father will send in my name, he will teach you all things, and bring to your remembrance all that I have said to you" (14:28). Jesus expands on the teaching ministry of the promised Holy Spirit: "When the Spirit of truth comes, he will guide you into all the truth; for he will not speak on his own authority, but whatever he hears he will speak, and he will declare to you the things that are to come" (16:13–14). Here the Holy Spirit conveys not only remembrance of the past but foreknowledge of the future, a uniquely divine prerogative (Isa 41:21–24). Moreover, "when he comes, he will convince the world concerning sin and righteousness and judgment" (16:8), inherently personal activities. The Holy Spirit "will bear witness to me" (15:26) and "will glorify me, for he will take what is mine and declare it to you" (16:14). We glimpse here the economic subordination of the Spirit to the Son, as of the Son to the Father.

In the Pauline correspondence, as well as the rest of the NT, the Holy Spirit is similarly presented as a divine person. Paul says that "When we cry, 'Abba! Father!' it is the Spirit himself bearing witness with our spirit that we are children of God" (Rom 8:14; cf. Gal 4:6). Such a dyadic relation of bearing testimony is necessarily an interpersonal relation. In a striking passage Paul writes, "The Spirit searches everything, even the depths of God. For what person knows a man's thoughts except the spirit of the man which is in him? So also no one comprehends the thoughts of God except the Spirit of God" (1 Cor 2:10–11). Clearly this statement entails that the Holy Spirit is both personal and fully divine. In fact, this statement might at first blush seem to imply that just as one's own spirit is not personally distinct from oneself, so God's Spirit is not personally distinct from God (the Father). But in Romans 8, in describing the intercessory ministry of the Holy Spirit on our behalf, Paul clearly differentiates the two: "Likewise the Spirit helps us in our weakness; for we do not know how to pray as we ought, but the Spirit himself intercedes for us with sighs too deep for words. And he who searches the hearts of men knows what is the mind of the Spirit, because the Spirit intercedes for the saints according to the will of God" (Rom 8:26–27). Here it is the Holy Spirit who acts as an intercessor between us and God the Father. It is the Father who knows the mind of the Spirit, rather than, as in 1 Corinthians, the Spirit who knows the mind of the Father. The Spirit takes our often misguided prayers and translates them into requests in accordance with God's will, and God the Father, knowing the Spirit's mind, answers our prayers appropriately. It is hard to avoid the implication, not only of the deity and personhood of the Holy Spirit, but of a diversity of persons within God.

It seems indisputable, then, that in the NT the Holy Spirit is taken to be both personal and divine, as divine as the Father and the Son. The only remaining question, then, is the one posed by Brown: is the Holy Spirit a distinct person from the Father and the Son? In places the lines of distinction between the persons can seem blurry. That raises the possibility that the Holy Spirit is personally identical with the Father or the Son. The second of these possibilities may be easily ruled out. As we have seen, the Holy Spirit is presented as standing in for Christ during his absence from this universe until the time of his parousia. In the economy of God's salvific plan the Holy Spirit continues and extends Jesus' ministry begun during his earthly lifetime and can therefore be denominated "the Spirit of Christ." That role helps to explain the blurriness of the lines of personal distinction between Christ and the Holy Spirit. For example, Paul writes,

> But you are not in the flesh, you are in the Spirit, if in fact the Spirit of God dwells in you. Any one who does not have the Spirit of Christ does not belong to him. But if Christ is in you, although your bodies are dead because of sin, your spirits are alive because of righteousness. If the Spirit of him who raised

Jesus from the dead dwells in you, he who raised Christ Jesus from the dead will give life to your mortal bodies also through his Spirit which dwells in you. (Rom 8:9–11)

Notice how Paul moves from speaking of "the Spirit" to "the Spirit of God" to "the Spirit of Christ" to simply "Christ." The Holy Spirit becomes so closely aligned with Christ that he can be spoken of simply as "Christ," even though he is expressly said to be "the Spirit of him who raised Jesus from the dead." So while Paul believes that we Christians are indwelt by the Holy Spirit, he can also say, "I have been crucified with Christ; it is no longer I who live, but Christ who lives in me" (Gal 2:20).

So could the Holy Spirit be, more plausibly, God the Father? This possibility is ruled out by the triadic formulae that pervade the NT, delineating exactly three divine persons.[45] We may mention just a few of the more famous passages. For example, Matthew 28:19 includes a baptismal formula that names all three persons instead of just Jesus: "Go therefore and make disciples of all nations, baptizing them in the name of the Father and of the Son and of the Holy Spirit (*eis to onoma tou patros kai tou hiou kai tou hagiou pneumatos*)." There can be no doubt that in the thinking of Matthew's community there are three persons listed here, as underlined by the repetition of the article, not merely two persons. By the same token it is unthinkable that there might have been a fourth person whom Matthew failed to mention.

Another well-known triadic formula is Paul's doxology in 2 Corinthians 13:14: "The grace of the *Lord Jesus Christ* and the love of *God* and the fellowship of the *Holy Spirit* be with you all." These are the three divine persons, and the only three divine persons, mentioned by Paul in his letters. If two of them were actually the same person, it would be gratuitous and highly misleading to mention three. Elsewhere Paul mentions the same three persons. To the Thessalonians he wrote, "We are bound to give thanks to *God* always for you, brethren beloved by the *Lord*, because God chose you from the beginning to be saved, through sanctification by the *Spirit* and belief in the truth" (2 Thess 2:13). To the Corinthians he wrote, "Now there are varieties of gifts, but the same *Spirit*; and there are varieties of service, but the same *Lord*; and there are varieties of working, but it is the same *God* who inspires them all in every one" (1 Cor 12:4–6). Again, "It is *God* who establishes us with you in *Christ*, and has commissioned us; he has put his seal upon us and given us his *Spirit* in our hearts as a guarantee" (2 Cor 1:21–22). To the Romans he wrote, "I appeal to you, brethren, by our *Lord Jesus Christ* and by the love of the *Spirit*, to strive together with me in your

---

45. For a fuller discussion see Wainwright, *Trinity in the New Testament*, chapter 13.

prayers to *God* on my behalf" (Rom 15:30). To the Galatians he wrote, "Because you are sons, *God* has sent the *Spirit* of his *Son* into our hearts, crying, 'Abba! Father!'" (Gal 4:6).

Other well-known triadic formulae in the NT include, for example, Ephesians 2:18: "through *him* [Christ] we both have access in one *Spirit* to the *Father*." Peter writes to those who are "chosen and destined by *God the Father* and sanctified by the *Spirit* for obedience to *Jesus Christ*" (1 Pet 1:2). Jude exhorts his readers to "pray in the *Holy Spirit;* keep yourselves in the love of *God;* wait for the mercy of our *Lord Jesus Christ* unto eternal life" (Jude 20–21). We have seen that in the Gospels the triadic pattern manifests itself at key moments in Jesus' life, such as his virginal conception, his baptism, his temptation in the desert, and his announcement at Nazareth. The Gospel of John, more than any other NT book, stresses the fact that Jesus is God and that the Holy Spirit is a divine person whose functions are distinct from those of the Father and Son.

Given that we have independent scriptural warrant for the deity and personhood of the Holy Spirit as well as of the Son, these pervasive triadic formulae exclude any realistic possibility that the Holy Spirit and the Father are in fact the same person listed twice. This is underscored by the different properties and roles attributed to each. The Father, in particular, cannot be the Spirit of Christ, any more than the Father can be sent by the Father.

Summary

In summary, we have strong scriptural grounds for affirming that

    i. There is exactly one God

and

    ii. There are exactly three distinct persons who are properly called God.

Now "a Trinity doctrine is commonly expressed as the statement that the one God exists as or in three equally divine 'Persons', the Father, the Son, and the Holy Spirit."[46] It therefore follows that, as commonly expressed, the NT teaches a doctrine of the Trinity.

---

46. See Tuggy, "Trinity."

Model Component

So far as the biblical doctrine of the Trinity is concerned, the model component more or less takes care of itself. Brower and Rea observe that there is nothing particularly philosophically problematic about the above statement of the biblical doctrine of the Trinity.

> The central claim of the doctrine of the Trinity is that God exists in three persons—Father, Son, and Holy Spirit. This claim is not problematic because of any superficial incoherence or inconsistency with well-entrenched intuitions. Rather, it is problematic because of a tension that results from constraints imposed on its interpretation by other aspects of orthodox Christian theology ... neatly summarized in ... the so-called Athanasian creed.[47]

It is these accreted constraints that occasion philosophical problems for the biblical doctrine of the Trinity. So one finds that philosophical articles on the subject of the Trinity very typically begin with quotations from later conciliar formulations of the doctrine, particularly the apparently incoherent Athanasian Creed. Protestants, however, bring all doctrinal statements, even conciliar creeds, especially creeds of non-ecumenical councils, before the bar of Scripture. To the extent that these formulations impose further constraints upon the above formulated biblical doctrine of the Trinity, I have no interest in defending them.

The biblical doctrine of the Trinity becomes logically problematic only if one interprets such statements as the following:

1. The Father is God
2. The Son is God
3. The Son is not the Father

as identity statements. Philip Bricker rightly warns, however, "Surface grammar often misrepresents the underlying logic: one must beware inferring logical from grammatical form."[48] The endemic ambiguity of ordinary language can make it very difficult to discern just when an author, especially one utterly unacquainted with the modern relation of identity, intends to make an identity statement. While biblical authors believed that the Son is God, they would have balked at the assertion that God is the Son, which suggests that we misinterpret them if we construe their initial belief as an identity statement. Similarly, the same author who affirms that the Father is "the only true God" (John 17:3) also affirms that Jesus Christ "is the true

---

47. Brower and Rea, "Material Constitution and the Trinity," 58.
48. Bricker, "Identity," 567.

God and eternal life" (1 John 5:20), which again suggests that we misconstrue these affirmations if we interpret them as statements of identity. Or again, the fact that the NT authors affirm that the Father is God and that Jesus Christ is God does not lead them to infer that the Father is Jesus Christ, in accordance with the transitivity of identity, showing once more that it is an anachronistic hermeneutical error to import the modern identity relation into these authors' statements. There is just no *prima facie* logical incoherence in the biblical doctrine of the Trinity.

As for the metaphysical coherence of the biblical doctrine, it seems to me that a disarmingly simple model of the biblical doctrine may be stated as follows: God is an immaterial, tri-personal being. That's it! No metaphysical mumbo-jumbo, no exotic stand-ins for the classical identity relation, no time-travelling fancy foot-stepping! God is an immaterial, tri-personal being, plain and simple.

We can gain some insight into this model by reflecting on the nature of the soul. Souls are immaterial substances, and many substance dualists hold that animals have souls. On such a view souls come in a spectrum of varying capacities and faculties. Higher animals such as chimpanzees and dolphins possess souls more richly endowed with powers than those of iguanas and turtles. What makes the human soul a person is that the human soul is equipped with rational faculties of intellect and volition which enable it to be a self-reflective agent capable of a first-person perspective and self-determination. Now God is very much like an unembodied soul; indeed, as a mental substance God just seems to be a soul. We naturally equate a rational soul with a person, since the human souls with which we are acquainted are persons. But the reason human souls are individual persons is because each soul is equipped with one set of rational faculties sufficient for being a person. Suppose, then, that God is a soul which is endowed with three complete sets of rational faculties, each sufficient for personhood. Then God, though one soul, would not be one person but three, for God would have three centers of self-consciousness, intentionality, and volition, as social Trinitarians maintain. God would clearly not be three discrete souls because the rational faculties in question are all faculties belonging to just one soul, one immaterial substance. God would therefore be an immaterial, tripersonal substance, just as each of us is an immaterial, unipersonal substance.[49] This model of the Trinity is straightforward, perspicuous, and

---

49. Christopher Hughes arrives at a model much like this, according to which there are three Trinitarian persons who all have God as their substance. Hughes even suggests that this relation of "ensubstancement" "in certain ways resembles the relation holding between 'multiple centers of consciousness' and a human person with a divided mind" ("Defending the Consistency of the Doctrine of the Trinity," 313).

explanatorily deep. Such a biblically consonant view of the Trinity, while not committed to all the later credal formulations, seems to give a clear sense to the classical formula "three persons in one substance."[50] As a name for this view I suggest "Tri-Personal Monotheism."

Conclusion

In conclusion, we have seen that the biblical doctrine of the Trinity affirms that (i) There is exactly one God, and (ii) There are exactly three distinct persons who are properly called God. Such a doctrine is *prima facie* logically unproblematic and can be straightforwardly modeled: God is an immaterial, tripersonal being.

---

50. William Hasker agrees: "The doctrine of the Trinity affirms that the three persons are together a *single concrete being*—that they share between them a single trope of deity, a single concrete instance of the divine nature. This claim can be modeled by the notion of a single mental substance, or soul, supporting simultaneously three distinct conscious lives, three distinct streams of experience" (*Metaphysics and the Tri-Personal God*, 257).

3

God and His Word and His Spirit Are One God

Beau Branson

Thou who art the Most Monarchial Trinity, not only because Thou alone reignest over all, but also because Thou hast one single origin in Thine own self, the origin prior to all origination, the only uncaused Monad, from whom originate and back to whom refer, timelessly and causelessly, the Son and the Spirit.

—St. Gregory Palamas[1]

God, and his Word, and his Spirit, are in reality one God.

—St. John of Damascus[2]

Introduction

In our opening essays, we are supposed to explain, and argue for, our views about the Trinity. Mine will be somewhat different in that, strictly speaking, I have no theory about *the Trinity*. If, like Moses or Isaiah, I had "stood in the [divine] council" and "seen the Logos" (Jer 23:16–18; 22), I could speak about the Trinity with confidence. Unfortunately, I haven't.

---

1. *Apodictic Treatises*, 61.
2. *On the Orthodox Faith*, 80.

I do have a view about *the doctrine of* the Trinity, a doctrine hotly debated during the fourth century. That's much easier to know about. Unlike knowledge about *the Trinity itself*, one needs no special prophetic abilities to investigate *an idea about* the Trinity—all one has to do is read! Then, like anything else in the history of ideas, one asks questions. "Is this idea logically coherent? What are its metaphysical commitments?" And so on. That will be my approach.

In contrast, rather than investigating *the doctrine of* the Trinity, in most philosophical literature on the Trinity, authors lay out *their own theory* or "model" of the Trinity and then argue about *its* coherence, plausibility, and so on. I've argued elsewhere such arguments have the logical form "A is Φ, therefore B is Φ."[3] In other words, most of the philosophical literature—whether for or against Trinitarianism—consists of non-sequiturs. So, rather than develop my own model of the Trinity, I'll evaluate the doctrine of the Trinity itself, as best I understand it.

I'm well aware many deny there is any such thing as "the" doctrine of the Trinity. While I understand the sentiment, such objections, once articulated, are typically either incoherent or irrelevant. They will certainly be irrelevant for us. The question is whether there is any view about the Trinity that is orthodox (not heretical) and meets whatever desiderata one has. The difference would only be whether one describes that as "a successful version of the doctrine of the Trinity" or "one successful model of the Trinity."

For an uncontroversially orthodox model (or version), I focus on St. Gregory of Nyssa, along with the other "Cappadocians" (St. Basil the Great and St. Gregory the Theologian) and St. John of Damascus, who summarized and systematized the views of earlier church fathers (particularly the Cappadocians). Gregory of Nyssa's theology was central to the final settlement of the Trinitarian controversy culminating in the Second Ecumenical Council (381), which issued the Nicene-Constantinopolitan Creed, and a handful of councils afterward that marked the beginning of the end of Arianism in the Roman Empire. Indeed, immediately after the council of 381, Roman law defined "catholic church" partly in terms of being in communion with Gregory of Nyssa personally.[4] Hence, to say that the stated Trinitarian theology of Gregory of Nyssa *doesn't count* as orthodox would be, if not incoherent, then bordering on it.

---

3. I.e., "my model of the Trinity is coherent, therefore the doctrine of the Trinity is coherent." See my "Ahistoricity in Analytic Theology."

4. See Pharr, *Theodosian Code*, 440.

Desiderata

One typically argues for or against a model of the Trinity by showing how it meets, or fails to meet, certain desiderata. I don't object to philosophically evaluating models of the Trinity, only to the unargued-for presupposition that there will automatically be some important relation between a given model of the Trinity and the doctrine of the Trinity itself. (Or, if one is allergic to talk about "the" doctrine, the presupposition that one's model is among the nebulous horde that count as orthodox, rather than those that count as heretical, like modalism and Arianism.)

What should our desiderata be? For some, the fact that a view is orthodox may be enough. In that case, its being stated by church fathers like the Cappadocians, or affirmed by ecumenical councils, suffices. Others may want to know more. Is it logically coherent? Does it involve implausible metaphysics? Is it scriptural? One way to investigate such questions is to see how a model stands up to the strongest objections against it. Although this approach is useful, much of the literature focuses so much on responding to objections that it loses sight of the original motivations *for* Trinitarianism. The doctrine of the Trinity becomes an "orphaned belief."[5] This is doubly problematic.

First, when we ignore the original motivations for Trinitarianism, Unitarianism can come to seem like a "default" view. If Trinitarianism faces difficulties, even if not insurmountable, one may be tempted to adopt Unitarianism as though it were unproblematic, or as though there were no motivation for Trinitarianism but tradition. But that's a misleading picture.

Second, for those who *do* construct their own models of the Trinity, their models risk drifting so far from the doctrine's original motivations as to become unrecognizable. Frankly, this is all too common. One frequently sees articles proposing new models of the Trinity that incorporate the latest fads from analytic metaphysics, but which bear little relation to the doctrine's original motivations and would likely be unrecognizable to its historical proponents. These often seem like metaphysical band-aids, as though the author knows they are supposed to affirm *something* called "the doctrine of the Trinity," but with little idea what that doctrine is, or what role it is supposed to play in a larger theological context. Hence, one desideratum must involve how a model relates to the original motivations for Trinitarianism.

---

5. Roughly, when a person (or group) bases belief y on belief x (or assigns a certain probability to y based on x), but later abandons (or forgets) belief x, but retains belief y (or fails to update the probability of y by downgrading it appropriately), y becomes an "orphaned belief."

Let's be specific. I'll focus on what seem to me to be the three most important issues: one major argument *for* Trinitarianism and two *against*. With respect to the former, I'll focus on what's sometimes called "Jewish Binitarianism," or the theology of "two powers in heaven." This theology was not uncommon in late Second Temple Judaism, and scholarship concerning the time period generally agrees it is the ground out of which Trinitarianism sprang.[6] This in turn is itself a deep issue, motivated by multiple considerations that can't all be canvassed briefly. So I'll focus even more narrowly on just one concern that seems to me to be, if not the most central motivation for both the Jewish and the Christian versions of this theology, at least one of the most prominent. Call it the "Theophanies Problem" (TP). The problem is simple. God tells Moses, "You shall not see My face" because "No man can see Me and live" (Exod 33:20). Yet many people see God—even "face to face" (e.g., Exod 33:11)—and live. How can these apparently contradictory claims be reconciled?

To elaborate, nowhere does Scripture ever tell us there are *different senses* in which one can "see" God (or not). And only in John 6:46 is any exception ever made to the quantifier—"*no*" man (the exception being Jesus, which is no help with Moses, Isaiah, or anyone else who saw God). What we *do* see in Scripture, however, is another figure, *the Angel of YHWH*, who is himself sometimes referred to as "God" or "YHWH."[7] It was therefore natural for many late Second Temple Jews to suppose the theophanies were not appearances of God himself, but of another figure, who for some reason is also sometimes called "God" or "YHWH." Various late Second Temple sources speculate about the identity and nature of this figure (often also imagined as God's "vice-regent").[8] Some took him to be a human exalted to divine status, like Enoch in the Book of Enoch, some a (created) angel like Metatron in the Talmud, and some a being who existed since before the creation of the world, and was even *the agent of* creation, like the Memra in the Targums.[9] So as not to beg any questions about the identity or nature of the figure directly seen in the theophanies, I will simply refer to "The Theophany Figure" (capitals, if assumed to be the same figure) or "a

---

6. E.g., Barker, *Great Angel*; Boyarin, *Border Lines*; Boyarin, "Gospel of the Memra"; Boyarin, *Jewish Gospels*; Heiser, "Divine Council"; Orlov, *Glory of the Invisible God*; Schäfer, *Two Gods in Heaven*; Segal, *Two Powers in Heaven*.

7. For just a few among many examples: Gen 16:7–14; 22:11–12; 31:11–13; Judg 13:21–23.

8. See Heiser, "Divine Council," especially sections 2.5–6 and chapter 8.

9. On the correlation between these late Second Temple Jewish theologies and the early Christian christological categories of adoptionism, Arianism, and proto-orthodoxy, see De Young, *Religion of the Apostles*, 14–15.

theophany figure" (lower case, if assumed that there were different figures involved in different theophanies). Another way to state TP, then, is to say a model of the Trinity should reconcile the apparently contradictory scriptural claims about the theophanies, and do so in a way that is not merely *ad hoc*, but rooted in Scripture itself and what we know about the late Second Temple Judaism out of which Christianity emerged.

Our second desideratum deals with the most common *objection* to Trinitarianism (in our day): the allegation that it amounts to tritheism. Call this the "Three Gods Problem" (3G). Our second desideratum is simple: a model of the Trinity should not be tritheistic. Less commonly discussed is how 3G generalizes. "God" is not the only word that can be predicated of more than one Trinitarian *hypostasis*, despite there being only one such thing. For example, Trinitarians say the Father is *the Creator* (e.g., Gen 1:1), but so is the Son (John 1:3; Col 1:16) and the Holy Spirit (Ps 33:6; 104:30; Job 33:4). Yet, there are not three creators, but one creator. Call this more general problem the "Three F's Problem" (3F).[10] 3F even affects Unitarianism. For the term "God," Unitarians deny the divinity of the Son and Spirit, and for "creator," their role in creation, but without a *general* solution to 3F, Unitarianism still faces objections involving other predicates. For example, Isaiah 43:11 and 45:21 say there is "no other *savior*,"[11] but the New Testament (NT) calls both the Father (Luke 1:47; Titus 1:3) and the Son (Luke 2:11; Titus 1:4) "savior." While we'll focus on the more common objection (3G), we'll also keep an eye on the more general problem (3F).

Finally, while most philosophical discussion of the Trinity focuses narrowly on 3G, I credit Dale Tuggy with pressing another objection, logically distinct from 3G (and 3F), but often incorrectly confused with 3G. Because of this confusion, it is not often directly addressed by Trinitarians. The objection is this. At least in the NT, when the word "God" is used, not as a common noun, but as a referring expression, it almost always refers to the Father. But some Trinitarians use "God" to refer to *any* of the persons equally, and others use "God" to refer to *the Trinity as a whole*, rather than *the Father*. Call this the "Who Is God?" Problem (WIG). The question is, what does the term "God" refer to when used as a referring expression? The Father? The Son? The Holy Spirit? The Trinity? Perhaps different ones at different times?[12]

10. I will refer to this as the *Three F's* Problem although, strictly speaking, some instances may only involve two of the divine *hypostases*. But the problem is similar in either case.

11. And in precisely the passages Unitarians often appeal to for the claim there is "no other god," e.g., Isaiah 43–45.

12. Jenson addresses this issue in detail in *Systematic Theology*, 44, 115. I am not aware of Tuggy having addressed Jenson's discussion in print.

This might seem like merely a semantic issue. The *evidence*, after all, is entirely semantic (how a particular *word* is used in the NT). As such, it might seem unimportant. One can construct a model of the Trinity and label the objects in it however one likes. Maybe the NT authors label things differently. So what? If the Unitarian insists on labeling things the same way the NT does, this might seem like just a silly superstition about words, rather than a substantive theological argument. Furthermore, it seems one could humor the Unitarian by leaving one's model entirely as-is and merely relabeling some objects in it.

I say this might *seem* unimportant. But when coupled with the substantive constraints of 3G, it can create problems for certain models. William Lane Craig's model is a useful example.[13] Intuitively, it would seem Trinitarians would want to say that the Father, Son, and Holy Spirit all have the divine nature, but *also* that God has the divine nature. Since Craig identifies God with the Trinity, rather than the Father, this creates a trilemma. Either:

A. God has the divine nature, but the Father, Son, and Holy Spirit don't,

B. the persons all have the divine nature, but God doesn't, or

C. there are four things instantiating the divine nature (rather than just one or just three).[14]

But (C) would be a *quaternity*, rather than a *trinity*. As for (B), what else would God's nature be, but divine? Craig opts for (A): God has the divine nature, but the Father, Son and Holy Spirit don't.[15]

Some consider this trilemma a decisive objection in itself (though naturally Craig does not). But the point (at the moment) is not to criticize Craig, but to show how a semantic requirement (WIG), can lead to substantive constraints when coupled with 3G. Suppose, to solve WIG, Craig *merely* relabels his model. Now "God" labels the Father rather than the Trinity. But now, *God lacks the divine nature too*—a "worst of both worlds" result. To fix that, Craig would need to make a substantive change to the theology, taking the divine nature away from the Trinity and giving it to the three persons.

---

13. Indeed, models like Craig's seem to be precisely Tuggy's target. A similar model would be that of Cornelius Plantinga, "Gregory of Nyssa and the Social Analogy of the Trinity."

14. Brian Leftow makes this argument, in a slightly different form, in "Anti-Social Trinitarianism," 221.

15. Though, according to Craig, one can be "divine" either by having the divine nature, or through something like analogical predication. See Moreland and Craig, *Philosophical Foundations*, 590–91.

But that would undermine his solution to 3G (namely, that there is only one god, because only one thing—the Trinity—instantiates the divine nature). Again, the point (at the moment) isn't to critique Craig, but to show how WIG, though a primarily semantic point, can join forces with 3G to produce additional substantive constraints on accounts of the Trinity. To be explicit then, for a model of the Trinity to "solve" WIG, it must either identify God with the Father or it must at least *be possible* to relabel its elements in that way, without resulting in incoherence.

To summarize, these are in my view the most important desiderata for a view about the Trinity: that it solves TP, 3G (and 3F generally), and WIG.

Linguistic Distinctions

Perhaps because the professional interests of most philosophers who deal with the Trinity lie in metaphysics, much of the literature has focused on giving metaphysically sophisticated responses to 3G. Less attention has been given to the philosophy of language (or simply grammar!), the philosophy of logic, or the philosophy of mathematics. Since it is assumed that sophisticated metaphysics is supposed to solve 3G, the metaphysics actually employed by patristic authors is often rejected as insufficient,[16] or it's assumed that the metaphysics must *really* be something beyond what is explicitly stated.[17] Discussions regularly overlook ambiguities and complexities of language, even when patristic sources discuss them explicitly and in detail, and explicitly state that they constitute, or are central to, a patristic author's response to certain objections. So, to get some clarity, I'll start by making some purely linguistic distinctions.

First, to avoid ambiguity about the "is" of identity and the "is" of predication, we can use the identity sign ("=") for identity and reserve the word "is" for predications.

Next, in English, it's traditional to capitalize "God" in reference to the *true* God and to use lower-case "god" in reference to *false* gods, regardless of whether "God" is used as a proper name or a common name (common noun). But since English otherwise typically uses capital and lower case letters to distinguish between proper and common names, this can create confusion, making it look as though "God" is used as a proper name, when it is in fact being used as a common name, as in "Thou art man, and not God" (Ezek 28:9), which really means "You are human, and not divine," but looks like "You are (a) man, and not the individual named 'God.'" So rather than

---

16. E.g., Pawl, "Conciliar Trinitarianism."
17. E.g., Kelly, *Early Christian Doctrines*, 236–37.

using lower-case and capital letters to distinguish between true and false gods, I'll use lower-case "god" for the *common noun* and capital-G "God" for the *referring expression*, with no implication that "a god" is necessarily a *false* god. Thus, I write Ezekiel 28:9 as "Thou art (a) man, and not (a) god" and I write Psalm 77:13 as "Thy way, O God, is in the sanctuary: who is so great a god as our god?" (with no implication that God is a false god!).

Next, "god" (the common noun) can predicate different things. The Greek word *polytheia* (polytheism) traces back to pre-Christian times.[18] Yet the first (and only two!) uses of *monotheia* (monotheism) that appear in a search of the *Thesaurus Linguae Graecae* do not occur until the fourteenth century,[19] while *polytheia* shows up almost eight hundred times across various centuries. Did Christians lack the concept of monotheism before the fourteenth century? Clearly not. They had the *idea*. But the *word* they used was not "*monotheia*," but "*monarchia*."[20] While we get the word "monarchy" from "*monarchia*," and it *can* be used to mean "a single rule(r),"[21] it can also mean "a single *source*." The latter was the sense in which Christians, from the beginning, were concerned to maintain there was "one god." Namely, that there was a single ultimate source of all things, the "*archē anarchos*," "*principium sine principium*," or "source without source." In terminology Tuggy has defined, there was a single "ultimate."[22]

I'll disambiguate different senses of "god" with subscripts. For a god in the sense of "ultimate source," I will write "god$_{\text{ULTIMATE-SOURCE}}$." Since part of the idea is that this being is the ultimate source *of everything else* (except itself), it follows logically that there couldn't be more than one. So, rather than speaking of "(a) god$_{\text{ULTIMATE-SOURCE}}$," we can speak of "*the* god$_{\text{ULTIMATE-SOURCE}}$."

Today, many take "*x* is (a) god" to mean *x has the divine nature*. It's noteworthy that this claim was rejected by every ante-Nicene church father

---

18. It is used for example by Philo, who was contemporaneous with Christ. See Philo, *Works*, 359.

19. Once in a work by Nicephorus Gregoras and once in a work by Gregory Palamas.

20. As noted by Prestige, *God in Patristic Thought*: "The word expressing the principle of divine unity is 'monarchy': Though modern writers have used the name Monarchian to denote a complex of heretical opinions, there is really nothing heretical whatever in its ancient application. 'Monarchy' is employed by the most respectable Fathers in the sense of what we call 'monotheism'" (xxv) and "The term expressive of the principle of monotheism was 'monarchy'" (94). See also Prestige, *Fathers and Heretics*: "'monarchy', in patristic language, being roughly equivalent to 'monotheism'" (165). Noted also by Lacugna, *God for Us*: "Monotheism was the same thing as 'monarchy' (*monē archē*)" (33).

21. See the epigraph from Gregory Palamas above, and my comments about Gregory Nazianzen in Oration 31 below.

22. See Tuggy, "On Counting Gods," 194–95.

who ever mentioned it. Gregory of Nyssa continues that tradition, explicitly denying it in literally every work he wrote on the Trinity.[23] Instead, like his ante-Nicene forebears, Gregory takes "x is (a) god" to mean *x performs an activity* of a certain type that is *characteristic of* the divine nature. Just as Plato and Aristotle held that natures are individuated by an associated "function" (or as I like to call it, a "characteristic activity"), Gregory supposes there is a type of activity characteristic of the divine nature, and performing it is what the word "god" properly and literally predicates. He notes that Scripture calls many things "gods" that do not have the divine nature (including demons).[24] Nor are these always "false" gods (God did not make Moses a *false* god to Pharaoh in Exod 7:1). Hence, the scriptural use of "god" cannot always and only mean "a thing with the divine nature." We'll revisit this below. For now, to disambiguate, I'll use "is (a) god$_{\text{NATURE}}$" to mean "has the divine nature" and "is (a) god$_{\text{POWER/ACTION}}$" for "performs a token activity of the characteristically divine type."[25] On Gregory's view then, Scripture does not use "god" as a *natural kind term* (god$_{\text{NATURE}}$), but as an *agent noun* (god$_{\text{POWER/ACTION}}$), like "shoemaker" or, more to the point, "savior" or "creator."

In "On Counting Gods," Tuggy usefully distinguishes between an "ultimate" (or what I've called a "source without source"), a "deity" (a supernaturally powerful self), and a "god" (an *ultimate deity*). Hence, Tuggy's definition of "god" parallels what I've labelled god$_{\text{ULTIMATE-SOURCE}}$, and his term "deity" parallels god$_{\text{POWER/ACTION}}$.[26] Neither corresponds to god$_{\text{NATURE}}$.

23. See Branson, *Logical Problem*, 136–39, 146–48, 174–78. Branson, "Gregory of Nyssa on the Individuation of Actions and Events," 135–37.

24. E.g., Ps 95:5 (96:5) LXX: "For all the gods of the gentiles are demons, but YHWH made the heavens."

25. Note that none of these distinctions is *ad hoc*. Grammar demands the syntactic distinction between the referential and predicative uses—"God" and "god." And even the Unitarian requires different meanings for the common noun "god," since other things besides God the Father are called "god" in the Bible—including, most problematically, *Jesus*. As noted below, Tuggy himself distinguishes between a "god" and a "deity," to mean roughly what I label "god$_{\text{ULTIMATE-SOURCE}}$" and "god$_{\text{POWER/ACTION}}$." See Tuggy, "On Counting Gods," 194–98.

26. Gregory defines "god" ("god$_{\text{POWER/ACTION}}$") in terms of *one particular type of activity*, while Tuggy defines "deity" in terms of a *set* of (types of) *powers*. Nevertheless, the definitions are close enough to be interchangeable for our purposes. Powers and their active uses are obviously correlated. And although Gregory suggests the activity associated with the word "god" may be a kind of power to behold hidden things, he also makes other suggestions and doesn't seem to have felt it important what the precise identity of the action type is. This makes sense, since his argument doesn't turn on *which* activity the term "god" (in the sense of god$_{\text{POWER/ACTION}}$) might express. So, whether we talk about "god$_{\text{POWER/ACTION}}$" or "deity," in either case these are not equivalent to god$_{\text{NATURE}}$, and the circumstances in which we *couldn't* use these interchangeably aren't germane in the current context.

Tuggy asks, "Is the property deity or divinity an essence? Is it a natural kind? It need not be either. Deity could be a status one can gain and lose, or could conceivably be had essentially. The concept is neutral."[27] In other words, Tuggy agrees with Gregory that being a god$_{\text{POWER/ACTION}}$ or "deity" does not conceptually entail being a god$_{\text{NATURE}}$, much less a god$_{\text{ULTIMATE-SOURCE}}$.

Finally, especially when discussing the Theophany Problem, we need to distinguish the ordinary use of referring expressions from the way we use them when the thing properly referred to *represents* or *is represented by* something else. Take Catherine Cook's example of a player in a role-playing game saying, "I rolled a one and I'm dead."[28] The first use of "I" refers to the human player; the second, to the played character. Or take this example from a transcript she examines:

> **Pete:** and I'll cast flame strike on him, and yes I know he doesn't cop fire damage
> **Phil:** he's not immune to fire Pete
> **Sean:** so you're gonna hit one of these guys
> **Gaz:** I'll do it Pete
> **Sean:** I'm sure Gaz'll dodge
> **Jake:** do it on Gaz
> **Pete:** No I'll just move up[29]

Pete's first and third uses of "I" refer to *the character played by* Pete, but the second refers to *himself*. The proper name "Gaz" refers to the *character played by* Gaz both times, neither time to Gaz himself. In general, when x is functioning as a representation of y, we treat either one as though it were the other. One might say, "I'm parked outside" when *one's car*, not *oneself*, is parked outside. We even do this with forms of the verb "to be." "I'm the thimble." Or (different tenses), "I was the thimble last time. I'll be the car this time." This can go the other way around too. "Who's the thimble?" "The thimble is Bob." When a referring expression is used in this way, to be perspicuous, we will write the term actually used *in speech or writing* as usual, then write a term that properly refers to the thing representing or being represented, as a subscript in brackets, indicating *it* is what should be looked at for the claim's truth conditions. For example, suppose Bob (the player) rolls a one and his character (Angbor) dies. I would write the truth conditions for "Bob rolled and one, and he died" as "Bob rolled a one, and he$_{\text{[ANGBOR]}}$ died."

With these linguistic distinctions in place, let's try to get clear on the Trinitarian views of the fathers we have in mind.

27. Tuggy, "On Counting Gods," 194.
28. Cook, "I Rolled a One."
29. Cook, "I Rolled a One," iii. I've deleted some symbols for clarity.

Theology I: The Monarchy of the Father

I call a "Monarchical Model" of the Trinity any model that affirms:

i. The Father is the *archē anarchos* [source without source], and

ii. there is a use of "God" as a singular term, such that it refers particularly to the Father *because* he is the *archē anarchos*.

I call the disjunction of all Monarchical Models of the Trinity, "Monarchical Trinitarianism" (MT). And I've argued that MT is what we see in Gregory et al.[30] It's well known that these fathers affirm that God the Father is the *archē anarchos* or god$_{\text{ULTIMATE-SOURCE}}$.[31] Many passages could be cited here; I will give just a few representative examples. Basil says:

> When I say "one substance" [*homoousios*] do not think that two are separated off from one, but that the Son has come to subsist from the Father, his principle [*archē*]. The Father and Son do not come from one substance that transcends them both. For we do not call them brothers.[32]

He also famously says, "There is one God because there is one Father,"[33] and "There are not two gods because there are not two fathers. Whoever introduces *two first principles* preaches two gods."[34] Given that Basil is discussing the number of "first principles," he clearly means there are not two gods$_{\text{ULTIMATE-SOURCE}}$, because there are not two fathers, but one

---

30. Branson, "One God, the Father."

31. I've called the claim that the Father is the *archē anarchos* (i.e., the first conjunct of MT) the "Weak Monarchy View," since it has been widely accepted by Trinitarians throughout Christian history. It's affirmed, for example, by the Nicene Creed, all seven ecumenical councils, Athanasius, the Cappadocians, Augustine, the Athanasian Creed, Pseudo-Dionysius, Maximus Confessor, John of Damascus, Aquinas, Luther, Calvin, the Westminster Confession of Faith, the 1689 Baptist Confession of Faith, and too many other sources to mention. It seems not to have been explicitly denied by anyone claiming to be Trinitarian before Herman Alexander Röell (1653–1718) in 1689. After he published his views, laws were passed to stop the spread of Röellianism, and five years after his death, his former colleagues in the theology faculty at Leyden published a condemnation of him for denying the divine processions, i.e., the monarchy of the Father. See Ellis, *Aseity of the Son*, 9, 14, 100, 110–12, 127–37, 128, 151, 160. Röell's rejection of processions was still widely considered heretical even among Reformed Protestants until Princeton theologians like B. B. Warfield (1851–1921) began to reconsider it in the late 1800s. See Waldron, "Scriptural Support."

32. Basil of Caesarea, *Christian Doctrine*, 295.

33. Basil of Caesarea, *Christian Doctrine*, 294.

34. Basil of Caesarea, *Christian Doctrine*, 295.

god_ULTIMATE-SOURCE because there is one Father, obviously identifying the Father as the one god_ULTIMATE-SOURCE.

Gregory of Nyssa also holds the Father is the one god_ULTIMATE-SOURCE:

> The persons of mankind do not have being directly from the same person, but some from this one, others from that.... In the case of the Holy Triad, however, this is not so. There is one and the same person, that of the Father, from whom the Son is begotten and the Holy Spirit proceeds. This is why we say legitimately and confidently that the one cause together with its caused is one God.[35]

Gregory Nazianzen also considers the Father to be "source and without source":

> Whose son would he in fact be if there were no causal relationship between his Father and himself? Nor again should we diminish the Father's status as source, proper to him as Father and generator.... The oneness of God would, in my view, be maintained if both Son and Spirit are causally related to him [God] alone... in the case of the Father, we think and speak of him as being both source and without source.... The Father, then, is without source: his existence is derived neither from outside nor from within himself.[36]

John of Damascus makes the same point in the *Dialectica*:

> The father, too, is prior to and greater than the son, because the father is causative of the son, in so far as the son is begotten of the father. It is for this reason that the blessed Gregory [Nazianzen] took in this sense what was said by our Lord in the Gospels, namely, "the Father is greater than I."[37]

Since they see the Father as the *archē anarchos*, the one god_ULTIMATE-SOURCE, from whom the Son is begotten and the Spirit proceeds, there is an obvious reason why, for these fathers, the typical referent of (capital-G) "God" in the NT is the Father.

Indeed, the Father is *also* typically the referent of "God" in the writings of the fathers themselves. While philosophers have often overlooked this issue, *theologians* have long noted that for the Eastern fathers, "God" is the Father, just as in the Bible and the Nicene Creed ("I believe in one God, the Father Almighty..."). As Karl Rahner puts it:

---

35. Gregory of Nyssa, *Trinitarian Works*.
36. See Gregory of Nazianzus, *Select Orations*, 111–12.
37. John of Damascus, *Writings*, 92.

If, with Scripture and the Greeks, we mean by ὁ Θεός in the first place the Father (not letting the word simply "suppose" for the Father), then the trinitarian structure of the Apostles' Creed, in line with Greek theology of the trinity, would lead us to treat first of the Father.... The Bible and the Greeks would have us start from the one unoriginate God, who is already *Father*.[38]

More recent scholarship has revealed less of a divide between East and West here than was once thought. God is also identified with the Father by Western fathers prior to Augustine and is still typically identified with the Father in Augustine's works outside of *De Trinitate*.[39] And no less a "Western" Christian than John Calvin asserts both the metaphysical and the semantic conjuncts of MT (albeit with a more egalitarian and essence-focused slant):

> Whenever the name of "God" is used indefinitely, the Son and Spirit, not less than the Father, is meant. But when the Son is joined with the Father, relation comes into view, and so we distinguish between the Persons. But as the Personal subsistence carry an order with them, the principle and origin being in the Father, whenever mention is made of the Father and Son, or of the Father and Spirit together, the name of "God" is specially given to the Father. In this way the unity of essence is retained, and respect is had to the order, which, however derogates in no respect from the divinity of the Son and Spirit.[40]

Calvin here echoes Gregory Nazianzen's *Oration 25*:

> Define our piety by teaching the knowledge of:
> One God, unbegotten, the Father; and
> One begotten Lord, his Son,
> referred to as "God" (θεός) when he is mentioned separately,

---

38. Rahner, *Trinity*, 16–17. In her introduction to this work, Catherine LaCugna writes, "Rahner relies on Greek theology according to which the Father is God; the Father is *fontalis*, the font and origin of divinity from whom Son and Spirit proceed. . . . Rahner follows Greek theology by using person (the person of the Father), not substance (shared divine essence), as the ultimate ontological category" (xx).

39. Ayres, *Augustine and the Trinity*: "This summary of Trinitarian belief also offers us Augustine's first use of the phrase *Trinitas quae Deus est* [the Trinity which is God—B.B.], a phrase not found in his predecessors. Interestingly this phrase is only once used by Augustine in his homiletic corpus. . . . Its absence from sermons, and from the record of his public debate with Maximinus, suggests that Augustine saw the phrase as, at the least, needing careful explanation because of its direct identification of *Trinitas* as *Deus*" (100). And later: "One constant strand of argument through this book has been that the Father's *monarchia*, his status as *principium* and *fons*, is central to Augustine's Trinitarian theology" (248).

40. Calvin, *Institutes*, 79–80.

but "Lord" when he is named together with the Father—
the first on account of the [divine] nature,
the second on account of the monarchy.⁴¹

In short, for all these figures, the answer to the question "Why would the word 'God' refer to the Father more frequently than to the Son (and especially in contexts in which the Father and Son are both mentioned)?" is obvious: the monarchy of the Father.

Theology II: The Theophanies

That it was Christ (not the Father) who spoke to Moses from the burning bush, and was seen by all the patriarchs and prophets, is the view seen consistently from pre- to post-Nicene fathers, including Justin Martyr, Melito of Sardis, Irenaeus, Basil, Gregory of Nyssa, John of Damascus, and too many others to list.⁴² As Alexander Golitzin puts it, "That Jesus, Mary's son, is the very One who appeared to Moses and the prophets—this is the consistent witness of the ante-Nicene Fathers, and remains foundational throughout the fourth-century Trinitarian controversies and the later christological disputes."⁴³

Now according to Basil, "God" (used referentially), when it refers to Christ, so refers in virtue of his being *the representation of* God. Basil refers

---

41. Quoted in Beeley, *Nazianzus on the Trinity*, 202.

42. Respectively: Justin Martyr, *First Apology*: "Our Christ talked with him [Moses] in the shape of fire from a bush" (101–2). In *On Pascha*, Melito of Sardis says Christ "gave command to Moses in Egypt" (40). Irenaeus, *On the Apostolic Preaching*, 69–71. According to Irenaeus, the figure seen by Abraham, Jacob, and Moses was not God the Father, but the Son of God. E.g., "This [the Son of God] is He who, in the bush, spoke with Moses and said, 'I have surely seen the afflictions of my people who are in Egypt, and I have come down to deliver them'" (70). Basil of Caesarea, *Against Eunomius*: "Didn't he find a designation well-suited for himself and fitting for his own eternity when he named himself He Who Is in his oracle to Moses his servant? He said: I am He Who Is [Exod 3.14]. No one will object when I say that these words were spoken in the person of the Lord" (155–56). Gregory of Nyssa, *Contra Eunomium III*: "The prophet, desiring to make luminously clear to mankind the mystery of Christ, uses the name 'angel' for Him who is, so that, with only the title of 'Him who is' appearing in the dialogue, the meaning of what is said might not be referred to the Father" (212). John of Damascus, *Three Treatises*: "No one, however, saw the nature of God, but the figure and image of One who was yet to come. For the invisible Son and Word of God was about to become truly human, that he might be united to our nature and seen upon earth" (101–2).

43. Golitzin, "Theophaneia," xviii.

to Christ as the "incorporeal image" and the "representation of the incorporeal [God]."[44] He gives this analogy:

> Whoever gazes at the imperial image in the forum and calls the one on the panel "emperor" does not confess two emperors, namely, the image and the one whose image it is. Nor when he points to the depiction on the panel and says, "This is the emperor," does he deprive the exemplar of the designation "emperor."[45]

Elsewhere he again argues:

> How, then, if they are one and one, are there not two gods? Because it is said that there is a king and the image of the king, but not two kings, for the power is not divided, and the glory is not portioned out.[46]

Suppose we have a photograph of King Charles II. Suppose we point to *the photograph* and say, "This is King Charles." Then King Charles walks by, and we say, "That's King Charles." Then suppose we are asked whether the photograph is King Charles. We admit, "The photograph is not King Charles." Have we contradicted ourselves? Basil says no. For what we thus assert is not:

This (the photograph) = King Charles.

That (King Charles) = King Charles.

But the photograph ≠ King Charles.

That would violate the logic of identity. Rather, the photograph functions as *a representation of* King Charles. Hence, what we assert (even pointing to the photograph when saying "this") is:

This$_{[\text{KING CHARLES}]}$ = King Charles.

That (King Charles) = King Charles.

And the photograph ≠ King Charles.

Now consider cases in which Scripture not only *describes* Christ as "(a) god" (*theos*, the common noun) but uses "God" (*o Theos*) or "YHWH" to *refer* to him. Two examples occur back-to-back in Hebrews chapter 1. The author writes in v. 8, "But concerning the Son, He says, 'Thy throne, O God, is unto the age of ages,'" and in v. 10, "He also says, 'Thou, YHWH, in the beginning

---

44. Basil the Great, *Christian Doctrine*, 273.
45. Basil the Great, *Christian Doctrine*, 296.
46. Basil, *Holy Spirit*, 80–81.

laid the foundation of the earth, and the heavens are the works of thine hands.'" Basil's readings of these would be something like: "But concerning the Son, He says, 'Thy throne, O God_[THE THEOPHANY FIGURE], is unto the age of ages'"[47] and "He also says, 'Thou, YHWH_[THE THEOPHANY FIGURE], in the beginning laid the foundation of the earth, and the heavens are the works of thine hands.'"[48]

The fact that this theology of Christ as The Theophany Figure, the "icon of the invisible God" (Col 1:15), underlies the theology of icons in the Seventh Ecumenical Council may partly explain why Protestant apologists don't make more use of it than they do. On the other hand, in sharp contrast to the tradition preceding him in the West, and continuing on in the East, Augustine was the first to *deny* the Old Testament theophanies were Christophanies, making them instead (created) angelophanies,[49] even denying the *possibility* of any vision of God in the present life.[50] This may partly explain its neglect among the scholastics. This loss of the theology of the theophanies is a tragedy. I say this not because of the doctrine's apologetic value, but because its rejection represents such a serious departure from the late Second Temple Judaism and early Christianity out of which Trinitarianism arose.[51] That Christ was The Theophany Figure was also the reason why both pre- and post-Nicene Christians (orthodox and Arian alike) could read Scripture as a seamless whole. The Old Testament was no less

---

47. Here I assume, in context, the author of Hebrews is saying that it is the throne *of the Son* that is "unto the age of ages." If that were being said of the Father, we would have "But concerning the Son_[FATHER] it says 'Thy throne, O God, is unto the age of ages.'" This wouldn't seem to serve the dialectical purpose of the passage, and the Father's speaking to himself would be awkward at best.

48. Here again, I assume the author of Hebrews is saying it is *Christ* who laid the foundations of the earth. If it were the Father, we would have "He also says, 'Thou, YHWH (=the Father), in the beginning laid the foundation of the earth, and the heavens are the works of thine hands.'" But then it would make no sense to say this was said "concerning the Son" (v. 8), and again the Father referring to himself as "thou" would be awkward. Also note that Hebrews is quoting from Psalm 102, which in v. 16 describes YHWH as "appearing," literally "*He will be seen*" in glory. Hence, it makes sense that the author of Hebrews would interpret the psalm as about The Theophany Figure, rather than God the Father.

49. *De Trinitate* II.16 and III, especially 11.

50. See Barnes, "Visible Christ," 329–55.

51. Not to mention raising problems for religious epistemology. If it was not one person of the Trinity that *was literally seen* by the prophets, then in what sense was God *revealed*? And how exactly do the prophets *know* what has been "revealed"? One sees the concern about this issue even in the Islamic tradition, in discussions of the Night Journey, in which Muhammad ascends into heaven and speaks to Allah directly. Without any such encounter, even Muhammad himself would simply be accepting the Qur'an based on testimony from another mere creature: the angel Gabriel.

Christocentric than the New. In comparison, much contemporary theology seems frankly Marcionite.[52]

The Desiderata Satisfied

Our desiderata, recall, involve the Theophany Problem (TP), the Who Is God? problem (WIG), and the Three God's and Three F's Problems (3G/3F, respectively). Let us now consider how the above theology fits with these desiderata, beginning with WIG.

WIG focuses on the NT's co-referring usage of the terms "God" and "Father." Tuggy opines that "God" used referentially "arguably does not admit of conceptual analysis."[53] If so, the assignment of a referent to it is merely a semantic choice, though, as Craig's model demonstrates, that choice can have substantive consequences. One might argue: a model of the Trinity *needn't* be formulated so that "God" and "Father" co-refer; but if it *can't* be, that's evidence it isn't consistent with the NT authors' thinking.

Suppose, however, the referential use of "God" *does* admit of conceptual analysis (perhaps it just means "*the* god$_{\text{ULTIMATE-SOURCE}}$"). If so, we could ask *why* "God" would (typically) refer to the Father in the NT. Since, for Gregory et al., the Father = the one god$_{\text{ULTIMATE-SOURCE}}$, it is not only *possible* for them to use "God" to refer to the Father (which they typically do), *it makes sense on their theology*. So, whether "God" admits of conceptual analysis or not, their theology meets our desiderata for WIG.

Moving on to TP, the fathers we've been discussing reconcile the apparently contradictory scriptural claims about the theophanies in precisely the same way as the Late Second Temple Jewish Binitarianism, out of which Christianity emerged. Namely, they affirm a straightforwardly literal interpretation of claims like:

No one can see YHWH and live,

No one has ever yet seen God, and

No one has seen the Father, except "he who is from God" (= Jesus).

And, just like the Jewish Binitarian sources, they read claims like,

Jacob wrestled with God,

Manoah and his wife saw God and lived,

---

52. For an overview and critique of these issues from an Orthodox Christian perspective, see Bucur, "Theophanies," 67–93.

53. Tuggy, "On Counting Gods," 190.

> Moses spoke to God face-to-face,
>
> The seventy elders saw the God of Israel,
>
> Isaiah saw YHWH sitting on a throne,

and so forth, as:

> Jacob wrestled with God[THE THEOPHANY FIGURE],
>
> Manoah and his wife saw God[THE THEOPHANY FIGURE] and lived,
>
> Moses spoke to God[THE THEOPHANY FIGURE] face-to-face,
>
> The seventy elders saw the God of Israel[THE THEOPHANY FIGURE],
>
> Isaiah saw YHWH[THE THEOPHANY FIGURE] sitting on a throne,

and so on. These fathers also agree with the Jewish Binitarian and early Christian traditions that:

> The Theophany Figure ≠ God,
>
> The Theophany Figure ≠ YHWH, and
>
> The Theophany Figure ≠ the Father.

Thus, just as in Jewish Binitarianism, no contradiction results, as it does for those who *do* identify YHWH, or God, or the Father with The Theophany Figure. The difference between Jewish Binitarianism and the theology of the church fathers does not lie in *the manner* in which they make sense out of the theophanies but in *the identity of The Theophany Figure*. Rather than Enoch, Melchizedek, Michael, or Metatron, they identify The Theophany Figure with *the Messiah* (and so, on a Christian view, Jesus).[54] Nor is this arbitrary. They take their cue from such NT passages as:

> No one has ever yet seen God. The only-begotten . . .[55] has revealed Him. (John 1:18)
>
> He that hath seen [Jesus] hath seen the Father. (John 14:8–9)
>
> Christ, who is the icon of God. (2 Cor 4:4)

---

54. As Boyarin puts it, "The earliest Christian groups (including, or even especially, the Johannine one) distinguished themselves from non-Christian Jews not theologically, but only in their association of various Jewish theologoumena and mythologoumena with this particular Jew, Jesus of Nazareth" (*Border Lines*, 105). And elsewhere: "The ideas of Trinity and incarnation, or certainly the germs of those ideas, were already present among Jewish believers well before Jesus came on the scene to incarnate himself" (Boyarin, *Jewish Gospels*, xiii).

55. Some manuscripts have "only-begotten son" and some "only-begotten god." Which reading one adopts is not relevant here, since I only assume that, whatever the exact phrase used, it is intended to refer to Jesus.

[the Son] is the icon of the invisible God. (Col 1:15)

[the Son of God] is . . . the exact image of [God's] *hypostasis*. (Heb 1:3)

Finally, 3G/3F. We'll start in the middle. It's uncontroversial that the Cappadocians and John of Damascus would affirm:

The Father ≠ the Son,

The Father ≠ the Holy Spirit, and

The Son ≠ the Holy Spirit.

Rejecting these would amount to modalism. Now, 3G seeks to derive a contradiction from the claims that the Father, Son, and Spirit are each "god" (though all non-identical) and the claim that there is only one god. But to say there is "one God" (used *referentially*) would be ungrammatical.[56] To count, one must use *a count noun*. And since we've identified three ways to disambiguate the term "god" (used as a common noun) there are three ways to disambiguate the claim that there is exactly one god:

There is exactly one $god_{ULTIMATE-SOURCE}$.

There is exactly one $god_{POWER/ACTION}$.

There is exactly one god_{NATURE}.

This yields three versions of 3G—which we'll call $3G_{ULTIMATE-SOURCE}$, $3G_{POWER/ACTION}$ and $3G_{NATURE}$—depending on which sense of "god" one employs when arguing Trinitarianism yields three "gods."

As mentioned above, Gregory denies that Scripture affirms the existence of only one $god_{POWER/ACTION}$, and he denies that Scripture uses "god" in the sense of god_{NATURE} at all.[57] It is *Gregory's opponents* who insist that Scripture uses "god" to predicate the divine nature or *ousia*. Gregory however cites numerous instances of "god" in Scripture that clearly do not predicate the divine nature. For example, Moses did not have the divine nature. So when Scripture calls him (a) "god" (Exod 7:1),[58] it cannot mean Moses was (a) god_{NATURE}, much less the $god_{ULTIMATE-SOURCE}$. Likewise, when Scripture says, "Let the gods who have not created the heavens and the earth perish"

---

56. This is so even if "God" contains descriptive content. "There is one *the* $god_{ULTIMATE-SOURCE}$" is ungrammatical. One would have to drop the article, thus, "There is one $god_{ULTIMATE-SOURCE}$." But that uses "$god_{ULTIMATE-SOURCE}$" *not* as a referring expression, but as a count noun.

57. See Branson, *Logical Problem*, 134–39.

58. Some translations insert "as," but the Hebrew simply says, "See, I have made you God (Elohim) to Pharaoh. . ." ". . . רְאֵה נְתַתִּיךָ אֱלֹהִים לְפַרְעֹה."

(Jer 10:11) and "I have said ye are gods, all of you sons of the Most High. Yet shall ye die like men" (Ps 82:6-7), these gods who did not create, and who are being condemned to die, obviously do not have the divine nature, much less are they gods$_{\text{ULTIMATE-SOURCE}}$. Nor would one say God made Moses a *false* god, nor that God *falsely* says, "I have said ye are gods, all of you sons of the Most High." So, we can only understand these as *truly* being gods, but gods only in the sense of gods$_{\text{POWER/ACTION}}$, rather than gods$_{\text{NATURE}}$ or gods$_{\text{ULTIMATE-SOURCE}}$. On the other hand, Gregory finds no evidence of Scripture using "god" in the sense of god$_{\text{NATURE}}$ at all. So, for example, when Scripture says "YHWH, He is god; there is no other besides him" (Deut 4:35), it cannot mean "YHWH, He is (a) god$_{\text{POWER/ACTION}}$; there is no other god$_{\text{POWER/ACTION}}$ besides him" on pain of contradicting Exodus 7:1 and Psalm 82:6-7. And if Scripture never uses "god" to mean god$_{\text{NATURE}}$, it cannot mean "YHWH, he is (a) god$_{\text{NATURE}}$; there is no other god$_{\text{NATURE}}$ besides him." So, we can only read it as "YHWH, he is (the) god$_{\text{ULTIMATE-SOURCE}}$; there is no other god$_{\text{ULTIMATE-SOURCE}}$ besides him." In other words, Scripture does not endorse "There is exactly one god$_{\text{POWER/ACTION}}$" nor, on Gregory's view, does it even *discuss* "There is exactly one god$_{\text{NATURE}}$." It endorses only "There is exactly one god$_{\text{ULTIMATE-SOURCE}}$."

Thus, *in the only sense in which the Bible is clearly monotheistic*, the monarchy of the Father obviously guarantees monotheism—no logical contradictions, no fancy metaphysics necessary. The first line of the Creed, and St. Basil's dictum that "There is one God because there is one Father,"[59] are strictly and literally true. To disambiguate, these claims are "I believe in one god$_{\text{ULTIMATE-SOURCE}}$, the Father Almighty" and "There is one god$_{\text{ULTIMATE-SOURCE}}$, because there is one Father", respectively.

Notice that, with WIG and TP solved, and with 3G *in the scriptural sense* (3G$_{\text{ULTIMATE-SOURCE}}$) solved, Arians and Trinitarians actually all agree with each other, as well as with Late Second Temple Jewish Binitarianism (*modulo* the Holy Spirit, and obviously minus the identification of The Theophany Figure with Jesus), and *most* of ante-Nicene tradition.[60] Given the widespread consensus on these points, even among groups that deeply disagree about other issues, any model that deviates from these solutions to WIG, TP and 3G is, from a historical point of view, highly unlikely to reflect the earliest Christian beliefs.

Now given that Gregory denies that Scripture ever claims there is only one god$_{\text{POWER/ACTION}}$ or only one god$_{\text{NATURE}}$, one might wonder why he

---

59. Basil the Great, *On Christian Doctrine*, 294.

60. The exception being modalists. But, with apologies to modalists, I think the evidence suggests that modalism arose later on, out of an anxiety about the *monarchia*, rather than tracing back to the NT or any pre-Christian Jewish theology.

addresses these claims at all. If 3G is already solved by the monarchy of the Father in the only sense in which Gregory admits that *Scripture* affirms there is "one god" (i.e., one god$_{\text{ULTIMATE-SOURCE}}$), why not just say that and move on? The answer is that it is not exactly these claims that he addresses. There's a much better way to press 3G$_{\text{POWER/ACTION}}$ and 3G$_{\text{NATURE}}$ than how they usually are today (and unsurprisingly that's just what the Arians did). While the Bible doesn't endorse the claims that *there exists* only one god$_{\text{POWER/ACTION}}$, or only one god$_{\text{NATURE}}$, we could ask slightly different questions. Not *are there multiple gods$_{\text{POWER/ACTION}}$, or multiple gods$_{\text{NATURE}}$*, but *are the Father, Son and Holy Spirit* one god$_{\text{POWER/ACTION}}$ and one god$_{\text{NATURE}}$, or are *they* three gods $_{\text{POWER/ACTION}}$ and/or three gods$_{\text{NATURE}}$?

Gregory thinks it is not only false to say the Trinity is three gods in either of these senses, he thinks it would be dangerously misleading to say so, as it would give the impression that it would be, at least conceptually, possible for the Trinitarian *hypostases* to disagree among themselves.[61] Thus he addresses these slightly modified questions in *ad Ablabium* and *Ad Graecos*. But to understand his response, we need to understand the difference between how we normally think of counting today, and how it was understood in antiquity.

Quantity: In Antiquity and Today

Introductory logic textbooks take for granted that we count by *identity*. However, from Aristotle through the end of the medieval period, it was thought we count by *division* (or *divisibility*). Only in the twentieth century did the current approach become dominant.[62]

To say we count by *identity* is to say the number of *F*'s is given in terms of logical subjects (terms or variables) that can have "*F*" predicated of them, and are such that each is *non-identical with* every other.[63] For example,

---

61. This is one reason not to classify the Cappadocians as Social Trinitarians. Social Trinitarians typically take it as essential to their position that the persons are, or have, "distinct centers of consciousness." This leads to one of the chief difficulties for Social Trinitarianism: how to secure the necessary agreement of the *hypostases*. Gregory et al. would answer that they *do not* have distinct centers of consciousness.

62. As Bertrand Russell put it, "The question, 'What is a number?' is one which has been often asked, but has only been correctly answered in our own time. The answer was given by Frege in 1884, in his *Grundlagen der Arithmetik*. Although this book is quite short, not difficult, and of the very highest importance, it attracted almost no attention, and the definition of number which it contains remained practically unknown until it was rediscovered by the present author in 1901" (*Introduction to Mathematical Philosophy*, 11).

63. More precisely, each of the things *represented by* the distinct terms or variables

when x is a dog, y is a dog, and z is a dog, and $x \neq y \neq z$, there are three dogs. Though often taken for granted, this creates numerous puzzles and paradoxes. I merely list some major ones. On this approach, it has been argued that:

i. One could only count with whole numbers (not fractions or irrationals).

ii. It would be mysterious why counting by mass nouns is ungrammatical.

iii. There could be a myriad of physical objects in *roughly* the same place at the same time (e.g., a myriad of clouds or cats where there seems to be only one).

iv. There could be multiple physical objects in *exactly* the same place at the same time (e.g., a lump of clay and a statue made out of it).

v. It would be impossible for one thing to become two, or for two things to become one.[64]

For these reasons and more, even some contemporary philosophers reject the identity approach to counting.[65]

To say we count by *division* is to say that the number of *F*'s is given by how *F*-ness is (or *the F's* are), or can be, *divided* into spatially discontinuous parts with "the same name" ("*F*") as each other and as the whole.[66] This view of discrete quantity as supervening on *divisibility* is discussed extensively by Aristotle and his commentators, and was accepted by everyone from Euclid, to Nicomachus of Gerasa, Theon of Smyrna, Boethius, John of Damascus, Islamic philosophers such as Ibn Rushd and al-Ghazali, down to Thomas

---

are non-identical with every other.

64. On (i), see Salmon, "Wholes, Parts, and Numbers." On (i)–(ii), see Liebesman, "We Do Not Count by Identity." On (iii), see Geach, *Reference and Generality*, 215–18; Unger, "Problem of the Many." The classic statement of the problem in (iv) is Gibbard, "Contingent Identity." Finally, (v) is a consequence of Leibniz's Law. Since x has always been identical with x, if x *became* identical with y, y would come to have always been identical with x. But in this case, it would not have *become* identical with x after all, which is a contradiction. Note that the Bible does describe things as "becoming one." The classic example is "The two shall become one flesh" (Gen 2:24; Matt 19:5; Mark 10:8; Eph 5:31). In the case of Ezekiel's "two sticks" (37:16–17), it's clear that the two become one precisely because, having been divided or separate, they come to be continuous.

65. In addition to Salmon and Liebesman, see Lewis, "Survival and Identity"; Lewis, "Many, but Almost One."

66. For details see Branson, *Logical Problem*, 129–34. See also Cross, "Gregory of Nyssa on Universals." For more background on common theories of universals at the time, and in what sense each was considered "divisible," see Lloyd, "Neoplatonic Logic I" and "Neoplatonic Logic II."

Aquinas and beyond.[67] In short, it was just as taken for granted from antiquity through the Middle Ages as counting by identity is today. The details of how this account of quantity applies concretely vary depending on one's metaphysics of universals. Let's consider some options.

If one were an austere nominalist, believing only in ordinary concrete particulars (but not particular properties), one way to analyze "F-ness" would be to identify it with the collection of concrete Fs. For example, doghood would just be the collection of all dogs. There would be three dogs when this collection is *divided into* x, y, and z, such that each of x, y, and z is a dog. And to say they are *divided* is just to say that they share no common boundary or part, i.e., they are all spatially discontinuous.

If one analyzes universals as collections, not of ordinary concrete particulars, but of particular property instances (tropes or modes), one would say universals are divided into these property instances, and the number of Fs would again correspond to these divisions. There are three dogs when the collection of property instances of doghood is divided into x, y, and z, such that each of x, y, and z is an instance of doghood, and these particular property instances are all spatially discontinuous.

Note however that in this last case, whether the number of Fs equals the number of logical subjects that are F-ish and non-identical,[68] will depend on whether one takes particular property instances to be individuated by their bearers or in some other way, say spatiotemporally. Let's use the term "modes" for particular property instances conceived of as individuated by their bearers, and "tropes" for particular property instances conceived of as individuated spatiotemporally.[69] On a modes view, the number of Fs would automatically equal the number of logical subjects that are F-ish and non-identical. But on a tropes view, the number of Fs might be fewer than that. This would occur in cases where some logical subjects x and y are non-identical, but not because of spatiotemporal discontinuity. In that case, they

---

67. To cite just the bookends, for Aristotle, see *Categories* 4b25–4b35; *Physics* 220a27; *Metaphysics* 1017a2–6, 1020a5–1020a15, 1052a15–1052b19, 1087b33–1088a14. For Aquinas, see *Summa Theologiae* I.Q11.a1: "I respond: One does not add any entity to being, but instead adds just the negation of division. For one signifies the same thing as undivided being."

68. Again, to be precise, the number of logical subjects (terms or variables) such that "F" can be truly predicated of them, and *the objects represented by* the terms or variables are non-identical. For short, I will just refer to these as "logical subjects that are F-ish and non-identical" in what follows.

69. For more on the individuation of tropes in the contemporary debate, and why most contemporary trope theorists prefer an account in which tropes are individuated spatiotemporally, rather than being individuated by their bearers, see Maurin, "Tropes," especially section 2.3.

could share (some) tropes. Take for example the famous case of the statue and the lump of clay out of which it is made. These are discernible (thus non-identical) since the lump can survive being smashed, but the statue cannot. But they are not *divisible*. On a tropes view, counting by division, the lump and the statue, although *not identical*, would be one physical object and, for example, one 1-kilogram object, since they share a single trope of physical objecthood and a single trope of weight.

Finally, if one believes there is literally one and the same *in re* universal *F*-ness, identical and *undivided* in all its instances, there would, strictly speaking, be only one *F*.[70] Needless to say, this was not a popular view in antiquity.[71]

To summarize, there are three types of cases we've considered according to their different results for counting. First, counting by identity, and counting by division on a modes view or an austere nominalist view, will yield as many *F*s as there are logical subjects that are *F*-ish and non-identical. Second, counting by division on a tropes view will yield the same as above when the (referents of the) logical subjects that are *F*-ish are themselves divided. But it can yield only one *F*, despite there being multiple logical subjects that are *F*-ish and non-identical, when (the referents of) those logical subjects are *undivided*, i.e., when they are individuated non-spatiotemporally (and their tropes of *F*-ness are not).[72] Finally, counting by division on an indivisible universals view will always yield only one *F*.

The Undivided Trinity

Neither Gregory nor any of his interlocutors counted by identity. Most also were not austere nominalists.[73] So the arguments about the Trinity being three gods$_{NATURE}$ or three gods$_{POWER/ACTION}$, hinge on whether the relevant universals are divisible or indivisible, and if divisible whether "divided" by

---

70. See Branson, *Logical Problem*, 123–34. See also Gregory of Nyssa, *Trinitarian Works*, 35–36.

71. See Lloyd "Neoplatonic Logic I," 59.

72. The fact that tropes are *also* individuated qualitatively explains why, when Arians accused the orthodox of having "three gods" in the sense of gods$_{NATURE}$, the orthodox said it was actually the Arians who had three gods (gods$_{NATURE}$). For the orthodox, if the persons of the Trinity are *both homoousious and* undivided (as is sung in the Orthodox hymn, "The Trinity, one in essence, and undivided") then the number of gods$_{NATURE}$ would be one. But if the Trinity was *not homoousious*, then *even if it was undivided*, there would still be three nature tropes, and thus three gods$_{NATURE}$ (since the Arians, despite a popular misconception, *did* affirm that Christ had "a" divine nature, just a *qualitatively different kind* of divine nature).

73. In any case, Gregory takes belief in some kind of properties for granted and most would have granted it.

their bearers or not. I.e., the argument hinges on whether we conceive of properties as modes, tropes, or (indivisible) universals.

In both *Ad Graecos* and *Ad Ablabium*, Gregory argues that *natures* are indivisible universals, hence, he concludes there is only one god$_{\text{NATURE}}$, and strictly speaking, there is only one man. This argument has been widely criticized for its conclusion,[74] but never based on a full reconstruction of the argument, which simply draws out the logical implications of his opponents' own premises (about counting) applied to his theology and metaphysics.[75]

Other fathers like Gregory Nazianzen and John of Damascus, as well as figures like Boethius and Aquinas (among many others),[76] say that three human *hypostases* are three men, because the human nature *is* divided among them, whereas the Trinity are one god$_{\text{NATURE}}$ because their nature is *not* divided.[77] In other words, they take what I've labelled the "tropes" view, with the result that there is a single god$_{\text{NATURE}}$, although there are three subjects, each of which "is (a) god$_{\text{NATURE}}$."[78]

So it is true that *at this point* we can begin distinguishing various church fathers' different metaphysics of universals, and thus different "models" of the Trinity. The problem is, regardless of their precise metaphysics, *all* of the Cappadocians, John of Damascus, and for that matter Augustine, Boethius, Thomas Aquinas, and *all* orthodox Trinitarians, East or West, affirmed that *the divine nature is undivided*.[79] To find anyone who thinks the divine nature *is divided* among the *hypostases*, one has to look to the likes of non-Chalcedonians like Severus of Antioch or John Philoponus (who,

74. See, e.g., Stead, "Why Not Three Gods?" Stead says Gregory's argument "resembles an accomplished conjuring trick more nearly than a valid theological demonstration" (149). See also Cartwright, "On the Logical Problem." Cartwright says Gregory "rather desperately suggested that strictly speaking there is only one man" (171).

75. See Branson, *Logical Problem*, 123–26. Note that Gregory recognizes *we can and do* count men in the plural. He only argues that we do so *catachrestically*, and that in mundane cases this carries less risk of yielding unwarranted inferences than in the case of theology, where it is much more important to avoid errors.

76. Respectively: Nazianzus, *Oration* 31.15; John of Damascus, *Writings*, 34–35 and *On the Orthodox Faith*, 80; Aquinas, *De Rationibus Fidei*, chapter 4. Note Aquinas labels the Father "God" here. Cf. the "Arabic" formula below.

77. Hence, the lump and statue analogy is not a bad illustration of this aspect of the doctrine.

78. Compare Aquinas, *Summa Theologiae* I.q39.a3.

79. See Cross, "Two Models of the Trinity?": "Once we take account of the divergent metaphysical presuppositions of the various writers I shall consider here, we discover that there is after all no significant difference between Eastern and Western views on the specific question I am interested in—despite the apparent divergence on the question of the divine essence as a universal" (276). I am putting the point in my own way here, but I believe what I am saying coheres with Cross's thesis in its essentials.

unsurprisingly, was considered a Tritheist). Despite differences in their metaphysics, the fathers we have in view all agree that:

There is only one god$_{\text{ULTIMATE-SOURCE}}$, the Father,

and:

The Trinity is one god$_{\text{NATURE}}$,

because the divine nature is *undivided* among the Trinitarian *hypostases*. Furthermore (as we will see below), they all also hold:

The Trinity is one god$_{\text{POWER/ACTION}}$,

because the Trinitarian *operations* are also undivided (or "inseparable") among the Trinitarian *hypostases*. Thus, no matter how we disambiguate "god," the result is that Trinitarians worship only one god. Compare Gregory of Nazianzen:

> When then we look at the Godhead, or the First Cause, or the Monarchia, that which we conceive is One; but when we look at the Persons in Whom the Godhead dwells, and at Those Who timelessly and with equal glory have their Being from the First Cause—there are Three Whom we worship.[80]

Inseparable Operations

What about the issue of three gods$_{\text{POWER/ACTION}}$? Given that "is (a) god$_{\text{POWER/ACTION}}$" means "performs a token activity of the characteristically divine type," and given the standard view of quantity in antiquity, what

The Father, Son, and Holy Spirit are one god$_{\text{POWER/ACTION}}$

amounts to is:

---

80. *Oration* 31.14, 322. Some have interpreted this as evidence that Nazianzen *equates* the Godhead with the First Cause and the Monarchia, as though the "or" introduces appositives. That's grammatically possible, but Nazianzen often uses "*monarchia*" in the sense of "single rule(r)" (hence, one god$_{\text{POWER/ACTION}}$) rather than "single source" (one god$_{\text{ULTIMATE-SOURCE}}$). So it's also possible to take him as making the same point I am making here, namely, that regardless of which of these three senses in which we ask whether God is one—one god$_{\text{NATURE}}$, one god$_{\text{ULTIMATE-SOURCE}}$, or one god$_{\text{POWER/ACTION}}$—we get the result that there is one god. And I think that interpretation fits better with clear statements elsewhere in his corpus.

The Father, Son and Holy Spirit perform a single (undivided) token activity of the characteristically divine activity type.[81]

And that is true, given the doctrine of inseparable operations *ad extra* (sometimes known as *synergy*). According to this doctrine, the activities of the divine persons *ad extra* ("to the outside") are rooted in the undivided divine nature, *not* the persons, as in standard Social Trinitarianism.[82] The persons are discernible (thus non-identical) due to the intra-Trinitarian relations of begetting and proceeding. But actions do not beget, or proceed from, other actions. So, while the persons themselves are not identical, their token activities *ad extra* are.[83] Hence, the persons share single, undivided token activities *ad extra*.[84]

Since *all* the Trinitarian activities *ad extra* will be undivided, what *particular* activity "god" in the sense of "god$_{POWER/ACTION}$" predicates won't matter. This is why Gregory's solution to $3G_{POWER/ACTION}$ generalizes to $3F$. Take for instance the claims that:

The Father is (a) savior.

The Son is (a) savior.

The Holy Spirit is (a) savior.

and:

The Father, Son, and Holy Spirit are exactly one savior.

This amounts to saying that each of the persons performs a token act of saving, but that they all perform a single, undivided token act of saving. And this will also be true, given inseparable operations.[85] To reiterate, Gregory

---

81. Roughly the idea would be that if the *A*-ers could be divided in such a way as to each *remain A*-ers, then the activity of *A*-ing would necessarily end up being divided as well (since there is no "action at a distance"). See Branson, *Logical Problem*, 189–93; Branson, "Gregory of Nyssa on the Individuation of Actions and Events."

82. Really *all* activities are rooted in natures, not *hypostases*, on this view, which just stems from Aristotle's definition of "nature" as an intrinsic source of motion and rest. This is not to say it is the nature that *performs* an activity. A *hypostasis* (individual) *performs* the activity. But it performs it *in virtue of* its nature. See Aristotle, *Physics* II.1.

83. See Branson, "Gregory of Nyssa on the Individuation of Actions and Events"; Branson, *Logical Problem*, 174.

84. Note that begetting and spirating are not "*ad extra*," nor are they conceived of as *energeiai* (actions), but as *scheses* (relations). See Gregory Nazianzen, *Oration* 29.16; Gregory of Nyssa, *Contra Eunomium I*, 251–69; and the discussion in Bradshaw, *Aristotle East and West*, 157–61.

85. That the doctrine of inseparable operations was a key component of pro-Nicene theology is affirmed by, to my knowledge, all serious patristics scholars. For a few

does not think Scripture uses "god" in the sense of god$_{\text{NATURE}}$ at all. Hence, he discusses the inseparable operations in *Ad Ablabium*. But those who *do* assume that "god" sometimes means god$_{\text{NATURE}}$ can refer back to the argument about the divine nature also being undivided.

God and His Word and His Spirit Are One God

With the main analysis completed, note how the above sheds light on a certain summary of Trinitarianism I'll call "the Arabic formula" (not because it only appears in Arabic,[86] but because it shows up so frequently in Christian authors who either wrote in Arabic,[87] or at least knew Arabic [like John of Damascus], during the first few centuries after the rise of Islam). The formula is:

God, and His Word, and His Spirit are one god.

This has an air of paradox about it. But we can now see how to analyze it. Namely, either:

God, and His Word, and His Spirit perform a single, undivided token activity of the characteristically divine activity type,

or

God, and His Word, and His Spirit share a single, undivided divine nature.

Neither is logically incoherent, nor is the metaphysics particularly exotic. Indeed, this is so even if we rephrase them as:

The one god$_{\text{ULTIMATE-SOURCE}}$, and his Word, and his Spirit perform a single, undivided token activity of the characteristically divine activity type,

or

The one god$_{\text{ULTIMATE-SOURCE}}$, and his Word, and his Spirit share a single, undivided divine nature.

---

examples, see Ayres, *Nicaea and Its Legacy*, 198, 236; Barnes, *Power of God*, 169–72.

86. It appears in Greek in John of Damascus before any Arabic-language theological writings we know of and follows Cappadocian triadology.

87. For examples, see Noble and Treiger, *Orthodox Church in the Arab World*, 42–58, 103, 229. More examples can be found throughout Griffith, *Church in the Shadow of the Mosque*; Bertaina et al., *Heirs of the Apostles*.

Conclusion

I'll conclude by making some brief remarks in comparing the Monarchical Trinitarianism of Gregory et al. to my interlocutors' views.

Let's begin with Tuggy. First, insofar as arguments *for* Unitarianism are often bound up with arguments *against* Trinitarianism, it's important to evaluate to what extent those are successful, and we've seen that the two biggest criticisms of Trinitarianism—3G and WIG—fail against Monarchical Trinitarianism. Note that this is so even on Tuggy's own terms. Tuggy calls a view monotheistic when it posits exactly one of what he calls a "god" (i.e., a god$_{\text{ULTIMATE-SOURCE}}$), and "mono*deistic*" or "poly*deistic*" depending on whether it posits one "deity" (one god$_{\text{POWER/ACTION}}$) or many.[88] But, says Tuggy, "'Polydeistic monotheism' is the view of *most* traditional Jews, Christians, and Muslims."[89] He continues, "Was first-century Jewish monotheism a distinctive version of high-god polytheism? Poly*deism*, to be sure. . . . But at least by the time the books of Deuteronomy and Isaiah were complete, the religion (or that branch of it reflected in those writings) was polydeistic monotheism."[90] Hence, Tuggy agrees with Gregory that Scripture affirms, and Christianity requires, not the belief that "There is exactly one god$_{\text{POWER/ACTION}}$" (mono*deism*), but "There is exactly one god$_{\text{ULTIMATE-SOURCE}}$" (mono*theism*). So by Tuggy's own definitions, Monarchical Trinitarianism is monotheistic.

Now to evaluate Unitarianism in itself. It surely solves WIG. And it doesn't face 3G, since it rejects the divinity of Christ and the Holy Spirit (though one might count that as a cost!).[91] It's less clear whether it can solve 3F. Are there two saviors, for example? Finally, I can't say how Unitarianism attempts to solve TP. But if it denies the pre-existence of Christ, it certainly doesn't solve TP in the way I would argue the NT authors do (i.e., by positing that The Theophany Figure = The Messiah).

Next, Craig's version of Social Trinitarianism solves 3G for "god" in the sense of god$_{\text{NATURE}}$, since for Craig the only thing that is god$_{\text{NATURE}}$ is the Trinity. Craig seems nonplussed about whether there is more than one god-$_{\text{ULTIMATE-SOURCE}}$ in his model, though I have never understood his response. Somehow, all the persons *and* the Trinity are *a se*? But somehow this isn't four things that are *a se*? I'm also unsure whether or how his account applies to there being one god$_{\text{POWER/ACTION}}$ or whether or how it generalizes to

---

88. Tuggy, "On Counting Gods," 203.
89. Tuggy, "On Counting Gods," 205.
90. Tuggy, "On Counting Gods," 206.
91. Assuming one considers the Holy Spirit to be a distinct *hypostasis* from the Father, which many Unitarians reject anyway.

3F. Is the Trinity as a whole the one savior of Isaiah 43–45? Is Jesus *not* a savior? Do we have two senses of "savior," one being something like "*part of a savior*"?[92] I won't repeat the issues with WIG noted previously, and I don't know Craig's views on the theophanies, but there are two obvious hurdles. First, if God is not the Father, but the Trinity, Christ would not be the icon of his Father, but of the Trinity. But since for Craig the Trinity *is* god$_{NATURE}$, but Christ *is not* god$_{NATURE}$, we get similar problems as with Arianism. How does Christ *reveal* God to us, if Christ and God have different natures? Craig could avoid that disconnect by making Christ the icon of the Father, instead of God. But that takes us back to WIG. If God is the Trinity, why does Scripture describe *the Father* as "the invisible God" of whom Christ is an icon? But that isn't so much a problem specific to TP as just another instance of the difficulties the model faces with WIG. A second issue is that there is obviously *some sense* of "subordinationism" in Jewish Binitarianism and early (or "proto-") Trinitarianism, which I think Craig will not like. Simply speaking of Christ as the image and God as the archetype (original) gives God (whether Father or Trinity) *some* sense of priority.

It should be no surprise I'm most sympathetic to Hasker's approach, rooted as it is in serious engagement with the patristic sources. Given that Hasker affirms the eternal generation of the Son and eternal procession of the Spirit (the monarchy of the Father), there is no obvious reason his view couldn't be formulated as a version of Monarchical Trinitarianism, thus solving WIG. And since for Hasker the persons have the divine nature, the "relabeling" issue isn't the problem it is for Craig. Further, although I have not seen Hasker address TP, I see no obvious reason he couldn't accept the views I've outlined above. Coming to 3G, although I have not seen Hasker address the logic and semantics of quantity/counting statements in detail, again there's no obvious reason he couldn't accept the ancient and medieval view of quantity discussed above. Indeed, it fits hand-in-glove with his view that the persons of the Trinity share a single trope of divinity. Where the view outlined above differs from Hasker's is that Hasker takes the Trinitarian *hypostases* to be "distinct centers of consciousness," thus denying the doctrine of inseparable operations. I've argued that inseparable operations are both Gregory's solution to the "god$_{POWER/ACTION}$" version of 3G, and what allows that solution to generalize to 3F. Hence, in my view, rejecting inseparable operations comes at a considerable cost.

In conclusion, the result of my reading of the Cappadocians and John of Damascus is an account of the Trinity that is logically consistent, solves

---

92. In *The Matrix*, does Neo's pale skin count as Choi's "savior" because it's *a part of* Choi's "personal savior," Neo?

WIG, solves all three disambiguations of 3G,[93] solves 3F, and solves TP in a way that flows naturally from the late Second Temple Jewish Binitarian theology out of which Christianity arose, along with the NT claims that Christ is the icon of God, the exact image of his *hypostasis*. As I'll argue in my responses to my co-authors, other models lose these features the further they depart from the historical doctrine of the Trinity.

---

93. In *The Logical Problem*, 197–251, I formalize Gregory of Nyssa's solution to 3G in terms of $god_{POWER/ACTION}$ (252–61, summarized in Appendix B, 325–35), and give a model-theoretic proof of its logical consistency. It's fairly trivial to extend this to 3F and to give a parallel account in terms of god_{NATURE}. It is also trivial to identify the Father with the one $god_{ULTIMATE-SOURCE}$ within that framework, thus solving WIG and the other version of 3G.

4

New Testament Theology Is Unitarian

Dale Tuggy

A Minority Report

SOMETIMES A CHRISTIAN MINORITY report turns out to be true. Do you believe in congregational church government, the priesthood of all believers, believer's baptism, either open theism or Molinism about divine providence, or conditional immortality (annihilationism) about hell? If so, you agree with me that sometimes God allows mainstream Christianity to stray from the truth, even for long periods of time.

Still, many find it hard to believe that God would allow most Christians to be mistaken about God being a Trinity; at first glance, such a suggestion seems like a conspiracy theory, given how widespread and longstanding official Trinitarian creeds are. However, a survey of popular creeds and statements of faith may mislead. These might suggest that 99 percent of all Christians currently believe that God is the Trinity, and that this has been so as long as there have been Christians. But nowhere near 99 percent of the laity are on board. Recent surveys of Christians show that 55–90 percent "Agree" or "Strongly Agree" that "There is one true God in three persons: God the Father, God the Son, and God the Holy Spirit." But this lip-service hides a lot of non-Trinitarian opinions. Thus, 58 percent of Evangelical American Christians also agree that "Jesus is the first and greatest being created by God," 27 percent agree that "Jesus was a great teacher, but he was not God," and 42 percent agree that "The Holy Spirit is a force but is not a personal being." In contrast, 99 percent of these Evangelicals agree that "There will be a time when Jesus Christ returns to judge all the people who have lived."[1] An obvious difference here is that Jesus' future, literal return is clearly taught in the New Testament (NT), but "the doctrine of the Trinity" is not.

In my view a Christian should start with the teachings handed down to her, and only budge from that when compelled by convincing reasons. This is what I did; I became interested in "the doctrine of the Trinity" for apologetics reasons. Surely, I assumed, this doctrine is central to Christianity and so has always been believed by all or almost all Christians, since it is clearly taught in the NT. *Surely* only rationalists and cultists would dare to deny this precious doctrine.

But I was shocked to learn that there is not really any one such doctrine, but rather there are some vague ideas and some required ambiguous words, sentences which various Christians interpret in clashing ways. I also found that no idea of God as tripersonal was required in mainstream Christianity until about the time of the council of bishops at Constantinople in 381.[2] And I learned that ever since the Reformation there has been a steady flow of fairly conservative and traditional Christians who agree that doctrines ought to be based on Scripture, who look there to find "the doctrine of the Trinity" and are surprised to learn that not only is it not there, but that what *is* taught there contradicts any such speculations. Many in the so-called "Radical Reformation" held to a theology like the sort I will defend in this book.[3] Indeed, despite some serious historical stumbles, this reforming movement is alive and well.[4]

How I Will Argue

I will defend *clear* NT teaching, and in other contexts I would simply quote a handful of verses to express it. Unlike Trinitarian theologies, a basic Unitarian view of God and Jesus can be stated in the very words of Scripture. But proof-text wars are futile; while the Unitarian has her favorite verses, the Trinitarian is taught by tradition to focus on a handful of texts (what I call "the canon within the canon") and to put them together to try to show that Scripture presupposes, logically implies, or at least is best explained by, some Trinity theory. And both sides will be quick to object that the other

---

1. See Ligonier Ministries' thestateoftheology.com.
2. Tuggy, *What Is the Trinity?*, chapter 5; Tuggy, "When and How?"
3. Williams, *Radical Reformation*.
4. Recently the movement is largely lay-driven and without institutional support. See for instance unitarianchristianalliance.org, biblicalunitarian.com, 21stcr.org, restitutio.org.

side, in citing their verses (as they understand them), are merely assuming what needs to be argued for. Both sides will urge that the other is coming to the texts with distorting assumptions that causes it inadvertently to misread them. Also, experience shows that various traditional Trinitarian arguments which purport to show that the Bible implies or assumes some Trinity theory are typically over-simplified and under-developed, and while I am willing to point out their many deficiencies, it is more important to show how they are poorly motivated with respect to the NT, even contradicting it in various ways.

In this chapter, therefore, I will adopt a style of arguing that can't be accused of begging the question, that is, of assuming *Unitarian* interpretations of key texts. I will focus on undeniable facts and consider them in light of two rival hypotheses, namely, that the NT authors assume a Trinitarian (tripersonal-God-involving) theology, and that they assume some Unitarian view, on which the one God just is the Father alone. Adopting a methodology from the sciences, we will reason that if a fact would be surprising or unlikely given one hypothesis, but not given the other hypothesis, then that fact confirms the second hypothesis over the first.[5]

I will define our two competing hypotheses in simple and mutually exclusive ways. Hypothesis T (for Trinitarian) is the conjunction of three claims about the NT authors: that they assume the numerical identity of the one God with the Trinity, the full deity of the Son, and the full deity of the Holy Spirit. The competing hypothesis U is that the NT authors assume the numerical identity of the one God with the Father, and that neither the Son nor the Holy Spirit is fully divine (i.e., divine in the way the Father is divine). Notice that it is manifestly impossible that both T and U are true. Notice too that neither includes all the claims that a given Trinitarian or a given Unitarian would be committed to; both allow for a range of positions that result from adding various further claims to the three mentioned. Rather, the definitions highlight what Trinitarians and Unitarians as such disagree about.[6]

---

5. Philosophers have called this the Prime Principle of Confirmation or the Likelihood Principle. See Forster and Sober, "Why Likelihood?"

6. I anticipate that at least one of my interlocutors will cry foul because the definition of U doesn't include the thesis that Jesus doesn't *in any sense* have a divine nature and that he came to exist at or after his miraculous conception. But to the contrary, this is as it should be, as Unitarians have long been split over the "pre-existence" of Jesus, and there is a long history of Unitarian scholars and organizations understanding Unitarianism so as to allow for both positions on that issue. Sometimes this is popularly expressed as talking of "Socinians" and "Arians" as two species of Unitarians. See e.g., Irons et al., *Son of God*, xiv–xv; Channing, "Unitarian Christianity," 295, 298; Christie, *Dissertations*, iii–x.

For most of the rest of this chapter I will highlight twenty undeniable facts (really, *classes of* facts), numbered F1–F20, each of which confirms U over T because it would be surprising given T but would not be surprising given U. An informed Trinitarian ought not deny any of these facts. And it is point-missing to urge (correctly) that each such fact is logically compatible with the truth of T. As we will see, the case that the NT authors assumed a Unitarian (and not a Trinitarian) view of God and Jesus is extremely strong. This shows that it is wrongheaded to try to logically derive a Trinity theory from the texts. To finish the chapter I shall briefly comment on these futile attempts.

Twenty Revealing Facts

F1. *There is no New Testament "Trinity passage."*[7] By a "Trinity passage" I mean a text in which the view that the one God just is the Trinity is clearly asserted, implied, or assumed. This would be a passage such that the editor of a modern study Bible could correctly insert as a section heading "God as Trinity." Even some enthusiastic proponents of Trinity speculations admit this.[8] This is quite surprising given T, especially if one holds that the claims of T are central and essential to Christian teaching, or even things that one must believe in order to be saved. But this fact is not at all surprising, but rather strongly expected, given U. Thus, this fact strongly confirms U over T.

F2. *No New Testament word or phrase was at that time understood to refer to a tripersonal God.* The Greek *trias* and the Latin *trinitas* date back, respectively, to around the last quarter of the second Christian century and to

---

7. This fact, like some others discussed below, is a "negative fact" about something which isn't there. Some may worry that in appealing to these I'm making fallacious arguments from silence. But no fallacy is being committed. If something isn't there, this is evidence against P in cases where *if* P were true, then *probably* the thing *would* be there. Thus, you don't see an elephant in the room with you, and this is strong evidence that your room is now elephant-free, for if there were one then probably you would see it. In contrast, you don't see any germs on your hands right now, but this is not good evidence that your hands are germ free, since it's false that you would see them if they were there. And in some scenarios it is not immediately clear whether this sort of "noseeum" inference is reasonable. See Wykstra, "Rowe's Noseeum Arguments." But I maintain that all of my inferences from negative facts in this chapter are of the first sort, with varying degrees of probability.

8. Erickson, *Making Sense of the Trinity*: "This teaching does not seem to be stated in the Bible" (13, 15). Similarly, Sanders, *Triune God*: "It is not directly proposed in the words of Scripture" (39).

the early third century.[9] But a Trinitarian need not call her triune god "the Trinity"; she may just coin a new use of the term "God," so that it refers to the Trinity.[10] Or she might even use a phrase, like "the Three who are One" or "the Three who are God" to refer to her tripersonal god. But we would be shocked if she had no word or phrase by which to refer to the Trinity. As best we can tell, the NT authors had no such word or phrase.

About the word "God" (Greek: *theos*), Trinitarian Evangelical New Testament scholar Murray J. Harris informs us, after surveying the usage of this word in the entire NT, that "When (*ho*) *theos* [i.e., "God" whether or not preceded by "the"] is used, we are to assume that the NT writers have *ho pater* [the Father] in mind unless the context makes this sense of (*ho*) *theos* impossible."[11] Perhaps the only phrase in all twenty-seven of these books which one might suppose refers to the Trinity is Jesus' command in Matthew 28:19 to "Go therefore and make disciples of all nations, baptizing them in the name of *the Father and of the Son and of the Holy Spirit*."[12] But there is no reason to suppose that the italicized phrase here is a singular referring term for the Trinity, and to the contrary, "the Father" and "God" are normally co-referring terms in the NT,[13] so reference is here made to three things, namely God, his human Son Jesus, and God's spirit, without any implication that they are equally divine or that somehow they compose or are in the one God.

If T were true, it would be shocking that these authors have no word or phrase by which to refer to their triune God. On the other hand, if U is true, it is unsurprising that they have no word for a triune God. Thus, our second fact strongly favors U over T.

F3. *Clear assumptions, assertions, and implications that the one God (formerly called "Yahweh") just is the Father, and no clear assumption, assertion, or implication that the one God just is the Trinity.* Given F2 it is no surprise that these authors never *assert* the numerical sameness of God with the

---

9. Theophilus, *To Autolycus*, 53 [2.15]; Tertullian, *Against Praxeas*, chapters 3, 12; Tertullian, *On Modesty*, chapter 21. Lest one misread the later singular-referring usage of *trinitas* back into these, see the passages and discussion in Tuggy and Date, *Is Jesus Human and Not Divine?*, 123–26, 142–45, 153–56, and my "Tertullian the Unitarian," or my "When and How?," 28–29.

10. This new usage is first observed around the last quarter of the 300s, on which see my "When and How?."

11. Harris, *Jesus as God*, 47.

12. Emphases added. Unless otherwise noted, all biblical quotations are from the NRSV-UE.

13. Harris, *Jesus as God*, 271, 282.

Trinity, as they lack the linguistic means to refer to the latter! Nor do they in any passage clearly *imply* or *assume* their numerical sameness/identity. Had they clearly implied or assumed that God is the Trinity, we would see believers in a triune God *far* earlier in Christian history than we do, that is, long before the second half of the 300s.

Granted, countless Trinitarian exegetes have urged that "the Trinity" is, *upon careful examination*, implied by and/or assumed by these authors. Even if they are correct, it is an undeniable fact that God being the Trinity is never *clearly* assumed, asserted, or implied in any portion of the Bible. This is why for any text that some Trinitarians think implies or assumes that God is the Trinity, we can find early Christians (c. 90–350 CE) interpreting it in non-Trinitarian ways, and we can find some later *Trinitarian* interpreters who *don't* think the text in question assumes or implies that God is the Trinity.[14] Further, as even some enthusiastic boosters of "the doctrine of the Trinity" admit, modern historical-critical interpretation has shown many of most popular Trinitarian proof-texts not to be Trinitarian when rightly understood in their original context.[15] This is why we see such a push for new-fangled philosophical and exegetical supports for the Trinity,[16] or at least for "the deity of Christ," hoping this gets one most of the way there.

In contrast, that the one God just is the Father himself, and not anyone else, does *frequently and clearly* seem to be assumed in the NT. In the Fourth Gospel Jesus refers to the Father as "the one who alone is God" (John 5:43–44) and as "the only true God" (John 17:1–3). While the peoples of the earth believe in various deities, Paul observes, "yet for us [Christians,] there is one God, the Father" (1 Cor 8:6). The assumption here would be rendered in our present-day logic as: for any x, x is a god only if x just is the Father.[17] In Acts, Peter preaches that the "God of Abraham and Isaac and Jacob, the God of our ancestors, has glorified his servant Jesus" (Acts 3:13). The god mentioned is, of course, Yahweh, the only god, according to the Old

---

14. Wilson, *Unitarian Principles*.

15. E.g., Sanders, *Triune God*: "[The] doctrine of the Trinity stands today at a point of crisis with regard to its ability to demonstrate its exegetical foundation. Theologians once approached this doctrine with a host of biblical proofs, but one by one, many of those venerable old arguments have been removed from the realm of plausibility" (162).

16. Swinburne explains that in his view Trinitarians need a philosophical proof that there must be a Trinity, since "even if you regard the New Testament as an infallible source of doctrine, you cannot derive from it a doctrine of the Trinity." See Swinburne, "Social Theory of the Trinity," 419. Alas, such philosophical attempts fail. See my Tuggy, "Antiunitarian Arguments."

17. In standard symbolism: $\forall x \, (Gx \supset x = f)$. On this see my "God and His Son" or my *Monotheism*, chapter 9.

Testament (OT),[18] and in Luke's view, this is none other than the Father (Luke 6:35–36; 10:21–22; Acts 2:33; 7:55–56).

In sum, while the Trinitarian labors at length and uphill to show that the Bible as a whole implies or assumes that God is in some way a Trinity, Unitarians simply state their view using the words of the NT. As Channing observed, "We are astonished that anyone can read the New Testament and avoid the conviction that the Father alone is God."[19] Put differently, in the NT, *at first glance*, the only god is supposed to be the one called "the Father," and there is no *clear* indication that the one God is the Father, Son, and Spirit. This is extremely surprising if T is true, but it is fully expected if U is true. Thus, this fact strongly confirms U over T.

F4. *Endorsement, not criticism or correction of core Jewish theology.* In Mark 12:28–34 Jesus passes up a golden opportunity to correct what the Trinitarian imagines to be a too-restrictive Jewish monotheism. Asked what the greatest commandment is, Jesus quotes the famous Shema, "Hear, O Israel: the Lord our God, the Lord is one." His interlocutor, a Jewish legal scholar, replies, "You are right, Teacher; you have truly said that 'he is one, and besides him there is no other.'" This Jew, who is *not* a disciple of Jesus, seems to agree with him about monotheism. Who is the "him" mentioned? It is of course Yahweh himself (Deut 6:4), who in the NT is called "the Father," "God the Father," or just "God."

Thus Paul writes that "I am grateful to God—whom I worship with a clear conscience, as my ancestors did," and the "God" here was just a verse before referred to as "God the Father" (2 Tim 1:2–3). And in the most quoted OT text in the NT, we read of "Yahweh's declaration to my lord, 'Sit at my right hand until I make your enemies a footstool for your feet,'" (Ps 110:1) and Yahweh, called "the Lord" in Greek and in most English translations, is none other than the Father himself.[20] In the NT, the young Jesus-movement and the rest of the Jews have a lot to disagree about, but this does not include who God is.[21] Thus Jesus says that "It is my Father who glorifies me, he of whom you say, 'He is our God'" (John 8:54).

---

18. The OT assumption is that there is only one god (one being of that kind), not that there is only one who can truly or properly or literally be addressed or referred to as "God" or "a god."

19. Channing, "Unitarian Christianity," 296, slightly modernized.

20. See Acts 2:33–35 where this verse is quoted (vv. 34–35) and just before (v. 33) the terms "God" and "the Father" are clearly used in a co-referring way (cf. F8 below).

21. Tellingly, the anti-Christian Jews in Acts 24:14–15 say nothing about Paul's theology, nor do they dispute Paul's claim to worship the same god they worship. And in Acts 3:13, Peter clearly is referring to the Father when he asserts that "the God of our ancestors, has glorified his servant Jesus." See also Acts 4:24–27, 5:28; Heb 1:1–2.

Long experience shows that Trinitarians feel the need to correct non-Christian Jewish monotheism as "too strict" or extreme or out of balance, or at any rate for having too few divine "persons." But the NT authors never do any such things, instead simply endorsing the core of Jewish theology, which would be very surprising if T were true. But it is to be expected if U were true. Thus, this fourth fact strongly confirms U over T.

F5. *No early monotheism controversies.* Whenever they encounter Trinitarian theologies, non-Christian Jews criticize them as polytheism, or just not good, or reasonable, or pure enough, or scriptural monotheism. But we see no such complaints in the NT, or anywhere in the first Christian century. The non-Christian Jews found plenty to complain about, as they rejected Jesus' claim to be God's Messiah/Christ, the disciples' claim that God raised Jesus from the dead, and Paul's claim that "Christ redeemed us from the curse of the law" (Gal 3:13). But they never, so far as we can tell, accused the Christians of being pseudo-monotheists, unscriptural monotheists, incoherent monotheists, crypto-polytheists, or Tritheists.[22]

This is very surprising given T. What is the chance the Jewish opponents of the (initially all-Jewish) Jesus-movement didn't know it was Trinitarian, or that they did but did not object to it? But this lack of any early Jewish-Christian controversy about monotheism is expected given U. Thus, F5 confirms U over T.

F6. *The New Testament usage of "God" (theos).* As we've seen, "God" (*theos*) in the NT nearly always refers to the Father. We can generously concede for sake of argument that as many as eight times in the NT *theos* refers to Jesus.[23] A naïve modern reader may be shocked that a man could be referred to as "God," but as Harris observes, *theos* "could be used to refer to deity in general, a particular heathen god or goddess, pagan deities at large (along with their images), angels, human rulers or judges, persons of valor or rank, godlike persons, as well as the one true God of Israel."[24] Traditional fixation on the few passages in which Jesus is allegedly called "God" prevents people from seeing the wider pattern of usage and its significance. It is an undeniable fact that more than 99 percent of the uses of *theos* in these books refer

---

22. Especially noteworthy is the failure of Jesus' Jewish opponents to accuse Jesus of claiming to be God or another god at his trials. Against the misreading that Jesus claims to be God himself or to be fully divine in Mark 14:62–64, see Bock, "Blasphemy and the Jewish Examination of Jesus."

23. See Harris, *Jesus as God*, 272, and F2 above.

24. Harris, *Jesus as God*, 29; cf. John 10:30–39.

to the Father.[25] It *never* refers to the Trinity, and *theos* perhaps twice refers to God's spirit (Acts 5:3; 1 Cor 3:16), which we will discuss below.

This pattern of usage is very surprising given T; we would expect a believer in a triune god to use the main God-word for that Triune God, and we would expect her to more evenly distribute the title "God" among the three equally divine persons. In contrast, this pattern of usage is not surprising given U. Thus, F6 confirms U over T.

F7. *The New Testament pattern of worship and/or honor.* As illustrated by Trinitarian liturgies, a Trinitarian worships God the Trinity, and also each of the divine "persons." But in the NT, the Trinity is never an object of worship; this is neither stated, nor implied, nor portrayed, nor presupposed anywhere. Neither is the Holy Spirit an object of worship. The main and ultimate object of worship is the Father, a.k.a. "God," whom we approach through Christ (Eph 5:20; Col 3:16–17; Heb 13:15). There is no attempt to spread around the worship equally between the three. Jesus, especially after his exaltation, is worshiped (or some would say *honored*) too, but the reason cited for this is not his divine nature but rather his exaltation by God because of his perfect, self-sacrificing service to God (Phil 2:9; Rev 5:9), and this worship of Jesus is explicitly said to be "to the glory of God the Father" (Phil 2:11). One would not expect *God* to be worshiped to the glory of someone above him!

F7 is *shocking* given T. It is *at most* a little surprising given U (because the man Jesus is honored or worshiped in addition to God).[26] Thus, F7 confirms U over T.

F8. *Pattern of stylistic name- and title-swapping.* Consider this paragraph:

> Joe Biden gave a speech. Then Joe Biden took a nap. Afterwards, Joe Biden met with his cabinet. Finally, Joe Biden went out for dinner.

Here is a slightly improved version:

---

25. Harris, *Jesus as God*, 30.

26. Trinitarians sometimes argue that for Jews of this era, it was unthinkable that religious worship should be given to anyone other than God, but this is not true. See Kirk, *Man Attested*. A leading proponent of the early worship of Jesus showing some amorphous "high" Christology stated that the NT reason for Jesus' worship is not his divine nature but rather God's will, as shown by his exaltation of Jesus. See Hurtado, *Lord Jesus Christ*, 641; Hurtado, *God in New Testament Theology*, 64, 107–8.

President Biden gave a speech. Then Mr. Biden took a nap. Afterwards, the President met with his cabinet. Finally, the Commander in Chief went out for dinner.

In the first paragraph I monotonously used the same singular referring expression ("Joe Biden") over and over. The second time I mixed up various co-referring names and titles. This sounds better in English, and, I assume, in most languages, including NT Greek. Observe now what the author of the Fourth Gospel does:

> It is written in the prophets, "And they shall all be taught by *God*." Everyone who has heard and learned from the Father comes to me. Not that anyone has seen the Father except the one who is from *God*; he has seen the Father. (John 6:45–46, emphases added)

The author artfully alternates between "God" and "the Father." This is not confusing because those terms in the NT are normally co-referring. In another passage, possibly this same author word-swaps for both God and Jesus:

> Everyone who does not abide in the teaching of *Christ*, but goes beyond it, does not have God; whoever abides in the teaching has both the Father and *the Son*. (2 John 1:9, emphases added)

The reader understands that not four but only two are mentioned: God/the Father and Christ/the Son. Co-referring terms are being switched to improve the style. In Acts, Peter is portrayed as saying,

> God has raised this Jesus. . . . Then, being exalted to the right hand of God, and having received from *the Father* the promised holy spirit, he has poured out this that you see and hear. (Acts 2:32–33, emphasis added)

Just having used the word "God" twice, Luke switches to "the Father" for the third mention. Similarly, James writes,

> But no one can tame the tongue—a restless evil. . . . With it we bless *the Lord and Father*, and with it we curse people, made in the likeness of *God*. (Jas 3:8–9, emphasis added)

As before, the meaning would be the same if just one referring term per referent were used throughout. But changing them just sounds better. In the NT, while terms like these *are* swappable: God/the Father/the Lord and Father—these pairs never seem to be swapped just for stylistic reasons: God/the Son, God/Christ, God/the Son of God, God/Jesus. This is surprising given T, but not given U. Thus, this pattern of word-swapping confirms U over T.

F9. *In the New Testament God-terms always take singular, personal words (verbs, adjectives, definite article, pronouns).* Authors can personify, that is, talk about something that is not a self *as if* it were. Thus one prophet likens Israel in his day to a prostitute (Hos 4:15). Similarly, an author can de-personify, talking about a person *as if* he were a non-person, an impersonal object. Thus Christ is likened to the cornerstone of a building's foundation (Isa 29:16; Acts 4:11; Eph 2:20; 1 Pet 2:6). Because of these common practices, the matching words don't *always* tell us what the author thinks the subject literally is.

But *usually*, they do. Suppose you're eavesdropping on a conversation at another table in a restaurant, and you hear, "I do love ___ so much!" (You couldn't make out that one word in the middle of the sentence.) Is this person expressing her love for one thing or many? And is this loved thing a person or not? A name or title (e.g., "David," "the principal") will tell you it is a single someone. So will a singular, personal pronoun: "him," "her." If it is an "it" she loves, it probably won't be a someone, but rather a mere something. If you can tell that what she loves is personal but not the number, a following sentence may easily clarify, e.g., "___ gives me so much joy!" Here, you didn't hear the first word, but the verb tells you that the subject is singular; if it were plural (e.g., "dogs") she would have said "give." Depending on the mechanics of the language, one might also fixate on other matching words, e.g., adjectives, the definite article, including their grammatical gender (masculine, feminine, or neuter). Adult human beings listening to their mother-tongue do this sort of interpretation mostly on autopilot, and we do it *very* reliably. It works in print as well as with spoken language, and it often works even when reading a translation from a very different language.

The NT titles for the only god[27] always take singular verbs, adjectives, and adverbs, and the single, masculine definite article (when one is used), and are replaced only by singular personal pronouns, the sort employed for individual selves. The overwhelming impression is that this god is a single self.[28]

---

27. "God," "Lord," "the Father," "God the Father," "the Father of mercies," "the Father of glory," "the Father of spirits," "the Father of lights," "your heavenly Father," "Abba," "the Almighty," "the Most High," "the Creator," "the Majesty on High," "the Lord your God," "the Lord God."

28. This is reinforced by the conceptual point that the common concept of a deity is of a certain sort of self. See Tuggy, "On Counting Gods."

F9 is expected given U. In contrast, F9 is *somewhat* surprising if T is true. While most Trinitarians normally speak of God the Trinity as if this were a single self, e.g., "The triune God has *self*-revealed in Scripture, and we should thank *him* for this," some will also speak of the Trinity as if they were a plurality of selves, e.g., "The Trinity *enjoy* [note the plural verb] one another in eternity; our communities should emulate *them*." For some Trinitarians, the word "persons" notwithstanding, the Trinity is a single self. For others, the Trinity is clearly a "they," and strictly not a self, although they may be thought of *as if* they were one. For others, no human term literally and properly applies to God, though we may improperly talk about God as a "he," "she," "it," or "they"; how many selves the Trinity is, is for them an ill-formed question. One theorist even has the Trinity literally being a self, while being composed of three other selves, which would make the Trinity both a "him" *and* a "them," though with respect to two different sorts of selves/persons.[29] The status quo among the laity is confusion, speaking of the Trinity sometimes as if it were a self and sometimes as if it were not.

Given all of this complexity, the very straightforward way the NT treats God-terms—they are singular and personal, full stop—is a bit of a surprise, and thus F9 at least weakly confirms U over T. "But doesn't the *Old* Testament contain hints—no, *adumbrations*—that God is a Trinity, or at least more than one self?" No. What it does is sometimes magnify God by pluralizing words relating to him; a thing that ancient Hebrew writers also do to other worthy selves and even things and non-human animals.[30] But suppose that such God-as-Trinity "adumbrations" *really are* part of the contents of the OT books. This would only highlight how surprising F9 is given T. One can't say that God *is revealed* in the OT to be a Trinity.[31] What God reveals, people actually believe, and this is nowhere observed in these books. God-as-Trinity, *if* it is divinely revealed, must have been revealed later, whether that is (as some popular apologists urge) "in between the testaments," in the NT, or at the council in 381.[32] If God is dropping Trinity-hints in the OT, then in the NT either he just has revealed, is revealing, or is about to reveal "the doctrine of the Trinity." Why then the step backward? Why not throw in *more* of these plural words relating to God, or at least as many? At any

---

29. McIntosh, "God of the Groups."

30. Smith, "Plural of Majesty."

31. Walton, *Old Testament Theology*, 286–89.

32. Here as on so many other things, Trinitarians disagree among themselves, with some even taking the hopeless position that the Trinity is revealed in the OT. E.g., Heiser, "Jewish Trinity." The first "official" triune-God-assuming creed is from the 381 council. See Tuggy, *What Is the Trinity?* chapter 5.

rate, these alleged hints do not affect the fact that F9 somewhat confirms T over U.

F10. *New Testament usage of "the Lord" and "the one Lord."* Use of "the Lord" (*ho kurios*) undergoes an interesting development in the NT. As is well known, in ancient Judaism before Jesus' time God's proper name, the Hebrew *Yahweh*, had fallen out of use. Thus, scholars who translated the Hebrew Bible into Greek substituted the title "the Lord" (*ho kurios*) for the proper name *Yahweh*.

Being avid readers of Greek version(s) of the Jewish Bible, the NT authors employ *ho kurios* in this sense (Matt 2:15; 4:7). But of course the generic term "lord" already had less exalted uses. A Greek speaker might use "lord" as a term of respectful address, which we translate as "Sir" (Matt 27:63). Again, "Lord" could refer to a human master, such as the Lord of a manor, a teacher, or a slave owner (Matt 6:24; 8:8, 25; 18:21). But to these three uses, the NT authors add a fourth. For them, often "the Lord" is a title for the risen and exalted Messiah, the Lord Jesus (Acts 9:27; 18:25).

Some today urge that the NT authors, in this new usage, hearkening back to the first usage mentioned (substituting *ho kurios* for the divine name), are hinting that the man Jesus is Yahweh himself, or that he "belongs to the divine identity."[33] But this is confused and confusing. In the NT, "the one Lord" is spoken of *in addition to and in contrast with* the one God. And the application, in a religious context, of "the Lord" to a man, which by itself would be surprising, is easily explained by these authors' enthusiastic application of Psalm 110:1 to the resurrected Jesus: "The LORD [Hebrew: *Yahweh*] says to my lord [Hebrew: *adoni*], 'Sit at my right hand until I make your enemies your footstool.'" Scholars think this was originally the opening line in a coronation song. God invites the speaker's master, the king, up to God's throne, to rule with and under him. NT authors consistently see a double meaning here; they take this text to also have a prophetic meaning referring to God's exaltation of the man Jesus after resurrecting him.[34] As Peter preaches in Acts, God has "made" this man "both Lord and Messiah" (Acts 2:36). The one they had mocked as "the King of the Jews" (Luke 23:38) now really is their king, and indeed the king of the whole world, under God. And notice that Luke shows his awareness of the ambiguity of the term "Lord," which can be used for God or for God's Messiah (Luke 1:32; 24:34; Acts 1:21; 4:26). But he neither confuses them together, nor is there any

---

33. For an evaluation of this obscure neologism, see my "On Bauckham's Bargain."

34. E.g., Matt 22:42–44; 26:64; Luke 20:42–44; Acts 2:34–35; Rom 8:34; 1 Cor 15:25; Heb 1:3, 13; 10:12–13; 12:2; Col 3:1; Eph 1:20.

reason to think that in using "Lord" in both ways he is hinting that somehow these two are the same being, or that they are equally divine. Occasionally a NT author will add a word to remove the ambiguity ("Lord *God*," "Lord *Jesus*") but generally the context alone makes clear which is meant. A handful of texts remain for scholars to argue about, whether the author means God or Jesus by *kurios*. In sum, although there are four meanings of *kurios* in NT Greek, when it comes to serious, religious contexts, there are two, and generally the reader is sure which is meant, God or his human Son.

When a Trinitarian says "the Lord," she may mean the Father, the Son, the Spirit, or the Trinity, so the ambiguity is greater than in the NT. And she often insists that in calling Jesus "Lord" the author is either asserting or hinting that Jesus "is Yahweh" or is divine. Given that, if T were true we would expect the Trinity and the Holy Spirit also to be called "Lord." But in the NT, they never are. Thus, F10 is surprising given T, but not surprising given U. So it confirms U over T.

F11. *Mere-man-compatible theses and "big reveals."* According to Trinitarians, the most important and profound facts about Jesus are that he is not only human but is also fully divine, and that he is the second "person" of the Trinity. Trinitarians never fail to mention these facts in presenting what they believe to be the important things to know about Jesus, when given enough time and opportunity.

The authors of the Gospels created medium-length, highly composed portraits of their central subject, and like any good (non-esoteric) non-fiction writers, they make clear the main theses of their books, and they also use various devices to dramatically reveal important facts about their central subject, the man Jesus. In the first of the Gospels, Mark, the author's main thesis is undoubtedly that Jesus is God's Christ, also called "the Son of God." This thesis is asserted using many different methods.[35] One is the big reveal when Jesus asks the disciples who *they* think he is. The answer comes from Peter, the leader of the apostles: "You are the Messiah" (Mark 8:29; Luke 9:20 has "the Messiah of God"). The author of Matthew amplifies this to "You are the Messiah, the Son of the living God" (Matt 16:16). The same main thesis is clearly stated in what is probably the original ending of the Fourth Gospel: "Now Jesus did many other signs.... But these are written so that you may continue to believe that Jesus is the Messiah, the Son of God, and that through believing you may have life in his name" (John 20:30–31). It is shocking to suggest that Trinitarian authors should so pointedly leave

---

35. See Tuggy, "Unfinished Business," 214–15.

out their central, most important claims about Jesus,[36] giving these much less exciting claims instead, especially given that these are not esoteric works, but rather popular writings which wear their main points on their sleeves. In contrast, if these authors are Unitarians, as defined above, then these are not only unsurprising facts, but they are even expected. Again, we have found a class of facts each of which strongly confirms U over T.

F12. Jesus is regularly called a "man" with no warning that this is only part of what he is (i.e., that he's not a "mere man"). Trinitarian authors are often reticent to call Jesus "a man." One reason for that reticence is just the traditional strong emphasis on his full deity. Another reason is the traditional view, most often seen in Roman Catholic sources,[37] that Jesus is "man" but not "a man." The motivation for this view is that the one self/person in the incarnate Christ is supposed to be the eternal, divine Son. The "complete human nature" he mysteriously unites with can't also be a self/person (a human one), otherwise in the incarnate Christ there would be two selves. Thus after the mysterious union, the Son is "man" (he can be called that) but is not *"a* man" (i.e., not a human person/self).

This teaching clashes with the NT, since in NT Greek, as with the English "man," the common nouns *anthropos* and *aner* normally refer to a human person or self. Many present-day Trinitarians are ignorant of this "man but not *a* man" tradition, or they know about it but conveniently ignore it, or they know about it but disagree. Thus many today *will* say that Jesus is "a man." But they will usually hastily add that he is *also* divine, or negatively, that he is not "a *mere* man" (i.e., a man who is not also divine).

But none of these habits are seen in the NT. These authors refer to Jesus as "a man" and then just keep going, showing no concern to rule out a "mere man" interpretation.[38] This nonchalance is surprising if they are Trinitarians, but is expected if they are Unitarians. Thus again, we find facts each of which confirms U over T.

F13. The use of titles or descriptions of Jesus normally assumes that the referent is a human being, with no warning that he is not a man (human person/self) or is not only a man. Similarly, the NT authors refer to Jesus,

---

36. Against the Athanasian-era point that Jesus must be "a real" Son of God who therefore must fully have the divine nature, see Kirk, *Man Attested*, chapter 2 and facts F12–F18 below.

37. Baker, *Jesus Christ*, 30–31.

38. E.g., Matt 8:27; Mark 6:2; 14:67; Luke 23:2, 4, 6, 13, 41, 47; John 1:30; 4:29; 5:11–12; 6:52; 7:25, 27, 31, 35; 8:40; 19:21; Acts 2:22–23; 5:28; 13:38; 17:31; Rom 5:12–19; 1 Cor 15:20, 47; 1 Tim 2:5.

unselfconsciously and with no warnings, as a prophet of God,[39] a servant of God,[40] and God's Christ/Messiah. But these were normally understood to be human beings.[41] Again, they claim that he is a descendant of David,[42] locating him within the human family tree. More specifically, he is "Jesus of Nazareth,"[43] which assumes that he is *a man* from Nazareth.

Further, in a great number of ways these authors constantly portray him as a real man, sometimes even seeming to show a concern to refute early Docetists.[44] He has a human body and a human mother (Matt 1:25; Luke 2:7).[45] He starts as a fetus, grows into a precocious child, and then into a man (Luke 1:31, 42; 2:21, 41–52). He eats and sleeps (Mark 4:38; Luke 22:8). He doesn't know things and so asks questions (Matt 15:34; Mark 5:9; 8:27; Luke 8:42–48). He suffers and is tempted (Heb 2:10–18). He worries about the future and prays to God (Mark 1:35; 6:46; 14:32; Luke 3:21; 5:16; 6:12; 9:18; John 17); he must put his trust in God and obey him (John 4:34; 6:38; 14:31; 15:10).[46] He is murdered by crucifixion, buried in a fancy tomb, then brought back to life by God (Matt 27:50, 60; 28:6; Acts 2:22–36; Eph 1:20).

All of this would normally betray the assumption that Jesus is a human person.[47] And yet the authors present Jesus in these ways without warning the reader not to infer that he is that, or *only* that, nor do they try to somehow confine these limitations to his "human nature," or give the reader any clear reasons for thinking that Jesus is also fully divine or has a divine nature. Again, we have discovered a large and varied class of facts such that each of them would be surprising given T, but would not be surprising given U, so each confirms U over T.

---

39. E.g., Matt 10:40–41; 21:46; Mark 6:4, 15; Luke 4:24; 24:19; John 4:19, 44; 9:17; Acts 3:22–23; 7:37.

40. E.g., Matt 12:18; Acts 3:13; 4:27.

41. I pass by here Jesus' title for himself "the Son of Man" because scholars disagree on what his use of that implies.

42. E.g., Matt 1:1; Acts 2:30; Rom 1:3; 2 Tim 2:8; Rev 22:16.

43. E.g., Luke 16:6; 24:19; John 18:5, 7; Acts 2:22; 10:38.

44. That is, people who thought that Jesus only appeared to be a man but was in fact something else.

45. Or a human mother and a human father: John 1:45; 6:42.

46. Tuggy, "Jesus as an Exemplar."

47. This is why we see "mere man" (or "humanitarian") views of Christ in early Christianity, especially in opposition to the then-new Logos speculations about God and Christ. Further, there is a plausible argument that such a "Dynamic Monarchian" Christology was the earliest. See Gaston, *Dynamic Monarchianism*.

F14. *Clear and unqualified claims that Jesus' mission, power, authority, knowledge, and kingdom were given to him by God (i.e., the Father).*[48] While historically many have supposed that Christ's miracles and teaching were sure signs that he had (or was) a divine nature, today many Trinitarians agree with the NT that Christ received his mission, his miraculous powers, his authority, and his knowledge from the Father. On the face of it, one who has received such things *needed* to receive them, as with other human servants of the Almighty. It is plausible that one who is fully divine would not need to be given the messianic mission, would be able to do Jesus-level miracles on his own, would as divine have authority to forgive sins and to do other astounding things, and would be essentially omniscient, and so not need to be informed by another.

Yes, it is arguably conceivable that a being who had all these endowments on his own would nonetheless choose to in some sense relinquish or not use them, so as to be empowered in these ways by another. If we see a participant in the marathon being pushed in a wheelchair, we assume that this is happening because she can't run, although it is conceivable that she can, but for some reason wants to finish the race by the power of her pushing friend. Of course, if she wants the rest of us to know that she actually can walk, she'll need to do more than just sit there!

Here is the problem for Trinitarians: these clear scriptural statements of Jesus' empowerment by God *suggest* that Jesus didn't already have any of these on his own. And the authors of the NT, knowing this, issued these statements *without the slightest warning* that the reader should not infer that Jesus *needed* to be so empowered. That they should do this seems unlikely given T, but likely given U. Thus again, we see a broad class of facts which confirm U over T.

F15. *Unqualified implications of the Son's limits.* Clear NT texts imply that Jesus is less than God in respect of power, knowledge, goodness, authority, immortality, impeccability, and greatness.[49] More precisely, these texts

---

48. For references to each, respectively: *mission* (Luke 10:16; John 5:20), *power* (Matt 12:28; Luke 1:32; 4:15; 11:20-22; John 3:2, 35; 5:19, 30; 14:10; Acts 2:22; 10:37-38; Heb 2:4), *authority* (Matt 9:8; 28:18; John 5:18, 22-23; Acts 17:31; 1 Cor 1:3; 15:24-28; Rev 2:26-27), *knowledge* (John 7:16; 8:28; 16:30; 17:8, 14; Rev 1:1), and *kingdom* (Heb 1:2; 1 Cor 15:24-28).

49. *Power* (Mark 10:37-40; John 5:19-20, 30), *knowledge* (Matt 24:36; Mark 5:30-32; 9:21; 13:32; Heb 5:8), *goodness* (Mark 10:18), *authority* (see above), *immortality* (Matt 27:50; Mark 12:37; Luke 23:46; John 19:30; Acts 5:30; Rom 5:6-10; Phil 2:8; Rev 1:18; 5:6), *impeccability* (cf. Matt 4:2-3, Heb 2:18; 4:15 with Jas 1:13), *greatness* (John 10:29; 14:28). For replies to some tortured Trinitarian interpretations see Emlyn, *Humble Inquiry*, 53-55; Wilson, *Scripture Proofs*, 63-64. With respect to impeccability, it is

imply that Jesus lacked essential omnipotence, essential omniscience, underived moral goodness, underived authority, essential untemptability, and essential immortality, as well as the divine attribute of being greater than all others—all of which are plausibly features that the absolutely perfect being must have.

Any competent writer would know, in authoring such texts, that they would lead the reader to think that God (a.k.a. the Father) is greater than Jesus and that Jesus is lesser than God in each of these respects. Thus, such a writer, if they believed that Jesus was as divine as is the Father, would warn the reader not to draw any such conclusions, or at least would offer some distinction intended to show that no such conclusions follow (e.g., that Jesus lacks essential omniscience "with respect to his human nature" only).

But these authors issue no such warnings or qualifications, in effect contrasting Jesus with God in these eight respects. If T were true this would be very surprising. But it is expected, or at least not at all surprising given U. Thus these facts too strongly confirm U over T.

F16. *The clear assumption and clear statements that the Father is Jesus's God.* The god of the Jewish Bible is by definition top-level, as it were an immovable King of the Hill. Necessarily, he is above or over any other beings there may be, and so anyone who is under a god is someone other than him. Further, in the highest sense of the word "God," there is only one, Yahweh himself (Isa 45:18; 46:9),[50] so there is no question of his being under a god (in the highest sense), since it is a contradiction to say that he is the god over himself (God-over is an irreflexive relation),[51] and there isn't and can't be another *god* (in the highest sense) in addition to him. And any "god" in a lower sense couldn't possibly be the "god" *over* Yahweh, the one true God (i.e., the only one who is "god"/"God" in the highest sense of the term). Being "God" in the highest sense is, given a metaphysics of natural kinds, to be the only one with the kind-essence *divinity/deity/godhood*.

The NT authors teach that the Father is the god over Jesus.[52] None of these texts contains any sort of qualification or warning designed to prevent

---

plausible that a being who is essentially perfect in power, goodness, and knowledge, and who necessarily exists and has his perfections independently of anything else in principle can't be tempted, so that divinity entails the impossibility of being tempted.

50. In the NT this is expressed by the title *pantocrator*, or "Almighty" (see 2 Cor 6:18; Rev 1:8; 4:8; 11:17; 15:3; 16:7, 14; 19:6), who is someone other than Jesus (Rev 21:22).

51. This, together with the clear NT teaching about to be mentioned, entails the falsity of relative identity Trinity theories. See Tuggy, *Monotheism*, chapter 10.

52. Matt 27:46; Mark 15:34; John 20:17; Rom 15:6; 2 Cor 1:3; 11:31; Eph 1:3, 17; 1 Pet 1:3; Heb 1:8–9; Rev 1:5–6; 3:2, 12; 5:10.

the reader from deducing that Jesus is not the unique god, and that he lacks the sort of divinity had only by God. This would be shocking given T, but it is expected given U. Thus, these facts strongly confirm U over T.

F17. *Use of "God the ____."* Trinitarians talk of "God the Trinity," "God the Father," "God the Son," and "God the Holy Spirit." Of these phrases, the NT authors use only the second. This is very surprising given T, but expected given U. Thus, F17 strongly confirms U over T.

F18. *Total lack of interest in the eternality of Son or the Spirit.* It is part of the Nicene orthodoxy first really established in 381 that both the Son and the Spirit, since each is fully divine, must be eternal, and so can't ever have come into existence. Famously, Arius is alleged to have taught about the Logos/Divine Son that there was a time before he existed.[53] But in earlier times some influential, mainstream Christian theologians thought that the Logos *had* come into existence (or come into existence *as a concrete, divine person*). This assumption is pretty clear in Justin Martyr,[54] and it is explicit in Tertullian.[55] And the reason that leading, mainstream Christian theorists could think this is that no NT author shows any clear interest in asserting the eternality of the Son or the Spirit of God. Even when telling us about the miraculous conception of Jesus, which would suggest that, as with human conceptions generally, Jesus came into existence, we are given no warnings not to infer that Jesus began to exist at some point during Mary's pregnancy (Matt 1:1; 18–25; Luke 1:26–38; Rom 1:3).

If one *assumes* their full deity, then their eternality follows from that. (But of course Christians like Justin and Tertullian did *not* assume the *full* deity of the Son or the Spirit.) Texts in which (allegedly) Jesus' pre-human existence is implied (e.g., John 17:5), or even his involvement in creation (e.g., John 1:1–3; Heb 1:3; Col 1:16), are irrelevant here. At most, such texts imply that he existed at that time "in the beginning" when creation occurred, or just before.[56] While it is true that "Jesus Christ is the same yesterday and today and forever" (Heb 13:8), this doesn't imply or assume that Jesus has always existed. There is no clear eternal-Son or eternal-Spirit text, which is why if one held, like Tertullian, that a finite time ago God oozed out a

---

53. Williams, *Arius*, 97–103.
54. Justin, *Second Apology*, section 6.
55. Tuggy, "Tertullian the Unitarian"
56. I grant Jesus' pre-human existence for the sake of argument when the topic is whether or not God is the Trinity. But like most today who claim the title "biblical Unitarian," in my view Scripture does not actually teach that. Divinity in the Bible does not imply timelessless or "being outside of time." See Mullins, *End of the Timeless God*.

portion of his material substance so that it also constituted the Logos, and then he (or they) oozed out a yet smaller portion to constitute also the Spirit,[57] then there just is no *easy* way to show why this scheme is false according to Scripture, again, given that (as Tertullian and others rightly saw) it nowhere implies the full divinity of both the Son and the Spirit.

This negative fact, this total lack of interest in the eternality of the Son and the Spirit is shocking if these authors are Trinitarians, but it is not shocking if they are Unitarians. Thus, it confirms U over T.

F19. *The spirit of God or "the Holy Spirit" is not clearly a divine self in the New Testament in addition to the Father (a.k.a. "God").* Sometimes God's spirit is described in ways that make it sound like a self or person in addition to God, perhaps even a divine one.[58] Yet more often it is compared with non-persons, such as wind, fire, breath, a dove, a letter's seal, water, or oil.[59] And looking at the whole NT, what is striking about this "spirit" is what is *not* there. It has no personal name, and we should remember that it is the translators who decide to capitalize, choosing "the Holy Spirit" over "the holy spirit." Paul never sends greetings from this spirit. It is usually the spirit *of God*,[60] and one would think that just as your spirit is you, not an additional self, so too God's spirit is just him (i.e., the Father), and not an additional self.[61] Mary is "found to be pregnant from the Holy Spirit," yet the resulting human is declared to be God's (i.e., the Father's) Son, not the Holy Spirit's (Matt 1:18; 3:17; 16:16; 27:54).[62] This spirit is never prayed to or worshiped.[63] Whereas the interpersonal closeness of God and Jesus is stressed—they cooperate and speak to one another—neither is clearly portrayed as enjoying an interpersonal relationship with "the holy spirit." This spirit is never said to love us.[64] While God has a throne, which he now shares with the exalted Jesus, this spirit is nowhere portrayed as enthroned.[65] Neither is

---

57. Tuggy, "Tertullian the Unitarian," section IV.

58. E.g., John 14:15–31. For other texts see Gregory, *Oration 31*, section 29.

59. Respectively: John 3:8; Matt 3:11; Job 33:4; Matt 3:16; Eph 1:13; John 7:37–39; Isa 61:1.

60. In a few passages we encounter "the spirit of Christ." In Rom 8:9 this seems to mean the power sent by Christ (and God)—see John 14:16; Acts 2:33; 10:45. In 1 Pet 1:11, the author seems to mean the power of God that was in the OT prophets and that later came to be in Christ.

61. Wallace, *Plain Statement*, 31–35.

62. Cf. Luke 1:30–37. See Morgridge, *True Believer's Defence*, 157.

63. Notice the spirit's absence in Rev 4 and 5.

64. Morgridge, *True Believer's Defence*, 156.

65. Notice also the spirit's absence in Acts 7:55–56.

this spirit taught in the NT to have been a participant in creation alongside God (or God and the pre-human Jesus). Again, this spirit is either absent or very faint as a personal character in the narratives of the NT.[66] There are many places where we'd expect a third divine person to be mentioned, given that there is one, but we don't see it (e.g., John 17:1–3; 1 Tim 5:21; 1 John 1:3; Rev 20:6; 21:23).

Especially striking is this spirit's absence in Jesus' statement that "no one knows about that day and hour, not the angels of heaven, nor the Son, but only the Father alone" (Matt 24:36).[67] What about the Holy Spirit, this purported third divine person? If the Father *alone* knows that day and hour, then it is false that this other person, the Holy Spirit, also knows it. But then, either he is a self who is not fully divine (so he needn't be essentially omniscient), or this "spirit" isn't literally a self, and so is out of view here when surveying potential knowers.

That this spirit is not *clearly* a divine self in addition to God is an undeniable fact. It is why Gregory of Nazianzus, though himself a Nicene, tells us that as late as 380, "Amongst our own experts, some took the Holy Spirit as an active process, some as a creature, some as God. Others were agnostic on this point *out of reverence*, as they put it, *for Scripture, which has given no clear revelation either way.*"[68] It is also why disagreement among Christians about God's spirit persists to the present day.[69] F19 is surprising given T, but it is not surprising given U, so it confirms U over T.

F20. *The "Triadic" New Testament passages.* In these texts each supposed "person" of the Trinity is somehow mentioned or is in view in (more or less)

---

66. In Acts this "spirit" usually seems like a power given by God and the exalted Jesus to believers (e.g., 1:2, 5; 2:4; 2:17–18; 4:8; 6:5). Acts 5:2–4, while consistent with Trinitarian views, is just as clearly consistent with Unitarian views. The idea is that God dwells in Peter by his (God's) spirit in Peter. Thus, Ananias lies not only to Peter, but to God. For scriptural parallels and exposition, see Clarke, *Scripture-Doctrine*, 8–9. In various books this spirit is said to do what only a self can do (e.g., Acts 8:2; 16:6; Eph 4:30; 1 Tim 4:1; Rev 3:6), but this is consistent both with its being a mere angel who acts on behalf of God, or rather God himself in action, so that he is strictly the only self involved.

67. Finnegan, "Unitarian View"; Morgridge, *True Believer's Defence*, 151; cf. Matt 11:27.

68. Gregory, *Oration 31*, 120, section 5. The translator here uses italics for quotations.

69. Most modern Unitarian Christians hold that God's spirit is not a self in addition to the Father (e.g., Finnegan "Unitarian View"; Wilson, *Scripture Proofs*, 93–106), although a minority views this spirit as an angel or a lesser divine being (Biddle, "XII Arguments"; Biddle, *Confession*, 18–24; Allfree, "Holy Spirit"). About the Trinitarian mainstream, see Ligonier Ministries' thestateoftheology.com.

close succession.[70] I agree that this phenomenon would be expected if the authors were Trinitarians. But this doesn't confirm T over U unless it would be surprising given U.

But the whole plot of the NT *according to a Unitarian* (or any other) Christian is that God the Father sends his human Son, empowering him by his spirit, eventually raising and exalting him, after which they send the spirit to all the Son's followers (e.g., Acts 2:32–33). The whole story is about what God does by his spirit: through prophets, then through his Messiah and his apostles, and then through all those within the new covenant. It's no surprise then that God, his human Son, and his spirit are often mentioned in close succession! These sorts of "triadic" passages are not even an at-first-glance difficulty for a Unitarian reading of the NT; they are expected by the Unitarian reader. Is then F20 neutral regarding our rival hypotheses T and U?

No, because so far I've stated F20 too abstractly, the way that Trinitarians often do, ignoring crucial details. When a Trinitarian enumerates the "persons" in God, she tends to do so (i) in the order Father-Son-Spirit (which fits hand in glove with traditional speculations about "generation" and "procession"), (ii) without repetition (e.g., mentioning Father, Son, Father, Son, and Spirit), and (iii) using those names[71] rather than using "God" and "Jesus" for the first two, and (iv) without interrupting the list with mentions of other things.

Matthew 28:19 ("Go therefore and make disciples of all nations, baptizing them in the name of the Father and of the Son and of the Holy Spirit") is *the only* NT text which meets all these expectations. No wonder it is the Trinitarian's favorite text![72] But it is an outlier. All the other "triadic" passages do not seem to imply, presuppose, or even hint at the one God being tripersonal. In Ephesians 4:1–6 we read,

> I, therefore, the prisoner in *the Lord*, beg you to walk in a manner worthy of the calling . . . making every effort to maintain the unity of the *Spirit* in the bond of peace: there is one body and one *Spirit*, just as you were called to the one hope of your calling, one *Lord*, one faith, one baptism, one *God and Father* of all, who is above all and through all and in all. (emphasis added)

---

70. Bowman, "Triadic New Testament Passages."

71. That is, using "Father," "Son," and "Holy Spirit" or "Spirit." Later Trinitarians also use "God the Father," "God the Son," and "God the Holy Spirit" or "God the Spirit," but in the NT, tellingly, only the first of these occurs.

72. The Trinitarian's second-favorite "triadic" passage is 2 Cor 13:13.

What is going on here? The author's concern is the unity of believers, and in this time there was no institutional unity such as the later one-bishop system, but only a loose network of assemblies founded by various apostles. So the author highlights the things all believers have in common, including God, his Son, and his spirit. This is one reason to mention what later readers suppose are the "persons of the Trinity," but there are many such reasons, given the plot of the NT.

Even the favorite outlier text—Matthew 28:19—ceases to seem Trinitarian when interpreted carefully, despite meeting the four expectations above. Considered in isolation (or presupposing a Trinitarian view of the NT), at first glance it is plausible that it reflects an assumption that the one God (whose "name" is gestured at?) in some sense "is" the Father, Son, and Holy Spirit. Many assume that the text presupposes some one name for the Three, but this is not so. As Bowman observes, "At most one could argue that a singular name for all three persons was possible, not that such is grammatically required."[73] But as we've seen, there is no such name or word or phrase in the NT. Many commentators have observed that this formula may reflect a later practice rather than Jesus' exact words,[74] but even so, what might these words have meant when this book was written, presumably in the last quarter of the first century, if not that God somehow "is" those three? First, observe that even in this context Jesus refers to his authority which has been given to him, obviously *by God*—something which a divine person would, as divine, not need, but would, as divine, necessarily have (Matt 28:18). Second, it's not true, as some readers suppose, that mentioning the three together implies their equal divinity (see 1 Tim 5:21) or that being mentioned in connection with baptism implies their divinity (see Rom 6:3; 1 Cor 10:2). Third, in this gospel (as in the others) the one God is none other than the Father himself (e.g., Matt 5:45, 48; 6:6, 8–15, 30–33; 15:13, 31; 16:15–17). The book should not be read as crypto-Trinitarian based on this one sentence. As I understand the passage, Jesus is referring to the authority by which his apostles will baptize, initiating people into the community: this authority is ultimately from God, but is now given to them by Jesus (after it had been given to him), which is (or will be) confirmed by God's spirit in them. The one God is mentioned here, but he's the first one in the list, not somehow all of them, in accordance with the normal NT usage of "Father" in religious contexts.

---

73. Bowman, "Triadic New Testament Passages," 29. As he points out, this sort of construction can refer to multiple persons with multiple names, e.g., Gen 48:16; Exod 23:13; Deut 18:20; 1 Chr 17:8; Luke 6:22.

74. Chandler, *God of Jesus*, 344.

In sum, the actual collection of "triadic" passages that we have in the NT (not the bare fact that there are any such), is somewhat surprising given T and not at all surprising given U, and so somewhat favors U over T.

Taking Stock and Comparing with Some Trinitarian Explanations

We've just surveyed twenty facts each of which confirms U over T. Has this been overkill? Yes. The six facts F1, F2, F3, F4, F7, and F17 are more than enough to confirm U over T. But T is so entrenched and so commonly assumed, merely asserted, or strenuously special-pleaded for that the full, twenty-fact nuclear option seemed appropriate.

Further, U explains a number of facts that T cannot, namely F2–F8, F10–F15, and F17–F18. And facts that T arguably *can* explain or help to explain—F1, F9, F16, F19, F20—U (or U with some related claims) explains better. In general, U-explanations of those are simpler and/or a better fit with other facts we know.

Thus, some Trinitarians will assert that what explains F1 is that all the NT authors *presuppose* that God is the Trinity. But the other facts we've surveyed show this claim to be false. F9 would be explained by these authors being one-self Trinitarians.[75] But a simpler explanation, and one better fitting other facts, is U. F16 is sometimes explained by claiming that the two-natured Christ must "as man" be under a god. It's unclear how two natures theory helps here, as full divinity seems to entail not being under or subject to another. But even if we think there is a T-consistent explanation here, it would seem much worse than a U-consistent one, which fits together with the other facts discussed here.

F19 has been explained by the dubious assertion that *somehow* the world was just not ready for a third divine person until the fourth century.[76] But that seems *ad hoc*. Exactly what changed in the fourth century to make the time right for this third-divine-person revelation? It's all too convenient to say the time was not right until around when the 381 council was the first to imply the full divine personhood of the Spirit. It seems better to just take NT spirit-talk to be a continuation of OT spirit-talk, which can all be understood without supposing it has to do with an additional divine person—which is consistent with U.[77]

---

75. See my "Trinity," section 1.
76. Gregory, *Oration 31*, sections 24–28.
77. Finnegan, "Unitarian View"; Wilson, *Scripture Proofs*, 325–32.

The Modern Biblical-Trinity Argument

In the face of this mountain of evidence that the NT authors were not Trinitarians, modern apologetics offers us this deductive argument.

- (1) The NT explicitly or implicitly teaches that (i) the Father is God, (ii) the Son is God, and (iii) the Holy Spirit is God, that (iv) the Father isn't the Son, (v) the Son isn't the Spirit, and (vi) the Father isn't the Spirit,[78] and (vii) that there is only one God.
- (2) To teach (i)–(vii) is to teach the doctrine of the Trinity.
- (3) Therefore, the NT teaches (at least by implication) the doctrine of the Trinity.

This sort of argument, popular though it is, has fatal problems. First, although the argument is valid, it is unsound because premise (2) is false. In (i)–(vii) no mention has yet been made of a tripersonal God, the signature idea of any Trinity theory. And do you think that "generation" and "procession" are essential components of "the doctrine of the Trinity"? If so, (2) is false. Either way, "The doctrine of the Trinity" has been dumbed down, over-simplified, to those seven claims.[79]

Second, (i)–(iii) are ambiguous, and some readings yield a demonstrably incoherent and so false theology (namely, taking [i]–[iii] to be making identity claims),[80] while other interpretations express views that are by definition not Trinitarian. A subordinationist Unitarian like Origen or Samuel Clarke would agree that each of the three "is God," though not in the same sense (which same sense [i]–[vii] do not require).[81] They would add that the one God is to be identified with the Father alone, not with the triune God, a god that Origen never heard of and which Clarke denied.[82] Likewise a modalist can easily accept an interpretation of (i)–(vii); the Father, Son, and Spirit are so many different modes as per (iv)–(vi), yet each "is God" in being a mode of the one God, as per (i)–(iii), and the one God (vii) is the tri-modal God.

Finally, this argument conveniently omits a clear and central theme of NT theology (part of fact F3 above), that the one God mentioned in (vii)

---

78. In other words, each of those is numerically distinct from each of the other two.
79. Warfield, "Trinity"; Tuggy, *Monotheism*, chapter 2.
80. Tuggy, "Trinity," section 1.4.
81. Clarke, *Scripture-Doctrine*, 1–35, 42–48, 150–51; Origen, *Commentary*, 98–103 (2.12–31).
82. Origen, *Commentary*, 2.21, 2.27; Origen, *Against Celsus*, 8.3–4, 14–15; Origen, *On First Principles*, 1.4; Clarke, *Scripture-Doctrine*, 1–35, 122.

is one and the same as the "God" mentioned in (ii). By identifying the one God with the Father alone, the NT doesn't leave open the possibility of identifying God with something else, such as this "Trinity"[83] which goes unmentioned in all the earliest Christian sources, including the NT books.

An Easy Reply?

Some will object: "The NT authors are still figuring things out; they lack the proper terminology. They're not *full blown* Trinitarians." If a half-blown (or whatever) Trinitarian is nonetheless a Trinitarian, then in effect T is being replaced with a more complicated hypothesis, call it H, which also somehow describes their lack of clarity. As best I can tell, the above arguments are going to work the same way—it's just that the likelihood gap for each fact between H and U will be a little lower than the gap between T and U. In the end, we would still have U well confirmed over H by the above twenty facts, or at least most of them.[84]

Perhaps others, when they say that these authors are "not full-blown Trinitarians" mean to say that strictly speaking they're not Trinitarians, though in retrospect they can be viewed as on a sort of trajectory in that direction. In reply, I agree that these authors are not Trinitarians. But it is clear to me that they're Unitarians as defined above. If you don't want to grant that they're Unitarians, you owe us some account of what their views are, one that better explains the known facts than U. I don't see how this can be done, so I can't see that this reply fares any better than the previous one. Further, I don't see any signs of the sorts of confusion, dissatisfaction, or searching for new theological horizons in these authors that many Trinitarians expect to find there.

Conclusion

Any Trinity theory dangles from a precarious chain of reasoning which tries to hang it from the NT, or rather from a fairly small number of texts in it, many of them unclear. But a careful look at the whole NT reveals the complete absence of any ideas about a tripersonal God. The NT explicitly states no such theory. Nor does it assume or imply any tripersonal God theory. Nor is any such theory the best explanation of what the NT authors do and

---

83. See Tuggy, *Monotheism*, chapter 3.

84. See my "Unfinished Business," in which I consider what I call hypothesis C, that the NT authors sometimes think of the only god as being identical with the Trinity, and sometimes they think of the only god as being identical with the Father alone.

do not say. As we have seen, there are at least twenty classes of facts that confirm that these authors identified the one God with the Father, not with the Trinity. Their teaching, which we Christians believe constitutes the best self-revelation of God to humankind (John 1:15–18), includes the claim that the one true God is none other than the Father himself, and so does not leave open the possibility that the one true God is the Trinity.

What, my Christian friend, is your primary theological authority? If it is the writings from the apostles and their circles, then your theology should be Unitarian, as this chapter has shown.[85] If you instead accept the teaching magisterium of the pope-led hierarchical church, then you must accept that God is somehow, mysteriously, "the Trinity,"[86] and that these dark claims are incapable of significant clarification.[87] If you accept only the so-called "ecumenical" councils accepted by the Eastern Orthodox churches, then you must accept a fairly specific and problematic Trinity theory.[88] For my part, I must stand with "the faith that was once and for all handed on to the saints" (Jude 3) in the New Testament era.

---

85. Some will perceive the argument of this chapter as a reason to leave Protestantism. "Surely we can't leave behind *the doctrine of the Trinity*, so we ought to base our doctrine fundamentally on something other than Scripture which includes that God is the Trinity" (Compare: Beckwith, *Return to Rome*, 80–81, 114). To this, I can only say briefly that first of all, NT theology and Christology stand quite well on their own without the baggage of later Trinity and two-natures theories. Second, there are good reasons to prefer Protestant Christianity to Roman Catholicism (Collins and Walls, *Roman but Not Catholic*), and some of these reasons, such as opposition to the post-biblical one-bishop system and the honoring of religious images and Christian "saints," apply equally to Orthodoxy.

86. See *Catechism of the Catholic Church*, 62–70; "Constitutions," 230–32.

87. See "Dogmatic Constitution," in Tanner, *Decrees*, 808–9.

88. Williams, "Discovery of the Sixth Ecumenical Council's Trinitarian Theology."

II. Ad *Hasker*

Shall We Proceed?

William Lane Craig

It is a great privilege to interact with William Hasker, an eminent Christian philosopher who has bequeathed to us a long and diverse legacy of important work in the philosophy of religion and the author of what, in my estimation, is the finest book on the doctrine of the Trinity currently available.[1] In his opening essay, he addresses both the probative and the model components of the doctrine of the Trinity.

Probative Component

With respect to the probative component, it is admirable that Hasker, a professional philosopher, should have taken the time and made the effort to understand the biblical grounds for the doctrine of the Trinity. His familiarity with and accurate exposition of the work of NT scholars like Larry Hurtado and Richard Bauckham is particularly commendable. Like them, Hasker emphasizes the early historical roots of a high Christology of Jesus Christ as fully divine. This approach contrasts with but complements my own opening essay, which emphasizes the high Christology of the canonical NT text. The eight NT affirmations he lists are, indeed, a "stunning constellation."

Hasker's taxonomy of Unitarian responses to these NT affirmations is less helpful. I take Unitarianism to be a diverse collection of views united by their common conviction that God is a single person.[2] Hasker's taxonomy obscures the fact that Arianism is itself a type of Unitarianism that identifies God with the Father and affirms the pre-existence of Christ as a supernatural but nonetheless created being. Monarchianism or Modalism was also

---

1. Hasker, *Metaphysics and the Tri-Personal God*.

2. According to Tuggy, Unitarians "hold God to be identical to one and only one divine self, the Father." See Tuggy, "Trinity," appendix, "Unitarianism."

an early brand of Unitarianism insofar as it denied a plurality of persons in God. Modalists held either that God the Father became incarnate, suffered, and died, the Son being at most the human aspect of Christ, or else that the one God sequentially assumed three roles as Father, Son, and Holy Spirit in relation to his creatures. Unitarianism was thus fairly well represented in early church history, being advocated by Modalists such as Noetus, Praxeus, and Sabellius and by Arians like Arius and Eunomius. These forms of Unitarianism differ from another important brand, namely, Socinianism, championed by the post-Reformation theologian Faustus Socinus and defended by Dale Tuggy, according to which Jesus Christ was merely a human being selected by God, raised from the dead, and then elevated to Lordship over creation.

Hasker is right to emphasize proto-Trinitarian as well as Trinitarian responses to the NT affirmations. According to the so-called Logos Christology of the early Greek Apologists, God the Father, existing alone without the world, had within himself his Word or Reason or Wisdom, which somehow proceeded forth from him, like a spoken word from a speaker's mind, to become a distinct individual who created the world and ultimately became incarnate as Jesus Christ.[3] The procession of the Logos from the Father was variously conceived as taking place either at the moment of creation or, alternatively, eternally. The danger courted by Logos Christology was subordinationism, since the Son was conceived to be derived from and dependent upon the Father. But it would be unfair to characterize such thinkers as non-Trinitarians because, despite their troubling affirmations of the Son's inferior status relative to the Father, they did not take such affirmations to deny that the Son and the Father both share a common divine nature and are therefore God.[4]

Model Component

Turning to the model component of the doctrine of the Trinity, Hasker builds his model "up from the New Testament writings" in nine successive steps (12n14). We thereby see his intent to have a biblically based model. Let us comment briefly on each step.

---

3. Although christological concerns occupied center stage, the Holy Spirit, too, might be understood to proceed from God the Father's mind.

4. On second-century proto-Trinitarians, see Grillmeier, *Christ in Christian Tradition*, chapters 2–3.

1. *Jesus is the eternal divine Son.* In contrast to Tuggy, Hasker argues on the basis of texts like John 17:3 that Jesus Christ is past-eternal. In saying that Jesus shared the Father's glory "before the world existed," it was surely John's intention to affirm Christ's eternal pre-existence, and it would be disingenuous to suggest that for John, Christ might have begun to exist, say, a thousand years prior to creation.

I do think that a qualification needs to be introduced with respect to the word "Son." Hasker's point is that Jesus was "the *very same individual* that co-existed with the heavenly Father from all eternity" (13). That is correct but does not imply Christ's eternal Sonship, for this role or office may belong to the economic Trinity and commence only with the incarnation of Christ. It will not be until step 6 that we find justification for thinking that Christ's Sonship is past-eternal.

2. *The Holy Spirit is a third, fully divine, Person along with the Father and the Son.* Hasker's emphasis here is that the Holy Spirit is a third, fully divine *hypostasis*. It will not be until step 3 that we see that the Holy Spirit is also a person in the sense of "a center of consciousness with the capacity for mental states, which may be cognitive, affective, or volitional, and with a capacity for relationships with other persons" (14). In my own opening essay, I explain the further significance of the triadic formulae mentioned briefly by Hasker in showing that there are exactly three persons who are fully divine.

3. *The Persons of the Trinity, the Father, the Son, and the Holy Spirit, are persons.* Again, in my opening essay I provide further NT data for the personhood of the Holy Spirit. Given the "I-Thou" relationships in which the persons of the Trinity stand to one another, some form of Social Trinitarianism is biblically obligatory. It is for this reason alone that Branson's Monarchical Trinitarianism is not acceptable.

4. *The Persons of the Trinity, the Father, the Son, and the Holy Spirit, are together the one God.* Hasker maintains that "it is essential to identify the entire Trinity as God if Trinitarianism is to be a form of monotheism" (17).[5] I agree that it is essential to identify God with that tripersonal, concrete, divine nature or substance later spoken of by Hasker. But here Hasker seems to endorse the identity claim "God = Trinity." This is what Brian Leftow calls Trinity Monotheism. Here I have misgivings. For the Trinity has obvious affinities to a group. Hasker himself speaks of the Trinity as "the group of

---

5. He also says that "the Trinity of Persons [is] to be described as, and to be, one single God" (18).

Father, Son, and Spirit" (17). The Trinity seems to be a plurality, not an individual, which is made up of the three divine persons. We naturally speak of the persons as members of the Trinity, which is the language associated with groups and classes. A group is composed of several individuals fulfilling certain constitution conditions. The Trinity would be an unusual group in that it has its members essentially, but it would seem to be a group nonetheless.

But if we do regard the Trinity as a group, as seems right, then we should not accept the claim that the Trinity is identical with God, for God is clearly an individual substance and, hence, an individual, not a group.[6] The Trinity is simply the group of the divine persons, which is not itself an individual or a substance. If we think of God as an individual substance, our view should not be called Trinity Monotheism, as Leftow has styled it; rather our view deserves a different name. I suggest Tripersonal Monotheism. I think Hasker would concur.

5. The divine Persons enjoy the closest possible communion and interpenetration. Not only is *perichoresis* among the persons of the Trinity an implication of perfect being theology, but Hasker's view also implies that we should reject the unbiblical and confused aphorism *opera ad extra sunt indivisa*. For, as he explains, the persons of the Trinity have differing individual wills and works, even though they all function in harmony with one another. The Father does not will to go to the cross but he concurs with the Son's will to go to the cross. Here again we see the superiority of Hasker's view to Branson's.

6. The Son is eternally generated from the Father; the Spirit eternally proceeds from the Father. This is the one aspect of Hasker's doctrine with which I am less than enthusiastic. It seems to me dispensable, if not deleterious. For although affirmed in creeds, the doctrine of the generation of the Son (and the procession of the Spirit) is a relic of Logos Christology which finds virtually no warrant in the biblical text and threatens to introduce a subordinationism into the Godhead that anyone who affirms the full deity of Christ ought to find very troubling.

---

6. *Pace* Richard Swinburne, "Trinity"; cf. Layman, *Philosophical Approaches*, 147–50, who, seeing the Trinity as a group, thinks of God as a social entity on the analogy of a nation. "The divine persons are bound tightly together by perfect love, by unity of purpose and will, and by certain relations [of personal procession] of metaphysical necessity" (152–53), which seems no better than Swinburne's view. Our editor reminds me, however, that most group agency realists, while denying that something as large and diverse as a nation can meet conditions of agency, hold that smaller groups, like corporations, might. McIntosh holds that if any group could meet conditions of agency, it would be the Trinity. See McIntosh, "God of the Groups."

The "positive theological rationale" (20) that Hasker offers for the doctrine of divine processions is one that all Social Trinitarians can affirm, regardless of their view of the reality of the processions. For as a maximally great being, God must, if Hasker is right, exhibit the communal love of the three persons rather than merely self-love or mutual love. Rejecting the doctrine of divine processions does not imply that "the three Persons have diverse origins, and only subsequently enter into the intimate union expressed in the doctrine of *perichoresis*" (19). Rather the attribution of origins is altogether inappropriate; to borrow an Athanasian term, all the persons are "unoriginate," both in the sense of uncreated (*agenētos*) and unbegotten (*agennētos*).

Since Hasker is here building his Trinitarian doctrine from biblical, not creedal foundations, he is exercised to provide biblical warrant for the doctrine of divine processions. Biblically speaking, the vast majority of contemporary NT scholars recognize that even if the word traditionally translated "only-begotten" (*monogenēs*) carries a connotation of derivation when used in familial contexts—as opposed to meaning merely "unique" or "one of a kind," as some scholars maintain[7]—nevertheless the biblical references to Christ as *monogenēs* (John 1:1, 14, 18; cf. Rev 9:13) do not contemplate some pre-creation or eternal procession of the divine Son from the Father, but have to do with the historical Jesus's being God's special Son (Matt 1:21–23; Luke 1:35; John 1:14, 34; Gal 4:4; Heb 1:5–6).[8] In other words, Christ's status of being *monogenēs* has less to do with the Trinity than with the incarnation.[9] John 5:26, adduced by Hasker, is probably his best prooftext, but even it is not connected to Jesus' origin so much as his resurrection from the dead and his ability to confer life.

I am not so sure that the Nicene fathers' response to Eunomius is convincing, that *gennētos/agennētos* is merely a "*personal property*" of the Son or Father, each of whom "enjoys the fullness of the divine nature (= *homoousios*) and so is fully God" (20). It is interesting to note that the church fathers interpreted the Arian proof-text, "The Father is greater than I" (John 14:28), not in terms of Christ's humanity, but as an expression of

---

7. See the fine summary discussion in Harris, *Jesus as God*, 84–103. That *monogenēs* in reference to Christ means more than just "only," but has a derivative connotation, is evident from the fact that while God the Father is called *ho monos theos* (the only God), he is not called (*ho*) *monogenēs theos*, as is the Son (John 1:18).

8. See discussion and literature in Bauer, "Son of God."

9. This primitive understanding of Christ's being begotten is still evident in Ignatius's description of Christ as "one Physician, of flesh and of spirit, begotten and unbegotten, . . . both of Mary and of God" (*Ephesians* 7).

his being generated from the Father.[10] But then is the Son not inferior to the Father? Basil, who sees the difficulty, would elude it by saying, "the evident solution is that the Greater refers to origination, while the Equal belongs to the Nature."[11] Even if the Father and the Son are equal in nature, however, why does the accidental property of being unbegotten, which inheres in the person of the Father alone, not make him greater than the Son, since it is admittedly a great-making property or perfection? If the Father is greater than the Son in any respect, not just in nature, then the Son is in that respect inferior to the Father. At the end of the day Basil must deny that having existence *a se* is a perfection or great-making property. He asserts, "That which is from such a Cause is not inferior to that which has no Cause; for it would share the glory of the Unoriginate, because it is from the Unoriginate."[12] I find this claim less than convincing, however, for to be dependent upon the Unoriginate for one's existence is to lack a ground of being in oneself alone, which is surely less great than being able to exist on one's own.

7. *The three Persons have in common a single instance of the concrete divine nature*. This point is, in my opinion, Hasker's most valuable contribution to Trinitarian debates. As he points out, if we say that each of the divine persons exemplifies a common abstract nature, then we are left with three instances of deity, or Tritheism. Instead, we should say that the persons share a common concrete nature, thereby averting Tritheism.[13] Hasker rightly explains (26),

> The doctrine of the Trinity affirms that the three persons are together a *single concrete being*—that they share between them a single trope of deity, a single concrete instance of the divine nature. This claim can be modeled by the notion of a single mental substance, or soul, supporting simultaneously three distinct conscious lives, three distinct streams of experience.

10. Athanasius, *Four Discourses against the Arians* 1.13.58.
11. Basil, *Fourth Theological Oration* 9.
12. Basil, *Fourth Theological Oration* 9.
13. So Marilyn Adams' characterization of Swinburne's model as "three numerically distinct souls of the divine essential kind" (quoted in McCall, *Which Trinity?*, 17) obviously does not apply to Hasker's model. The single soul that God is serves to allay Layman's worry that, absent a body, such as we have in the case of conjoined triplets, it is hard to see how the three divine persons could be one of the same being of some type (Layman, *Philosophical Approaches*, 142). Thus, the model avoids Carl Mosser's concern that, whatever insights Social Trinitarianism may provide, "God should not be portrayed as a community of divine Siamese triplets," for then it would be just "a sophisticated form of tritheism" (Mosser, "Fully Social Trinitarianism," 145).

I have called this view Tri-Personal Monotheism.[14]

8. *The Three Persons are each constituted by the single divine nature.* We can agree with Hasker that the doctrine of the Trinity is incompatible with a strong doctrine of divine simplicity. Aquinas' contention that each of the three persons has the same divine essence entails, given divine simplicity, that each person just is that essence. But if two things are identical with some third thing, they are identical with each other. Therefore, given divine simplicity, the Father, Son, and Holy Spirit cannot be distinct persons or relations.[15]

Hasker agrees that a model of God as a soul endowed with three sets of cognitive faculties, each sufficient for personhood, gives a better understanding of the classical formula "three persons in one substance" than any other proposal of which he is aware. Still, Hasker would like to have "a more precise, or at least more philosophically developed, account of the relation between the three Persons and the one divine substance" (24). For my part, I do not see much need for further precision or philosophical development, which is apt to become needlessly controversial.[16] Hasker tentatively proposes adding another layer to his account by maintaining that the divine soul *constitutes* the three persons in a suitable sense.[17] It is not clear to me, however, that Hasker's account of the constitution relation provides an informative account of the relation between the concrete divine nature and

---

14. Christopher Hughes arrives at a model much like this, according to which there are three Trinitarian persons who all have God as their substance. This relation of "ensubstancement" neither is nor implies strict identity. Unlike the identity relation, it is irreflexive, asymmetric, and non-Euclidean. Hughes even suggests that this relation "in certain ways resembles the relation holding between 'multiple centers of consciousness' and a human person with a divided mind" (Hughes, "Defending the Consistency, 313; cf. 310–12).

15. See the trenchant critique by Hughes, *On a Complex Theory*, 218–38, who argues that Aquinas' theory of the Trinity is fundamentally incoherent as a result of his desire to have a God who is at once triune and free from all composition (188). Hughes shows that Aquinas is forced by his commitment to divine simplicity to deny the relation of identity in order to safeguard his doctrine of the Trinity. "The moral is that Aquinas' theory of the Trinity is logically flawed at the core" (238).

16. Hasker's account becomes especially controversial if he, with Brower and Rea, takes the constitution relation to entail the relation of numerical sameness without identity, so that the Father, Son, and Holy Spirit are non-identical but nonetheless numerically one object. For a withering critique, see Hughes, "Defending the Consistency," 303–8. This same critique also applies to Branson's Monarchical model, which likewise makes use of the analogy of the statue and the mass to affirm that the persons are non-identical but nevertheless one object.

17. Hasker, *Metaphysics and the Tri-Personal God*, 238–45; Hasker, "One Divine Nature."

the Trinitarian persons. Hasker explains the way in which the divine nature constitutes a Trinitarian person as follows: "The divine nature constitutes the divine Trinitarian persons when *it sustains simultaneously three divine life-streams*"[18] or, in this essay, when "the divine nature supports, e.g., the Son-life-stream" (26). It seems evident that what is really doing the work here is the relation of *sustaining* or *supporting*, which seems to be a primitive but well-understood relation,[19] which I also affirm. "We shall say, then, that the one concrete divine nature sustains eternally the three distinct life-streams of the Father, Son, and Holy Spirit, and that in virtue of this the nature *constitutes* each of the persons although it *is not identical* with the persons."[20] It is *sustaining* that is fundamental.

In a series of exchanges with Leftow, Hasker rightly emphasizes that "my overall Social conception of the Trinity does not stand or fall with my use of constitution."[21] For his part, Leftow champions a "deflationary" account of constitution, according to which at least one of the relata is a mind-dependent, conventional, or socially constructed reality.[22] So, for example, in the case of the mass of gold and the statue, the statue is an artifact, a mind-dependent object like money or a doorstop. All that really exists is the mass of gold, which we regard as a statue in virtue of its being sculpted by someone. So there really is no constitution relation. Given my proclivities toward deflationary theories of reference and truth,[23] I find Leftow's deflationary account quite attractive. If he is right that such an understanding disqualifies constitution for use in the doctrine of the Trinity, we may happily leave it aside.

Conclusion

In short, Hasker has provided for us a perspicuous, viable, and biblically defensible doctrine of the Trinity.

---

18. Hasker, *Metaphysics and the Tri-Personal God*, 243.

19. Hasker, *Metaphysics and the Tri-Personal God*, 228; cf. Hasker, "One Divine Nature," 66-68.

20. Hasker, *Metaphysics and the Tri-Personal God*, 244.

21. Hasker, "Constitution, Identity, and the Trinity," 165.

22. Leftow, "Can the Constitution be Saved?," 160-61.

23. See my *God and Abstract Objects*, 438-75.

One Movement of Three *Hypostases*

Beau Branson

> There is one springing forth and one movement of the three *hypostases*, which is something that it is impossible to observe in created nature.
>
> —JOHN OF DAMASCUS[1]

I'M FORTUNATE TO HAVE had correspondence with Hasker about the Trinity (and wish that time permitted more), and delighted at the opportunity for this exchange. Of all my interlocutors, I'm most sympathetic to Hasker, and appreciate his serious engagement with patristic sources.

     Before my criticisms, I'll reiterate our main disagreement concerns inseparable operations. Unlike Craig, Hasker accepts the eternal processions/ Monarchy of the Father (MoF). Hence, *modulo* inseparable operations, the differences between Hasker and Monarchical Trinitarianism (MT) are primarily semantic. I'll respond to a remark of Hasker's:

> [I]t is essential to identify the entire Trinity as God if Trinitarianism is to be a form of monotheism. If we insist on the identification of the one God with the Father alone, and if we also assert that the Son and the Spirit are fully divine (as we must if we are to be Trinitarians), we will have, in addition to God, two other fully divine Persons. This, it seems, is no longer monotheism. Or if not that, then we must demote the Son and the Spirit to a sort of quasi-divine status—but that is to abandon Trinitarianism for subordinationism or Arianism. (17)

Obviously, I don't think this follows. On MT, God = the Father, and God ≠ the Trinity, but the Son and Spirit are also fully divine. So it follows there

---

1. John of Damascus, *On the Orthodox Faith*, 96.

are "in addition to God, two other fully divine Persons." But it doesn't follow that this "is no longer monotheism," because there's no sense of "god" on which there's more than one god (whether $god_{ULTIMATE\text{-}SOURCE}$, god_{NATURE}, or $god_{POWER/ACTION}$).[2] As John of Damascus puts it, "God, and His Word, and His Spirit, are one God."[3] Nor does this demote the Son and Spirit to a "quasi-divine status" unless MoF itself does, but Hasker himself accepts MoF (as he should!).[4] But suppose it *did* follow. Then if we say God = the Trinity, rather than God = the Father, we'd have *three* fully divine persons "in addition to God." No improvement there!

Is there *any* sense in which "The Persons of the Trinity, the Father, the Son, and the Holy Spirit, are together the one God" (17)? Yes, if "one God" means one god_{NATURE} or one $god_{POWER/ACTION}$.[5] But even Hasker can't say the Persons of the Trinity "are together the one $god_{ULTIMATE\text{-}SOURCE}$," because he accepts MoF (as he should!). For Hasker, as for MT, the one $god_{ULTIMATE\text{-}SOURCE}$ is the Father.

I don't know whether Hasker will be happy with that. But there it is. And it's worth emphasizing, given Tuggy's criticisms. Tuggy presents these as *substantive* issues that apply to Trinitarianism *generally*. But it seems they're *largely semantic* and apply only to *certain versions* of Trinitarianism (or certain formulations of them). Tuggy argues Hasker's theology conflicts with the New Testament.[6] Would it *not* if we merely switched some labels around? Similarly, Tuggy has sometimes suggested that MT isn't genuinely Trinitarian. Would it be if we merely switched some labels around? As I argued in my opening essay, some models (like Craig's) collapse if relabeled to solve WIG. But if some (like Hasker's) don't, why are *mere labels* so important?

The Real Disagreement: Inseparable Operations

What separates Hasker and MT more substantively than semantically is inseparable operations.[7] Elsewhere I've argued that Gregory of Nyssa has

---

2. See p. 62 for explanations of these.

3. John of Damascus, *On the Orthodox Faith*, 80.

4. See pp. 19–20.

5. Note that, as Tuggy uses "the one god" it means "the ultimate deity," roughly equivalent to "the one $god_{ULTIMATE\text{-}SOURCE}$" in my terminology.

6. Tuggy, "Hasker's Tri-Personal God."

7. When I say "inseparable operations," I mean, for example, that the event of the Father's creating the universe = the Son's creating the universe. I don't know if Hasker wants the *term* "inseparable operations" for his own view. If so, the reader should substitute "the view of inseparable operations I attribute to Gregory and other church fathers" for "inseparable operations."

a broadly Davidsonian ("coarse-grained") account of action individuation.[8] Actions are individuated by their own *idiomata*, just like *hypostases*, not merely by the *hypostases* performing them. Hence, "the Father's creation of the universe = the Son's creation of the universe" can be literally true. As I read Gregory, that's part of his solution to $3F$ and the $3G_{POWER/ACTION}$. Hasker, however, takes the *hypostases* to have distinct token actions, which are "inseparable" only in the sense of intimate cooperation and direction towards a common goal. And he believes that's the correct interpretation of fathers such as Gregory and Augustine.

Hasker has a lengthy debate with Scott Williams about both the coherence of inseparable operations and the interpretation of Gregory.[9] I'll leave the proper interpretation of Gregory aside due to space constraints. My main question is: How does Hasker solve $3F$ and $3G_{POWER/ACTION}$? Would Hasker say that there are, strictly speaking, three Creators, three Saviors, and so on (even if we can legitimately *act as if* there was only one)? And is there *some* sense in which the Persons *are* three gods (namely, three gods$_{POWER/ACTION}$)?

Perhaps Hasker will say, strictly speaking, only the Son creates, redeems, judges, and so forth, the Father merely directing these activities. It's not clear to me that this isn't still a case in which the Son's creation = the Father's creation.[10] Suppose I give my realtor power of attorney to purchase

8. See Branson, "Gregory of Nyssa on the Individuation of Actions and Events"; Branson, *Logical Problem*, 174–84.

9. See Williams, "Indexicals and the Trinity"; Williams, "Unity of Action"; Hasker, "Can a Latin Trinity Be Social?"; Williams, "In Defense of a Latin Social Trinity"; Hasker, "Is the Latin Social Trinity Defensible?"; Williams, "Conciliar Trinitarianism"; Hasker, "'Latin' or 'Conciliar,' but Still Incoherent."; Williams, "Discovery of the Sixth Ecumenical Council's Trinitarian Theology."

10. In an important passage in *To Ablabius*, Gregory of Nyssa does seem to espouse what we might call a "hierarchical" or "ordered" view of the divine *energeiai*, rather than what we might call a "symmetrical" or "coordinate" view: "For just as having learned about the God of the whole of things from the Scripture, which says that he judges all the earth, we therefore say that he is judge of the totality, and again having heard that 'the Father judges no one,' we do not believe that the Scripture fights with itself, for he who judges all the earth through the Son, 'to whom he has given all the judgment,' makes this, and everything that comes to be from the only-begotten has reference to the Father, so he is both judge of the totality and judges no one because, as it has been said, he has given all the judgment to the Son and all the judgment of the Son is not alienated from the paternal will, and one may not reasonably say either that there are two judges or that the one is alienated from the authority and power in judgment." Gregory of Nyssa, *Trinitarian Works*, 44. But again, it's not immediately obvious to me that the hierarchical view isn't still one of inseparable operations. Also, see below on the *filioque*. If spiration *were* a divine *energeia*, it would seem, on a hierarchical view, one would get a procession from the Father "through" the Son, but not "*ex utroque . . . tanquam ab uno principio et unica spiratione*," unless the "*uno principio*" is ultimately just the Father.

a home. I go into a coma the day before closing and wake up the day after. In one clear sense, only my realtor performed any action the day of the closing. Yet, it's still true that *I* purchased the house, despite there being a sense in which I did nothing that day. And the day I purchased the house was the day my realtor signed the documents. One way to analyze all this is that *my realtor's* purchasing the house (or signing the documents) = *my* purchasing the house. Both describe the same event, which is an action (directly) performed by my realtor, and also (indirectly) performed by me. We bear different relations to the action. But it's still *one* action. The same would seem to hold of an act performed by the Son as an agent of the Father. Perhaps Hasker sees things differently.

Deeper Questions

What motivates Hasker's rejection of inseparable operations? His main stated reasons concern indexicals. The Father can say (or think) "I am the Father." But if the Son said (or thought) "I am the Father," it would be false. In Hasker's and Williams' lengthy exchange, Williams develops an account of mental content where the semantics of the same token indexical ("I") and token copula ("am") in a mental language shift as used by different persons. Hasker rejects Williams' account, but there is no space to do it justice here. Interested readers may consult their exchange, but I find it uncomfortably anthropomorphic. Does God literally have propositional thought, even a "language of thought"? Does God think discursively, as we do, rather than in some "all-at-once" intuition? And would the church fathers affirm any of that? I'm open to seeing evidence, but I'm not holding my breath. Given the widespread patristic view that we cannot know what God is like in himself, but only through his activities in the world, I'd be surprised if any of them thought we could know what God's inner mental life is like (if we can even describe God in those terms).[11]

So, I don't find the debate over indexicals very moving. This raises a question: Is this as deep as the motivation behind rejecting or accepting inseparable operations goes? Or does a deeper issue animate both sides? Specifically, whether causal powers are *natural* or *hypostatic*, i.e., grounded in a nature-trope, or "directly" in a *hypostasis* (or non-nature tropes of a *hypostasis*).[12]

---

11. Perhaps the disconnect stems from the fact that I assume God is timeless, which Hasker rejects.

12. Traditionally, non-nature tropes are called "accidents." But in contemporary parlance, this has the connotation of *contingency* (in antiquity, it was recognized that there

Although actions are *performed* by *hypostases*, and powers are *had* by *hypostases*, one might take activities and powers to be grounded primarily in *the properties of* those *hypostases*, specifically tropes (particular property-instances). As Anna-Sofia Maurin puts it:

> It is after all not the whole stove that burns you, it is its temperature that does the damage. And it is not any temperature, nor temperature in general, which leaves a red mark. That mark is left by *the particular temperature had by this particular stove now*. It makes sense, therefore, to say that the mark is left by the stove's temperature-*trope*, which means that tropes are very good candidates for being the world's basic causal relata.[13]

Sometimes tropes are shared. Hasker agrees. The mass trope in a lump of clay causes it to press down on a scale, which reads "1kg." The statue constituted by the lump does the same. Why does the scale only read "1kg" instead of "2kg"? Because it's the same trope of mass in both the lump and the statue, and the causal power is grounded in, and individuated by, the trope, not the subjects that have the trope. That's just to repeat part of my discussion of 3*F* (77).

Perhaps Hasker thinks token powers attach "directly" to *hypostases*, not mediated via tropes. Or, perhaps Hasker thinks powers are grounded not in the shared nature-trope,[14] but in non-nature tropes, so they might be divided among the Persons.[15] Hasker says:

> [E]ach divine person performs his own cognitive and volitional acts, acts which are "incommunicable" in the sense that they are not and cannot be the acts of any other person. And this means that each divine person has his own set of cognitive and volitional powers, which are likewise incommunicable. (Call this the "multi-power" view.) Williams holds that this is a mistake: on his view, all divine acts are communicable, and in fact are common to all three divine persons. Correspondingly, there is only one set of divine cognitive and volitional powers, grounded

---

were "inseparable" accidents.) So as not to confuse the issue of contingency vs. simply not being a nature, I'll refer to "non-nature tropes."

13. Maurin, "Tropes."

14. This raises questions about divine simplicity—must *any* property that is both essential to, and intrinsic to, God be grounded in the divine nature?

15. Traditionally, it's been thought that all there is to the divine persons is the divine nature-trope and the *idiomata* of begetting, being begotten, "spirating," and proceeding.

in the one concrete divine essence or substance which is common to the three persons. (This is the "one-power" view.)[16]

This raises the question of what a nature is.

Natures

Analytic philosophers often use "nature" for a list of necessary and sufficient conditions for belonging to some (natural) kind. It's assumed that (natural) kind-membership is essential to particulars, so "nature" is also often conflated with "essence," and both with a definition or list of essential properties.

However, in antiquity "nature" didn't *mean* "definition." Aristotle notes that certain things (like beds and coats) "have no innate impulse to change."[17] Whenever they change, something *external* to them causes the change. Other things (like plants and animals), have *within themselves* "a source of motion and rest." Aristotle calls this a "nature," defined as "a principle or cause of being moved and of being at rest in that to which it belongs primarily, in virtue of itself and not accidentally."[18] So this isn't a list of properties. It's *dynamic*. It's something literally powerful.

Aristotle later argues (given his hylomorphism as a background assumption) that the natures of plants and animals must be their substantial forms, rather than their matter. And substantial forms are essences. So, all natures are essences (though not all essences are natures—artifacts have essences, but their essences aren't their natures, but their matter). Next, all essences have definitions. But a nature isn't a definition. It's an internal source of power and action. So there's an association between nature and definition. But they're not equivalent.

So what's the point of positing things called natures, rather than just token causal powers? Why not *merely* posit powers, then reduce natures to (i.e., identify them with) sets of powers? Here's an Aristotelian response. Consider humans. Most humans have powers to walk, talk, see, hear, eat and digest, speak and understand language, and so on. Is that just coincidence? Are powers divvied out to individuals at random, and do we simply choose, as a matter of convention, to group together and label "human" individuals that, by chance, happen to share enough powers in common? Is it also a coincidence that the individuals we happen to group together by shared powers all turn out to share a common ancestor? And what about the fact

---

16. Hasker, "Can a Latin Trinity Be Social?"
17. *Physics* II.1.
18. *Physics* II.1.

that in cases where a human lacks one of these powers (say, someone can't see, or can't digest certain foods) there's almost always a *cause*: a person's eyes were damaged by disease or injury; a genetic disorder interferes with digestion, and so on. It's unlikely enough that the powers characteristic of human beings clump together as frequently as they do just by chance. That these similarly powered individuals also happen to descend from a common ancestor, and that deviations from the whole set of powers are rare and always or almost always have a cause (i.e., they don't just happen randomly), is even less likely to be mere coincidence. There must be *something* to unify, and thereby explain, the patterns of distribution of causal powers we see among biological organisms.

That's what natures are for. We posit a "nature" (in this case, human nature), to ground the whole set of causal powers characteristic of human beings as such. In the process of generation ("begetting") a parent's nature-trope is divided. One resulting trope remains with the parent, the other belongs to the offspring. Since they result from division of one trope, the resulting tropes will be of the same generic *type*. Hence, a father begets a son *homoousious* with himself, but (unlike the case with the Trinity), divided/separated from him. In a sense, a nature is like metaphysical DNA. Natures ground all the "clumped" powers of *hypostases* and explain the connection between the clumped powers and a common ancestor. Aristotelians would argue the explanatory payoff of natures outweighs any metaphysical cost.

So, much of the point of natures is to unify otherwise inexplicably similarly clumped sets of causal powers, powers characteristic of certain natural groupings of individuals. In ecclesiastical terminology, powers characteristic of *homoousious hypostases*. Regardless of whether any powers are hypostatic, at least the powers characteristic of individuals of a certain kind, *qua* that kind, should by hypothesis be natural, i.e., grounded in their nature-tropes, rather than hypostatic. For example, perhaps the power to speak *Russian* is hypostatic. But the ability to speak *in general* (characteristic of humans *qua human*) is surely natural.

Hasker and MT agree that, for the Trinity (unlike creatures), the nature-trope is not divided in divine generation and procession. Hence, presumably we should have inseparable operations for any powers grounded in the nature-trope. I suspect this is the deeper issue between adherents and opponents of inseparable operations. If token powers and activities are hypostatic, they should be divided; if *natural*, they should be inseparable.[19]

---

19. This is likely at the root of some other issues. If token powers are hypostatic, rather than natural, it's unclear how Christ could have "two wills," or "two (natural) energies (activities)" as affirmed by the Fifth and Sixth Ecumenical Councils. Monothelites argued two wills entailed Nestorianism. But that makes sense only if the will

Would Hasker agree that powers of thought and speech are characteristic of divine Persons *qua* divine? Or does the Father have those powers not in virtue of his divinity, but in virtue of his fatherhood or begetting (and the Son has them due to his being begotten, and so on)? If the latter, how are power of thought and speech grounded in properties like begetting, spirating, being begotten, and proceeding? If the former, how can there be multiple powers of thought and speech grounded in a single nature trope? What would individuate them?

The *Filioque*

Finally, Hasker mentions, but wants to avoid, the infamous *filioque*,[20] claiming "the essential questions concerning the Trinity can be engaged while leaving that question open" (19). I don't think that's right, and it seems odd to reject inseparable operations, yet affirm the *filioque*. A typical argument for the *filioque* runs something like this:

(1) Spiration is (or can be treated as) a divine activity (not just a relation).

(2) All divine activities are grounded in the divine nature-trope, and so are inseparable.

(3) The Father and Son share the divine nature-trope.

(4) Therefore, the Father and Son inseparably spirate the Spirit ("as a single principle").

Rejecting (3) would be at least *semi*-Arianism. A common Eastern Orthodox response rejects (1)—processions are not activities (*energeiai*) but relations (*scheses*).[21] So, unlike the activities *ad extra*, which are natural, the relations *ad intra* are hypostatic. In particular, being the "wellspring of divinity,"[22]

---

is hypostatic, rather than natural. See Maximus, *Disputation with Pyrrhus*, especially 57. So it's no surprise when Social Trinitarians, who describe the Persons as "distinct centers of consciousness"—thus, apparently taking powers to be hypostatic—typically find fault with dyothelitism as well. It's also no surprise that Scott Williams recently (re)discovered that the Sixth Council explicitly affirms the doctrine of inseparable operations. If the fathers of the Sixth Council took the faculty of will to be natural, rather than hypostatic, of course they would affirm both dyothelitism, and inseparable operations. Had they taken powers to be hypostatic, they would have rejected both instead.

20. I.e., the proposition that the Holy Spirit proceeds from the Father "and from the Son" (in Latin: *ex patre "filioque" procedit*).

21. Gregory Nazianzen argues this in response to Eunomius, for reasons unrelated to the *filioque*. See his *Oration* 29.16. See also Bradshaw, *Aristotle East and West*, 159, 216.

22. Pseudo-Dionysius, *Divine Names*, II.V and II.7; see *Complete Works*, 62–64.

is the *idioma* of God the Father. Hence, any true predication concerning a divine person has as its truth-maker either the shared nature-trope or an unshareable *idioma*. Hence, either the Holy Spirit spirates himself,[23] or only one of the Persons (the Father) spirates the Spirit.[24] Thus, on a characteristically Western view (on which spiration is natural), the *filioque* is necessary, while on a characteristically Eastern view (on which spiration is hypostatic), it's impossible.[25]

I don't expect to settle the *filioque* debate here. But I want to point out the oddness of rejecting (2) yet accepting (4) anyway. Without inseparable operations, what would motivate the *filioque*?[26] I doubt the *filioque* is coherent. But if an old-school Thomist defends it as necessary for Thomas' system, I at least understand the argument and its motivation. "I believe that *you* believe it," as the proverbial psychiatrist says. But why affirm the *filioque* while rejecting the apparatus that originally motivated it?

Last of all, even supposing both the Father and Son spirate, why do they not count as *two spirators*? The typical scholastic argument just applied the solution for $3F/3G_{POWER/ACTION}$ here. Father and Son are "one spirator" or "one source" for the Spirit, for the same reason Father, Son, and Spirit are "one creator"—because the operation is inseparable. Without that response, why aren't they "two sources" (hence, also violating MoF)?

Conclusion

To recap, I've asked Hasker how to solve $3F$ and $3G_{POWER/ACTION}$ without inseparable operations; why the Son acting as agent of the Father shouldn't be analyzed as inseparable operation;[27] whether divine powers of thought and speech are natural or hypostatic; what would motivate the *filioque* if not all

---

23. If the shared divine nature-trope is the truth-maker for "*x* spirates the Holy Spirit."

24. If an (unshareable) *idioma* is the truth-maker for "*x* spirates the Holy Spirit."

25. Of course there are more "dovish" positions on both sides. The point is that it's naïve to simply assume, without argument, that any coherent compromise position can be found, or that one could take a position on the *filioque* with no consequences for one's overall metaphysics of the Trinity or vice-versa.

26. Some propose additional arguments. Aquinas, for example, argues that only asymmetric relations can individuate the persons (so you need one between the Son and Spirit). But this requires further assumptions, like a very strong understanding of divine simplicity, no *intrinsic* difference between begetting and spirating, and so on. But Hasker and most Social Trinitarians reject these auxiliary assumptions.

27. In other words, why adopt a more fine-grained account of event/action individuation?

divine powers/activities are natural (and especially if *none* are!); and how it would be possible for the Father and Son to count "as a single source" of the Spirit if their spiration is not an inseparable operation.[28] I don't expect Hasker to settle the *filioque* debate in a few pages! But I look forward to more detail on his views about powers, natures, and *hypostases*.

---

28. Note how this returns us to question 1 but with "spirator" as the predicate.

The "Faith Once Delivered"?

Dale Tuggy

"THE DOCTRINE OF THE Trinity" is many, not one. Words that did not clearly express a single theology were mandated by a meeting of bishops convened by the emperor,[1] and so still 1,642 years later Trinitarians (or rather, a tiny percentage of highly educated ones) still labor to determine their meaning, putting forward incompatible interpretations.[2] Hasker has done more than anyone to advocate what I call a "three-self" Trinity theory, on which the "Persons" of the Trinity are so many selves, concrete beings who are intelligent agents, knowers and choosers, capable of interpersonal relationships with other such beings. Hasker seems sympathetic to philosophical arguments that there can't be only one divine self (see 20–21). As I've critiqued such arguments elsewhere,[3] I'll leave those aside. I'll also mention but not here pursue this concern: if three-self Trinitarians like Hasker are right, and the one true God turns out to be *a group of* selves that only resembles a self, then it looks like God, or rather the selves that compose it, intentionally deceived the Jews via Old Testament (and New Testament—see my opening essay) revelation, both of which seem calibrated to present God as a perfect, single self.[4]

I disagree with how Hasker sorts theologies and theologians. As I explain in my opening essay (100), subordinationists are naturally grouped together with Unitarians based on the contents of their views; what Hasker calls "proto-Trinitarians" (e.g., Tertullian, Origen) I call "subordinationist

---

1. Tuggy, *What Is the Trinity?* chapter 5.
2. See Baber, "Trinity"; Howard-Snyder, "Trinity"; Tuggy, "Trinity."
3. Tuggy, "Antiunitarian Arguments."
4. Tuggy, "Divine Deception, Identity, and Social Trinitarianism"; Hasker, "Has a Trinitarian God Deceived Us?"; Hasker, "Deception and the Trinity"; Tuggy, "Divine Deception and Monotheism: A Reply to Hasker"; Tuggy, "Divine Deception and Monotheism."

Unitarians," as for them the one true God just is the Father, not the triad. As many do, Hasker lumps them in with the Trinitarians so that there will be someone who *kind of looks like* a Trinitarian before the second half of the fourth century. I protest that we should sort views by their contents, not by retrospective judgments about them as stepping stones to orthodoxy.[5]

Hasker's chapter is extremely sophisticated, reflecting his long work on this topic. First, he admits not only the obvious point that no Trinity theory is explicitly taught in the Bible, but in addition that no Trinity theory is *implicitly* taught or assumed in the Bible. This is a needed corrective to those who try to logically deduce "the doctrine of the Trinity" from Scripture. In Hasker's view, some such doctrine will be *the best explanation of* what is and what is not in Scripture, but he does not claim that his theory is included in the contents of those writings.[6] Second, aiming to have the best explanation, Hasker knows that he must put forward clear claims, not merely intone traditional language. Third, Hasker doesn't follow the modern tradition of dumbing down "the doctrine of the Trinity" into just a few seemingly simple sentences, which are (allegedly) easy to show are implied by or assumed in Scripture. No, he presents his whole, hard-won understanding of what catholic traditions are supposedly getting at. Fourth, nor is Hasker a freewheeling speculator; for the most part he tries to build upon the views of earlier mainstream theologians. All of this is bold, careful, and serious, and it puts Hasker in a different class than many would-be defenders of "the Trinity."

What then, is this doctrine, in Hasker's view? By my count, it includes more than three dozen claims. Each Person is fully divine (claims 1-3). Each Person is a self (4-6). No Person is identical to any other (7-9). Each stands in a relation of "*perichoresis*" with each of the others (10-12). The Father eternally generates the Son (13). The Spirit eternally proceeds from the Father (14). The Father exists *a se* (15). The Father has a concrete (non-abstract) divine nature, which is also had by the other two Persons (16-18).[7] It is false that any Person just is (i.e., is numerically identical with) the divine nature (19-21). The divine nature shares one improper part with each Person (22-24).[8] If anything with the primary kind *divine nature* is

---

5. For Hasker's objections to my way of sorting these, see Hasker, "Trinity and the New Testament."

6. That is why, in his view, we have "constructed," not discovered, such a doctrine.

7. And 17 and 18 (the Son and Spirit having the divine nature) would be because of 13 and 14, respectively.

8. The idea is that each of those things lacks multiple, "proper parts" (parts that are less than the whole), but each just is a proper-part-less whole, in the lingo of modern mereology (theory of parts and wholes), an improper part. This one part they, though not numerically identical, share in common.

in divine-person-favorable circumstances, then an object of primary-kind *divine person* shares all its parts with that thing (25). The divine nature is in the divine-person-favorable circumstances of supporting a "life-stream" for each Person (26–28). There is the requisite sort of causal activity required for there to be divine Persons with the divine nature (29). The divine nature constitutes each Person (30–32).[9] The divine nature includes or implies tripersonality (33). Each Person is a proper part of the one God, i.e., the Trinity (34–36). The Trinity is like a single soul supporting three conscious lives (37).[10]

Seeing this, one can sympathize with the typical Christian (and even the typical pastor), who wants nothing to do with this confusing morass of speculations. We could lay out all of these claims and date them, that is, specify about when in history they entered into the minds of at least some Trinitarians.[11] Is this supposed to be part of "the faith which was once for all delivered to the saints" (Jude 3)? When God reveals something to humans, we find many of those human recipients believing the claims in question. If "the doctrine of the Trinity" is best understood to be claims 1–37, then we can be sure that it was not revealed by God to humankind in the first century, nor in any of the first twenty Christian centuries, for we do not see people who believe all of 1–37 until the twenty-first century! If Hasker is right, "the doctrine of the Trinity" is not a God-revealed doctrine, even though some of its component claims (any Christian should agree) are.

I agree that no theology involving a tripersonal God has been divinely revealed. Trinitarians generally intend to in some sense "ground" their theory in the Bible—thus Hasker assures us that the NT is "the primary theological basis" (5) for it. Even those who like Hasker admit that not all of the component claims of the doctrine are taught in Scripture, still generally want the doctrine to be consistent with its teachings, so that no claim within "the doctrine of the Trinity" contradicts any clear biblical teaching.

For such, I bear bad news: any triune-God theory clashes with the clear NT teaching of the numerical sameness of the one God with the one the NT calls "the Father," "God the Father," or just "God." The Trinitarian as

---

9. The claim here about the Father is supposed to be implied by: 22, 25–26, 29. About the Son: 23, 25, 27, 29. About the Holy Spirit: 24–25, 28–29.

10. I take it that for Hasker all of these thirty-seven claims are true of metaphysical necessity, and so eternally, but for the sake of simplicity I have omitted these pre-fix "Necessarily," for each claim.

11. Claim 37 originated in 2003 with Moreland and Craig, *Philosophical Foundations*, chapter 31. Claims 30–32 originated in 2005 with Brower and Rea, "Material Constitution and the Trinity." Claims 25–29 in 2013 with Hasker, *Metaphysics and the Tri-Personal God*, chapter 28.

such is committed to the one God and the Trinity being one and the same. But the NT teaches that the one God is none other than the Father himself; in other words, the one God and the Father are one and the same. But it is self-evident that things that are numerically identical with the same thing must be numerically identical with one another. Thus, it would follow that the Trinity and the Father are one and the same. But all sides should agree that this can't be true. There either is or isn't a Trinity. If the triune God is a fiction, then it won't be true to say it is one and the same with the Father, whom we agree is real. If there is a Trinity, then it will not be one and the same with the Father, as they will qualitatively differ.[12] So one must pick between the NT's identification of God with the Father, and catholic tradition's identification of God with the Trinity. For my part, as a disciple of Jesus, I'm compelled to go with the NT here.

Sometimes Trinitarians confuse the NT identification of God with the Father with the linguistic point that these authors nearly always use the word "God" to refer to the Father. That linguistic point is correct and indisputable, but the subject has been changed from theology to language. That language (using "God" mostly for the Father) is, as Hasker has pointed out,[13] consistent with holding to a Trinitarian theology, although that is not a typical Trinitarian practice.

I agree with some leading Trinitarian analytic theologians that processions as traditionally understood imply the ontological inferiority and lack of full divinity of the Son and Spirit;[14] these implications didn't bother the early adopters of such innovations, but they ought to bother all who bind themselves to the 381 "Nicene" Creed.

I also agree with the growing consensus among biblical scholars that contrary to catholic traditions dating back to about the time of Origen, the Bible offers no support at all for claims 13 or 14 above.[15] Hasker asks us what could be going on in John 5:26 if not eternal generation.[16] In reply, the

---

12. Among other differences: the first is and the second is not tripersonal. It is self-evident that numerical identity forces absolute intrinsic qualitative sameness, so if we know that $a=b$, we know that a and b can't ever simultaneously differ from one another. Metaphysicians call this principle "the indiscernibility of identicals." The word "simultaneously" in the previous sentence is important, as we know that things may change (not merely be replaced) as time goes on.

13. Hasker, *Metaphysics and the Tri-Personal God*, 247–48.

14. Mullins, "Hasker on the Divine Processions"; Craig, "Is God the Son Begotten in His Divine Nature?"

15. See e.g., Craig, "Is God the Son Begotten in His Divine Nature?," 26–27. It is striking how little defenders of biblical processions have to work with in the biblical texts; e.g., Dahms, "Generation of the Son."

16. See p. 21 above, and also Hasker, "In Defense of the Trinitarian Processions."

chapter has nothing to do with divine attributes or "processions." Rather, to have life in oneself here is to possess the life of the age to come ("eternal" life), so that one can give it to others. Jesus here asserts that he can give this life in two senses, first, by preaching God's life-giving words to people in the present age, and second, by resurrecting them to face their divine judgment through Jesus (John 5:19-29).

Hasker disagrees with the position taken nowadays by many scholars that *monogenes*, traditionally translated as "only begotten" (which suggests that the Father causally produced the Son), means only "one of a kind."[17] In reply, if he's right about that, then there is a natural place to find God's begetting/production of Jesus in the NT: God's miraculous begetting of Jesus, which is his miracle of causing Mary to become pregnant. Matthew describes Jesus' *genesis* (origin or birth), introducing him as a descendent of David and Abraham, proceeding to fill in a genealogy in which each parent "begets" their offspring (Matt 1:1-17). The reasonable background assumption here is that a child is brought into existence by the reproductive actions of his or her parents. Mary did her part with Jesus, bearing him, and it turns out that God did the rest, making a human father unnecessary (Matt 1:20-21). Jesus is the child conceived in her (Matt 1:21, 25), and the reader knows that it's at conception time (or maybe a little after, but no earlier) that a human begins to exist. Similarly, in Luke, Mary is told "you will conceive in your womb and bear a son, and you will name him Jesus," and it is made clear that God will perform this by his spirit (Luke 1:31, 34-35). No "eternal begetting" is mentioned, but only Jesus' temporal conception within Mary, nor is there the slightest hint of Jesus around this time traveling from heaven down to earth to become incarnate. On the face of it, this is when the man Jesus begins to exist.[18]

The standard objection to "social" Trinity theories is that they imply Tritheism.[19] No Trinitarian sets out to construct a Tritheistic theology, but sometimes we fallible theologians end up implying things we are deliberately trying not to imply. In past jousts with Hasker, I have objected that his Trinity theory unfortunately implies Tritheism.[20] Hasker has wrestled with this problem in a long series of publications. As I see it, his position has evolved to contain a clear answer to such objections, albeit at a severe cost.

17. Brown, *Gospel according to John*, 13; Brant, *John*, 35.

18. Brown, *Birth of the Messiah*, 140-42, 160-61, 291; Kuschel, *Born before All Time*, 316-23; Kirk, *Man Attested by God*, 363-73, 387-93; Chandler, *God of Jesus*, 361-72. For the weakness of the argument of Gathercole, *Preexistent Son*, see Dunn, "Review of Gathercole."

19. For primary source references see Tuggy, "Trinity," section 2.3.

20. Tuggy, "Hasker's Quests"; Tuggy, "Hasker's Tri-Personal God."

Let's first clarify the problem, which slightly pre-dates Trinity theories. There is no reference in the writings of Basil of Caesarea (d. 378) to a triune God, but he does wrestle with the implications of Nicene speculations about the Son and eventually too the Spirit being one in *ousia* with the Father. We know from Basil's late writings that he was repeatedly confronted about his perceived Tritheism.[21] Here is an argument that it seems occurred to those critics. I call it Basil's Bane.[22]

(1) Regarding the sort of divinity which implies being a god, the Father is divine, the Son is divine, and the Spirit is divine.[23]

(2) Therefore, the Father is a god, the Son is a god, and the Holy Spirit is a god.

(3) It is true that any a and any b are the same F only if the following three things are true: a is an F, b is an F, and a just is b.[24]

(4) None of these claims is true: the Father just is the Son, the Son just is the Spirit, the Spirit just is the Father.[25]

(5) Therefore, none of the Father, the Son, or the Spirit is the same god as either of the others.

(6) Therefore, there are (at least) three gods.

Any monotheist must deny (6), so we all agree that the argument goes wrong somewhere. But where? Steps (2), (5) and (6) are validly inferred from prior steps, so it would be point-missing to only deny one or more of those. We must diagnose a problem farther back, denying at least one of: (1), (3), or (4). But some of those seem undeniable. Premise (3) seems to me, and probably to most analytic philosophers, to be a self-evident truth.[26]

---

21. Basil of Caesarea, *On the Holy Spirit*, chapter 18; Basil of Caesarea, "Homily Against," sections 3–7 in *On Christian Doctrine*; Basil of Caesarea, Letter 189 in *Letters and Select Works*; Basil of Caesarea, Letters 210 and 236 in Stevenson, *Creeds*. Basil tried out several replies, but as best I can tell, none are well-motivated and effective.

22. Hasker gestures at basically this problem on p. 17 above.

23. Premise (1) does not imply that there actually are multiple kinds of divinity, although it is compatible with such claims. So if you hold that there is but one sort of divinity, you should not object to the first clause of (1).

24. Put differently: being the same F requires being the same thing. The letter 'F' here stands in for any kind-term, e.g., god, human, wife, tree, planet.

25. In other words, it is incorrect to identify (assert the numerical sameness of) any two of those.

26. If, for instance, Peter and Cephas are the same apostle, this requires three things, that Peter is an apostle, that Cephas is an apostle, and that Peter and Cephas are one and the same (so that counting them as two realities would be over-counting).

And the Trinitarian, as such, is committed to (4); it is equivalent to the antimodalist portions of Trinitarian confessions which insist that Father, Son, and Spirit are all numerically distinct (not numerically identical).

Given what is actually in the NT, the most obvious way out is to deny (1). This is my response to the argument, and this is the response implied by all the ancient subordinationists, such as Justin, Origen, Tertullian, and Novatian.[27] Oddly enough, Hasker agrees with us in denying (1).[28] But he goes further; following Craig,[29] Hasker posits two kinds of divinity,[30] one had by the Trinity (but not by the Persons) and one by each Person (but not by the Trinity). This clashes with the 325 Nicene Creed, which begins thus: "We believe in one God the Father all powerful, maker of all things."[31] This asserts that the Father *is* a god, the only one.[32] But then, he would have the sort of divinity that implies being a god and not only "divine Person" divinity. Later in that creed we're told that the Son is "God from God . . . true God from true God, begotten not made, consubstantial with the Father."[33] This seems to say that the Son too is a god, as he has the same sort of being-a-god divinity the Father has. We're not told that each is a "divine Person" which is not a god.[34]

But Hasker could argue that since the 325 Nicene Creed never mentions or implies a tripersonal god, whereas arguably the revised creed from the 381 Council of Constantinople *does* presuppose that the only god is triune, we should interpret the latter creed's God-talk differently,[35] so that being called "God" or "true God" *doesn't* presuppose that one is a god, but rather that one is a divine Person—something with Person-divinity, not god-divinity. I think this is plausible, so long as one is willing to admit a

---

27. For some primary sources, see my reply to Branson, p. 187n27.

28. The denials, though, are for different reasons; we hold that the Father alone has the said kind of divinity, whereas Hasker denies that any of the Persons has it.

29. Moreland and Craig, *Philosophical Foundations*, 589–90; Hasker, *Metaphysics and the Tri-Personal God*, chapter 23.

30. The point is not merely that "divinity" can mean various properties. It can. But the claim here is that there are two divinity properties, two ways to be divine.

31. Tanner, *Decrees of the Ecumenical Councils*, 1:5.

32. Compare Rea, "Trinity," 405–6.

33. Tanner, *Decrees of the Ecumenical Councils*, 1:5.

34. Many Trinitarians agree that each Person *is* a god, and go on to argue that they are all *the same* god. This is problematic as concerns logical consistency (see Tuggy, "Trinity," sections 2.1, 1.4.) and consistency with the NT (see Tuggy, *Monotheism*, chapter 10). For similar points regarding another much-used standard of orthodoxy, the "Athanasian" creed, see Brower, "Problem with Social Trinitarianism."

35. Tuggy, "When and How?"

shocking change of theological ideas in the mainstream between 325 and 381.

Unfortunately, a metaphysical and theological problem looms large. The monotheistic concept of a god implies ultimacy.[36] God, the necessarily unique god, is supposed to be the source of and farthest back explanation for all else, but is not supposed to in any sense come from or depend on or exist because of or be explained by anything else.[37] For the Trinitarian the only god and the Trinity are one and the same; thus, Hasker holds that only the Trinity has the sort of divinity that implies being a (and the) god.

But if Hasker's thirty-seven claims above are correct, then the Trinity exists because of other things, as do, in various ways, each of the Persons. The only metaphysically basic thing here, and the only thing that could be ultimate, is the divine nature; the Persons, being constituted by it, exist *because of* it, and since the Persons are (or are like?) proper parts of the Trinity, it would seem that the Trinity exists *because of* the Persons (and so ultimately *because of* the divine nature). Although Hasker asserts the Trinity to be identical with the only god, it can't be, as it is (on his theology) not ultimate. Thus, the scheme is a species of what I have called polydeistic ultimism;[38] the ultimate reality (here, the divine nature) is not a deity, and so is not a god. There are three omniscient and omnipotent and morally perfect Persons, but these will be mere deities, none being ultimate. Therefore, this Trinity theory implies the falsity of monotheism, but is not, properly speaking, Tritheism, but rather trideistic ultimism, which is actually a variety of non-naturalistic atheism![39] Hasker's Trinity can be neither a deity nor a god. It is a thing we don't really have a good concept or word for, a conglomeration of deities that is not itself a deity. In his chapter here he clearly asserts that the Persons are selves but "God" (the Trinity) is not. Thus, any "divine" attribute that requires being a self—such as omniscience, omnipotence, and perfect moral goodness—will belong to each Person but not to God.

On such a theology "the one true God" doesn't know, intentionally act, or love.[40] I don't see how the theological pain of this is lessened by pointing

---

36. Tuggy, "On Counting Gods," 3–11. Our good editor has raised very similar concerns about aseity for both Hasker's and Craig's views. See McIntosh, Review of *Metaphysics and the Tri-Personal God*; McIntosh, Review of *God over All* and *God and Abstract Objects*.

37. This criterion of ultimacy is more demanding than the sort of "aseity" which requires only existing independently from "anything external." See Mullins, "Hasker on the Divine Processions," 196–99.

38. Tuggy, "On Counting Gods," 16–17.

39. Tuggy, "On Counting Gods," 12–18.

40. Howard-Snyder, Review of *Metaphysics and the Tri-Personal God*, 113–15. For

out that on the present theory *the proper parts of* God or members of the Trinity can do those things. My son can love me, and so can my daughter, but strictly speaking this thing can't: *my-son-and-my-daughter*.[41] But I invite Dr. Hasker to clarify what the divine attributes are and how they divide up among the two kinds of divinity, and so between the Persons and this "God" which is the Trinity.[42] Hasker says we are to "worship, and obey, and love" (27) the Trinity, but these are all "I-thou" (self to self) relations, and this thing isn't a self, though Hasker urges that it is *similar to* one. This is not, as Hasker hopes, what the "Christian church knows God as" (3).

Hasker's unsatisfying attempt to answer this difficulty, see his *Metaphysics and the Tri-Personal God*, 249–50, 258.

41. I'm not suggesting there actually is such an entity as *my-son-and-my-daughter* in reality, although for some present-day metaphysicians any two things whatever compose a whole.

42. Craig has, not entirely clearly, done this in *Philosophical Foundations*, chapter 31.

III. Ad Craig

We Do Need the Processions

William Hasker

It is hoped that both readers and editor will forgive me if I have comparatively little to say about William Craig's contribution to this volume. The reason for this is, that I am in virtually complete agreement with what he has presented. By far the greater part of his essay is devoted to what the editor has called the "probative" aspect of the doctrine of the Trinity. That is to say, he is mainly concerned with the various biblical texts that provide important support for the doctrine. He has some excellent things to say about the fact that, in the New Testament, the word "God" refers, in the majority of its uses, to the Father. (Contrary to what Dale Tuggy would have us believe, this usage in no way detracts from the doctrines of the Trinity and the deity of Christ.) Most of Craig's effort, however, is directed at the comparatively few New Testament texts in which, arguably, Jesus is said to be "God."

Now, some of these texts also figure in my own essay, but there is less redundancy here than one might at first suppose. The references to those texts in my essay are mainly directed at establishing a broad historical and theological context, a context that will assist the reader in grasping the theological import of the texts for the doctrine of the Trinity as a whole. Craig, in contrast, pursues in much greater depth a detailed exegesis of the various passages, citing a number of highly regarded exegetes as he discusses various possible readings of the particular passages. It should be clear that these two approaches are in no way in conflict with each other. In view of the great intrinsic importance of these particular texts, both ways of approaching them are thoroughly justified. Careful, detailed exegesis is especially needed when particular biblical texts have important theological implications: Craig is careful to point out the existence of possible alternative interpretations that might not have the christological and Trinitarian implications that follow from his preferred understanding of the texts. On the other hand, these passages do need to be set in historical and theological context: in some cases, this is needed to keep us from casually taking for granted, as a result of familiarity, the truly astonishing nature of what is being asserted. So I welcome and celebrate Craig's explanations of this biblical material.

As Craig makes clear, he has comparatively less to say about the "model" component of the doctrine of the Trinity. However, I find little to complain of in what he does say about this. Far from it! As I made clear, both in my main essay and in my book, *Metaphysics and the Tri-Personal God*, I accept and affirm his central claim: God is "an immaterial, tripersonal substance, just as each of us is an immaterial, unipersonal substance" (53). In my essay I pointed out that Craig, in other writings, has stated his disagreement with the doctrine of processions, which claims that the Son is eternally generated from the Father, and the Holy Spirit is eternally "spirated" from the Father. Craig has not chosen to introduce that issue into the present discussion, so I will say no more about it here. (There is a brief discussion of the processions in my main essay.)

Another point of difference (though not necessarily of disagreement) can be found in my introduction of the metaphysical idea of "constitution" in explaining how it is that the three divine Persons, though each distinct from one another, can share in their possession of the one concrete divine nature. This, I should perhaps say, is a view that I favor, but I do not wish to insist that such a view is essential to the doctrine of the Trinity. I like my "constitution Trinitarianism," and have good hopes for its success, but I have no objection if others have different proposals for explicating the doctrine at this point. So, allowing for these differences between our views, we nevertheless stand together in affirming a biblical, coherent, and Social stance on the doctrine of the Trinity.

Socialist Trinitarianism

Beau Branson

What the honorable member is saying, is that he would rather the poor were poorer, provided the rich were less rich.

—MARGARET THATCHER, NOVEMBER 22, 1990

I'M DEEPLY HONORED TO be in a book with William Craig. Craig has devoted his life to defending Christianity. He's argued powerfully for theism, the historicity of Christ's resurrection, and too many other topics to list. Like many, I've benefited greatly from his profoundly erudite and meticulously analytical work. Moving from general or "mere" Christianity to specific doctrines, however, I confess some deep misgivings. As an Orthodox Christian, I applaud Craig's motives: to adhere strictly to Scripture, and to defend Christ's divinity. I'm less enthusiastic, though, about the results.

Around 90 percent of Craig's chapter argues for the divinity of Christ and the Holy Spirit in the New Testament (NT). As anyone would expect, he makes a devastating case. Would that he had spent more space on the "model" component, where I think there are more problems than Craig lets on. Craig says, "So far as the biblical doctrine of the Trinity is concerned, the model component more or less takes care of itself" (52). He quotes Brower and Rea that, "The central claim of the doctrine of the Trinity . . . is not problematic because of any superficial incoherence or inconsistency, . . . it is problematic because of a tension that results from constraints imposed on its interpretation by other aspects of orthodox Christian theology" (52). Craig avers, "It is these accreted constraints that occasion philosophical problems for the biblical doctrine of the Trinity. . . . Protestants, however, bring all doctrinal statements, even conciliar creeds . . . before the bar of Scripture. To the extent that these formulations impose further constraints upon the above formulated biblical doctrine of the Trinity, I have no interest in defending them" (52).

As a description of Protestant practice, perhaps these words are accurate. But they're not flattering. Here the profound lack of prudence in the Protestant instinct to reinvent theological wheels is, it seems to me, on full display. Craig claims, "the biblical doctrine of the Trinity becomes logically problematic *only if* one interprets such statements as the following:

1. The Father is God.

2. The Son is God.

3. The Son is not the Father.

as identity statements" (52). But, with all due respect, this is patently false. And without saying more, what Craig describes as a "disarmingly simple model" (call it "DSM")—that "God is an immaterial, tri-personal being"—provides no help on *any* of 3G, 3F, WIG, *or* TP.[1] His discussions of the Trinity elsewhere help some. But, I'll argue, not enough.

The Three Gods$_{\text{NATURE}}$ Problem

Start with 3G$_{\text{NATURE}}$. Craig rightly takes "is God" in 1 and 2 as predications, not identity claims ("is (a) god" rather than "is God" in my capitalization convention). Read thus, 1–3 are indeed not inconsistent with each other. But they're at least *apparently* inconsistent with:

4. There is exactly one God

which Craig includes in the "biblical doctrine of the Trinity" (54). And not only are 1–4 *apparently* inconsistent, they would be *actually* inconsistent if:

A. 3 is a *non*-identity claim (i.e., the Son ≠ the Father),

B. 4 has the logical form attributed to it by standard logic textbooks,

C. "Father" and "Son" are univocal throughout 1–4, and

D. "God" is univocal throughout 1–4.

(A)–(D) all at least *seem* reasonable, even if one or more is ultimately false. So it's not the case that there's "no *prima facie* logical incoherence" here (53). Of course there is. And lots of things are *prima facie* incoherent, but turn out to be true (e.g., the Banach-Tarski Paradox, the relativity of simultaneity, or wave-particle duality), so there's no reason not to admit it. Elsewhere,

---

1. See my opening essay for explanations and definitions of these and other terms.

even Craig acknowledges the *apparent* incoherence and addresses it.[2] He clearly accepts (A) and (C),[3] and apparently accepts (B). So, it's unsurprising he rejects (D).[4] In my terminology, DSM says there's only one god$_{NATURE}$, because only "the Trinity as a whole" is (a) god$_{NATURE}$—the divine persons *aren't*.

In what sense can a divine person be called "God"? Craig gives an analogy to a cat and its parts (like its DNA or skeleton).[5] All can be called "feline," but there is only one *cat*. The *whole cat* is "feline" in the sense of having the feline *nature*. The skeleton and DNA are "feline" in the sense of *being parts of* a cat. Call this the "Equivocation Solution" (ES).[6]

Now, Craig's essay revolves around Christ's divinity. And elsewhere Craig states that Christ "exemplifies *two . . . natures*, one human and *one divine*."[7] Yet DSM says Christ *doesn't* have the divine nature. Space precludes canvassing all the theological problems with that. But I'll present some straightforward philosophical and biblical problems.

First, unclarity. Do the persons have a nature at all? If so, is it divine or non-divine? If they have no nature, or only a non-divine nature, how could Christ have two natures, one divine? If they have *a* divine nature—but only the Trinity has "the" divine nature—are there two qualitatively different divine natures—one for the persons, and one for the Trinity?[8]

Second, biblical problems. Colossians 2:9 says, "In [Christ] dwelleth all the fullness of the Godhead bodily." The Greek *"theotes"* ("Godhead") means precisely *the divine nature*. Greek distinguishes between *"theos"* (a

---

2. Moreland and Craig, *Philosophical Foundations*, 575–95, esp. 577 and 583.

3. Rejecting (A) yields modalism. Rejecting (C) would be a heresy so unusual it has no name.

4. Moreland and Craig, *Philosophical Foundations*, 589–95. Craig says there is "more than one way to be divine. . . . The Father, Son and Holy Spirit *are not instances of the divine nature*, and that is why there are not three Gods. The Trinity is the sole instance of the divine nature, and therefore there is but one God" (590; emphasis mine). In Branson, "No New Solutions," I show that, given some fairly uncontroversial constraints, there are ultimately *only* two ways to solve any version of 3G within classical logic: either equivocate on "God" in exactly the way Craig does (i.e., reject [D]), or count by a relation other than identity (i.e., reject [B]).

5. Moreland and Craig, *Philosophical Foundations*, 591.

6. Typically, one appeals to analogical predication as not involving outright equivocation, i.e., unrelated senses of a word. Nevertheless, analogical predication is not univocal predication and is a species of equivocation. My point doesn't turn on how related two senses of "god" are.

7. Moreland and Craig, *Philosophical Foundations*, 606; emphasis mine.

8. If so, this only exacerbates my final point below—that ES doesn't solve 3G anyway.

god), and "*theios*" (divine).[9] But *theotes* is the abstract form of *theos*, not *theios*. It isn't "divine-ish-ness." It's *god-hood*. Craig himself makes a parallel point about John 1:1 (39–40). Yet ES *denies* Christ has the divine nature. The Son may have the nature of *the Father* (if he has a nature), but on ES that *is not* the nature of God. Ultimately Craig, no less than Tuggy, must reject the straightforward readings of Colossians 2:9, John 1:1, and the like.

Finally, barring an alternative view of counting, ES can't solve any version of 3G anyway. For, given ES alone, although *there's a sense* in which there is only "one God" (the Trinity) *there's also a sense in which there are three gods* (the persons). And we can't downplay that sense—it's the only sense in which the Father, Son, or Spirit "is God." So, to the extent that there's any good sense in which each "is God," there's a good sense in which there are three Gods.

The Three *F*s Problem (and 3G$_{POWER/ACTION}$)

Replace "God" with "Savior," "Creator," "Redeemer," or what have you, and you get exactly parallel apparent contradictions, and parallel potential solutions for 3*F* (and 3G$_{POWER/ACTION}$). But again, while there's *a sense* in which there is only "one Savior" (the Trinity), *there is also a sense in which there are three* (the persons).

The Three Gods$_{ULTIMATE\text{-}SOURCE}$ Problem

Moving on to 3G$_{ULTIMATE\text{-}SOURCE}$, we can recast Leftow's argument against Trinity Monotheism, or DSM, in terms of aseity, rather than divinity. Thus, for DSM, either the Father, Son, and Holy Spirit are each *a se*—but God isn't; God is *a se*—but the Father, Son, and Holy Spirit aren't; or *all four*—the Father, Son, Holy Spirit, *and* God—are *a se*. But the first option contradicts the unassailable view that God is *a se*, and the second contradicts Craig's own view that the Son and Spirit must be *a se* to be "fully divine."[10] As far as I can tell, Craig actually holds to the third option. He says concerning divine attributes like aseity that "the persons have these properties because God as a whole has them. For parts can have some properties in virtue of the wholes of which they are parts."[11] I don't know what it means for some-

---

9. Which doesn't necessarily imply *having the divine nature*. The liturgy is called "the divine liturgy," for example.

10. Despite his claim that they lack the divine nature, more on which below.

11. Moreland and Craig, *Philosophical Foundations*, 591.

thing to be *a se* "in virtue of" something else. That seems to violate the definition of aseity.[12] But anyway, assuming we count by identity, we have four gods$_{\text{ULTIMATE-SOURCE}}$. And that's three too many.

The "Who Is God?" Problem

DSM also gets WIG wrong. As powerful as Craig's case for Christ's divinity is, Tuggy's case that in the NT God = the Father is just as strong. Even Craig admits that in the NT "God" *typically* refers to the Father. The truth is, *both* Tuggy's *and* Craig's arguments are cogent. But what they support, taken together, is neither of their proposals, but Monarchical Trinitarianism (MT).

The Theophanies Problem

The failure on WIG produces a failure on TP. Christ is "the icon of God" (2 Cor 4:4; Col 1:15). But if Christ is the icon of *the Trinity*, rather than *the Father*, we get problems similar to Arianism. Does Christ represent God naturally (like an icon) or merely conventionally? If merely conventionally, how can he *reveal* God?

If I show you a picture of my wife and say, "This is my wife," you can read facts about my wife off the picture. If I had an exact duplicate of my wife, you could read *any* fact about her off the duplicate, save the fact that one is the duplicate and one the prototype. If we're playing Monopoly and, pointing to the hat, I say "This is my wife," it may represent her by convention, but you can't read facts about my wife off the hat. You can act *as if* the hat were blonde, human, female, and so on. But you'd need some independent way of knowing my wife's features to know what features to act as if her representation had. The moral is, natural representations (like the Nicene Christ) *reveal*; they *provide* knowledge. Merely conventional representations (like the Christ of Arianism, Unitarianism, and DSM) don't; they *presuppose* knowledge.

Since Craig admits "God" typically refers to the Father in the NT, he could read "icon of God" as "icon of the Father." But if, speaking precisely, *the* God is really the Trinity, what's the point of one *part* of God revealing *a*

---

12. And normally we take wholes to be dependent on their parts. But that yields the first option, not the third. One might take a holist view where the whole ("God the Trinity") is more fundamental than the parts (the persons). But that would be the second option, not the third. It's unclear how a whole can neither be more fundamental than its parts nor its parts more fundamental than it—and how the whole and all the parts can each be independent of each other. But that seems to be what this view amounts to.

different part? If *the* God isn't the Father, then Christ, as icon of *the Father*, doesn't reveal *God* to us, which is central to NT theology.

Relabeling DSM

Does DSM need only minor tweaks? Or is it irreparably flawed? We could "relabel" DSM so the Father is God, instead of the Trinity, solving WIG and TP. But since, on DSM, the Father lacks the divine nature, this bizarrely results in *God* lacking the divine nature.

We could shift the nature back to the persons. Then God would have the divine nature, as would all three persons. But since now God = the Father, we can no longer solve 3G with ES. The predicate "is God" can't mean one thing as applied to God and something else as applied to the Father, if God = the Father. The only other solution to 3G was to reject:

B. 4 has the logical form attributed to it by standard logic textbooks.

Hence, we must count by a relation other than identity. But at this point, we have MT in everything except the Monarchy of the Father (MoF).[13] But, without MoF how can we interpret the NT claim that there is "one god, the Father" (1 Cor 8:6)? Here "god" is a count noun, not a name or definite description. Given MoF, we could read this as "there is one $god_{ULTIMATE-SOURCE}$, the Father." But if all three persons are *a se*, we can't. (And on *any* Trinitarian view, the persons are equally god_{NATURE} and $god_{POWER/ACTION}$, so the NT authors shouldn't single out the Father as "the one god" in either of *those* senses.)[14] So it seems we need MoF. Thus, after all the necessary tweaks, we transform DSM into MT.[15]

---

13. And perhaps inseparable operations, if there's another way to solve 3F. See my response to Hasker for more on that.

14. It would also be unclear *why* "God" (used as a proper name or definite description) typically refers to the Father in the NT. Without MoF, we would avoid inconsistency with the NT, but *prima facie* at the expense of making the NT's way of stating things inexplicable or arbitrary.

15. Note that MT also has multiple senses of "god," but that is not its way of addressing $3G_{NATURE}$ or $3G_{POWER/ACTION}$, as it is for DSM. Rather, MT counts by division, rather than by identity. For MT, the distinction in senses of "god" has to do with WIG and $3G_{ULTIMATE-SOURCE}$.

What Motivates DSM?

So, DSM fails literally *all* our desiderata. And it doesn't differ from the NT merely semantically, because relabeling it generates new absurdities, and correcting them all collapses it into MT. So, one might wonder, what exactly motivates DSM? Elsewhere Craig argues against the orthodox, Nicene Trinitarian doctrine of eternal generation.[16] But he mostly argues the doctrine *isn't supported by Scripture*. Little positive argument against it is presented, other than very brief remarks about aseity and "subordinationism." Craig writes, "Despite its protestations to the contrary, Nicene orthodoxy does not seem to have completely exorcised the spirit of subordinationism. . . . Protestants bring all doctrinal statements, even Conciliar creeds, before the bar of Scripture. Nothing in Scripture warrants us in thinking that Christ is begotten of the Father in his divine nature."[17] Now, as an Orthodox Christian, my Bible says, "From the womb, before the morning star, I have begotten Thee" (Ps 109:3 LXX). That certainly sounds like eternal generation. But as a Protestant, Craig's Bible says something like "From the womb, from the morning, Thou hast the dew of Thy youth"—whatever that means (Ps 110:3 Masoretic Text).[18] Even several Protestant scholars have mounted scriptural defenses of eternal generation that seem more substantial than Craig lets on.[19]

Given the scriptural argument is far from conclusive, and provides no reason to reject the doctrine anyway, why reject it? As far as I can reconstruct it, the argument against eternal generation is something like:

(1) God has aseity necessarily (not merely contingently).

(2) Therefore, aseity is part of God's nature.[20]

---

16. Craig, "Is God the Son Begotten in His Divine Nature?"

17. Craig, "Is God the Son Begotten in His Divine Nature?," 29.

18. Many study Bibles footnote this verse, pointing out the Hebrew seems garbled, or at best unclear. See Bratcher and Reyburn, *Handbook on Psalms*, 949–50 for a discussion of the many difficulties with the Masoretic text of this verse. So, to conclude there is *no scriptural warrant* for the doctrine of eternal generation, we need to know why we should reject the clear text preserved in the Septuagint (and some Hebrew manuscripts) in favor of the unclear, and potentially garbled, Masoretic text.

19. See e.g., Irons, "Lexical Defense"; Letham, *Holy Trinity*, 193–94. And for a useful outline of the history of the doctrine of eternal generation and of the origin of Evangelical Christian objections to it, see Waldron, "Scriptural Support."

20. Craig writes, "the fact that God alone exists *a se* would not seem to be a contingent matter. . . . Thus, we should take God's being the sole ultimate reality as belonging to God's nature." Craig, *God over All*, 30–31.

(3) Therefore, if the Son and Spirit have the same nature as God, they must be *a se*.

(4) The Son and Spirit do have the same nature as God.

(5) Therefore, the Son and Spirit must be *a se*.

But first, the inference from (1) to (2) is invalid. x could be necessarily F for a number of reasons, including:

(a) F-ness is entailed by x's *kind essence* (roughly corresponding to *ousia* in patristic terminology)[21] or

(b) F-ness is entailed by x's *individual essence* (roughly corresponding to *idioma* in patristic terminology).[22]

So, from God's non-contingent aseity, we can at most conclude either aseity is entailed by God's *ousia*, or aseity is entailed by God's *idioma*.[23] So the argument *presupposes* aseity *isn't* entailed by God's *idioma*, which simply begs the question against Nicene Trinitarianism. Furthermore, the proposition that aseity *isn't* entailed by God's *idioma* requires that aseity is not, itself, one of God's *idiomata*, which in turn entails there are possible worlds in which something other than God exists *a se*. But this undermines the whole idea that, necessarily, everything else depends on

---

21. A.k.a. "Aristotelian" essence, a set of properties necessary and sufficient for membership in a certain natural kind. Critically, these are *shareable*. And I say "roughly" because an *ousia* (essence) or *physis* (nature) isn't *really* just a set of properties, as kind essences are often treated in contemporary philosophy. See my response to Hasker for more (128ff).

22. A.k.a. "Leibnizian" essence, a set of properties necessary and sufficient for being *numerically identical to a certain* hypostasis. Critically, these are *unshareable*. See Plantinga, *Nature of Necessity*, 70 for a discussion of individual or Leibnizian essences (which Plantinga simply calls "essences" *simpliciter*). See Loux and Crisp, *Metaphysics*, 112 for a discussion of the distinction between Aristotelian/kind essences and Leibnizian/individual essences.

23. According to Gregory of Nyssa, (divine) Fatherhood is God's *idioma*: "God, Who is over all, alone has, as one special mark of His own *hypostasis*, His being Father, and His deriving His *hypostasis* from no cause" (Erroneously listed as Basil's 38th Epistle in *Nicene and Post-Nicene Fathers*, 2nd series, 8:139). Note that it's *analytic* that if God's *idioma* is to be the source of divine persons, then God, and only God, is *a se* in every possible world, and hence aseity is one of his *idiomata*. For if something was God's source, it would have God's *idioma* of divine Fatherhood, and thus would just *be* God himself. So, God is no less necessarily *a se* on the patristic view that Fatherhood is God's *idioma* than on a view that stipulates aseity to be part of God's *ousia*.

God for its existence. That's a mighty high price to pay just to hang God's necessary aseity (which God has on either view anyway) on his *ousia*, rather than his *idioma*.

Second, DSM rejects (4) anyway, so Christ's divinity can't very well be the *real* motivation for DSM. So what *does* motivate it? It's hard to see what could other than a basic opposition to MoF itself, an *a priori* distaste for the lack of "equality" between the Trinitarian persons. What should we make of this?

Socialist Trinitarianism

Critics of economic socialism argue that it reduces inequality only by diminishing the wealth of everybody—including the poor. A free(er) market, it's claimed, makes the poor mostly better off, even if it makes the rich *even better* off (hence increasing inequality). I'm not an economist and take no stand on the economic argument. But it provides a useful metaphor.

In Monarchical Trinitarianism, the persons are each (a) god_{NATURE}. But certain critics we might call "Socialist Trinitarians" complain that because on MT the Father = God but the Son ≠ God and the Spirit ≠ God, MT solves all our desiderata at the cost of in some sense "privileging" the Father. Socialist Trinitarians call this "subordinationism" and decry the lack of absolute equality between the persons.

But notice, in Socialist Trinitarianism *it's still the case* that the Son ≠ God and the Spirit ≠ God, since neither = the whole Trinity. No divine person is *better off* in that respect. It's just that now the Father ≠ God *either*. Equality is achieved, not by *giving something to* the Son and Spirit, but by *taking something away* from the Father.

What's worse, in Socialist Trinitarianism, the "divine" persons don't even have the divine nature either! "From him who has not, even what he has shall be taken away." Now no divine person is identical to God, and no divine person even has the divine nature. Apparently no divine person is "God" in any but an analogical sense. Like a dystopian dictatorship in which everyone is equally wealthy only because they're equally poor, in Socialist Trinitarianism, the persons are "equally God" only because they're equally *not* God.

Craig insists that in his model the persons still have various divine *attributes* and argues "their deity seems in no way diminished because they are not instances of the divine nature."[24] Eunomius—the most infamous, extreme Arian of the fourth century—said literally the same thing:

---

24. Moreland and Craig, *Philosophical Foundations*, 591.

> Now don't anyone interrupt or let his mind be troubled. We have not used these expressions[25] in order to take away the godhead of the Only-begotten, or his wisdom, or his immortality, or his goodness, but rather to distinguish them with respect to the pre-eminence of the Father. For we confess that the Lord Jesus is himself "Only-begotten God," immortal and deathless, wise, good.[26]

Like Socialist Trinitarians, Eunomius denied Christ had the divine nature. And, like Socialist Trinitarians, he ascribed divine *attributes* to Christ. Indeed, like Socialist Trinitarians, he even ascribed to Christ "divinity"—*of a sort*. As we might put it, "*a*" divine nature, just not *the* divine nature. Like Socialist Trinitarians, Eunomius merely distinguished the way these apply to *Christ* from the way they apply to *God*. Comforted? I'm sure not. Eunomius and modern Socialist Trinitarians make precisely the same move—distinguishing the divinity of *Christ* from the divinity of *God*. But Socialist Trinitarians go further. They distinguish even the divinity of *the Father* from the divinity of God, thus reducing even God the Father to the status of the Arian Christ.

Conclusion

Socialist Trinitarianism is (forgive me) a philosophical and theological train wreck. It fails every desideratum we set, and even manages to generate additional absurdities and novel heresies along the way.[27] So it seems disingenuous to say "the model . . . takes care of itself" (52), or to blame difficulties on "constraints imposed . . . by . . . orthodox Christian theology" (52), and to claim it's "these accreted constraints that occasion philosophical problems" (52). Socialist Trinitarianism's problems are of its own making—the blame doesn't lie with the church fathers or the Nicene Creed. And as they say, "If

---

25. Eunomius had just been noting NT references to the Father as "the only true God," "the only wise God," "who alone is good," "alone mighty," "who alone has immortality," etc., apparently implying the exclusion of the Son from those attributes. Hence, Eunomius reminds us he isn't trying to exclude the Son from having those attributes *in some sense*, just *a different sense* from that in which God has them. In other words, Eunomius employs equivocal or analogical predication between God and Christ, just as Craig does. Only for Eunomius God = the Father, while for Craig God = the Trinity.

26. Eunomius, *Extant Works*, 61.

27. Like being unable to ascribe the divine nature to Christ, to the Holy Spirit, and even to God the Father—as far as I know, a heresy unprecedented in any Abrahamic religion. Even Tuggy doesn't deny the divine nature to God the Father.

it ain't broke, don't fix it." Or as a wiser man wrote, "Remove not the ancient boundaries, which thy fathers have set" (Prov 22:28).

Though traveling very different routes, Tuggy and Craig begin and end in similar places. Both reject the Nicene Creed and the orthodox doctrine of the Trinity it canonized. Both, ultimately, deny Christ has the divine nature. And both do so for the same reason: a particularly freewheeling version of *sola scriptura* and apparent lack of concern for historical Christianity.[28] But Tuggy wears his heresy on his sleeve. And there's something to be said for truth in advertising.

I've been highly critical of Craig's Socialist Trinitarianism. So I'll end where I began, reiterating—quite sincerely, I emphasize—both my immense admiration of Craig personally, and my deep gratitude for his lifelong defense of Christianity. I pray the future finds him defending a more orthodox form of it.

---

28. For a far more sensible version of *sola scriptura*, and a critique of the extreme version of it typically found within American Evangelicalism, see Mathison, *Sola Scriptura*. Most of Mathison's critical arguments are directed against Roman Catholicism and Evangelicalism. Unfortunately, he spends only a few pages critiquing Orthodox Christianity and leaves it entirely unclear in what way, if any, the view he develops differs from Orthodoxy.

Changing the Subject, Cognitive Faculties, and "God"

Dale Tuggy

I HAVE LEARNED MUCH from Dr. Craig's work on many topics over the years. Unfortunately, I found the arguments of this chapter lacking. Let's start with the end, where he lays out what is supposed to be a "biblical doctrine of the Trinity" (54). This is:

i. There is exactly one God.

ii. There are exactly three distinct persons who are properly called God.

In my opening essay, I complain about a modern trend of dumbing down "the doctrine of the Trinity" to what are obviously too few claims in order to show how it's allegedly derivable from the Bible (110). Craig boldly takes this trend to a new low, offering a mere two sentences, one of them partly terminological, about the word "God."

But this definition is a non-starter. A subordinationist Unitarian like Origen would agree with both claims,[1] as would some modalists, yet none of them are Trinitarians. For Origen, the most prestigious champion of catholic orthodoxy in his time, the one God just is the Father himself, so (i) is true. And he believes in three distinct (to various degrees divine) persons, each of whom is properly called "God." Yes, they are each called "God" (*theos*) in a different sense, but each of these is a proper and true sense. A modalist may think that the one God is the Father-Son-Spirit, with each of the modes being called a "person" who, being a mode of God himself,

---

1. For good summaries of Origen's views on God (a.k.a. the Father) and the Logos, see Gaston, *Dynamic Monarchianism*, 31–32; Martens, "Origen's Christology." These views are the most clear in Origen's writings which have not been "corrected" by his Nicene Latin translator Rufinus (*Commentary on John*, 2.12–21; *Against Celsus*, 8.1–26; "On Prayer," 15.1–16.1).

is properly called "God."[2] So if Craig has shown that the authors of the New Testament (NT) are committed to (i) and (ii) above, he has not come anywhere close to showing that they are orthodox Trinitarians. Notably absent is any mention of a tripersonal God, a shared divine *ousia*, or eternal generation and procession.[3] If Craig should protest that the only "proper" use of "God" is for someone having the divine essence, first, we should remind him that the modalist's "persons" each have the divine essence, and that Origen's persons each have it to some degree or in some way, but more importantly, such a claim is refuted by the relevant lexicons.[4] More on this below.

Towards the end of his chapter Craig also offers us his model of what "the Trinity" is supposed to be: "a soul which is endowed with three complete sets of rational faculties" (53). I believe Craig is the first person in the history of Christian theology to understand "the doctrine of the Trinity" in this way. Here we have a version (or two—see below) of the tripersonal God idea, and perhaps also of the same-essence idea, since there is only one soul here and it presumably has an essence. First, notice that such a theology on the face of it is not supported at all by the NT. Nor is it obviously the only or best way to cash out the supposedly "biblical" Trinity doctrine just sketched. Craig crows that this model is "straightforward, perspicuous, and explanatorily deep" (54), presenting nothing "philosophically problematic" (52).

---

2. Even a hypothetical ancient Second Temple era Jew, call him Schlomo, might count as "Trinitarian" on this definition, since Schlomo thinks that Yahweh is the only God, and that there are three ancient prophets or judges or sages, call them Larry, Curly, and Moishe, each of whom is properly referred to as a *theos*, having received the word of God (John 10:34–35). After all, this threadbare definition doesn't say who these properly-called-"God" persons are!

3. In my view Craig is right in thinking that traditional doctrines about "procession" imply the ontological subordination of the Son and Spirit to the Father, but I also agree with Hasker and Branson that such speculations are central to catholic Trinitarian traditions.

4. The most authoritative New Testament Greek lexicon gives five meanings for *theos*: 1. a "deity, god, goddess." 2. "Some writings . . . use the word *theos* with reference to Christ (without necessarily equating Christ with the Father)," 3. a title of "God in Israelite/Christian monotheistic perspective," 4. for "that which is nontranscendent but considered worthy of special reverence," i.e., various humans (John 10:34f), some peoples' bellies or appetites (Phil 3:19), or even 5. "a title of Satan (2 Cor 4:4)" (BDAG, 398–400). Only the third usage clearly and always involves a thing with the divine essence, and there is no reason to think that the point of the second usage is to assert that Christ has the divine essence or is fully divine. In fact, regarding use 2, this entry highlights that a "fundamental semantic component" of *theos* is "the factor of performance, namely saviorhood or extraordinary contributions to one's society," which is extremely relevant to Christ, given his mighty, world-changing deeds (Rev 5:9–14).

To the contrary, it is opaque in what sense there are "three persons" in this model. If this soul has three cognitive faculties, each of which is "sufficient for personhood" (i.e., sufficient to make *that soul* a person), then that soul is overdetermined to be *a* person! And yet Craig clearly intends to be in the three-self or "social" Trinitarian camp.[5] Consider Ralph the bad husband.[6] He has three qualities, each of which is sufficient for being a bad husband: he cheats on his wife, he's a chronic liar, and he's a coward. But these qualities make him only one bad husband, not three. Or consider a sci-fi scenario where a man gets some cognitive upgrades. Since he has a large derriere, he decides to put it to good use, and has a donated brain installed in the left cheek, and another in the right. He now has to be careful how he sits, but it's worth it, since each of these brains gives him another set of cognitive capacities. Of course, it is not a brain which thinks, but rather the person whose brain it is, using the brain. Now, he can use three brains at once. But this doesn't make him three persons! Rather, he's just one, one who is over-determined to be a person; even if he lost any two of the brains, he'd still be a person, for any one would be sufficient.[7] Analogously, if Craig's imagined God could lose two of his cognitive faculties, he'd still be a single person, just not one who is twice over-determined to be a person.

Perhaps Craig imagines that personhood is the result not of a soul having a cognitive faculty, but rather that somehow persons supervene *on the cognitive faculties themselves*, at least, when they're had by some underlying soul. If so, I don't know what to make of such an unintelligible speculation. A faculty is just a complex property, a set of powers. But a person is a thinking thing, a thing that *has* powers. How would the existence of a set of powers, had by some concrete thing (here, the soul) somehow imply the existence of another concrete thing which is now somehow "in" that first thing? In sum, what Craig dubs "Tri-Personal Monotheism" (formerly "Trinity Monotheism") seems to be an undesirable one-self Trinity theory,[8] contrary to his intentions, or else it is an implausible and under-developed three-self theory.

---

5. See (53) and Moreland and Craig, *Philosophical Foundations*, 586–94.

6. I have raised this sort of objection before in "Hasker's Quests," 180.

7. I stipulate for my example that having a functioning human brain is necessary for being a human person. But the dualist who thinks a person is strictly speaking a soul can modify the example like this: a "complete" or normal and embodied human person must have at least one functioning human brain. Our three-brained man would, then, be over-determined to be a "complete" human.

8. I assume that Craig would agree that it would be a theological disaster and would seriously misfit the NT picture of the Father and the Son to say that there is but one self between them.

The bulk of Craig's chapter follows a common apologetic strategy. Everyone agrees that the Father is fully divine, so set that aside. Now argue that also the Son, even though a distinct person from the Father, is also fully divine, and likewise with the Spirit. Spike the ball; do a touchdown dance.

But the celebration is premature. Positing three distinct beings, each of which has all it takes to be a god (and so *is* a god)—is positing three gods. What I call Basil's Bane (see 138) still haunts today's Trinitarian apologists. Even if the above apologetic strategy is successful, how do we conclude that there is a single, tripersonal god? That is, after all, the key idea for any Trinity theory. Three divine persons who are three divine beings, that is, three gods, do not get us there.

Still, let's evaluate Craig's arguments about the Father, Son, and Spirit. Yes, everyone agrees that the Father is fully divine. But the highest or fullest way one can be divine is to be a god. And as I show in my opening essay, the NT clearly teaches and everywhere assumes that the one god is none other than the Father himself.[9] The one called "Yahweh" in the Old Testament turns out to be "God the Father" in the NT. When one manages to set aside the distorting spectacles of later traditions, this is about as clear as the biblical authors' views that Abram is none other than Abraham. As Craig says, "Jesus thought of God as his heavenly Father" (29), and here "God" and "his heavenly Father" refer to one and the same someone, the one true God of both testaments, Yahweh/the Lord God.

Craig spends the bulk of his chapter arguing that in the NT Christ is fully divine. Conveniently, he ignores what seem to be qualities Christ has which rule out his being fully divine, such as his dying, his being tempted to do wrong, and his being less than omniscient.[10] In a footnote Craig refers us to a work of popular apologetics which argues that the NT Christ must be fully divine because he has the Honors, Attributes, Names (and titles), Deeds, and Seat (i.e., throne) of God—the HANDS argument.[11] But a Unitarian understanding of Jesus explains the phenomena that a "deity of Christ" proponent supposes can only or best be explained by his two-natures theory. The Bible is quite explicit in saying that it was the one God

---

9. The sentence "*a* is the only *F*" implies that "*a* is an *F*." Thus, that the Father is the only god entails that the Father is a god. To say that he is a god is neither to imply nor to suggest that he is but one of several.

10. For a fuller list, see Moreland and Craig, *Philosophical Foundations*, 595, and for a yet fuller list and a thorough evaluation of Craig's unique incarnation theory, see my "Craig's Contradictory Christ."

11. Bowman and Komoszewski, *Putting Jesus in His Place*.

himself who generously empowered and awarded Jesus with the aforementioned amazing things.[12]

Craig suggests that the full deity of Christ is the best explanation for the NT authors' applications of what were originally texts about Yahweh to Christ. First, it must be said that many a lesser apologist nowadays instead concludes from this phenomenon that Yahweh and Christ are one and the same person. I have called this "the fulfillment fallacy," and it is clearly a beginner's error of NT interpretation. But Craig's error is almost as obvious. Given that inspired texts about Yahweh, as other scriptural texts, can have multiple meanings and so multiple fulfillments—which the NT authors clearly assume[13]—why couldn't a second meaning and a second fulfillment be about one who is less than fully divine? Where is it written that if the original meaning was about a fully divine person, then an additional meaning (perhaps known to God but not to the human author) must also be about a fully divine person? Craig's inference requires such a principle, but I have no idea how this could be justified.

Again, Craig is impressed by the NT use of "Lord" (*kurios*) for Jesus. But why think that this implies, assumes, or even hints that Jesus is fully divine? The lexicons tell us there are fundamentally two meanings in the NT for *kurios*: owner (of things and/or people), and "one who is in a position of authority, lord, master."[14] Among the possible referents in this second sort of use can be either God or Jesus, but also a husband, a government official, an angel, or a lesser deity of the pagans. To be sure, a frequent use of *kurios* in the NT is for God, particularly in Old Testament quotations, reflecting the ancient practice of substituting a word (often the Hebrew *adonai* or the Greek *kurios*) for God's proper name ("Yahweh"). And it certainly is striking that particularly after his resurrection and exaltation, *kurios* is a main title for the man Jesus. But as James Dunn has pointed out, "Paul speaks of God . . . as 'the *God* of our *Lord* Jesus Christ' [Eph 1:17. Cf. 2 Cor 1:3]. . . . [T]he

---

12. *Honors*: Rev 5; Phil 2:11. *Attributes*: the NT does not say that Jesus has any essential divine attribute, though it says that God gave him some *typically divine* attributes, namely the authority to forgive sins (Matt 9:8), to judge the human race (John 5:21-27; Acts 17:31), and to receive the sort of honor normally due to God alone (John 5:23). *Names*: Acts 2:36; Phil 2:9. *Deeds*: John 5:36; 14:10-12; Luke 4:18-21. *Seat*: Acts 2:34-35; Rev 5. See also Tuggy and Date, *Is Jesus Human and Not Divine?*

13. Hos 11:1 ("son" = Israel) and Matt 2:15 ("son" = Jesus); Isa 7:14; 8:8, 10 ("Emmanuel" = some ancient person, perhaps Hezekiah) and Matt 1:23 ("Emmanuel" = the man Jesus); Ps 45:6 ("God" = the king whose wedding it is) and Heb 1:8 ("God" = the risen and exalted Jesus). On the interpretations of each pair, see Beale and Carson, *Commentary*, 3-4, 7, 936-39, and for the first pair also see Enns's comments in Kaiser et al., *Three Views*, 198-202.

14. *BDAG*, 511; Danker and Krug, *Concise*, 210-11.

kyrios title is not so much a way of *identifying* Jesus with God, as a way of *distinguishing* Jesus from God."[15] Nor is this Lord only *numerically* different from God. Unlike God, he was mortal (Rom 5:6), temptable (Luke 4:1–13), subject to some degree of ignorance (Mark 13:32), under the authority of God (Mark 14:36; John 5:19; 20:17; 1 COR 11:3; 15:28), and a product of human ancestors (Matt 1:1–17; Luke 1:32; Rev 22:16). This is a man, not a second fully divine person. And the authors never soften the blow by ascribing these limitations to only one of his natures.

For Craig, it seems that the most important evidence that Christ is fully divine is that he is arguably called "God" eight times in the NT. Since he tells us that just one such instance is enough to prove his case, he seems to think that being called "God" implies being fully divine. But observe the gap between this premise and conclusion:

(1) Jesus is appropriately referred to as "God."

(3) Therefore, Jesus is fully divine.

This is an invalid argument; it is conceivable that (1) is true even though (3) is false. What's needed to close the gap is another premise, so that the whole argument is:

(1) Jesus is appropriately referred to as "God."

(2) For any x, x is appropriately referred to as "God" only if x is fully divine.

(3) Therefore, Jesus is fully divine. (1, 2)

This argument *is* valid; *if* (1) and (2) were true, *then* 3 would have to be true too. Unfortunately, there is nothing to be said in favor of (2)! (2) is neither self-evident, nor is it taught anywhere in Scripture, nor is it supported by any other sort of evidence. Even worse, according to the relevant lexicons, (2) is false; being appropriately and truly called "God" does *not* require having a divine nature.[16] And Jesus himself, or at least, the author of the Fourth Gospel, tells us as much (John 10:34–36).

And in case one thought that had only to do with the plural form "gods" (*theoi*), the reader can just figure out for herself that even the singular *theos* can refer to one who is less than fully divine by reading Hebrews 1.[17]

---

15. Dunn, *Did the First Christians Worship Jesus?*, 110.

16. See Danker and Krug, *Concise*, 168–69.

17. All of the plausible Jesus-as-"God" passages feature significant textual, translation, and/or interpretive problems. For the translation issue here, see Harris, *Jesus as God*, 192–202.

Here, the author quotes one of a string of Old Testament prophecies which, he urges, is fulfilled by Jesus.

But of the Son he says, "Your throne, O God, is forever and ever, and the scepter of righteousness is the scepter of your kingdom. You have loved righteousness and hated lawlessness; therefore God, your God, has anointed you with the oil of gladness beyond your companions" (Heb 1:8-9). Portions of Psalm 45 are quoted here, which seems originally to have been addressed to a human king, "the most handsome of men" and someone under God, who thus will not have been fully divine. The reader knows then that the "God" in Psalm 45:6 was originally a man who is under the only God, who is his god, that is, the god over him (Heb 1:9/Ps 45:7).

What about the fulfillment in Jesus though? The original subject, the king, wasn't supposed to be fully divine, but does the author of Hebrews think that Jesus is? The context tells us that he does not. For him the Son is like God and is the one through whom God has revealed himself in these latter days, but he is not the creator (the ultimate source of all else) even though in some sense God made the worlds or ages through him (v. 2). If this means that God made the cosmos through the pre-human Jesus, this *rules out* that Jesus is the creator in the biblical sense.[18] After "he had made purification for sins" (the reader knows: by his atoning death on the cross), this Son of God "sat down at the right hand of the Majesty on high, having become as much superior to angels as the name he has inherited is more excellent than theirs" (Heb 1:3-4). A fully divine person is necessarily and always "superior to angels," but this one was *given* that position by God. The main argument of the chapter is that now, post-resurrection and post-exaltation, Christ is superior to angels, something the author would feel no need to argue if he and his audience agreed that Christ is fully divine. In the next chapter we learn that through this man's death God has redeemed us, the Son's "brothers and sisters" (Heb 2:17). But the Almighty God, the reader knows, is essentially immortal, is not a human being, and is not a servant of God (or of anyone else). Further, this man exhibited heroic trust in God (Heb 12:2), something a fully divine person can't do.[19]

In this way the reader can see for herself that the first "God" mentioned in Heb 1:8-9, the (formerly) mortal man of whom God is the god, isn't himself literally a god (i.e., one who is fully divine/has the divine nature). The word "God" is ambiguous in these verses, being used once for God and

---

18. Here I grant for the sake of argument that the author thinks that God (i.e., the Father) created the physical cosmos through the pre-human Jesus, although I don't think this is his meaning; see Tuggy and Date, *Is Jesus Human and Not Divine?*, 117-19, 145-48; Tuggy, "Podcast 258"; Tuggy, "Podcast 259."

19. For more on this, see Tuggy, "Jesus as an Exemplar."

once for this other one, God's less-than-fully-divine yet unique and exalted human Son.

In sum, I grant for the sake of argument that the word *theos* is applied to Jesus in the eight texts Craig argues for. Those don't weaken my case a bit, nor do they strengthen his. The Bible is throughout in favor of monotheism (there's only one god) but it everywhere assumes the falsity of what I call mono-theos-ism (there's only one being which can truly be called "God" or "god"). The mainstream tradition was right in the late 100s to insist against the modalists on the folly of collapsing together (numerically identifying) Jesus and God. But Jesus' full deity was only really established as mainstream by the force of the emperor in 380–81[20]—which shows that, correct or not, the Bible does not *clearly* teach the full deity of Christ[21]—which it must if that were a belief required for salvation.[22]

A reader of Craig's chapter might think, for all she reads there, that Craig has never so much as heard of the literary device of personification. This is the cure for much of what he says about "the Holy Spirit." But for lack of space, I will instead say a few things about John 1. Craig assures us that "It is indisputable that John identifies the Logos with the pre-incarnate Christ" (39), thus calling Jesus "God" in verse 1.[23] To the contrary, that was an assertion of the second–fourth centuries. Logos theorists, who wanted Jesus to be the incarnation of a second, lesser "god" or deity (not the one true god), and it was, rightly, vigorously disputed in those times by other mainstream Christians. As I've argued at length elsewhere,[24] for John's original audience the key to this text would not have been, as Craig urges, Middle Platonism, but rather earlier Jewish literature, particularly of the wisdom genre, in which God's "word" or "wisdom" (and sometimes these characters are merged) is personified and said to have been with God at creation, or even to be the one through whom he created.[25] It is *this* that "was God" at the beginning and was "with" God, and who later as it were "became flesh"

20. For the basic historical facts here, see Tuggy, *What Is the Trinity?*, chapter 5; Freeman, *A.D. 381*, chapter 7.

21. *Clear* implications of a text are understood immediately by most competent readers.

22. In the NT this is not a required belief, as is evidenced by all the gospel preaching portrayed in Acts.

23. I assume that by "identifies with" Craig means to say that the author holds the man Jesus and the Logos to be one and the same, or at least to be the same person/self.

24. See my "What John 1 Meant."

25. For how most of the ideas at play in the Prologue to John, rightly understood, are found in previous Jewish writings (mainly, in the Hebrew Bible and the deuterocanonical writings), see Boyarin, "Logos, a Jewish Word," and my "What John 1 Meant." The one earlier text which is most similar to the Prologue is Sirach 24.

in the man Jesus. That this "Word" is a literal person who is the same person as the man Jesus is only an assumption that people, following the Logos theorists, bring to the text. And it is only traditional cherry picking that results in the Jesus of the Fourth Gospel being either God himself or fully divine. In fact, this gospel author *firmly* distinguishes Jesus from God, even while closely associating them, and for this author the Father is *explicitly* the only true god, and the god over the man Jesus. But this is another large argument for another time.

In conclusion, Craig has not even tried to show that a "doctrine of the Trinity" worthy of the name is either taught in or is the best explanation of what is revealed in Scripture.

IV. Ad Branson

The One God Is the Trinity

William Hasker

IN THE INTRODUCTORY SECTION of his essay, Beau Branson criticizes many other discussions of the Trinity on the ground that their authors are guilty of a *non sequitur*; they argue, "my model of the Trinity is coherent, therefore the doctrine of the Trinity is coherent" (56)—or, as paraphrased by Branson, "A is F, therefore B is F." I believe, however, that Branson is offering an incomplete picture of the thinking of his (many) interlocutors. I suspect that at least some of them mean to be claiming something more along the lines of:

(1) My model of the Trinity is an acceptable interpretation of the doctrine of the Trinity.

(2) My model of the Trinity is coherent. *Therefore,*

(3) The doctrine of the Trinity is coherent.

If indeed this is what they are meaning to argue, no logical fallacy is involved: if a doctrine has an acceptable interpretation that is coherent, that is enough to show that the doctrine itself is coherent. Now, it may be Branson's view that most, or even all, of the authors he is referring to are offering models that are *not* acceptable interpretations of the doctrine of the Trinity, so that an argument of the form given above would be unsound. But that, of course, would need to be argued on a case-by-case basis; a general condemnation of the sort offered by Branson would not suffice.

Branson's assertions concerning his own view are puzzling. He claims to have no theory about the Trinity. (He is not a prophet like Moses or Isaiah!) He does not propose to investigate *the Trinity*, but rather to study the *doctrine of the Trinity*, which is "much easier to know about . . . all one has to do is read! Then, like anything else in the history of ideas, one asks questions. 'Is this idea logically coherent? What are its metaphysical commitments?'

And so on. That will be my approach" (56). Branson, then, portrays himself as carrying on the sort of scholarly study of the doctrine of the Trinity that might equally well be done by someone who has no personal belief in that doctrine, someone like Adolph Harnack or, in our own time, Dale Tuggy.

But this can't possibly be an accurate statement of what is going on in Branson's essay. No one can read the essay without receiving the impression that Branson himself is *endorsing* Monarchical Trinitarianism—that he regards it either as the *truth* about the Trinity, or at least as close to the truth as we humans are likely to get. Notice that he laments as "a tragedy" the loss, due to Augustine, of the "theology of the theophanies" (70). No one writes like this about a view they are merely surveying in a detached scholarly inquiry. So why doesn't Branson's version of Monarchical Trinitarianism count as his theory of the Trinity?

It is also worth pointing out that Branson's view concerning what is most important to investigate concerning the doctrine of the Trinity seems somewhat idiosyncratic. To be sure, one cannot disagree that 3G, the "three Gods problem," is one of the most important objections to the doctrine that needs to be addressed. WIG, the "Who is God? problem," no doubt merits attention, but it is doubtful that it represents the next most important difficulty for the doctrine after 3G. It borders on the bizarre, however, to suppose that TP, the "Theophanies Problem," is the one, central, most important reason for affirming the doctrine of the Trinity. (This would suggest that, in the Western church, the doctrine was largely unmotivated once the theology of the theophanies had been abandoned!) One could, I suggest, search long and hard in recent and contemporary literature without finding anyone who agrees with that assessment![1]

It is evidently impossible for me, in this brief comment, to respond to all of the points made by Branson in his complex presentation. In view of this, I will limit myself to two items that bear especially on the relationship between Branson's Monarchical Trinitarianism and my own Social Trinitarianism. And at this point I need to make a retraction. In my main essay, I wrote, "'Monarchical' Trinitarianism . . . still insists on using 'God,' in a nominative sense, as referring only to the Father" (18). I now recognize that this statement represents a misunderstanding on my part. Branson lays out the core of Monarchical Trinitarianism as follows: "I call a 'Monarchical model' of the Trinity any model that affirms:

---

1. As a matter of information, my own stance on the theophany issue is agnostic. I don't dispute that the theophanies occurred, but I take no position as to whether the entity or entities that appeared consisted of one or more divine Persons, or an angel, or something else entirely.

i. The Father is the *archē anarchos* [source without source], and

ii. there is a use of 'God' as a singular term, such that it refers particularly to the Father *because* He is the *archē anarchos*" (65)

Thus Branson affirms that *there is* such a use of "God," but not that this is the *only* nominative use of that term. Social Trinitarians have no difficulty with the first of Branson's points, so long as they affirm the doctrine of processions (as I do). Social Trinitarians, furthermore, will recognize that there is an extremely common use of "God" as a singular term referring to the Father. They may not have held that the term so refers "*because* He is the *archē anarchos*"; they may have had in mind other reasons for this reference (such as the historical fact that Jesus taught his disciples to pray to God as his and their Father). But once the doctrine of processions is in place (as it was not for Jesus' disciples), there is no reason why this should not supply an additional reason why "God" is often used in referring to the Father. In view of this, Social Trinitarianism can easily qualify as a version of Monarchical Trinitarianism—as Branson himself notes (see 84). (Social Trinitarians may not, however, agree with John of Damascus and Gregory of Nazianzen—and perhaps with Branson?—that, in virtue of the eternal generation of the Son, the Son is inferior to the Father [66].)

The other main difference between Monarchical Trinitarianism and Social Trinitarianism is not, however, so easily overcome. I will introduce the problem by labeling it, following Branson's lead, as the WIDP problem—the "What is a divine Person?" problem. Anyone at all familiar with the recent discussion of the doctrine will recognize this question as a central focus of that discussion. I have given a clear and concise answer to that question by stating that the divine Persons are "centers of consciousness with the capacity for cognitive, affective, and volitional mental states, as well as the capacity for relationships with other persons." This, I believe, is a statement all Social Trinitarians will agree with. In contrast, I do not find anywhere in Branson's paper any similar clear, concise statement of what, ontologically, a divine Person *is*, according to his Monarchical Trinitarianism. I would go further, and hazard the conjecture that one will not be able to find in his paper anything that will provide a basis for a concise and informative answer to the WIDP question. (Of course, it is open to Branson to prove me wrong about that!)

However that may be, it is clear that he rejects my claim that each of the Persons is a distinct center of consciousness, a claim that, as he understands the matter, requires me to deny the doctrine of inseparable operations (see 84). On his view, then, there is only a single "center of consciousness"—a single person, in our sense of "person"—for the Trinity as a whole. This is a fundamental disagreement, and I maintain that it leaves Branson with major, perhaps insoluble, difficulties. I begin with an observation from Brian Leftow, who was criticizing a view according to which the divine Persons have only one set of mental states among them. Leftow writes, "Did the whole Trinity will, 'the Son shall become incarnate?' The Son could not learn from that that *he* would become incarnate unless he could also think to himself, in effect, 'I am the Son, so *I* shall become incarnate.'"[2] The Son, then, must have (or must be) a distinct center of consciousness, different from that of the Father, who thinks rather, "I am not the Son, so I shall not become incarnate." Clearly, no single center of consciousness can coherently have both of these incompatible thoughts.

Leftow, of course, is no Social Trinitarian, and cannot be supposed to be biased in favor of that view. It may be, however, that as a contemporary his views will not carry great weight with Branson. So let us turn to a source Branson regards as unimpeachable, Gregory of Nyssa. In "On Not Three Gods," Nyssa wrote,

> For as when we learn concerning the God of the universe, from the words of Scripture, that He judges all the earth, we say that He is the Judge of all things through the Son: and again, when we hear that the Father judgeth no man, we do not think that the Scripture is at variance with itself,—(for He Who judges all the earth does this by His Son to Whom He has committed all judgment; and everything which is done by the Only-begotten has its reference to the Father, so that He Himself is at once the Judge of all things and judges no man, by reason of His having, as we said, committed all judgment to the Son).[3]

In a previous writing, I commented on this passage as follows: "The upshot of this is: the Father delegates the work of judging to the Son; this delegation is an act of the Father alone, not of the Son. . . . Also, the Son performs the task of judging, not the Father; it is explicitly said that the Father does not, himself, perform this task."[4] But what, then, of the "inseparable operations"? The two Persons operate "inseparably" in that *each contributes towards the common project*—the project of *seeing to it that all persons are judged in wisdom and in justice*—and each does this in his own way, the Son by performing the act of judgment, and the Father by delegating that task to the Son. What could be more harmonious? And once again, there is no way that a single person, a single center of consciousness, could coherently have

---

2. Leftow, "Anti Social Trinitarianism," 70.
3. Gregory of Nyssa, "On Not Three Gods," 334.
4. Hasker, "Is the Latin Social Trinity Defensible?," 507.

both the thought that "I will not myself perform this task, but will delegate it to my Son," and also the thought that "I will perform this task, since it has been delegated to me by my Father." If Gregory had agreed with the view that there is only one center of consciousness in the Trinity as a whole, what he asserts in this passage would be metaphysically, and indeed theologically, impossible.[5]

The real bottom line for this discussion, however, is the depiction in the New Testament of the personal relationship between Jesus and his heavenly Father. All patristic writers, I believe without exception, understood this as a *relationship between Father and Son within the Trinity*. There are many, many instances in all four of the Gospels where this relationship is portrayed. An especially striking instance is found in the words of desolation from the cross: "My God, why have you forsaken me?" (Matt 27:46; Mark 15:34). There are also the closing chapters of the Fourth Gospel, where Jesus both describes in the most intimate terms his relationship with the Father (chs. 14–16), and addresses the Father directly in prayer (ch. 17). Jesus will ask the Father, and he will give to the disciples another Advocate (14:16). Those who love Jesus will be loved by his Father (14:21). Jesus does as the Father has commanded him, so that the world may know that he loves the Father (14:31). If the disciples keep Jesus' commandments, they will abide in his love, just as he has kept his Father' commandments and abides in his love (15:10). When the Advocate (the Holy Spirit) comes, whom Jesus will send from the Father, he will testify on Jesus' behalf (15:26). All that the Father has belongs to Jesus (16:15). If the disciples ask anything of the Father in Jesus' name, the Father will give it to them (16:23). The Father himself loves the disciples, because they have loved Jesus and have believed that he came from God (16:27). Addressing the Father in prayer, Jesus says, "Father, the hour has come; glorify your Son so that the Son may glorify you" (17:1). "All mine are yours, and yours are mine" (17:10). "I am not asking you to take them out of the world, but I ask you to protect them from the evil one" (17:15). "As you, Father, are in me and I am with you, may they also be in us" (17:21). "Righteous Father, the world does not know you, but I know you, and these know that you have sent me" (17:25). The Father's role in the dialogue is less perceptible to readers, but is seen in his speaking from heaven in endorsement and approval of his Son: at Jesus' baptism (Mark 1:11) and at the transfiguration (Mark 9:7): "This is my Son, the Beloved; listen to him!"

---

5. For additional discussion of Gregory's views in this connection, see my exchange with Scott Williams.

Altogether, this biblical evidence leads very directly to the point made in the argument presented in my main essay: "The early Christians perceived God the Father and Jesus Christ as distinct persons—as distinct centers of knowledge, will, love, and action." So far as I can see, Branson has no reason to disagree with any of the other premises of that argument. If that is so, then presumably he ought to agree with the conclusion of that argument: "There is a valid and acceptable version of monotheism in which there is more than one divine person." If Branson understands these texts differently, I should very much like to hear his alternative explanations, as well as his reasons for disagreeing with all of the church fathers about this matter.

Why Complicate Things?

William Lane Craig

Beau Branson claims to be interested in the *doctrine* of the Trinity, rather than in the *Trinity* itself.[1] This raises the question as to what the doctrine of the Trinity is. In contrast to my interest in the biblical doctrine of the Trinity,[2] Branson is interested in what we may call the creedal doctrine of the Trinity, that is to say, the statements of the Nicene and Constantinopolitan Creeds, which are the object of their confessional affirmations. Given that interest, it is surprising that Branson does not state the doctrine for us, though perhaps he thinks it too familiar to require citation. Here are the relevant portions:

> We believe in one God, the Father Almighty, Maker of heaven and earth, and of all things visible and invisible;
>
> And in one Lord Jesus Christ, the Son of God, the Only-begotten, Begotten of the Father before all ages, Light of Light, Very God of Very God, Begotten, not made; of one essence with the Father; by whom all things were made: . . .
>
> And we believe in the Holy Spirit, the Lord, and Giver of Life, who proceeds from the Father, who with the Father and the Son together is worshipped and glorified, who spoke by the prophets.

Whether we think it of vital importance to defend the coherence and truth of these statements will depend upon whether we take them to be authoritative for Christian faith. I do not. I take Scripture alone to be authoritative in matters of Christian doctrine, since it alone is inspired of God. I take

---

1. It is doubtful, however, that he is able to maintain this clean bifurcation throughout his essay. He seems to have plenty to say about the Trinity itself.

2. I.e., that there is exactly one God and that there are exactly three persons who are properly called God.

the ecumenical creeds to represent the accumulated wisdom of the first few centuries of the church and therefore worthy of our attention and respect; but they are not infallible. They are, in my view, what Michael Bird has called "a consultative norm" for Christian theology.[3] They must be assessed in light of their accord with inspired Scripture. Where they go beyond the Scriptures, they are not obligatory for Christian faith, and where they are inconsistent with Scripture, they should be rejected.

This is doubtless a very different perspective on the ecumenical creeds than Branson's, but the source of doctrinal authority is not the subject of our discussion here. Although a defense of the creedal doctrine of the Trinity is not my concern, nevertheless I am quite happy to hear Branson out in his defense of the coherence and truth of the creedal statements. I am simply not overly wrought about what conclusions we come to. What matters is the coherence and truth of the biblical doctrine of the Trinity.

Probative Component

Before we look at what Branson calls a "Monarchical Model" of the Trinity, let us say a word about the probative component of his case, the single argument he presents for belief in the Trinity. Oddly, it does not appeal to scriptural affirmations of the deity and individuality of the Trinitarian persons, but to what he calls the "Theophanies Problem," namely, that whereas the Scriptures testify that no man can see God and live, there are nonetheless many theophanies recorded in the Scriptures in which God is seen by surviving witnesses.

I am astonished that Branson considers Jewish "Binitarianism" or the theology of "two powers in heaven" to be "the ground out of which Trinitarianism sprang" and the Theophanies Problem to be "the most central motivation for both the Jewish and the Christian versions of this theology" (58). Branson's claim ignores what was the decisive influence, namely, the overwhelming impact of Jesus of Nazareth and belief in his teaching, death, and resurrection upon the movement that followed in his train. Jewish belief in intermediate figures, like exalted patriarchs and principal angels, or in personifications of divine attributes, like Wisdom, were part of what Larry Hurtado calls the "forces and factors" contributing to the background of the worship of Jesus in the early church, but do not suffice to explain it.[4] As a result of his extensive research, Hurtado concluded, "Although there were conceptual resources in ancient Jewish tradition that were likely drawn upon

3. Bird, *Evangelical Theology*, 64.
4. Hurtado, *Lord Jesus Christ*, chapter 1.

WHY COMPLICATE THINGS? 177

by earliest believers, there was not really a full analogy or precedent for the intensity and nature of the cultic expressions of devotion to Jesus."[5] In particular, the Jewish theology of two powers in heaven is a later development of rabbinic Judaism, which may even have reference to the beliefs of Jewish Christians. "None of the various 'chief agent' figures in second-temple Jewish texts gives us a full precedent or analogy for the more thoroughgoing way that the exalted Jesus was linked with God in early Christian devotion, and neither individually nor collectively do they represent a major mutation in ancient Jewish monotheism comparable to the cultic veneration of the exalted Jesus."[6] Rather the worship of Jesus can be understood only in the context of Christians' religious experience of the risen Christ.[7] "The only reasonable factor that accounts for the central place of the figure of Jesus in early Christianity is the impact of Jesus' ministry and its consequences."[8]

But let that pass. The more important point is that a plausible solution to the Theophanies Problem does not require Monarchianism or, for that matter, even Trinitarianism. At the heart of Branson's Monarchianism, as we shall see, is the procession of the Son and Holy Spirit from the Father, the sole ultimate reality (*archē anarchos*). The Theophanies Problem is said to be dissolved by holding that while God the Father is never seen, the pre-incarnate Christ is. The problem is that this solution is available to any Social Trinitarian, not just to Monarchians. One might go so far as even to deny the procession relations between the Trinitarian persons while affirming that the biblical theophanies were, in fact, Christophanies. Indeed, as Jewish monotheism itself bears witness, one need not affirm a plurality of divine persons at all in order to resolve the Theophanies Problem. One might appeal to a principal angel or another *ersatz* figure for God who appears to people in such experiences. Even more plausibly, I think, one might hold that such theophanies are merely visions of God, mental projections of the percipient's mind caused by God, or, on occasion, materializations of a humanoid figure caused by God, rather than sightings of God himself, who

---

5. Hurtado, *One God, One Lord*, 140–41.

6. Hurtado, *One God, One Lord*, 154. He explains, "Moreover, the high status of Jesus in earliest beliefs and devotional practice seems to represent a novel development in the Jewish religious matrix in which it first appeared. Although (as I contend) early notions of Jesus' status *vis-à-vis* God drew upon traditions about various 'chief agent' figures in ancient Jewish tradition, nevertheless, the Jesus-devotion reflected already in Paul's letters comprises a significant further development, a novel 'mutation.' This is reflected most dramatically in the novel 'dyadic' pattern of devotional practice already presumed in Paul's letters" (172).

7. Hurtado, *One God, One Lord*, 156; cf. Hurtado, *Lord Jesus Christ*, 64.

8. Hurtado, *Lord Jesus Christ*, 54.

as an incorporeal being does not reflect photons and so cannot be literally seen.

Branson will later pose a number of questions about such solutions (68ff). Is Christ the representative of the Trinity in such appearances? Probably not, since in the OT "God" or "the Lord" is used to designate the Father. Why does Scripture describe the Father as "the invisible God" of whom Christ is an icon? Since in typical NT usage *theos* refers to the Father, it is not in the least surprising that Christ is described as the image of the invisible God, though the relevant passage (Col 1:15) has nothing to do with theophanies. Branson is right to surmise that I feel uncomfortable about the nascent subordinationism not only in proto-Trinitarianism but also in Monarchical Trinitarianism; but such subordination, as comes to expression in the Father-Son relation, is unproblematic if it is confined, as explained in my opening essay, to the economic Trinity rather than extended to the ontological Trinity.

Hence, there is no reason to think that it is the responsibility of the doctrine of the Trinity to explain the apparently contradictory scriptural claims about the theophanies. In other words, whatever the church fathers may have thought, resolving this problem is not a *desideratum* of the doctrine of the Trinity. The Theophanies Problem fails to supply a convincing argument for the doctrine of the Trinity, much less for Monarchianism.

Model Component

But what about the Monarchical Model itself? According to Branson, this model affirms that

i. The Father is the *archē anarchos* [source without source], and

ii. there is a use of "God" as a singular term, such that it refers particularly to the Father *because* he is the *archē anarchos*" (65)

(i) implies that the Father is the sole *archē anarchos* or that the Father alone is the *archē anarchos*. It entails, given the doctrine of the Trinity, that the Son and the Spirit are derivative in their being, proceeding in some way from the Father, and (ii) affirms that "God" can be used as a singular term designating the Father, just as it is typically so used in the NT.[9] As stated, the "model" does not differ from Unitarianism. As an expression of Nicene orthodoxy,

---

9. On such a usage, see my opening essay. Singular terms include proper names like "Yahweh" and "Jesus Christ," definite descriptions like "the only begotten God" or "the only true God," and demonstratives like "*This* is the true God and eternal life," and serve to designate in a certain context of use a particular individual.

however, it is entailed by William Hasker's model of the Trinity, but Hasker does us the additional service of providing a model of the Trinity to make sense of Nicene doctrine rather than simply repeating it.

Branson considers two objections to Trinitarian doctrine. First, the allegation that it amounts to Tritheism (the Three Gods Problem), and, second, the ambiguity of the word "God" when used as a singular term (The "Who Is God?" Problem). Let us consider these objections in reverse order, since the second problem is, I think, easily dismissed.

"Who Is God?" Problem

What is the referent of the singular term "God"? Singular terms like proper names and definite descriptions depend for their reference on their context of use. The proper name "John Kennedy" in one context refers to the former president, but in another context to the current U.S. senator from Louisiana. Similarly, the definite description "the current U.S. senator from Louisiana" depends for its reference on the context of its use. In the same way the word "God" varies in its reference with its context of use. As explained in my opening essay, in the first-century Jewish context of use the word *theos* typically designates God the Father. But not always: in some contexts it clearly designates something or someone other than the Father. Thus the ambiguity of the referent of "God" taken in isolation is just the way of singular terms. There is no problem here at all. Singular terms have different referents in different contexts of use.

In an attempt to illustrate the significance of this alleged problem, Branson points to my response to Brian Leftow's dilemma for Trinity Monotheism. My response does, indeed, illustrate how "God" can be used in a different context to designate the Godhead rather than the Father. For I wrote,

> The persons of the Trinity are not divine in virtue of exemplifying the divine nature. For presumably *being triune* is a property of the divine nature (God does not just happen to be triune); yet the persons of the Trinity do not exemplify that property. It now becomes clear that the reason that the Trinity is not a fourth instance of the divine nature is that there are no other instances of the divine nature. The Father, Son, and Holy Spirit are not instances of the divine nature, and that is why there are not three Gods. The Trinity is the sole instance of the divine nature, and therefore there is but one God. So while the statement "The

Trinity is God" is an identity statement, statements about the persons like "The Father is God" are not identity statements.[10]

It is evident that in this context of use, "God" does not refer to the Father. Unfortunately, Branson represents me as affirming that "God has the divine nature, but the Father, Son and Holy Spirit don't" (60).[11] This is a mistake, apt to mislead our readers. What I affirm is that according to Trinity Monotheism the persons of the Trinity are not three cases or instances of the divine nature; there is only one God and so only one such instance. But I affirm, like Hasker, that the three persons share one, concrete divine nature and so have the divine nature without being instances of the divine nature.

In short, Branson's supposed difficulty for the doctrine of the Trinity is purely imaginary. The fact that singular terms like "God" shift their reference with their context of use is unremarkable and unproblematic.

The Problem of Tritheism

So let us turn to the first problem, the allegation that the doctrine of the Trinity is Tritheistic. Branson thinks that the only sense in which the Bible is monotheistic is that it affirms that there is a sole ultimate reality, which, given the Bible's alleged commitment to the divine processions, it identifies with the Father. He says, "*in the only sense in which the Bible is clearly monotheistic*, the monarchy of the Father obviously guarantees monotheism" (74). So he says that "Arians and Trinitarians actually all agree with each other, as well as with Late Second Temple Jewish Binitarianism," presumably in affirming that the Father is the sole ultimate reality. Since neither the Arian Logos nor the Jewish intermediate figures were uncreated beings, it seems to follow that Trinitarians believe that the Father alone is uncreated and the Son and Spirit are creatures, which would be not only an absurd interpretation of the Cappadocians, but also incompatible with the biblical witness to the equal deity of the Son and Spirit with the Father. But Branson

---

10. Craig and Moreland, *Philosophical Foundations*, 590. For revision of Trinity Monotheism's identity claim, see my opening essay and reply to Hasker.

11. Branson also says that "according to Craig, one can be 'divine' *either* by having the divine nature, *or* through something like analogical predication" (60n15), a doubly inaccurate statement. For I say that one can be divine either by being an instance of the divine nature or by being in some sense a distinctive part of God, which makes no appeal to analogical predication with respect to God. Interestingly, Branson suggests that I could merely relabel my model, which is exactly what I have done in my opening essay. I now prefer the label "Tripersonal Monotheism" over Leftow's label "Trinity Monotheism." But this relabeling is unproblematic.

saves the day by holding that the Father, Son, and Spirit, and only they, share the same divine nature. He says (80),

> Despite differences in their metaphysics, the fathers we have in view all agree that:
>
> There is only one god$_\text{ULTIMATE-SOURCE}$, the Father,
>
> and:
>
> The Trinity is one god$_\text{NATURE}$,
>
> because the divine nature is *undivided* among the Trinitarian *hypostases*.

I take this to be basically the same view stated and defended more perspicuously by Hasker, that only the Father is unbegotten, the Son and Spirit proceeding from him, and that there is only one concrete, divine nature which is shared by all the persons. When Branson talks about the modern view of "counting by identity," what he is talking about is the commonsensical conviction that if *x* and *y* are not identical, then they are not the same object. But Branson seems to affirm that the Trinitarian persons are non-identical but nonetheless numerically one object, which leaves him open to the same objections attending Brower and Rea's model of the Trinity based upon the weird relation of numerical sameness without identity, objections that Branson does not address.[12] Rather than pin Trinitarian doctrine to an obscure and controversial theory of counting, Hasker and I explicate the Trinitarian persons' being *homoousios* in a way that is both clear and plausible.

Branson complains, "Craig seems nonplussed about whether there is more than one god$_\text{ULTIMATE-SOURCE}$ in his model, though I have never understood his response. Somehow, all the persons *and* the Trinity are *a se*? But somehow this isn't four things that are *a se*?" (83). Since in my context of use, "God" refers to the entire Godhead, there is, indeed, one "god$_\text{ULTIMATE-SOURCE}$," namely the triune God. The persons are not Gods. Similarly, the persons are not substances and so not "things" in any objectionable sense. It is possible to count even "things" that do not really exist, such as Wednesdays in March or holes in the ground or hours before dawn or drawbacks to the plan. In such a lightweight sense, it is not problematic to speak of four "things" that are *a se*.

Branson's further claim that the operations of the divine persons *ad extra* are one and inseparable is a superfluous add-on that finds no justification in the creeds. Indeed, he admits that this claim is incompatible with there being three centers of self-consciousness in God, implying a one-self

---

12. See the trenchant critique by Hughes, "Defending the Consistency of the Doctrine of the Trinity."

view of the Godhead that is inadequate and unbiblical. This is to meet the threat of Tritheism by needlessly collapsing into Unitarianism.

Branson adds, "I'm also unsure whether or how [Craig's] account applies to there being one god$_{\text{POWER/ACTION}}$ or whether or how it generalizes to 3F. Is the Trinity as a whole the one Savior of Isaiah 43–45? Is Jesus *not* a savior? Do we have two senses of 'savior,' one being something like '*part of a savior*'?" (83–84). In reply, I reject as wholly implausible and unbiblical the view that the persons' *opera ad extra sunt indivisa*. This is especially the case if Branson is right that the indivisibility of divine action implies that the divine persons "*do not* have distinct centers of consciousness" (75n61). For then we do not have three persons. In Isaiah 43–45 "the LORD your God" doubtless refers, in line with customary OT usage, to God the Father. He is Israel's Savior. Of course, in another context of use, Jesus is also our Savior. No, there are not two *senses* of "Savior," but the *referent* of "Savior" varies, as is typical with singular terms, with its context of use.[13]

Conclusion

In conclusion, while I am open to the creedal doctrine of the Trinity, Branson has not done a very good job in motivating it, particularly the doctrine of the divine processions. The "Who Is God?" objection appears to me to be a straw man, which need trouble none of us. But the "Three Gods" objection is handled more persuasively by Hasker, while Branson's affirmation that the external acts of the Trinity are indivisible smacks of Unitarianism.

---

13. We do well to keep in mind Gottlob Frege's important distinction between the sense and reference of singular terms. Just as "God" and "Father" may in certain contexts have the same referent even though they do not have the same sense, so "Savior" may have the same sense in different contexts of use while having different referents. For further explanation, see note 3 of my opening essay.

An Ancient, Triadic, Unitarian Theology

Dale Tuggy

I'M GRATEFUL FOR DR. Branson's carefully argued and historically informed work on Trinity theories. In his chapter here he goes some way towards showing what ancient theologians like Gregory of Nyssa were thinking. I shall argue, though, that he does not come close to giving a contemporary Christian a believable "doctrine of the Trinity."

    As an Orthodox analytic theologian, Branson's main concern seems to be not biblical support, but that an account of the Three should be orthodox, i.e., in keeping with the teachings of the ecumenical creeds, and this is secured in his view by what he lays out as being the view of the so-called Cappadocian fathers.[1] In my view Branson does not have any account of *the Trinity*, i.e., the tripersonal God. But he does have an account of the triad, i.e., God, God's Son, and God's Spirit. In Branson's view the one true God is *not* the Trinity, but rather the Father alone; I say that makes him a Unitarian, one with views broadly similar to famous early modern Unitarians (sometimes smeared as "Arians") such as Samuel Clarke, John Biddle, and Thomas Emlyn.[2] Now, Branson has argued that my view that no theology counts as "Trinitarian" unless it involves a tripersonal God is a crazy, gerrymandered mis-definition.[3] For my part, I think his attempts at defining the concepts *Trinitarian* and *Unitarian* are non-starters. But I don't have room to make that case here, so I'll just note this disagreement to set it aside.[4]

    1. These are the bishops and Nicene polemical authors Basil of Caesarea (d. 379), Gregory of Nyssa (d. 395), and Gregory of Nazianzus (d. 390).

    2. On these see Clarke, *Scripture Doctrine*; Pfizenmaier, *Trinitarian Theology*; Biddle, *Confession of Faith*; Biddle, *Testimonies*; Emlyn, *Humble Inquiry*.

    3. Branson, "One God, the Father," 13–20.

    4. I hope to publish a paper in which I criticize Branson's definitions of the concepts *Trinitarian* and *Unitarian* and address his interesting criticisms of my past attempts.

Speaking of definitions, Branson's "Monarchical Trinitarianism" is defined both broadly and oddly.[5] Naturally, Branson's brand of subordinationist Unitarianism, or if one likes, Nicene triadology, will count as "Monarchical Trinitarianism." But so will any tripersonal God theology, so long as it includes traditional speculations about "processions." So Hasker would be in, but Craig would be out. Who else is "in"? Me! Any Unitarian Christian will agree with "Monarchical Trinitarianism," for all of us think that the Father is ultimate, and that there is a singular referring use of "God" on which it refers to the Father because he's ultimate, since he's the only god. Many readers will think this is an abuse of the word "Trinitarian." Note too how odd a definition it is. Its first requirement is metaphysical, basically that the Father is what I call ultimate,[6] whereas the second requirement has to do with how the word "God" is used.

In Branson's view, the most important challenges to a Trinitarian theology are: what should we think the usual referent of the word "God" is when it is used as a singular referring term,[7] and what Branson calls "3G." One might think that 3G is the metaphysical/theological difficulty of why exactly "the doctrine of the Trinity" doesn't imply three gods. But no, Branson explains, "3G seeks to derive a contradiction from the claims that the Father, Son, and Spirit are each 'god' [i.e., called that] (though all non-identical) and the claim that there is only one god" (73). This problem isn't directly metaphysical or theological, but is a concern about words, about how "god" (etc.) is used. But monotheism (that there's only one god) doesn't imply mono-theos-ism (that only one can be truly referred to as "god" or "God"), since beings other than the one God can be referred to as "gods" or "god" or "God." Says who? The lexicon authors,[8] the authors of both testaments,[9]

This requires discussing uncontroversial desiderata for these types of concept definitions for purposes of classification.

5. In earlier unpublished works Branson advocated a definition of "Monarchical Trinitarianism" which included the strict identity of the one god with the Father, a usage of the term that survives in online discussion and in Sijuwade, "Building the Monarchy of the Father," 436–38. Why not instead define "Monarchical Trinitarianism" as requiring what for Branson (and me) is a very important truth, namely, that the one God is one and the same with the Father alone? I take it, because this would rule out many present-day Orthodox theologians as holding to what Branson thinks is the historically orthodox theology (Tuggy, "When and How?," 45).

6. "An ultimate is a being/entity which is unique and unsurpassable in reality (degree and/or kind) and/or in explanatory priority. Roughly, an ultimate is supposed to be the highest, most basic, most real, or 'farthest back' being" ("On Counting Gods," 9).

7. What Branson calls WIG, the "who is God?" problem—really, the who is "God" problem.

8. *BDAG*, 398–400.

9. Gen 31:19; Exod 7:1; 15:11; Num 25:2; Deut 10:17; Pss 45:6–7; 82:6; John 10:35; Heb 1:8–9; 2 Cor 4:4.

the more learned "fathers,"[10] and well-informed Unitarian and Trinitarian Christians.[11]

Branson generously credits me with raising the "who is God?" problem. But as he means that, I have long taken the answer to be: for NT authors and for most ancient theologians before the time of Augustine, the main and usual referent of "God" is the Father.[12] It then, as I've documented, shifts somewhat to the Trinity.[13] But these are facts that any Trinitarian should admit.[14] Rather, what I've long focused on is not a question about any word,[15] but rather this: for the NT authors, who or what do they identify with Yahweh, with the only god, the one who created the cosmos on his own?[16] To round out his triad of "most important desiderata" when it comes to triadology, we have this question: who should a Christian think "the theophany figure" is? To me these are *far* from being the most pressing issues for a Trinitarian, or for a Nicene triadologist like Branson.[17]

About this "Theophany Problem," the NT authors believe that God has worked through angels (Acts 7:53; Gal 3:19; Heb 2:2), but they show no anxiety about identifying who exactly "the angel of the LORD" was,[18] and in

---

10. Origen, *Commentary on the Gospel according to John*, 2.2.12–32; Tertullian, *Against Marcion*, 1.7; Novatian, *Trinity*, 76–78.

11. Chandler, *God of Jesus*, 324; Emlyn, *Humble Inquiry*, 47–50; Harris, *Jesus as God*, 21–50.

12. "When *(ho) theos* ['(the) god'] is used, we are to assume that the NT writers have *ho pater* [the Father] in mind unless the context makes this sense of *(ho) theos* ['(the) god'] impossible" (Harris, *Jesus as God*, 47). In my view this usage reflects their theological assumption that the only god and the Father are one and the same.

13. See my "When and How?"

14. Hasker, *Metaphysics of the Tri-Personal God*, 246–47.

15. However, as I briefly explain in my opening chapter, I do think this fact about the early usage of "God" needs explaining, and that the best explanation seems to be that they identified the Father alone with the one true God. But just the fact of usage itself is logically consistent with any Trinity theory.

16. Gen. 1–2 (and note the singular verb "created" in 1:27); Isa 44:24; 45:12; Ps 33:6–9; Mark 10:6; 13:19; Rom 1:20; Acts 4:24; 14:15; 17:24–31; Heb 11:3; Eph 3:9; 1 Tim 4:3–4; Rev 4:11; 10:6; 14:7. Though I don't have the space to discuss them here, I would urge that the alleged Christ-creator NT texts be considered in light of these *clear* texts which ascribe creation to Yahweh/the Father alone.

17. Far more pressing for today's Christian are: Why does this alleged triune God never get mentioned as such in the NT? Why is there no passage that clearly teaches that God is triune? Why are eternal generation and eternal procession never taught there? And do the texts really require that the Father and Son (and Spirit) are equally divine?

18. Nor do they clearly assume, and nor should anyone assume, that "the messenger/angel of Yahweh" is one and the same someone in all the texts where such a phrase appears.

contrast to Justin,[19] they never say that any "God" or "Lord" seen must have been the pre-human Jesus. They would deny that Christ is any angel (Rom 5:15, 18; Heb 1:5–14), and in their view, *"in these last days* he [God] has spoken to us by a Son" (Heb 1:2 NRSV-UE; emphasis added). Aside from some texts traditionally interpreted as saying that God created the cosmos through the pre-human Jesus (or through the Logos),[20] there is no NT text that ascribes activity to Christ in OT times.[21]

I am grateful for Dr. Branson's careful engagement with my article on the concepts of monotheism, polytheism, and atheism. Its main point is that what the "polytheist" says there are many of is not quite the same as what the monotheist insists there is only one of. With an eye towards understanding the views of many religions, I distinguish the concept of a deity, roughly, a supernaturally powerful self, from the concept of a god, a deity who is ultimate.[22] In monotheistic contexts the unique god is supposed to be a god, not a mere deity. Thus, when someone like the ancient Nicene bishop Basil says that "There are not two gods because there are not two fathers,"[23] he is repeating what was then a well-worn strategy. Justin, seemingly the initiator of Logos theories, spoke of the Logos as "another god" who is "distinct in number" from God (i.e., the Father).[24] So too Origen held that the Logos is "a second god."[25] This new doctrine, the Logos theorists tell us, was met with resistance, particularly from less philosophically sophisticated Christians, who insisted that there was only one god and only one creator.[26] Now, had quotation marks been invented, the Logos theorists might have responded: that there is only one god and only one creator—these truths don't require that only one is called "god" or "God" or "creator." But what they do when challenged on the monotheistic credentials of their theology is to point out

---

19. Justin Martyr, *Dialogue with Trypho*, chapters 126–27.

20. For some early catholic authors, like Origen, these are not the same, although a standard understanding of Chalcedonian Christology is that the Logos/divine Son is the same self as the man Jesus, and the only self within the complex, two-natured, incarnate Christ.

21. No, not 1 Corinthians 10:4, on which see Dunn, *Christology in the Making*, 183–84; and no, not Jude 5, on which see my "Jude 5" and Wasserman, *Jude*, 262–66.

22. Tuggy, "On Counting Gods," 3–11.

23. As quoted by Branson, p. 65.

24. Justin Martyr, *Dialogue with Trypho*, chapters 50, 55–56, 62.

25. Origen, *Against Celsus*, 5.39, 6.61, 2.9.

26. Tertullian, *Against Praxeas*, 3; Origen, *Commentary on the Gospel according to John*, 2.2.16–18; Novatian, *Trinity*, 30.16; Origen, *Dialogue*, sections 1–4.

the uniqueness of the Father.[27] In short, only he is divine in the highest sense, the sense that implies being a god (and not only a deity).

Basil, then, deploys this old move. But because of the Nicene Creed it no longer clearly works! This says that the Father eternally shares full and complete deity or divinity with two others. But divinity or deity is that property in virtue of which its owner is a god. This looks, on the face of it, like a Tritheistic scheme, on which one god eternally causes the existence of a second and a third god.

Here, Branson would point out that in my view, such a scheme should count as "monotheistic polydeism" (83), on which the Father is the one god, each of the persons is a deity, but the Son and Spirit are not also gods. Quite so! But the Cappadocian bishops, over-reacting to the late non-Nicene ("Arian") Eunomius, deny that divinity includes aseity, or not being from any other. So while on my view, being eternally generated or spirated rules out being a god (because it rules out being ultimate), making the Son and Spirit mere deities, for these later Nicenes (and for traditionalists like Branson), it is full divinity, not some lesser sort, which the Father eternally gives to the Son and Spirit. In short, the old monotheism-defending move has expired; the signature Nicene claim, the much-vaunted *homoousion*, has rendered it point-missing. After 381, mainstream theologians will no longer allow that the Logos and the Spirit are less divine than the Father.

I have never understood what Branson's answer to this apparent implication of Tritheism is. It's all well and good to proclaim with the NT that the one God just is the Father, but then when you add that God gave everything it takes to be a god to two others,[28] why doesn't that imply Tritheism? I invite him to answer that question, perhaps giving an answer to what I called "Basil's Bane" in my response to Hasker (see 138).

In the meantime, let's review and then evaluate the ancient answer he provides. First, counting things as two because they're non-identical is a mistake; the ancients assumed that counting should be by "division." And doing that, we should only count the persons as being one god_{NATURE}—i.e., "god" in the sense of a thing having the divine nature. Or if you want to use the word "god" in the sense of a thing performing the characteristic god-action (whatever that is!), then the persons must be counted as only

---

27. Justin Martyr, "First Apology," 26, 30–31 45, sections 6, 12–13, 32; Tertullian, "Against Marcion," 1.3–7; Origen, *Against Celsus*, 8.1–14; Novatian, "Trinity," chapters 30–31; Lactantius, "Divine Institutes," 4.6–8, 29–30; Arnobius, *Case*, 1.29–42; Athenagoras, "Embassy," 10; Irenaeus, *Against Heresies I*, 1.10; Irenaeus, *Against the Heresies II*, 2.28.4–6.

28. I hold (and Craig concurs) that this metaphysically impossible, as a property like aseity is in principle such that it can't be given to another.

one god$_{POWER/ACTION}$—i.e., "god" in the sense of one who does the aforesaid action—because in anything that they do regarding this world, we can only (supposedly!) discern one token action.

Branson says that the important "fathers" denied that "god" means "thing with the divine nature." Now it is true that *if* that's what the word "god" meant, then if there were three things each of which had the divine nature, then it would follow that there were three gods. But this point about the meaning of "god" is a mere distraction. Even if it is false that "god" means "thing with the divine nature," this can still be true: something is a god if and only if it is a thing with the divine nature.[29] As best I can tell, Branson *agrees* with this, so denouncing the definition of "god" as "thing with the divine nature" is not to the point. The biconditional (if and only if) statement just given says that having the divine nature is necessary and sufficient for being a god. Three numerically distinct things, each of which has all it takes to be a god: yes, that's three gods![30]

Here Branson urges that counting things by identity leads to paradoxes, seemingly to lend credibility to the rival "division" approach. Space doesn't permit a full rebuttal. I'll just register my agreement with John Hawthorne that identity is an unproblematic and basic concept we have, and so "Puzzles that are articulated using the word 'identity' are not puzzles about the identity relation itself."[31] Of the five problems Branson asserts (76), (i) is really about mereology (theories about parts and wholes), (ii)–(iv) are really about the metaphysics of material objects, and (v) is really about our concept of change.

The problem with urging that things ought to be counted using some relation less demanding than identity, is that the weaker relation will allow simultaneous qualitative differences between things which we're being told to count as one and the same. We'll reply, "but we can *see* the differences," whether that is literally or metaphorically true. How is it supposed to be that the Trinitarian knows that the Father and the Son are *not* the same divine person? It is by simultaneous differences, e.g., the Son is crucified while the Father is not. Here we apply the principle called the distinctness of discernibles,[32] and it goes hand in hand with counting by identity. The anti-

---

29. In other words, if anything is a god, then it has the divine nature, and anything with the divine nature is therefore a god.

30. And this must of necessity be false, since a god (in contrast to a mere deity) is by definition unique.

31. Hawthorne, "Identity," 99.

32. I would formulate this as: necessarily, for any x and any y, if x and y could possibly simultaneously intrinsically differ, then $x \neq y$. It is logically equivalent to the indiscernibility of identicals, which says that necessarily, for any x and y, $x = y$ only if

modalist premise of Trinity theories commits the Trinitarian to counting by identity. She must deny that "Father" and "Son" are co-referring names like "Abram" and "Abraham." Each name ("Father," "Son") does refer, but the things to which they refer are *not* one and the same, not identical. Rather, one name refers to this person, and the other to a numerically distinct person. How do we know they're not *the same* person? Because they simultaneously differ.

Despite its impressive ancient pedigree, it seems that counting by divisibility is a mistake. Suppose that a man marries two women who happened to be conjoined twins who are *so* conjoined that spatially separating them would instantly kill both. If we count by division, we must count them as one living woman and one living wife—which they clearly are not, despite their overlapping bodies. (If one objects that the divisibility in question need only be divisibility in principle, i.e., "in at least one possible world," change my example here so that God has somehow made these women so that *necessarily* they can't live while separated. Counting them as one will still be mistaken.)

Finally, let us address the implausible claim that the persons of the Trinity must be the same god because the universal nature or essence divinity/deity is not spatially divided among the persons. This is implausible because it has at its heart an implausible claim of impossibility, that multiple gods could not share a not-spatially-divided divine nature. But why on earth not?[33] Suppose that angels are wholly non-physical and non-spatial. One would think that the Almighty could create two such angels, which will share the universal angelic nature such that it is not spatially divided between them. Why would things be different when it comes to divine persons? If Branson thinks it is true that "The Trinity is one god$_{NATURE}$, because the divine nature is *undivided* among the Trinitarian *hypostases*" (80), then he needs to support the impossibility claim that would keep this from being a non sequitur,[34] by showing us how a contradiction would follow from these premises:

---

it is impossible that x and y should intrinsically differ. The concept of possibility or impossibility in each is metaphysical. Roughly put, in short, even possible difference guarantees distinctness, and sameness requires no possible difference. The underlying intuition is that we know that one and the same thing at a single time (or in timeless eternity) can't intrinsically be a certain way and also not.

33. I'm not assuming here that it is metaphysically possible that there be many gods; rather, I'm asking how any contradiction follows from the said scenario which has been asserted to be impossible. This is one way we judge that some scenario is metaphysically impossible; we show how it implies at least one contradiction.

34. In other words, if it is true that the divine nature is undivided between the persons, it doesn't seem to follow that those persons are one and the same thing with the divine nature.

(1) $a \neq b$

(2) a is an F

(3) b is an F

(4) F-ness is not spatially divided between a and b

(5) a and b are *not* the same F

I don't see how this can be done. That's why it seems to me implausible that having the same universal divine nature which isn't spatially divided should make the persons the same god. What is needed is a derivation of a contradiction from (1)–(5); this would show that (1)–(5) could not all be true when F = the property of being a god.

In conclusion, let's briefly review the dispute in this book about what or who the unique God of the Bible is. As I showed in my chapter, this unique someone is called "Yahweh" in the OT and "God the Father" in the NT. This clashes with the mainstream tradition, dominant since around 381, of identifying the one God with the Trinity. Craig and Hasker defend this claim by denying that any of the persons is a god (since the Trinity is the only god). Other Trinitarians urge instead that there are "relative" identity relations that don't reduce to absolute ones, for instance the Father and the Son can be the same god while being different persons (god-identical but not person-identical).[35] Others urge that, while clearly the persons are distinct (i.e., no pair are absolutely numerically identical), they are "to be counted as one."[36] The ancient position Branson discusses falls into this category. But it's no good to tell the reader to "count as one" things that she knows to simultaneously (or timelessly) differ.

"The doctrine of the Trinity" is touted in countless popular sources as that by which the "triune God has revealed himself to us"[37] in Scripture. But it is neither explicitly nor implicitly taught in Scripture; it arose in the late-fourth Christian century after a lot of theological speculations that culminated in the so-called "Arian" controversy.[38] If God didn't reveal "the doctrine of the Trinity" in the Bible, did he do this instead in the late fourth century?

---

35. For these see my "Trinity," section 2.1; Branson, "No New Solutions." For how these claims clash with the NT, see my *Monotheism*, chapter 10. In my view Hasker and Craig are right to not put any stock in such solutions (Hasker, *Metaphysics of the Tri-Personal God*, chapter 15; Moreland and Craig, *Philosophical Foundations*, 591).

36. Brower and Rea, "Material Constitution and the Trinity"; Tuggy, "Constitution Trinitarianism."

37. Reeves, *Delighting in the Trinity*, 12.

38. Hanson, *Search for the Christian Doctrine of God*.

Protestants should demur (Jude 3), but so should anyone. The Almighty is a competent revealer; when he reveals something people "get it" and believe it, and it doesn't prove to be an unending source of avoidance, confusion, and disputes. But this is what "the Trinity" is. Is it implied by Scripture or not? Does it require "processions" and the idea of a tripersonal god, or are those optional? Does it or doesn't it require "counting as one" things we know to differ? Does expressing it require two sentences or many more? Is it monotheistic and not polytheistic because only the Trinity is a god, or because each person is a god, but they should be considered the same god? And are the "persons" of the Trinity selves or something less?[39]

In contrast, followers of Jesus have always believed that the man Jesus is God's Messiah, that God confirmed this by the miracles he did through him, that God raised him from the dead and exalted him, and that he's coming back to rule some day, after which by him God will raise and judge. There are, to be sure, philosophical and theological puzzles to be investigated here, and a minority of Christians who question a few of these. But the widespread agreement in these matters greatly contrasts with "the doctrine of the Trinity," which is widely avoided by the many and disputed among the learned.

Against Craig, Hasker, and most "Trinitarian" theologians, how can these traditions require us to disagree with the NT authors about the only god (the Father vs. the Trinity)? Here, Branson and I side with the NT (and most early catholic theologies) against later catholic traditions and our two interlocutors. But for Branson, being more Orthodox is the way, committing to the theology of its founding fathers. For me, Protestantism shows the best way forward. When catholic traditions, particularly late, confused, and confusing ones, conflict with the New Testament, we ought to prefer the latter, going back to apostolic teaching, even when so many great theologians have backed these sorts of speculations.

---

39. The Trinitarians in this discussion all hold the "persons" to be selves, but it is common for Trinitarian theologians to hold that strictly the Trinity is a single self, and God's "persons" are something like ways God is (Tuggy, "Trinity," section 1.).

V. Ad *Tuggy*

T vs. U? A Mis-Framed Debate

William Hasker

DALE TUGGY DEVOTES ALMOST all of his entire essay to a single argument. He puts forward two hypotheses, "T" for Trinitarian, and "U" for Unitarian, and asks which of them is more predictive with respect to a selection of phenomena in the text of the New Testament (NT). The good news for Tuggy is that the argument is sound: hypothesis U predicts the selected phenomena much more successfully than hypothesis T. The bad news is that, in spite of its soundness, this argument contributes very little towards Tuggy's ultimate goal, which is to show that the NT is more supportive of his Unitarian view than of the Trinitarianism represented by William Craig and me.[1] The reason for this failure is found in certain flaws in the way the argument is set up. There are three main flaws:

1. *It is problematic to reduce the issues in play to a simple binary choice between two competing hypotheses.* Clearly the relevant data in the NT text are numerous, complex, and potentially confusing. There are at least ten principal authors, likely more, writing in different styles, at different times, with different purposes, and to different groups of Christian believers. The development of doctrine in the early Christian church was complex and is at present highly contested. Reducing this complexity to a single choice between alternatives runs a risk of over-simplifying the issues and overlooking significant alternative possibilities. If such a reduction is attempted, it is evidently important that the hypotheses presented represent the best, most accurate alternative ways of viewing the perspectives that are in dispute. As we shall see, this is not the case for Tuggy's alternatives.

---

1. I do not include here Branson's view, because I am unclear as to what that view amounts to, in virtue of Branson's failure (as I see it) to answer the "What Is a Divine Person?" problem. (See my response to Branson.)

2. *The "Trinitarian" hypothesis, T, represents an extreme position that no reasonable, well-informed Trinitarian will endorse.* "Hypothesis T (for Trinitarian) is the conjunction of three claims about the NT authors: that they assume the numerical identity of the one God with the Trinity, the full deity of the Son, and the full deity of the Holy Spirit" (88). This comes very close to attributing to the NT authors (all of them?) the fully developed Nicene doctrine of the Trinity. But on Tuggy's own accounting, the identity of the one God with the Trinity was not accepted until late in the fourth century. If we were to assume that the NT authors already accepted Nicene Trinitarianism, we might well expect them to have said things differently than what we actually find in the NT writings. So it is completely unsurprising that this assumption has very low predictive power with respect to various features of those writings. On the other hand, it will be very hard—likely impossible—to find among intelligent, well-informed, contemporary Trinitarians anyone who embraces hypothesis T. Frankly, it is hard to understand why Tuggy thought it worth his while to refute a hypothesis when the refutation will affect only a vanishingly small proportion of his opponents.

Still, it is perhaps understandable that someone does a less than optimal job of formulating the position of an opponent. Presumably, Tuggy will have been more successful in stating his own favored alternative, and if that alternative shows impressive success in predicting important features of NT discourse, that will constitute important evidence in favor of his overall position. Maybe so; we shall see.

3. *The "Unitarian" hypothesis, U, falls short of providing an adequate statement of the position that needs to be defended, because it is ambiguous between two significantly different views.* "Hypothesis U is that the NT authors assume the numerical identity of the one God with the Father, and that neither the Son nor the Holy Spirit is fully divine" (88). Here the problem is not that Tuggy, and Unitarians who agree with him, will have difficulties in accepting U. The problem, rather, is that U will be welcomed also by many others whose views are in serious disagreement with Tuggy-style Unitarians. In terms of the typology set forth in my main essay, Tuggy is a "classical Unitarian," one who affirms a "human-only" Jesus, one who ontologically is a human being and nothing more, and insists that such a view is consistent with what the NT says about him. But U is also acceptable to subordinationists or Arians, according to whom Jesus is a supremely great, supernatural being, but ontologically he is a creature, not God. This is a much different position than that of classical Unitarians, and we might wonder why Tuggy has chosen to defend a hypothesis, U, that fails to distinguish the two. One possibility is that lumping them together results in a much stronger

presence in the ancient church for "Unitarianism" so described. Classical Unitarianism had a very small footprint in the early Christian centuries, but if we add in subordinationism, we get a much more impressive picture. In view of Tuggy's restriction of Trinitarianism to something close to the full Nicene doctrine, we get a picture in some of Tuggy's writings in which not only Tertullian and Origen, but also Basil of Caesarea and even Athanasius, count as Unitarians! Evidently, this classification is a monstrous distortion of the historical development that actually occurred. But there is another possible reason for choosing U as the hypothesis to be tested. If instead of U we had a hypothesis that insisted on Jesus being, ontologically, human and nothing more, there would be a great many NT passages that would give trouble, and the predictive power of such a hypothesis would be seriously diminished. One of the things I have learned from studying this topic is that one can make a fairly impressive case in favor of Arianism from the NT. I don't say that Arianism gives the best interpretation of the NT overall; on that question I am firmly committed to Trinitarianism. But there are a great many passages that ascribe to the Son attributes that are super-human but do not clearly imply the Son's divinity. A hypothesis that does not conflict with those passages does much better in prediction than one that does cause such conflicts.

A careful reading of Tuggy's essay reveals yet another, startling fact: the Unitarian position that Tuggy himself holds, and presumably wants to defend, is never clearly affirmed in the entire piece! But perhaps I am too quick in assuming what position he wants to defend. He states, "I anticipate that at least one of my interlocutors [presumably me, WH] will cry foul because the definition of U doesn't include the thesis that Jesus doesn't *in any sense* have a divine nature and that he came to exist at or after his miraculous conception" (88n6). So perhaps Tuggy is interested in defending only the hybrid view that Jesus was *either* merely human *or not a human being at all* but rather an exalted, supernatural (but not divine) creature. Of course, the more disjuncts are added, the harder it becomes to come up with counter-evidence. But at other times he seems to ignore the disjunctive character of U: F12 states, "*Jesus is regularly called a 'man' with no warning that this is only part of what he is (i.e., that he's not a 'mere man')*." Tuggy thinks this would be misleading if Jesus were divine as well as human, but it would be even more misleading on an Arian view in which the place of a human soul in Jesus was occupied instead by the created (and not divine) Logos. U interpreted as including the latter possibility does a poor job of predicting F12.

So far as I can see, most of the "undeniable facts" about the NT appealed to by Tuggy really are facts, but in some cases this might be questioned.

One possible exception is F5, which states that non-Christian Jews "never, so far as we can tell, accused the Christians of being pseudo-monotheists, unscriptural monotheists, incoherent monotheists, crypto-polytheists, or tritheists" (93). Here we might think of John 5:18, which recalls that the Jews were seeking to kill Jesus because he was "calling God his own Father, *thereby making himself equal to God.*" This does not formally contradict F5, but it comes close enough that it should merit some attention. Also of interest is F18, which claims there was a "*Total lack of interest in the eternality of Son or the Spirit.*" What then of John 17:6, where Jesus asks the Father to "glorify me in your own presence with the glory that I had in your own presence *before the world existed*"? Or John 8:58 "before Abraham was, *I am.*" Here the contrast is telling between the past tense for Abraham, and the present—may we say, the "eternal present"—for Jesus. And then there is John 1:1: "In the beginning was the Word." Of course, the Word here is Jesus (see 1:14). If "in the beginning" doesn't go back far enough to satisfy Tuggy, what would it take?

These examples suggest a larger point: almost none of the crucial biblical texts discussed by Craig and by me in our essays get talked about by Tuggy. Instead, we are told that Trinitarians "focus on a handful of texts (what I call 'the canon within the canon')" (87). Presumably there is something bad about this, but what exactly is the problem? In fact, what happens is that Trinitarians, like adherents of other controversial views, tend to focus on texts that are especially clear in teaching the doctrines they want to emphasize. What is wrong with that? Tuggy, however, is ignoring a primary requirement for responsible argumentation: *In defending a controversial view, one needs to confront the strongest evidence adduced by one's opponents.* If this is not done, it becomes difficult to take seriously whatever positive case someone is making for their own position. Yet Tuggy has virtually nothing to say about the "Jesus is God" passages that Craig so carefully analyzes.[2]

Near the end of his essay, Tuggy finally gets around to recognizing that sensible Trinitarians will not accept T as a thesis implied by their position. Perhaps then, he suggests, they think the early Christians were not Trinitarians, but rather "half-Trinitarians." Tuggy states, however, "it is clear to me that [the early Christians are] Unitarians as defined above. If you don't want to grant that they're Unitarians, you owe us some account of what their views are, one that better explains the known facts than U" (111). He doesn't think this can be done; I, on the other hand, think it not only *can* be done but *has been* done (ignoring the patronizing reference to

---

2. On his website (trinities.org), Tuggy has discussed some of the relevant passages. For commentary, see Hasker, "Trinity and the New Testament."

"half-Trinitarians"). Here are a couple of examples. For a careful, deeply researched and highly respected account of what was going on in the first two centuries, I recommend Larry Hurtado, *Lord Jesus Christ: Devotion to Jesus in Earliest Christianity*. For a slightly later period, see Lewis Ayres, *Nicaea and Its Legacy: An Approach to Fourth-Century Trinitarian Theology*. These, and other comparable volumes, present accounts of the ways of understanding Jesus held by Christians throughout the period between Jesus' first appearance in Galilee and the full-blooded Trinitarianism of the Niceno-Constantinopolitan Creed. These accounts, it need hardly be said, are infinitely subtler and more nuanced than the stark alternatives offered by T and U.

Is Socinianism Biblical?

William Lane Craig

I AM AFRAID THAT few, if any, biblical scholars will be persuaded by Dale Tuggy's essay. As I explain in my opening essay, New Testament (NT) scholars, whether Christian or non-Christian, conservative or liberal, are virtually unanimous in thinking that by at least the later stages of the NT, biblical authors believe and assert that Jesus Christ is "fully divine (i.e., divine in the way the Father is divine)" (88). Nonetheless, laymen are apt to be impressed by Tuggy's long and complex argument. So, before we examine that argument, I want simply to ask such persons: If, as Tuggy claims, his view represents "*clear* New Testament teaching" based upon "undeniable facts," then why is the movement he champions "largely lay-driven" (87n4) and without scholarly support? Already the alert layman ought to be suspicious that something is fundamentally amiss with Tuggy's view, since scholars are not convinced by it.

The Argument in General

We shall examine Tuggy's argument in detail, but first it is worth remarking upon its general defects. In general Tuggy attempts to exploit the resources of confirmation theory in order to defend an inference to Unitarianism as the best explanation of NT data. His argument is based on a standard principle of confirmation theory called the *likelihood principle*. According to this principle, the evidence E supports a hypothesis H_1 over a competing hypothesis H_2 if E is more probable on H_1 than on H_2: $Pr(E \mid H_1) > Pr(E \mid H_2)$. The probability is interpreted in epistemic terms as the degree to which one ought to expect E given H_1 or H_2. If E is more to be expected on H_1 than on H_2, then E confirms H_1. The strength of E's confirmation will depend upon the degree to which $Pr(E \mid H_1)$ exceeds $Pr(E \mid H_2)$.

Tuggy proposes two competing hypotheses, the Trinitarian hypothesis T and the Unitarian hypothesis U, and assesses the degree to which we should expect certain facts, labeled F1 to F20, relative to each hypothesis. He argues that each of F1 to F20 is more to be expected (or less surprising) on U than on T, and so the evidence confirms the truth of U as opposed to T. He thinks, moreover, that E strongly confirms U rather than T.

Unfortunately, Tuggy's attempt to import the method of hypothesis-testing from the natural sciences into literary criticism and, in particular, into biblical hermeneutics is misconceived. Morna Hooker's famous title "On Using the Wrong Tool" seems to be an apt description of Tuggy's method.[1] Literary interpretation is not conducted according to the likelihood principle. Rather than engage in speculations about what the NT *would* say if our interpretive hypothesis were correct, we exegete the NT text to see what it *does* say. In determining what the NT teaches, there is no substitute for a close and careful reading of the text. Tuggy's method diverts attention from the task of textual exegesis, determining what the text says, to futile speculations about what we would expect the text to say if the author held to a certain belief. The result is a paucity of textual exegesis on Tuggy's part in favor of repeated arguments from silence.[2]

But even if we take Tuggy's argument at face value, there is the problem that, because confirmation is so easy to obtain, such arguments may be very weak.[3] In particular, they do not show the confirmed hypothesis to be more probable than not; H may remain highly improbable despite its confirmation by E. E's confirmation of H may contribute to H's probability without sufficing to make H more probable than not. Thus, the argument is inconclusive. So Tuggy's argument that E confirms U rather than T, even if successful, remains inconclusive. More needs to be said.

But the problems with Tuggy's attempt to employ confirmation theory run deeper than that. First, he considers the probabilities of each of the relevant facts F1, F2, F3, . . . , F20 separately or independently relative to T

---

1. I do not mean to imply that Hooker was talking about Tuggy's method.

2. On the weakness of arguments from silence see McGrew, "Argument from Silence." *N.B.* that Tuggy's F1–F20 kicks off with five straight arguments from silence. Some of Tuggy's arguments are especially problematic because he fails even to demonstrate that the relevant sources are silent. Here his lack of careful exegesis becomes paramount.

3. I vividly recall the late Keith Yandell explaining to me why he found arguments from mere confirmation to be so weak. "Suppose that my hypothesis is that Leah, the invisible, seven-foot Queen of the leprechauns, likes to go about putting paper cups on tables," he said. Pointing to the paper cups on our table, Yandell proclaimed, "There! We have confirmation of my hypothesis!" For the hypothesis was more probable on the evidence of the paper cups on our table than it would have been without them. Confirmation just comes too easy.

and U—Pr (F1 | T) compared to Pr (F1 | U); Pr (F2 | T) compared to Pr (F2 | U); etc. The problem with this method is that the facts taken in isolation might each fail to confirm a hypothesis but nonetheless confirm the hypothesis when all the facts are taken together. By way of analogy, consider a prosecuting attorney who presents a cumulative case in support of the claim that Jones is guilty of murder. Jones' defense attorney would argue in vain if he contended that the fingerprint evidence alone fails to confirm Jones' guilt, that the eyewitness testimony alone fails to confirm Jones' guilt, that the videotape evidence alone fails to confirm Jones' guilt, that motive alone fails to confirm Jones' guilt, etc. For the prosecutor would simply point out that what is at issue is the degree to which the cumulative evidence confirms Jones' guilt. Similarly, even if each fact F_1 to F_{20} taken individually were surprising relative to the Trinitarian hypothesis T, that fails to prove that (F_1&F_2&F_3& . . . F_{20}) is surprising relative to T. This failing of Tuggy's formulation is not fatal to his argument, but it does require the argument's reformulation and defense if his argument is not to be inconclusive.

A more fatal objection to Tuggy's argument concerns the selectivity of his evidence. It is entirely possible that despite the conjunction of the twenty selected facts' being more probable on U than on T, nevertheless when other relevant facts are considered, it turns out that the total relevant facts are more probable on T than on U. To return to our courtroom analogy, suppose that the prosecutor is able to show that the evidence he has presented is far more probable on the supposition that Jones is guilty rather than innocent; but then the defense attorney presents evidence of a fail-safe alibi for Jones, namely, at the time of the murder Jones was chairing a board meeting in another city. That single, additional fact would overturn the prosecution's case and exonerate Jones at least from committing the murder himself.

This failing is not a mere possibility for Tuggy's argument. As I show in my opening essay, there are multiple NT data explicitly and unambiguously affirming the full deity of Christ, which cannot be accommodated by U. These data strongly confirm T and disconfirm, even falsify, U. Of course, Tuggy will be given the opportunity to respond to my essay, but I am confident that, given the consensus of NT scholarship concerning the passages adduced, he will not be able to show the data to be more probable or expected on U rather than on T.

The Argument in Detail

In addition to these general problems with Tuggy's argument, more specific problems arise. First, Tuggy's statement of T is tendentious and not one with which all Trinitarians, including me, concur. T is the hypothesis that the NT authors assume (i) the numerical identity of the one God with the Trinity, (ii) the full deity of the Son, and (iii) the full deity of the Holy Spirit. While (ii) and (iii) are unobjectionable, I strongly suspect that most Trinitarians would deny (i). Most would probably deny that the NT authors have a clear conception of the Trinity. My reservation runs even deeper: the NT authors did not even have a clear conception of the logical relation of numerical identity. As explained in my opening essay, this relation was virtually unknown in antiquity and would have been particularly foreign to the missionary-pastors who wrote the NT. Most people even today do not understand what is meant by "numerical identity." Even if I thought (which I do not) that God is numerically identical to the Trinity, I should not presume to ascribe such a belief to the NT authors. Rather NT authors believed (i) that there is exactly one God and (ii) that there are exactly three persons who are properly called God. It follows, then, that Tuggy's argument is a non-starter. He is arguing that the NT data are improbable relative to a hypothesis that few Trinitarians hold to. He needs to reformulate T and show that the NT data are surprising given this more accurately reformulated hypothesis T*.

Second, Tuggy's formulation of U, that the NT authors assume the numerical identity of the one God with the Father, and that neither the Son nor the Holy Spirit is fully divine, shows that my allegation is correct that the nerve of Unitarianism lies in the attribution to the NT authors of a conception of the modern relation of identity—a relation that, I maintain, would have been foreign to them and could not have been intended by them in light of their explicit statements that Christ is God but is not the Father. Sever that nerve, and Unitarianism atrophies and dies. Moreover, U is fatally ambiguous. A generic Unitarianism cannot be true unless some specific brand of Unitarianism is true.[4] But some versions of Unitarianism will be incompatible with certain NT data and other versions not. For example, Tuggy's Socinian brand of Unitarianism is incompatible with Christ's pre-existing his conception, whereas Arianism is not. I think that no brand of Unitarianism is compatible with all the relevant NT data.[5] Tuggy needs to show that some such brand is.

---

4. To illustrate, the generic hypothesis "Reptiles live in Los Angeles" cannot be true unless some specific hypothesis is true, e.g., "Lizards live in Los Angeles" or "Snakes live in Los Angeles," etc.

5. Including Christ's vicariously bearing the suffering that we deserved as the punishment for our sins. If Christ was merely human, then such substitutionary atonement for the sins of the human race is impossible, as Socinus recognized in espousing a moral-influence theory of the atonement. The failure of Unitarianism to provide an

But, now, what about F1–F20? Tuggy needs to show two things with respect to each fact F*n*: (i) that F*n* is, indeed, a fact and (ii) that F*n* is significantly more probable on U than on T. It is interesting that Tuggy tends to say very little in support of (ii); rather he just asserts it, which is surely inadequate as an argument. In our space remaining let us look briefly at each one of Tuggy's alleged facts.

F1. *There is no New Testament "Trinity passage."* This is a fact but is not at all surprising on T*. What we do find in the NT is a constellation of passages that together affirm that there is exactly one God and that there are exactly three persons who are properly called God.

F2. *No NT word or phrase was at that time understood to refer to a tripersonal God.* I'm not sure that this is true, given our limited knowledge. *Theos* could on occasion have referred to the tripersonal God.[6] No reason has been given to think that it is surprising that NT authors had not yet coined a new term for the Trinity.

F3. *Clear assumptions, assertions, and implications that the one God (formerly called "Yahweh") just is the Father, and no clear assumption, assertion, or implication that the one God just is the Trinity.* The first clause does not state a fact, for it assumes anachronistically and contrary to the data that "The Father is God" is an identity statement. The second clause is irrelevant because what we find are assumptions, assertions, and implications that Christ is fully God, which is incompatible with U but not improbable on T*.

F4. *Endorsement, not criticism or correction, of core Jewish theology.* This is not a fact, for as Hurtado and Bauckham have shown,[7] belief in the deity of Christ represents a significant "mutation" of Jewish monotheism.

---

adequate doctrine of Christ's atoning death is just one more of its deficits which are not discussed here. But see my *Atonement and the Death of Christ*.

6. Tuggy's quoting Murray Harris out of context (90, 185n12) illustrates Tuggy's tendentious use of scholarship. For Harris, in using the term "impossible," obviously did not intend the word to be taken strictly, since he also argues that it is "certain" that Christ is called *theos* in John 1:1; 20:28, and "very probably" also in Rom 9:5; Heb 1:8, Titus 2:13; 2 Pet 1:1. He was obviously using the word "impossible" in the same colloquial sense in which we might say that it's impossible for the Chiefs to win the Superbowl without Mahomes.

7. Hurtado, *Lord Jesus Christ*; Hurtado, *One God, One Lord*; Hurtado, "Binitarian Shape." Hurtado unfolds a constellation of devotional actions constitutive of the cultic worship of Jesus in the early church that represent the sort of reverence that devout Jewish monotheists otherwise reserved for God alone. Hurtado emphasizes two

F5. *No early monotheism controversies.* This is neither a fact nor surprising. Evidence of such controversies is already present in John's Gospel, where Jews protest, "You, being a man, make yourself God" (10:33; cf. 5:18; 19:7). Moreover, given the fact that the Christian proclamation of Jesus as the Messiah, who inaugurated the long-awaited kingdom of God, was already an insurmountable stumbling block, it is no surprise that controversy over monotheism, which Christians affirmed, would not occupy center stage.

F6. *The New Testament usage of "God"* (theos). Harris' book *Jesus as God* demonstrates that *theos* is multiply applied to Christ in the sense of full divinity.[8] This single fact decisively disconfirms U.

F7. *The New Testament pattern of worship and/or honor.* As Bauckham and Hurtado have shown, Jewish monolatry required that worship be accorded to God alone, and therefore the Christian practice of worship of Jesus implies his full deity.[9]

F8. *Pattern of stylistic name- and title-swapping.* Of course, words like "God" and "Father" are often swappable, though not always (e.g., John 1:18). But then it is also true, as explained in my opening essay, that words like "Christ"

---

things about these phenomena: (i) They form a constellation of devotional practices, the collective force of which constitutes a so-called "mutation" in Jewish monotheistic practice; and (ii) these phenomena are the actual devotional practices of adherents of a known religious movement, functioning as the identifying marks of their devotional life (Hurtado, "Binitarian Shape," 193). Cf. Bauckham, "Biblical Theology and the Problems of Monotheism"; Bauckham, *Jesus and the God of Israel*, 1-59.

8. Again, the misuse of scholarship on Tuggy's part: Harris argues *in extenso* that the generic use of *theos* is not at issue in NT descriptions of Christ as (*ho*) *theos*. See also Hurtado's work cited above. Tuggy is engaged in quote-mining, not scholarly engagement.

9. Tuggy's misuse of Hurtado's work is inexcusable (94n26). Hurtado emphasizes that the devotional actions constitutive of the cultic worship of Jesus in the early church evince the sort of reverence that devout Jewish monotheists otherwise reserved for God alone (Hurtado, *Lord Jesus Christ*, 138; cf. Hurtado, "Binitarian Shape," 187-213). The fact that Jesus Christ as well as the Father was worshipped by the NT church leads to a startling conclusion: early Christ-devotion was "a 'binitarian' form of monotheism: there are two distinguishable figures (God and Jesus), but they are posited in a relation to each other that seems intended to avoid a ditheism of two gods" (Hurtado, *Lord Jesus Christ*, 52-53). Hurtado wants to differentiate his view from Bauckham's by insisting that worship of Jesus was not an *inference* from his divine identity but arose from his followers' religious experience. But Bauckham is not giving an etiological account of Christian worship but drawing out some of its necessary conditions, with which Hurtado fully concurs.

and "God" or "Jesus Christ" and "God" are sometimes interchangeable in the NT, which decisively disconfirms U.

F9. *In the New Testament God-terms always take singular, personal words.* This fact is hardly surprising, given the precedent set by historic Jewish monotheism. Even today Trinitarians almost never refer to God using plural words like "they."

F10. *New Testament usage of "the Lord" and "the one Lord."* The startling and ingenious device of NT Christians of using the name of Yahweh in Greek (*kyrios*) to refer to Jesus Christ, so as to avoid any misunderstanding that Jesus is the Father incarnate, is powerful evidence that they regarded Christ as fully divine. Especially significant are two phenomena: (i) the interpretation of OT texts about Yahweh as applying to Jesus Christ (e.g., Heb 1:8); and (ii) the retrojection of the person of Christ into historical situations in the OT about Yahweh (e.g., John 12:41; Jude 5). This fact decisively disconfirms U.

F11. *Mere-man-compatible theses and "big reveals."* As biographies of Jesus, the Gospels of course focus on the events of his life and especially his atoning death on the cross. But John's statement that the purpose of his Gospel was to engender faith that "Jesus is the Messiah, the Son of God, and that through believing you may have life in his name" (20:30–31) was thought by John to imply Christ's deity, as the christological bookends of his Gospel, namely, the Prologue and the appearance to Thomas, and 1 John 5:20 reveal.

F12. *Jesus is regularly called a "man" with no warning that this is only part of what he is (i.e., that he's not a "mere man").* Oh, my goodness, the NT is suffused with warnings that Jesus, though human, was not merely a man but was also divine, exercising the prerogatives of God and deserving of worship![10]

F13. *Titles or descriptions of Jesus such that their use normally assumes that the referent is a human being, with no warning that he is not a man (human person/self) or is not only a man.* Same point applies here as to F12.

F14. *Clear and unqualified claims that Jesus' mission, power, authority, knowledge, and kingdom were given to him by God (i.e., the Father).* This fact is unsurprising given the subordination of the Son to the Father in the so-called economic Trinity, as discussed in my opening essay with regards to Hebrews 1–2 and Philippians 2:5–11. Though ontologically on a par with the Father,

---

10. See note 2 of my opening essay.

the Son in virtue of his incarnation enters what is classically called his "state of humiliation," which lasts through his death and is ended by his exaltation by his Father. On Tuggy's Socinian Christology, Christ, though a mere human being, is exalted by the Father to lordship and is worshiped, which would have been idolatrous and blasphemous in Jewish thinking.

F15. *Unqualified implications of the Son's limits.* But, of course, these limits are qualified by the NT authors. For example, in the very gospel in which we find Jesus' assertion, "The Father is greater than I" (John 14:28), we find the affirmation that Christ is God, the Creator of all things (John 1:1–3). Unlike Tuggy, John saw no incompatibility between such claims.

F16. *The clear assumption and clear statements that the Father is Jesus's God.* This fact is not so surprising when we keep in mind the incarnation and humiliation of Christ. Jesus of Nazareth was not like Superman disguised as Clark Kent. Rather he embraced fully our humanity and as a human being worshiped and was dependent upon God the Father. Notice, moreover, that Christ is called "God over all" (Rom 9:5).

F17. *Use of "God the ____."* Again, given Jewish precedent, it is not surprising that God is typically referred to as "the Father." But Tuggy fails to take account of passages in which Jesus Christ (not to mention the Holy Spirit) is referred to as God. Only Christ is referred to as "the only begotten God" (John 1:18).

F18. *Total lack of interest in the eternality of Son or the Spirit.* Tuggy evidently means "past-eternality," since the NT authors certainly take the Son and Spirit to be future-eternal. But Christ and the Spirit's being God *entails* their past- and future-eternality, so that it goes without saying. Moreover, Christ's role as cosmic Creator plausibly implies his past-eternal existence.[11] This

---

11. In John 1:1–3 the uncreated Word (*Logos*), the source of all created things, was already with God and was God at the moment of creation. It is not hard to interpret this passage in terms of the Word's eternal unity with God—nor would it be anachronistic to do so, given the first-century Jewish philosopher Philo's doctrine of the divine *Logos* and Philo's holding that time begins with creation (Philo, *On the Creation of the Cosmos according to Moses*); for a discussion of the similarities between John's prologue and Philo's *On the Creation* 16–19, in which his *Logos* doctrine of creation is described, see Dodd, *Interpretation of the Fourth Gospel*, 66–73, 276–77. In Jude 25 we find the doxology, "to the only God, our Savior through Jesus Christ our Lord, be glory, majesty, dominion, and authority, *before all time* and *now* and *forever*" (*pro pantos tou aiōnos kai nun kai eis pantas tous aiōnas*). The passage contemplates an everlasting future duration but affirms a beginning to past time and implies God's existence, using an almost inevitable *façon de parler*, "before" time began. Similar expressions are

fact alone is fatal for Socinianism. As for the Holy Spirit, the author of Hebrews speaks of "Christ, who through the eternal Spirit [*pneumatos aiōniou*] offered himself without blemish to God" (Heb 9:14).

F19. *The spirit of God or "the Holy Spirit" is not clearly a divine self in the New Testament in addition to the Father (a.k.a. "God")*. Tuggy does not dispute that in the NT the Holy Spirit is taken to be both personal and divine, as divine as the Father and the Son. The only question is whether he is the same person as the Father. That possibility is ruled out by the triadic formulae which pervade the NT, delineating exactly three divine persons. It would be bizarre if in these formulae one person is actually listed twice! This fact is underscored by the different properties and roles attributed to the Father and the Holy Spirit.[12]

F20. *The "Triadic" New Testament passages*. What Tuggy does not dispute is that these passages show that there are exactly three persons involved. That is their significance for the doctrine of the Trinity. There can be no doubt that such formulae are to be expected given the NT authors' belief in the biblical doctrine of the Trinity.

---

found in two intriguing passages in the pastoral epistles. In 2 Tim 1:9 we read of God's "purpose and grace, which were given to us in Christ Jesus before age-long time (*pro chronōn aiōniōn*)." Similarly in Titus 1:2–3 we read of those chosen by God "in hope of eternal life (*zōēs aiōniou*) which God, who never lies, promised before age-long time (*pro chronōn aiōniōn*) but manifested at the proper time (*kairois idiois*)." Bauer's *Greek-English Lexicon of the New Testament* renders *pro chronōn aiōniōn* as "before time began" (*BDAG*, s.v. "aiōnios"). Evidently it was a common understanding of the creation described in Gen 1:1 that the beginning of the world was coincident with the beginning of time or the ages; but since Christ already existed with God at the moment of creation, it therefore follows that he existed "before" the beginning of time. NT authors speak of Christ and the Father's relation "before the foundation of the world" (*pro katabolēs kosmou*) (John 17:24; Eph 1:4; 1 Pet 1:20).

12. Moreover, in Romans 8, in describing the intercessory ministry of the Holy Spirit on our behalf, Paul clearly differentiates the Father and the Spirit: "Likewise the Spirit helps us in our weakness; for we do not know how to pray as we ought, but the Spirit himself intercedes for us with sighs too deep for words. And he who searches the hearts of men knows what is the mind of the Spirit, because the Spirit intercedes for the saints according to the will of God" (Rom 8:26–27). Here it is the Holy Spirit who acts as an intercessor between us and God the Father. It is the Father who knows the mind of the Spirit (*ho phronēma tou pneumatos*), rather than, as in 1 Cor 2:10–11, the Spirit who knows the depths of the Father (*ta bathē tou theou*). The Spirit takes our often misguided prayers and translates them into requests in accordance with God's will, and God the Father, knowing the Spirit's mind, answers our prayers appropriately. It is hard to avoid the implication, not only of the deity and personhood of the Holy Spirit, but also of a diversity of persons within God.

Conclusion

I am gratified that Tuggy has chosen to focus on the biblical testimony to the doctrine of the Trinity. This is truly where the emphasis properly belongs. Unfortunately for him, his attempt to show that the biblical data confirm the Unitarian hypothesis is not only generally flawed but, in the estimation of the vast majority of NT critics, wholly implausible in the details.

The Icon of the Invisible God

Beau Branson

Adonai is at Thy right hand
He struck down kings
in the day of His wrath
He shall judge among the gentiles

—PSALM 110:5–6

The Father judgeth no one.

—JOHN 5:22

THERE'S MUCH TO ADMIRE about Tuggy, and his work. Contrary to what critics might expect, he's motivated by a deep concern for Scripture. Although I reject his interpretations, I appreciate his motive. And Tuggy has significantly advanced philosophical discussion about the Trinity. Most focus on the "Three Gods" Problem (3G), but Tuggy has pressed the "Who Is God?" problem (WIG). Many haven't fully appreciated the distinction, or how WIG complicates 3G. Tuggy deserves credit for this—and for keeping Trinitarians honest.

His current argument further advances discussion, focusing on inductive, rather than deductive, argumentation. There *are* deductive arguments about Trinitarianism. But interpretation of Scripture, councils, and church fathers (always matters of probability) are crucial. Tuggy compares two hypotheses, T and U:

T. The New Testament authors assume:
   i. the numerical identity of the one God with the Trinity,
   ii. the full deity of the Son, and
   iii. the full deity of the Holy Spirit.

U. The New Testament authors assume:
   i. the numerical identity of the one God with the Father, and
   ii. that neither the Son nor the Holy Spirit is fully divine (in the way the Father is divine).

He then presents evidence confirming U and disconfirming T,[1] noting "it is point-missing to urge (correctly) that [Tuggy's evidence] is logically compatible with the truth of T" (89). He's right. That suffices for deductive arguments. But for inductive arguments, if E is *more likely* on H_1 than H_2, it confirms H_1 relative to H_2. That H_2 and E are logically compatible only shows their joint probability is non-zero. It doesn't restore the lowered probability of H_2. For that, one must show E is *just as likely* on H_1 as H_2.

This goes both ways. Trinitarians can't merely argue Tuggy's evidence is compatible with T. Unitarians can't merely argue Craig's evidence (or mine, below) is compatible with U. One must show the total evidence is more likely on a given hypothesis than on its alternatives. Here's another alternative hypothesis:

MT_{NT}. the New Testament authors assume:
   i. the numerical identity of the one God with the Father, and
   ii. the full deity of the Father, Son, and Holy Spirit.[2]

Tuggy argues powerfully the NT authors assume God = the Father.[3] I think Craig argues powerfully they assume the deity of Christ. Naturally Tuggy disagrees; I simply note, while *prima facie* Tuggy's evidence disconfirms T

---

1. To "confirm" or "disconfirm" is to raise/lower the probability of, not to decisively prove/disprove.

2. I.e., each is (a) god_{NATURE}. Note that MT says Monarchical Trinitarianism *is true*; MT_{NT} says the NT authors *assumed* MT.

3. By "the one God" Tuggy means "the Ultimate Deity," i.e., roughly my "$god_{ULTIMATE-SOURCE}$" or capital-G God. Hence, the first clause of MT_{NT} says the NT authors assumed the Father = God = the one $god_{ULTIMATE-SOURCE}$.

and Craig's disconfirms U,[4] neither seems to successfully disconfirm MT_{NT}. Arguably, the total evidence confirms MT_{NT} over these alternatives.[5]

Space constraints dictate focusing on a mere handful of challenges I'd like to make. Readers may know little about Unitarianism except that it rejects Trinitarianism. So, hopefully the challenges below provide Tuggy the opportunity to display more positive details of Unitarian theology, revealing its explanatory power. Since Unitarianism solves WIG and two versions of 3G ($3G_{ULTIMATE-SOURCE}$ and $3G_{NATURE}$), my challenges focus on the Three Fs Problem (3F) and $3G_{POWER/ACTION}$, the Theophany Problem (TP), and the divinity of Christ, with a final challenge about Scripture.

The Three *F*s Problem and $3G_{POWER/ACTION}$

Briefly: Is the Father a savior (Luke 1:47; Titus 1:3)? Is the Son a savior (Luke 2:11; Titus 1:4)? Are there two saviors (Isa 43:11; 45:21)? Likewise for any shared predicate (e.g., "redeemers," "lords") including what Tuggy calls "deities" (what I've called "$gods_{POWER/ACTION}$")." Should Christians not worship Jesus? Or should they worship "two deities" (two $gods_{POWER/ACTION}$)? Can Unitarianism resolve this without simultaneously resolving it for MT?

The Theophany Problem

The Theophany Problem (TP) involves the apparent contradiction in the Old Testament (OT) saying "No one shall see me [God] and live" (Exod 33:18–23) yet saying some people *have* seen God and lived (e.g., Exod 24:9–11; Isa 6:1). There are three aspects to the logical forms of these claims:

1. A quantifier: "No one"/"someone"

2. A relation: seeing

3. An object of the relation: God

Correspondingly, there are three obvious strategies for resolving it:

---

4. Since Craig denies that Christ has the divine nature (likewise for the Father and the Spirit), his view does not technically accord with hypothesis T. Hence, much of the evidence Craig presents actually counts against his own view as much as it counts against Tuggy's. See my response to Craig for more.

5. Tuggy does present arguments intended to disconfirm the divinity of Christ in the NT, but in my view, those arguments are not as strong as the arguments that the NT authors identified God with the Father. More importantly, I think they're not as strong as Craig's arguments for Christ's divinity in the NT.

RQ. Restricting the quantifier,

2S. Introducing distinct senses, times, ways, and the like such that God can be seen in one sense, time, way or what have you, but not in another, or

2P. Treating the Theophany Figure as a distinct person also referred to as "God" (or "YHWH").

Consider two hypotheses:

FT_{NT}. The NT authors assume The Theophany Figure = the Father. Call this "Father theophany" theology (FT).

ST_{NT}. The NT authors assume The Theophany Figure = the Son. Call this "Son theophany" theology (ST).

Given FT_{NT}, the NT authors can't resolve TP with 2P. So we'd expect them to utilize RQ or 2S (or both) and we'd be highly surprised if they rejected both. Given ST_{NT}, the NT authors could theoretically adopt RQ or 2S, but they wouldn't need to. So we'd strongly expect them to use 2P, and be somewhat surprised if they used RQ or 2S.

For a baseline of what to expect from FT adherents addressing TP, consider Mormon scripture.[6] It's precisely what we expect: *lots* of RQ and 2S, *no* 2P. Here are several relevant passages (my emphases) with strategies in brackets.

> Thou canst not see my face *at this time* [2S]. . . . [T]here shall no man among them see me *at this time* [2S]. . . . [N]o *sinful* man [RQ] hath at any time, neither shall there be any *sinful* man [RQ] at any time, that shall see my face and live. . . . [M]y face shall not be seen, *as at other times* [2S]. (Exod 33:20–23, Joseph Smith translation)

> And he [Moses] saw God face to face, and he talked with him, and *the glory of God was upon Moses; therefore Moses could endure his presence* [2S]. (Moses 1:2)

> But now mine own eyes have beheld God; but *not my natural, but my spiritual eyes* [2S] . . . but *his glory was upon me* [2S]; and I beheld his face, *for I was transfigured before him* [2S]. (Moses 1:11)

---

6. Note that my argument presupposes neither that Mormonism is true nor that it's false. It only presupposes what anyone, Mormon or not, would grant: that Mormonism teaches FT.

> For behold, I could not look upon God, *except his glory should come upon me, and I were transfigured before him* [2S]. (Moses 1:14)

> For no man has seen God at any time *in the flesh* [2S], *except quickened by the Spirit of God* [2S]. Neither can *any natural man* [RQ] abide the presence of God, neither *after the carnal mind* [2S]. (Doctrine and Covenants 67:11–12)

> And *without the ordinances thereof, and the authority of the priesthood* [2S] . . . no man can see the face of God, even the Father, and live. (Doctrine and Covenants 84:21–23)

The LDS website states

> The Prophet's inspired revisions of those verses explain that *sinful* people [RQ] can't see God—*only those who believe* [RQ]. And even then, a righteous person *must be changed—transfigured* [2S]—to see God.[7]

So, precisely what's expected from FT adherents: *lots* of RQ and 2S, but *no* 2P. Given FT$_{NT}$, we'd expect the same in the NT. Instead, we get the exact opposite.

> Neither knoweth any man the Father, save the Son [Quantifier Restricted *only for Jesus*], and he to whomsoever *the Son* [2P] will *reveal him*. (Matt 11:27; cf. Luke 10:22)

> *No man* [Unrestricted Quantifier] hath seen God *at any time* [Rejects 2S], *the only-begotten* [2P], which is in the bosom of the Father, *he hath revealed him*. (John 1:18)

> Ye have neither heard his [the Father's] voice *at any time* [Rejects 2S], nor seen his form. (John 5:37)

> Not that *anyone* hath seen the Father, *except he who is from God* [Quantifier Restricted *only for Jesus*], he hath seen the Father. (John 6:46)

> He who sees *me* [2P] *sees him who sent me*. (John 12:44–45)

> If ye had known *me* [2P], ye should have *known my Father also*. . . . Philip saith unto him, Lord, *show us the Father*. . . . Jesus saith

---

7. See "How Can I Respond When My Friends Say That No Man Can See God?" on churchofjesuschrist.org.

unto him, Have *I* [2P] been so long time with you, and yet hast thou not known *me* [2P], Philip? He that hath seen *me* [2P] *hath seen the Father.* (John 14:7–9)

No man [Unrestricted Quantifier] hath seen God *at any time* [Rejects 2S]. (1 John 4:12)
The one who does not love his brother whom he has seen, cannot love God *whom he has not seen* [No RQ; No 2S]. (1 John 4:20)

Christ [2P], who is *the icon* of God. (2 Cor 4:4)

[*Christ*] [2P] is *the icon* of the *invisible* [No 2S] God. (Col 1:15)

Now unto the King eternal, immortal, *invisible* [No 2S], the only wise God. (1 Tim 1:17)

... dwelling in the light which *no man* [Unrestricted Quantifier] can approach unto; whom *no man* [Unrestricted Quantifier] hath seen, *nor can see* [Rejects 2S]. (1 Tim 6:15–16)

God ... Hath in these last days spoken unto us by *His Son* [2P], ... the brightness of his glory, and *the exact image* of his *hypostasis.* (Heb 1:1–3)

So, precisely what's expected from ST adherents and precisely opposite what's expected from FT adherents: no RQ (or quantifiers restricted *only* for Jesus—*not* OT theophany recipients like Moses or Isaiah); no 2S (indeed, several 2S strategies are specifically rejected—e.g., for Paul, God is simply "invisible" or "unseen"; he even says it's *not possible* to see God, eliminating possible "ways" or "situations" in which one could see God); and lots of 2P, namely frequent mention of a second figure (Christ) described in "ocularcentric"[8] vocabulary: "the icon of God," "the icon of the invisible God," "the exact image of his [God's] *hypostasis,*" who "reveals" the Father, so if you've *seen* him you've *seen* the Father. Hence, explicit NT discussion of TP *highly* confirms ST_{NT} over FT_{NT}.

There's also a "big picture" feature of the NT that fits better with ST_{NT} than FT_{NT}: the total absence of Father theophanies in the Gospels. That would be highly unexpected from Father-Theophany adherents. *Beyond* unexpected, though, is that in the NT the Father never reveals himself *even to Jesus*. A theophany was the zenith of any OT prophet's career. If Jesus

---

8. The term is from Orlov, *Glory of the Invisible God*.

were not, himself, The Theophany Figure, we'd unquestionably expect him to be a *recipient* of a theophany. Yet, in the most clearly theophanic scene of the Gospels—the transfiguration—the Father remains invisible, manifesting only as a voice. While that would be highly unexpected from Father-Theophany adherents, for Son-Theophany adherents the difference between OT and NT is minimal. The Theophany Figure is just revealed *more directly* in the NT (not less directly!). And though he doesn't reveal his divine glory publicly prior to the crucifixion, he does so privately (at the transfiguration). Finally, 2P was not an uncommon strategy for resolving TP in Late Second Temple Judaism anyway. So it's *a priori* unsurprising to find it in the NT.

I'll consider two Unitarian responses that don't work, and one that *could*. First, arguing that the OT assumes FT commits the fallacy of missing the point. If successful, it would follow that the NT authors misinterpreted the OT, not that they had a different interpretation of it than what the evidence shows. Second, agreeing that the NT rejects FT but denying it assumes ST also misses the point. If a second divine person makes two gods, it doesn't matter if that second person is Jesus, an angel, or your next-door neighbor. (Nor does it fit the evidence. The only figure mentioned in connection with TP in the NT is Jesus. And there is no theophanic angel in the NT—the only figure given theophanic attributes in the NT is Jesus.) A more viable option is admitting that the NT authors assume ST but maintaining the Theophany Figure (Jesus) is a creature—in other words, good old-fashioned Arianism. Space precludes a full critique of Arianism, but one issue is straightforward. Given ST, the one who called himself "I Am That I Am" at the burning bush, led the Exodus, descended on Mt. Sinai, gave the Torah to Moses, and made the covenant with Israel, was Christ. But it's hard to believe *that character* was a creature. In Gregory of Nyssa's memorable phrase, Eunomius (an Arian) "says that He Who Always Is, once was not."[9] This brings us to a third challenge to Tuggy.

Craig's Evidence for Christ's Divinity in the NT

Tuggy has sometimes treated Christ's divinity as separable from the doctrine of the Trinity. Now, on Tuggy's definitions, Christ's divinity in the NT isn't sufficient for T. But it *is* sufficient to show that U is false. And it gets about 2/3 of the way to MT_{NT}. So the arguments in Craig's essay can't be ignored. Which leads to a fourth challenge.

---

9. "τὸν ἀεὶ ὄντα ποτὲ μὴ εἶναι λέγει" (*Gregorii Nysseni Opera*, 1:55).

The *Nomina Sacra*

Craig argues certain NT passages are best interpreted as calling Jesus "*Kyrios*" in the sense of "YHWH." But there's also an argument based not on interpretation but on the presence in the text itself of *nomina sacra*—"sacred names" written very distinctively in Christian manuscripts. Non-Christian Greek manuscripts usually abbreviate "by 'suspension,' the first letter or two written, and the rest omitted, with varying marks to indicate the abbreviated word."[10] *Nomina sacra*, however, are typically written as the first and last letters of a word, with a horizontal overline.[11] Also, non-Christian manuscripts typically abbreviate commonly occurring words, to save time and manuscript space. But *nomina sacra* weren't intended to save time or space,[12] and they don't abbreviate commonly occurring words but a specific set of words with special religious significance. Fifteen eventually became standard, but eleven began being written as *nomina sacra* only later, and are less consistently treated so. Four, however, (sometimes called *nomina divina*—"divine names") trace back to the earliest NT fragments that exist, and are written as *nomina sacra* with only very rare exceptions throughout the manuscript tradition.[13] They are:

Lord	(Κύριος)	written	$\overline{ΚΣ}$ ($\overline{κc}$)
God	(Θεός)	written	$\overline{ΘΣ}$ ($\overline{θc}$)
Jesus	(Ἰησοῦς)	written	$\overline{ΙΣ}$ ($\overline{ιc}$)
Christ	(Χριστός)	written	$\overline{ΧΣ}$ ($\overline{χc}$)

The original intent seems to have been to avoid profaning divine names.[14] Two issues seem noteworthy. First, in the earliest NT manuscripts, "Lord"

10. Hurtado, "Origin of the *Nomina Sacra*," 658.

11. A convention ordinarily indicating the letters should be interpreted as numbers rather than as spelling (or abbreviating) a word.

12. Colin Roberts explains: "The purpose of the system was demonstrably not to save either space or the scribe's time; a free space is often left round the abbreviation and the time saved by writing a four-letter word in two letters would be occupied in drawing the line. Thus there is no connection with the abbreviations by suspension found in Greek documents or with those found not in ordinary literary papyri but in working copies and a few technical texts. The words in question are certain proper names and some other terms which for religious reasons only are given special treatment in writing" ("*Nomina Sacra*," 26–27).

13. Thanks to Daniel Wallace for pointing out to me that there are a few rare exceptions in the manuscript tradition and saving me from some other mistakes. Any errors remaining in what I've said here are my own.

14. "The aim is clearly to express religious reverence, to set apart these words visually

is written as the divine name $\overline{K\Sigma}$ when applied to Jesus.[15] It would be highly surprising if *Unitarian* scribes could easily and unambiguously distinguish "lord" in the sense of "master" or "sir" from "Lord" in the sense of "YHWH," but *consistently* applied the "YHWH" version to Jesus, rather than the "master"/"sir" version. So this highly disconfirms that any early Christian scribes were Unitarian. Second, the earliest NT manuscripts also treat "Jesus" and "Christ" as, themselves, divine names, just like "Lord" and "God." This is also highly unexpected if the earliest Christian scribes didn't consider Christ divine in the way the referents of "$\overline{K\Sigma}$" (= "YHWH") and "$\overline{\Theta\Sigma}$" (= "Elohim") were, but expected if they did.

Finally, as Hurtado notes,

> The origin of *nomina sacra* appears to take us back beyond the second-century manuscripts, in all likelihood well back into the first century. By the second century, the four divine epithets (Ἰησοῦς, Θεός, Χριστός, Κύριος) are consistently written as *nomina sacra*, and allowing even minimal time for the practice to gain sufficient recognition and standardization would require an origin no later than the late first century.[16]

If the NT authors themselves were Unitarian, it's highly unexpected that these scribal practices should develop and become so widespread so early and that *not even a single fragment* from an alternative tradition should ever be discovered.

---

in the way they are written." Hurtado, "Origin of *Nomina Sacra*," 659. Compare how some people today write "G-d," rather than "God," or manuscripts of the Talmud or Targums with "YY" instead of "YHWH."

15. For example *Codex Sinaiticus* has Romans 10:9 as, "εαν ομολογησῃς εν τω στοματι σου $\overline{κν}$ $\overline{ιν}$" ("if you will confess in your mouth that $\overline{ιν}$ is $\overline{κν}$. . ."). *Codex Vaticanus* has the same, but with diacritical marks. Similar remarks hold for 1 Cor 12:3 and Phil 2:11. One of the oldest NT fragments in existence, $\mathfrak{P}^{46}$, contains Romans 10:9, cut off in the middle of the *nomina sacra*, but originally had "$\overline{κν}$ $\overline{ιην}$ $\overline{χρν}$." The "$\overline{χρν}$" is still visible, as is the final "$\overline{ν}$" of "$\overline{ιην}$" and the horizontal overlines for "$\overline{κν}$" and "$\overline{ιην}$." Hence, *Institut für Neutestamentliche Textforschung* transcribes it as "εαν ομολογησης εγ τω στοματι σου $\overline{κ}[\overline{ν}]$ $[\overline{ιη}]\overline{ν}$ $\overline{χρν}$" (i.e., "if you will confess in your mouth that $[\overline{ιη}]\overline{ν}$ $\overline{χρν}$ is $\overline{κ}[\overline{ν}]$."). Instances of "god" and "lord" that clearly *don't* refer to the God of Israel may or may not be abbreviated. Earlier manuscripts are more likely to differentiate than later ones. For example, for Genesis 24:12, *Codex Sinaiticus* has "$\overline{κε}$ ο $\overline{θc}$ του κυριου μου αβρααμ" ("Oh, $\overline{κε}$, the $\overline{θc}$ of my lord Abraham"). I.e., it writes "κυριος" ("κυριου") *plene* when describing Abraham as "my lord," but writes the *nomen sacrum* "$\overline{κε}$" for the translation of "YHWH." *Codex Vaticanus* has the same, but with diacritical marks. For Psalm 110(109):1, *Codex Sinaiticus* has "ειπεν ο $\overline{κc}$ τω $\overline{κω}$ μου καθου εκ δεξιων μου" ("$\overline{κc}$ said to $\overline{κω}$, 'sit at my right hand'. . ." i.e., "YHWH said to YHWH, 'sit at my right hand'). Again, *Codex Vaticanus* has the same, but with diacritical marks. .

16. Hurtado, "Origin of *Nomina Sacra*," 659–60.

Explicit Affirmation of the Trinity and Christ's Divinity in Some New Testaments

Finally, Tuggy states, "Any Trinity theory dangles from a precarious chain of reasoning which tries to hang it from the New Testament. . . . The New Testament explicitly states no such theory" (111). But *which* New Testament? If we set aside literally the entire history of all Christians outside Western Europe, then we can say that Protestants (eventually)[17] settled on a NT canon inherited from Roman Catholics, so there's (more or less) one NT in Christian traditions deriving from medieval Western Europe. But *global* Christianity has never enjoyed a consensus on just one single NT canon.[18] And *multiple* non-European NTs *do* explicitly affirm the doctrine of the Trinity, and the divinity of Christ.

For example, although most of the Ethiopian Orthodox Tewahedo Church's "broader" NT canon has never been translated into English,[19] parts have. Ethiopic *Didascalia* describes Jesus as "our Lord and our God."[20] Also as "our Lord and our Savior, our God, and our King, even Jesus Christ."[21] Another passage says, "Let the Bishops and Priests offer up sacrifices and oblations to the Lord our God, the Lord Jesus Christ, who died for us."[22] *Sinodos* describes Christ as "our Lord and our God," says "God was born" on Christmas, and "the Divinity of our Lord Christ" was revealed at his baptism, while the people who stood by said, "This is God in truth, the Son of God in truth."[23] A pre-baptismal creed in *Sinodos* states, "I believe in one

---

17. Martin Luther famously rejected the apostolic authorship of James, and classed Hebrews, James, Jude, 2 Peter, 2 and 3 John, and Revelation as *antilegomena*. On the other end of the spectrum, Wycliffe, the "morning star of the Reformation," included the Epistle to the Laodiceans in the NT.

18. Besides the Protestant canon(s) and the Ethiopian canon (discussed below), we can note several other NT canons. The Peshitta historically lacked 2 Peter, 2 John, 3 John, Jude, and Revelation. Gregory Nazianzen's canon also lacks Revelation. The Armenian NT at some points contained the epistle *from* the Corinthians to Paul, and the Third Epistle of Paul to the Corinthians. Third Corinthians still appears in an appendix of the 1805 Zohrab edition. Although not reflected in manuscript evidence, Grigor Tat'evatsi's canon included the Doctrine of Addai/Acts of Thaddaeus, the Apocryphon of James, the *Didache*, the Acts of Justus, Dionysius the Areopagite, and the Acts of Peter. See Nersessian, *Bible in the Armenian Tradition*, 29.

19. In addition to the twenty-seven books familiar from most NT canons, the so-called "broader" canon of the Ethiopian NT includes four books of *Sinodos*, two books of the Covenant, Ethiopic Clement, and Ethiopic *Didascalia*.

20. Platt, *Ethiopic Didascalia*, 20.

21. Platt, *Ethiopic Didascalia*, 54.

22. Platt, *Ethiopic Didascalia*, 60–61.

23. Horner, *Statutes of the Apostles*, 213–14.

God, the Father almighty, and in his only Son, our Lord and Saviour Jesus Christ, and the Holy Spirit, giver of life to all creation, the Trinity equal in Godhead."[24]

Those are dramatic examples. But not the only ones. The Epistle of Barnabas is in numerous early canons and some ancient NT codices.[25] Grigor Tat'evatsi's canon (Armenian) includes the Acts of Peter,[26] and even Dionysius the Areopagite.[27] Protestants often downplay the problem of the canon. But this is a case study in why it can't be ignored. The Trinity isn't in everybody's Bible. But it isn't absent from everybody's Bible either. Tuggy sometimes appeals to sola scriptura. But even if an Ethiopian Orthodox Christian accepted sola scriptura, he'd still (have to!) accept the doctrine of the Trinity. The issue isn't the "sola." It's the "scriptura."

Now, Unitarians arguing for their canon over others because the others teach the Trinity would be circular. And if Unitarians simply take the Protestant canon as basic, why shouldn't Ethiopian Orthodox take theirs as basic? Indeed, why shouldn't *Protestants* take the Ethiopian canon as basic, if they like?[28] Early Protestants like Luther had a more fluid canon. Why should Protestants owe more allegiance to the Roman Catholic Church than to the Ethiopian Orthodox Church? Appealing to current scholarly consensus on authenticity, on the other hand, would certainly get rid of 2 Peter, probably Paul's pastoral epistles, and likely more. So the question is, what non-circular, non-arbitrary criterion counts as canonical or authoritative the Unitarian's preferred NT canon, but none of those that explicitly teach the Trinity or Christ's divinity (and that doesn't simply count the doctrine

---

24. Horner, *Statutes of the Apostles*, 153.

25. Barnabas interprets "Let us make man in our own image" (Gen 1:26) as God speaking to Christ (Barn. 5:5). That's consistent with Arian Christology, but not Tuggy's human-only Christology. And I'm an incrementalist. I'd be happy to at least nudge Unitarians up the christological scale to Arianism, for now.

26. In *The Acts of Peter*, Paul refers to "Jesus the living God," Peter addresses Jesus as "O God Jesus Christ," and Ariston refers to "the Lord Jesus Christ, our God." See Elliott, *Apocryphal New Testament*, 400, 403, respectively.

27. See Pentiuc, *Oxford Handbook of the Bible in the Orthodox Christianity*, 106.

28. For that matter, why shouldn't a Christian accept the doctrine of the Trinity itself as basic? Globally and historically, Christians have *always* had greater consensus about the doctrine of the Trinity than about the role of Scripture, or even what books count as Scripture. All ancient churches—Orthodox, Assyrian ("Nestorian"), Miaphysite, and Roman Catholic—have at least slightly different canons of Scripture. But *none* of them disagree about the doctrine of the Trinity as formulated at Nicaea and Constantinople. So why take one particular canon of Scripture that has *never* been universally accepted among Christians and pit it against a doctrine that has *always* been more widely accepted than that particular canon of Scripture?

of the Trinity itself as a canonical or authoritative doctrine)? Or is the argument not intended for Christians in general?

Conclusion

I've issued five challenges to Tuggy. I won't hold it against Tuggy if he can't address all of them in a limited space. But hopefully addressing some of these provides an opportunity to reveal more of the richness and explanatory power of Unitarian theology. No doubt Tuggy's response will advance discussion once more, regardless of which side one is convinced of.

VI. Final Replies

God Ultimate and Triune

William Hasker

READERS BY NOW WILL have become accustomed to the fact that William Craig and I are for the most part in supportive agreement in our respective views of the Trinity. This continues to be the case with Craig's comments on my essay; most of the disagreements he notes are fairly minor. But there is one major point of disagreement between us, namely the doctrine of processions—the eternal generation of the Son, and the eternal procession (or spiration) of the Holy Spirit. This is a doctrine I affirm, but which Craig rejects. In rejecting it, he opens a wide gap between his own doctrine and the main Trinitarian tradition. Now, I agree with Craig in refusing to ascribe infallibility to any man-made creeds or traditions. I believe, however, that in this instance he would do well to accord greater respect to the tradition than he so far has done. At present, I will limit myself to elaborating slightly on what I said on this topic in my main essay.

Opponents of the doctrine of eternal generation, like Craig, tend to be Protestants who complain that the doctrine is not taught in Scripture. It is true, of course, that we do not find in the Bible clear, explicit affirmations of this doctrine, any more than we find clear, explicit affirmations of the doctrine of the Trinity as a whole. What we should be looking for are statements about the *derivation* of the Second Person from the First Person, as well as the *dependence* of the former on the latter. To be sure, the very terms "Father" and "Son" apparently imply such derivation and dependence. But additionally, we need statements where the derivation/dependence in question does not originate with the Son's appearance in his earthly life. A pertinent example is Hebrews 1:2, which speaks of "a Son . . . through whom also he created the worlds." The Sonship referenced here is not plausibly supposed to have commenced only with the Son's earthly life. Another example is John 17, where Jesus, self-identified as the Son, refers to "the glory that I had in your presence before the world was made." The Father–Son relationship is the fundamental background presupposition of the entire passage; it would make little sense to suppose that this relationship was not in effect in the time before the incarnation.

Alongside the Father–Son texts, there are other passages that strongly imply a relation of ontological dependence between the beings in question. Consider John 1:1: "In the beginning was the *Logos*." The notion of Word, or Reason (however *Logos* is best understood) clearly implies dependence. "Word" and "Reason" are not free-standing entities; a *logos* is the word or reason *of someone*: in this case, of *God*, which is to say, of the Father. The text from Hebrews cited above continues by saying that the Son is "the radiance of God's glory and the exact representation of his being" (NIV); both "radiance" and "representation" imply a relation of dependence. In Colossians 1:15, Christ is "the image of the invisible God, the firstborn of all creation." Each of these texts deserves, and requires, careful exegetical work in order to bring out the nuances of what is being said about Jesus. All of them, however, express a relation of dependence, which can be given a formulation in the doctrine of processions.[1]

Craig's proposed explanation of John 5:26 is, I maintain, far from satisfactory. Which is the more plausible account of "having life in oneself"? That this is an essential, fundamental divine attribute? Or that it is merely a contingent property, "the ability to confer life," derived somehow from the Son's resurrection from the dead, which however had not yet occurred at the time of this utterance? Was the Second Person, then, unable to "confer life" before he was raised? And since the Father, and the Spirit, were never raised from the dead, how shall we account for their ability to confer life, assuming that they had it? In minimizing the importance of "having life in oneself," this interpretation cuts against the grain of the passage in John. I believe the interpretation I gave in my main essay is far more plausible.

According to Dale Tuggy, "to have life in oneself" in John 5:26 is to "possess the life of the age to come ('eternal' life), so that one can give it to others" (137). Perhaps so, but this life is possessed *in the same way* by the Father and the Son, so it must be an essential attribute rather than a mere contingent enhancement. That this is so is confirmed by 1:4: "In him [the *Logos*] was life, and the life was the light of men." The commentator C. K. Barrett observes concerning 5:26, "This does not contradict the words of the Prologue (1:4, *en auto zoe en*), since the giving (*edoken*) is not a temporal act but describes the eternal relations of Father and Son."[2] These "eternal

---

1. These two paragraphs are adapted from my "In Defense of the Trinitarian Processions." This article is a reply to Mullins, "Trinitarian Processions," in the same issue.

2. Barrett, *Gospel according to St. John*, 262.

relations," of course, include the eternal generation of the Son. The crucial question is whether "having life in oneself" is a contingent enhancement of the Son's powers, or an inherent divine attribute. Even Rudolph Bultmann, no friend of Trinitarian orthodoxy, says "*zoen echein* can of course also be said of men who believe; but the latter have life 'in him' while God and the Revealer have life 'in themselves', i.e., they possess the creative power of life."[3] Other exegetes who support this interpretation of 5:26 include F. F. Bruce[4] and D. A. Carson.[5]

All this having been said, however, I remain extremely happy about the general correspondence of Craig's view of the Trinity and my own. I am delighted to have him as a fellow-traveler on this topic and look forward to continuing to explore the relevant issues along with him.

It is good to hear that Beau Branson feels comfortable with at least parts of my view of the Trinity. Clearly there are disagreements between us, but I must confess to some difficulty in telling exactly where the disagreements lie. Branson thinks we disagree about "inseparable operations," but I am not sure that is correct. According to Branson, there is a sense of "same action," derived from Gregory of Nyssa, such that the Father's delegating the judging of the world to the Son, the Son's actual judging of the world, and (let's assume) the Spirit's convicting the persons judged of the wisdom and justice of the judgments made—all this counts as one single action, performed inseparably by the three Persons. My response is: given this sense of "same action," I agree entirely with this. I will point out, however, that this is not the usual way actions are individuated in ordinary, present-day English. In our everyday speaking and writing, the Father's delegating, the Son's judging, and the Spirit's convicting would be seen as three distinct actions. In that case, the Persons are operating "inseparably," in that each of their actions plays an indispensable role in carrying out a single project, namely the work of divine judgment. They are not, however, acting *indistinguishably*, so if that is what is being insisted on, I must demur. But then, in Branson's illustration, he and his realtor do not act indistinguishably, so I don't suppose that is what is required in the case of the Trinity.

There are some points about methodology that require brief mention. In various places, Branson seems to imply that everything we say in theorizing about the Trinity must have a basis in statements from church fathers who are recognized authorities on the topic. ("And would the church fathers affirm any of that? I'm open to seeing evidence, but I'm not holding my

---

3. Bultmann, *Gospel of John*, 260.
4. Bruce, *Gospel of John*.
5. Carson, *Gospel according to John*.

breath," 126) However, it seems that the fathers were not always entirely clear, or at least explicit, in their assertions, so we need a variety of new notations to clarify this—for example, Branson's "god$_{\text{SUBSCRIPT}}$" notation. I'm afraid I don't see this as helpful. It may be useful for Branson himself, as he seeks to gain a better understanding of the fathers, but it tends to place an additional obstacle—or perhaps two additional obstacles—in the way of contemporary students and theorists of the Trinity. First, we have to train ourselves to speak always in precise agreement with the fathers on various topics. (For instance, by agreeing with Gregory of Nyssa about the individuation of actions.) Then, we have to incorporate into our thinking the neologisms coined by Branson in order to clarify our understanding of those fathers. All this, before we are allowed to say anything of our own about the Trinity. I'm sorry, but I am just not on board!

But returning to the main point, where if anywhere are the real, serious disagreements between Branson's view and mine? His lengthy discussion of natures, powers, and actions would require a similarly lengthy reply, something I don't have space for here. A few very quick remarks may help to clarify some of my views about this. It is important, as I make clear in my responses to Williams,[6] that there are (at least) two senses of "power" that are relevant to this discussion. In one sense, I agree that "All divine activities are grounded in the divine nature-trope" (126). The capability (or power) of any Person to perform any activity has its source in the common, concrete divine nature. It is also true, however, that often the ability of a Person to perform some action is a power to act that is *unique to that Person*: only the Son, for example, has the power to respond to the Father's love with love of his own, and to carry out the Father's will by giving his life for the sins of the world. Recognizing these two senses of "power" obviates many of the puzzles about powers that can otherwise arise.

One really clear, and important, difference between us is the one highlighted in my comments on Branson: he rejects my claim that each of Father, Son, and Spirit is a distinct "center of consciousness." But how, I ask, can he account for the fact that in the NT the relationship between Jesus and the Father is represented as a relationship between the eternal Father and his eternal Son, who seem to be viewed as distinct persons and therefore as distinct centers of consciousness? Apparently Branson is uninterested in arguments involving pronouns, but I should have thought that it is of some importance whether, when Jesus asks the Father, "Why have you forsaken

---

6. I concur with Branson in recommending that readers consult my exchange with Williams.

me?," he was speaking to himself or to another person. I hope Branson will clarify his views on this in his own final response.

Finally, I have to insist that if we affirm, with full intent, that the Father is the one and only God, but then go on to add that the Son and the Holy Spirit are both fully divine persons—if we say this, I submit that we have too many divine entities to count as monotheists. When John of Damascus said, "God, and His Word, and His Spirit, are one God," what he said can only be coherent if the two occurrences of the word "God" differ in reference. The first occurrence, I submit, represents the conventional use of "God" to refer to the Father; the second occurrence of "God" must refer to the Trinity. The final answer to the question, "What is God?" can only be that the Trinity—Father and Son and Holy Spirit—is God.

In a way it is refreshing to turn to Dale Tuggy's critique: it is quite clear both what his views are and how they differ from mine. Briefly, I am a Trinitarian and he is not; he seeks to make the case that the entire enterprise of Trinitarian thought is a mistake. Tuggy is a tough controversialist; engaging with his polemics is bound to elicit carefully honed thinking from his Trinitarian opponents.

Tuggy does not believe that Jesus, the person who lived in Palestine two thousand years ago, existed with God, his Father, before the world was made (John 1:1–2; 17:3). He does not believe that all created things were made through Jesus (John 1:3; Heb 1:2), nor that, in some way that is difficult for us to grasp, it is through him that all things "hold together" (Col 1:17; Heb 1:3). He does not believe that Jesus, existing in what is termed the "form of God," and "equality with God," "emptied himself" in order to be born in the likeness of humans (Phil 2:6–7). Now, I am not entirely surprised that Tuggy does not believe these things. The things we Trinitarians say about Jesus are indeed amazing, astonishing, and, some would say, unbelievable. What I do find surprising, however, is Tuggy's claim that none of the writers of the NT believed these things either! That claim is something I have difficulty in wrapping my mind around! It is, I submit, quite significant that Tuggy is unable to cite reputable NT scholars who agree with him that the NT throughout presents a "human-only," Unitarian Jesus.[7]

Another point on which I seriously disagree with Tuggy is the way he classifies the views of early Christian thinkers about Jesus. On his accounting, almost all the major thinkers in early Christianity were "Unitarians," because they affirmed that the Father is the "one God." From a Unitarian standpoint, things were going along nicely until, near the end of the fourth

---

7. Tuggy does, however, proffer his own explanations for some of these texts. For discussion of some of these explanations, see my "Trinity and the New Testament."

century, someone (perhaps the two Gregories, of Nyssa and Nazianzen), invented Trinitarianism, which identified the one God with the Trinity. Unfortunately, the emperor Theodosius I intervened by calling the Council of Constantinople (381), which produced our "Nicene Creed," and the true faith of Unitarianism never recovered from this blow.

I disagree with this account of the history, and I think it is significant that Tuggy is unable to cite a single reputable contemporary scholar of the history of Christian doctrine who agrees with his way of sorting that history.[8] As an example of mainstream thinking on this topic, I cite an older work, J. N. D. Kelly's *Early Christian Doctrines*, which devotes an entire chapter to "Third-Century Trinitarianism." For Tuggy, there is no third-century Trinitarianism. He insists that "we should sort views by their contents, not by retrospective judgments about them as stepping stones to orthodoxy" (134). I reply that this sorting is heavily determined by the definitions we take as normative, and Tuggy's definitions are carefully crafted to get the results he desires. As a counter to his maxim, I maintain that, in narrating historical controversies, we should attach considerable weight to the affinities and alliances as they were perceived by the participants at the time. If certain individuals and groups perceive themselves as being in mutual support, they should figure as such in our reconstructions. And groups that perceived each other as opponents should likewise be recognized as such. Viewed in that light, it seems clearly absurd to group Athanasius and Basil with Arius and Eunomius as Unitarians, in opposition to the Gregories, Augustine, and later Trinitarians! It is commonly accepted that the "Nicene" Creed, adopted by the council of Constantinople in 381, differs only in relatively minor ways from the creed of Nicaea in 325. Tuggy, however, sees them as opposed, with the earlier creed counted as "Unitarian" rather than Trinitarian!

Especially problematic is Tuggy's definition of "Unitarian." Under this head he groups together "human-only" Unitarianism, held by Tuggy's "biblical Unitarians" and most others in recent times who wear that label, with the Arian/subordinationist views held by a good many in the ancient church. Now these views do have one important point in common: both of them are opposed to Trinitarianism. But in other respects they are sharply opposed. Modern Unitarians (sometimes called Socinians) lay great emphasis on the humanity of Jesus, in opposition to views that they think may

---

8. A few years back, when we were discussing this topic, Tuggy called to my attention Alvan Lamson, *Church of the First Three Centuries*, second edition revised by Henry Lerson, and published by the British and Foreign Unitarian Association in 1875. (A facsimile version has been produced by the University of Toronto Libraries.) I have no way to assess the scholarly quality of this work, judged at the time when it was issued. Lamson clearly plays no role in the present-day discussion of early Christian theology.

call that into question. But for Arian/subordinationists, *Jesus is not a human being at all!* Rather, he is the embodiment of a powerful, exalted, created super-being, who is really neither human nor divine. These views are strongly opposed, and so far as I know the biblical Unitarians do not make common cause with, or cooperate in practice, with that much larger group of modern "Unitarians," the Jehovah's Witnesses.

In fact, the motivation for this definition is not at all obscure. In the ancient Christian church, human-only Unitarianism was extremely rare; views of this sort simply failed to establish themselves as credible. On the other hand, subordinationist views of various kinds were quite common. Now it would hardly enhance the claim of present-day Unitarians to represent the true, original form of Christian teaching if they were to admit that their views had very little prevalence in the early centuries of Christianity. Adopting the early subordinationists as "really" Unitarians yields a much more impressive pedigree! But it does so at the price of ignoring the contours of ancient controversy as they actually developed.

There is yet another biblical text that I would call to Tuggy's attention. In John 16:13–15, Jesus says to his disciples, "When the Spirit of truth comes, he will guide you into all the truth. . . . He will glorify me, because he will take what is mine and declare it to you. All that the Father has is mine. For this reason I said that he will take what is mine and declare it to you." It seems to me (and to many others) that, if we are looking for a fulfillment of this promise, a likely place to look for it is precisely in the doctrine of the Trinity. Here, at what is widely regarded as the most central part of Christian doctrine, we have a conception that has received wide acceptance from all the main Christian churches. We also have a specific formulation, the Nicene Creed, which enjoys wide acceptance, regardless of differences concerning its precise ecclesiastical status. Unitarians, however, are bound to regard the Spirit's efforts in this regard as having resulted in a catastrophic failure. Is this not, I ask, a rather severe embarrassment to their overall position? Tuggy, I suppose, might want to say that the Spirit has succeeded in bringing about agreement in other respects, including perhaps some matters in ethics, and that in view of this the failure with regard to matters Trinitarian is less significant. I reply that this failure can hardly be insignificant by any measure. For part of what is at stake in the debate over the Trinity is precisely *monotheism*, and no Unitarian can afford to regard that as less than supremely important. If the Spirit couldn't lead the church to get that right, it is hard to see how we can rely on that guidance as having been successful elsewhere!

At this point, however, I need to address Tuggy's criticisms of my own position. I have argued that his view is flawed, both with regard to the NT understanding of Jesus and with regard to the development of doctrine in the early centuries of the church. But even if I am right about this, that does not refute his finely crafted assault on my Trinitarianism. Space is lacking, however, to work through all of Tuggy's objections (by my count, there are fourteen of them), so let us consider his final, climactic, criticism of me. Tuggy, I am happy to say, no longer thinks I am a Tritheist, as he did earlier. Now he finally realizes that I am an atheist—albeit, a "trideistic atheist"! However, I have to say that I don't seem, to myself, to be an atheist, nor do I worship and pray as one would expect from an atheist. So how does Tuggy reach this conclusion? His argument to this effect is a remarkable piece of dialectic:

> The monotheistic concept of a god implies ultimacy. God, the necessarily unique god, is supposed to be the source of and farthest back explanation for all else, but is not supposed to in any sense come from or depend on or exist because of or be explained by anything else. For the Trinitarian the only god and the Trinity are one and the same; thus, Hasker holds that only the Trinity has the sort of divinity that implies being a (and the) god.
>
> But if Hasker's thirty-seven claims above are correct, then the Trinity exists because of other things, as do, in various ways, each of the Persons. The only metaphysically basic thing here, and the only thing that could be ultimate, is the divine nature; the Persons, being constituted by it, exist *because of* it, and since the Persons are (or are like?) proper parts of the Trinity, it would seem that the Trinity exists *because of* the Persons (and so ultimately *because of* the divine nature). Although Hasker asserts the Trinity to be identical with the only god, it can't be, as it is (on his theology) not ultimate. Thus, the scheme is a species of what I have called polydeistic ultimism; the ultimate reality (here, the divine nature) is not a deity, and so is not a god. There are three omniscient and omnipotent and morally perfect Persons, but these will be mere deities, none being ultimate. Therefore this Trinity theory implies the falsity of monotheism, but not, properly speaking, Tritheism, but rather trideistic ultimism, which is actually a variety of non-naturalistic atheism! (140)

Call this the argument from Ultimacy and Godhood. Godhood, it claims, requires ultimacy. The candidate for Godhood put forward by Trinitarians is the Trinity. But the Trinity can't be God, because it is not ultimate; the Trinity exists because of the Persons, and so, ultimately, because of the divine nature. And the divine nature can't be God, because it is not a person. So there is no God; hence, "atheism."

Let's unpack this a bit more. As depicted in my reconstruction of Trinitarian doctrine, the Persons are constituted by the divine nature, and in virtue of this they are not ultimate. So neither the Persons nor the Trinity satisfy the ultimacy requirement; neither the Persons nor the Trinity can be God. One thought that comes to mind is that the argument really doesn't depend on there being a Trinity. If there were only one divine Person constituted by the divine nature, that Person would still lack ultimacy in virtue of being so constituted. We might term this "Unitarian atheism"; this suggests that Tuggy's own view has a problem here. He will no doubt reply that he does not adhere to the constitution doctrine, so the argument will not apply to his Unitarian view. But escaping from the argument is not that easy. In the case of a human being, I don't think he will deny that there is such a thing as a human body and brain (and perhaps a soul; I don't know his views on the materialism/dualism issue), which can be termed a "human nature." Perhaps he will also admit that there is a *person* only if this human nature is capable of supporting mental acts of cognition, affection, and volition. But this capability can in principle be lacking, if for instance the human nature in question is in a state of profound and irreversible coma. So we can say that, in the normal case, the person exists *because* the human nature both exists and is capable of supporting personal functioning, as seen in the various kinds of mental acts. And by analogy, we can say that the one divine person exists *because* the divine nature exists and has the capability to support divine mental acts. So the one divine person is not ultimate, and cannot be God.

Tuggy, however, has a good answer available to him at this point. He may admit that, under exceptional circumstances, a human nature may exist without being able to support mental activities, so that there is no human person. But, he will insist, in the case of the divine nature that is simply impossible; there simply *cannot be* a situation that exists where there is a divine nature but no divine person. It is necessary in the strongest possible sense that, if there is a divine nature, there is a divine person. The nature and the person together form, one might say, a package deal. There is no logical space between them through which one might draw a line and say that one but not the other is ultimate. What is ultimate is the nature and the person together. In this way, Tuggy has an effective and successful answer to the Ultimacy and Godhood argument.

It should be noticed, however, that *exactly the same answer is available to the Trinitarian!* The Trinitarian will point out that it is necessary in the strongest possible sense that if the divine nature exists, there are the three divine persons and therefore the Trinity. Nature, persons, and Trinity are a package deal, and there is no logical space between them through which one might draw a line and say that the nature, but not the persons or the Trinity, is ultimate. The lesson to be drawn from this is that, in spite of Tuggy's sweeping assertion, not every internal distinction within the Godhead negates the ultimacy of some of the items thus distinguished. A divine being can have some kinds of internal complexity, as seen in our account of the Trinity. But if the various components of the being are absolutely inseparable, that divine being as an undivided whole can have the ultimacy required for being "a god," that is, for being God. The Ultimacy and Godhood argument does not defeat Trinitarianism.

Tuggy insists, however, that there is an even simpler, and more basic, reason why the Trinity can't be our God:

> Hasker says we are to "worship, and obey, and love" (27) the Trinity, but these are all "I–thou" (self to self) relations, and this thing isn't a self, though Hasker urges that it is *similar to* one. This is not, as Hasker hopes, what the "Christian church knows God as" (3).

This is very strange. Does Tuggy think it is impossible to love a group of people—say, a family? Of course, it helps if all the members of a group are lovable, and even more if they have no tendency to be jealous of one another. Worshiping a group (or venerating, if the group is non-divine) doesn't seem all that much of a stretch either. Obeying a group may be more problematic—unless, of course, we can be assured that the members will not be giving us contradictory orders. But what in all this seems to be impossible?

One would think that if worshiping a group were impossible, Trinitarians would have experienced this difficulty in practice. But this does not seem to have been the case. The *Gloria Dei* and the *Te Deum Laudamus* are ancient forms of worship that to all appearance involve worshiping the Trinity. Each of these begins with praise and adoration for "God"—that is, for the Father. Each then goes on to address Jesus, the Son, celebrating his inherent greatness as well as his saving actions on behalf of humankind. Neither addresses the Spirit directly, but in each case the Spirit is acknowledged in a way that recognizes his status as a member of the Trinity. Amazingly, the millions upon millions of worshipers who have used these forms over the centuries do not seem to have noticed the incongruities that trouble Tuggy.

I conclude as I began: The Christian Church knows, and loves, and worships God as the Holy Trinity of Father, Son, and Holy Spirit.

In Defense of Biblical Trinitarianism

William Lane Craig

Introduction

THE CENTRAL POINT OF my opening essay was to show that the NT contains a rudimentary doctrine of the Trinity to the effect that (i) there is exactly one God and (ii) there are exactly three distinct persons who are properly called God. For all the interlocutors in this book, (i) is uncontroversial.

In (ii) the word "properly" is carefully chosen. I mean to distinguish thereby the sense in which the Father, Son, and Spirit are called God from the sense in which intermediate figures in Judaism, such as exalted patriarchs and principal angels, are only improperly called God.[1] By "properly," then, I mean something like "in truth," where truth is intended to be literal truth. Christ, in particular, is not, *pace* Tuggy, called God merely hyperbolically or figuratively but in truth. He is called God in the same sense that the Father is called God.[2]

Thus, we need not offer a philosophico-theological analysis of the divine nature but simply say that just as the Father is called God so is the Son also called God. The probative burden of this claim will be carried by a

---

1. See my remarks on Hurtado and Bauckham's work on Jewish monotheism and monolatry in response to Tuggy (205), and Hasker's in his opening essay (5ff). While Tuggy cannot respond to everything, his failure to reply to Hurtado's claims is noteworthy.

2. Thus Tuggy has failed to formulate correctly my argument. A more accurate formulation would run:

(1) Jesus is properly called God by NT authors.

(2) If Jesus is properly called God by NT authors, then Jesus is fully divine.

(3) Therefore, Jesus is fully divine.

Premise (2), given our commitment to biblical inspiration and authority, is true by definition of "properly." The whole debate then hinges on premise (1), which is the focus of my contribution. I seek to show that Christ is called God in the same way that the Father is called God.

careful exegesis of specific NT passages and their contexts. I focused on passages in which Christ is explicitly referred to as God because NT affirmation of the deity of Christ, while not sufficient for a full-blown Trinitarianism, is nonetheless a dagger in the heart of Unitarianism, and in particular of Tuggy's Socinian brand of Unitarianism, which, violating as it does Jewish monolatry, is blasphemous and idolatrous, enjoining worship of a creature, a mere man.

Is my biblical Trinitarianism too thin to qualify as Trinitarian, as Tuggy alleges? It is difficult to see why, given Tuggy's own statement that "A Trinity doctrine is commonly expressed as the statement that the one God exists as or in three equally divine 'Persons', the Father, the Son, and the Holy Spirit."[3] It therefore follows that biblical Trinitarianism qualifies as a doctrine of the Trinity as commonly expressed. Tuggy complains, "A subordinationist Unitarian like Origen would agree with both claims, as would some modalists, yet none of them are [sic] Trinitarians" (110). Yes, Origen would qualify, and therefore historians of dogma take Origen to be a Trinitarian, despite his subordinationism. But no, modalists would not qualify, for modalists did not believe there to be three distinct persons who are God.

To be perfectly candid, Tuggy *wants* the doctrine of the Trinity to be as complicated as possible so that he can assail it as incomprehensible and unjustified. I shall leave it up to Branson and Hasker, who want to add additional doctrinal layers to the biblical doctrine of the Trinity, to defend their views against Tuggy's criticisms. But Branson, Hasker, and I all agree on the biblical doctrine of the Trinity, since it is entailed by their more complex theories. They may regard it as theologically or philosophically inadequate and so in need of expansion and elaboration, but they do not regard it as false, as Tuggy does.

Probative Component

Christ as Theos

So does the NT teach the biblical doctrine of the Trinity? I anticipated that Tuggy would devote the lion's share of his response to a serious, detailed, exegetical discussion of the eight key christological passages that constitute the centerpiece of my opening essay. But as I read Tuggy's response, the image that came to my mind was that of a deer caught in the headlights. As if immobilized, he has almost nothing to say in response to my exegesis

---

3. Tuggy, "Trinity." The reader is invited to assess Tuggy's statement by the same standard applied in the derisive second paragraph of Tuggy's "Response to Craig."

of the eight passages. He agrees that each of these passages does, indeed, refer to Christ as God (93). Excellent! His only recourse, then, is to interpret (*ho*) *theos* in every passage as ascribing some sort of diminished divinity to Christ consistent with his being merely a creature. Anticipating that strategy, I sought to foreclose this escape route by showing that the most plausible interpretation of the relevant passages is that such a diminished divinity is not in view.

Tuggy deals with only two of the eight passages examined, namely, Hebrews 1:8 and John 1:1-3. In discussing the first of these passages, Tuggy points out that Hebrews 1:8 cites Psalm 45:7, which in the Hebrew may well have been addressed to the king. But such hyperbolic use cannot be plausibly carried over to Hebrews 1:8, since, as I say, "The parallelism of the Son's being addressed as both 'God' and 'Lord' and the exalted descriptions of him in his superiority to angelic beings make it clear that Christ is not addressed merely in the way that a Jewish king might be called *elohim*" (35). In Judaism angels were as high as it gets among intermediate beings, and Christ exceeds them all and is worshipped by them all. Christ's being the mediate cause of creation does distinguish him from the Father but in no way diminishes his deity (cf. John 1:1-3; Col 1:16). Tuggy protests that Christ is exalted only post-mortem to Lordship. No, the author of Hebrews holds that Christ's Lordship is possessed from the moment of creation: "In the beginning, Lord, you founded the earth" (1:10). Moreover, Tuggy ignores what I say concerning the themes in Hebrews of the humiliation and exaltation of Christ via the incarnation and resurrection, which relate to Christ's human nature.

Of the Johannine texts I examine, Tuggy interacts briefly with only John 1:1, claiming that the background to the Prologue is not Middle Platonism, as I have argued, but Jewish wisdom literature, which featured personifications of figures like Lady Wisdom in Proverbs 8. I think that that provenance is unlikely in light of the many striking parallels between the Johannine Prologue and Philo of Alexandria's Logos doctrine and the fact that it is not Sophia but Logos who is in the beginning with God and is God.[4] But let that pass. The more important point is that by interpreting the Logos to be a personification of a divine attribute, Tuggy concedes the full deity of

---

4. See the lengthy discussion in my *God over All*, chapter 2. Tuggy says that Sirach 24 is his best parallel. But Sirach speaks, not of Logos, but of Sophia. Indeed, in Jewish Wisdom literature, Logos is never personified. Moreover, in contrast to the Johannine Logos, who is said to have created all things, Wisdom is said by Sirach to have been herself created by God in the beginning. Note that while Wisdom comes to dwell in Israel, there is no thought that the female figure of Wisdom becomes a concrete, historical person like the Johannine Logos.

Christ, denying instead his distinct personhood in his pre-incarnate state. The fatal flaw in this idiosyncratic interpretation is that a literary personification cannot become flesh and live among us as a real person (John 1:14).[5] John 1:18, which Tuggy does not discuss, reveals that prior to the incarnation the Son was a distinct and fully divine person with the Father. Similarly Jesus' talk of "the glory that I had in your presence before the world existed" and of "my glory, which you have given me because you loved me before the foundation of the world" (John 17:5, 24) makes little sense with respect to a literary personification. Yes, John explicitly states that the Father is "the only true God" (John 17:3), just he also states that the Son "is the true God and eternal life" (1 John 5:20). That John can affirm both truths shows that these cannot be identity statements but are predications of deity to the Father and Son.

That is the extent of Tuggy's comments on my exegetical discussion of the eight NT passages that are the focus of my attention. He clearly has much more work to do if he is to turn back the force of my argument.

Christ as Kyrios

In addition to the teaching embedded in these christological passages, there is abundant NT evidence, as I noted, indicating that Christ is regarded by various NT authors as fully divine. Consider, for example, Christians' seizing upon the term *kyrios* to refer to Jesus Christ. The theological import of *kyrios* in reference to Christ is conveyed by two unsettling practices of the NT authors: quoting OT prooftexts about Yahweh in application to Christ and retrojecting Christ into OT narratives about Yahweh. With respect to the first, we saw three examples of passages about the Lord cited as applying to Jesus. Tuggy responds that "Craig is impressed by the NT use of 'Lord' (*kurios*) [sic] for Jesus" but asks, "Given that inspired texts about Yahweh ... can have multiple meanings and so multiple fulfillments ... why couldn't a second meaning and a second fulfillment be about one who is less than fully divine?" (162). Context will be our guide. For example, the promise, "If you confess with your lips that Jesus is Lord and believe in your heart that God raised him from the dead, you will be saved" (Rom 10:9) is vouchsafed by the proof text "Every one who calls upon the name of the Lord will be

---

5. If persons are essentially persons, then Jesus could not possibly have once been a literary personification. Jesus did not replace a literary personification at his birth; rather the supposed literary personification "became flesh and dwelt among us, and we beheld his glory" (John 1:14). Ironically, Boyarin, cited by Tuggy, *agrees* that for John Jesus is the Logos become flesh ("Logos, a Jewish Word," 691).

saved" (Joel 2:32). Salvation is from the Lord alone. Unless Jesus is fully divine, then the assurance that everyone who calls upon Yahweh will be saved would not ratify the promise that everyone who calls upon Jesus will be saved. Tuggy agrees that "it certainly is striking that particularly after his resurrection and exaltation, *kurios* [sic] is a main title for the man Jesus," but thinks that, citing Dunn, "the *kyrios* title is not so much a way of *identifying* Jesus with God, as a way of *distinguishing* Jesus from God" (162–63).[6] Right, if "God" here refers to the Father! As I explained, by means of this ingenious ploy Christians could distinguish the Son from the Father while regarding them as equally divine.

As examples of the second unsettling practice of retrojecting Christ into OT narratives about Yahweh, consider the following:

> Isaiah said this because he saw his [Christ's] glory and spoke of him. (John 12:41)

> Now I desire to remind you, though you are fully informed, once and for all, that Jesus, who saved a people out of the land of Egypt, afterward destroyed those who did not believe. (Jude 5)

According to these passages, it was none other than Jesus whom Isaiah saw high and lifted up in the temple and who delivered the Israelites out of bondage and judged the Egyptians. Tuggy does not discuss these shocking passages.[7]

It is futile for Tuggy to try to blunt the force of these *kyrios* passages by pointing to other passages about Jesus' human limitations (163), for the NT authors agree that Jesus was truly human as well as truly divine.

Christ's Deity Equal to the Father's

There are, in addition, various NT passages in which equal divinity is ascribed to the Son as to the Father. Consider, for example, Paul's statement in Philippians 2:6 that Christ Jesus, "though he was in the form of God, did

---

6. N.B. that the accurate quotation of Dunn is "as the *God* . . . of our *Lord* Jesus Christ," where the ellipsis points stand in for "and Father." See Dunn, *Did the First Christians Worship Jesus?*, 110.

7. In his response to Branson, Tuggy does reference Wasserman's discussion of the text of Jude (186n21). So incredible is Jude's assertion that earlier textual critics and translators defied the much weightier attestation of the Greek and versional witnesses to *Iēsous* and chose to read *kyrios* instead. Similarly, Wasserman says, "The reading Ἰησοῦς has the best manuscript support and is indeed a difficult reading to the point of impossibility" (266). But now the UBS[5] and NA[28] as well as the SBLGT and THGNT are united in preferring the reading *Iēsous*, a reading reflected in more recent translations.

not count equality with God a thing to be grasped." Here Christ is explicitly said to be equal (*isa*) to God, that is, to "God the Father" (v. 11). Being in the form of God (*en morphē theou*) concerns his divine nature or status, which, as the following verse indicates, he already possessed in his pre-incarnate state. Christ is thus said to be equally divine with the Father.

Or consider John 5:18, the closest NT parallel to Philippians 2:6, where John explains in his own voice, "This was why the Jews sought all the more to kill him, because he not only broke the sabbath but also called God his own Father, making himself equal with God." Here John explicitly affirms Jesus to be equal to God (*ison tō theō*), that is, to God the Father. Such an affirmation represents John's own Christology. But such a claim is regarded by fellow Jews as blasphemous, displaying their grasp of the import of Jesus' words.[8]

Finally, consider the striking statement in Colossians 2:9: "in him the whole fullness of deity dwells bodily." Christ's is not some watered-down divinity; rather the incarnate Christ is said to embody *to plērōma tēs theotētos* (cf. 1:19). The use of the word *plērōma* is decisive. This is deity in its fullest sense. Moreover, this fullness of the divine nature is not said to be merely in Christ as the indwelling Holy Spirit is in believers but is said adverbially to dwell bodily (*sōmatikōs*) in him. This is a startling, almost incomprehensible, affirmation—how can the divine nature, which is incorporeal, dwell bodily? Yet that is that we have in the incarnate Christ: all the fullness of God dwelling bodily.

The full deity of Christ is especially evident in the worship accorded to Christ by NT believers. I mentioned previously that the earmark of Jewish monotheism was its monolatry, the worship of God alone. But among NT believers worship is accorded to Christ just as to God the Father without the abandonment of their inherited Jewish monotheism. As Bauckham and Hurtado have argued, the cultic beliefs and practices of the NT church are powerful evidence for their embrace of the full deity of Jesus Christ within a monotheistic context. Tuggy reminds us that it is God the Father who

---

8. The passage also shows that Jesus' being the Son of God is in John's mind tantamount to claiming to be equal to God. That is why, in Jewish thinking, "he ought to die, because he has made himself the Son of God" (John 19:7). Holding Jesus to be *theos* or *monogenēs theos* or *huios theou* is to ascribe to him equality with God the Father. Jesus' fully divine status is woven into the fabric of the Fourth Gospel from the Prologue to Thomas' post-resurrection confession, including Jesus' personal invocation of the divine name (8:58) and claim to oneness with the Father (10:30), both of which are regarded by Jews as blasphemous "because you, being a man, make yourself God" (10:33). But in John's mind, since Jesus is in fact equal to God the Father, all people should "honor the Son, even as they honor the Father" (5:23).

enjoins worship of the Son and bestows glorious titles upon him (102).[9] But Tuggy just does not seem to appreciate that on his Socinian view of Jesus as merely a man, this is to attribute to God the command to commit idolatry and blasphemy, which is absurd. It is so telling, then, that after affirming that Jesus Christ "is the true God and eternal life" (1 John 5:20), the apostle John warns tersely, "Little children, keep yourselves from idols" (1 John 5:21).

Model Component

The model I propose for the biblical doctrine of the Trinity is that God is a spiritual substance endowed with three sets of rational faculties, each sufficient for personhood. Tuggy flatters me by saying that I am "the first person in the history of Christian theology to understand 'the doctrine of the Trinity' in this way" (159). I think this is intended as a criticism, but when doing modeling, as opposed to formulating doctrine, originality is no vice. I have never thought of myself as much of an original thinker, so I feel certain that others have so conceived of God. Perhaps the reason that such a model has not been popular is that by far and away most Trinitarian theorists are trying to model, not the simple biblical doctrine of the Trinity, but a more complex doctrine featuring layers of doctrinal accretion characteristic of the creedal doctrine of the Trinity, including doctrines like the divine processions, divine simplicity (the doctrine that God lacks not only separable parts but even metaphysically inseparable parts), each Trinitarian person's being somehow equal to the Trinity as a whole, and the persons' inseparable operations. Tuggy's claim that my simple model "is not supported at all by the NT" (159) is vacuous in light of his failure to engage in serious exegesis of the relevant passages.

The Problem of Overdetermination

Tuggy criticizes the model because the divine soul "is overdetermined to be *a* person!" (160) What does he mean? The key to understanding Tuggy's criticism is the notion of overdetermination. In cases of causal overdetermination two separate causes are alleged to be each sufficient to bring about a single effect, for example, two matches' simultaneously lighting a single candle. But in the case at hand, there is no causal overdetermination. For

---

9. Perhaps here is the best place to register my distaste for Tuggy's condescending characterization of defenders of Christ's deity in the NT (161). The fact is that the weight of scholarship lies decisively with those who affirm that NT authors ascribe full deity to Christ.

each set of rational faculties is sufficient for being a person, but not for being the *same* person.[10] Tuggy's illustration of the man with three brains perfectly illustrates the point.[11] He would be three distinct persons. In fact, in the case of Siamese twins, we do have two persons, not one, each with a distinct self-consciousness, will, and intentionality. The model holds that God is too richly endowed to be *a* person but is rather three persons. If, *per impossible*, God lost two sets of his rational faculties, then Tuggy is right that God would, indeed, be a person; but if he lost only one set, he would be bipersonal. I'm quite open to Tuggy's suggestion that personhood supervenes on complete sets of rational faculties, that is to say, the set could not be exemplified without personhood's being exemplified, just as consciousness is thought to supervene on healthy brains. I see nothing unintelligible about this suggestion, nor does Tuggy present any argument against it.

The Problem of Tritheism

Branson, for his part, complains that my simple model "provides no help on *any*" of the problems he identifies (148). Therefore, his more complicated model is needed. Indeed, Branson almost seems bent on making the doctrine of the Trinity as difficult and incomprehensible as he can (no doubt to Tuggy's delight). My simple model certainly leaves many questions open for further exploration. But are we compelled to abandon it for Branson's model?

Consider first whether my model is threatened by the spectre of Tritheism, the most serious objection to Social Trinitarianism. Branson says that the following claims, affirmed by the model, are at least *apparently* inconsistent:

1. The Father is God.

2. The Son is God.

---

10. I wonder if Tuggy's difficulty is occasioned by his construing the model to hold that the divine "soul has three cognitive faculties, each of which is 'sufficient for personhood' (i.e., sufficient to make *that soul* a person)" (160). For example, freedom of the will, a first-person perspective, and moral agency are each sufficient for personhood but not for three distinct persons. We are talking, however, not about individual faculties but whole sets of faculties, each set being sufficient for being a person, i.e., for that soul to be personal or at least one person, but not excluding being multiply personal.

11. Indeed, it recalls my own illustration of Cerberus, the three-headed dog guarding the gates of Hades. See Craig and Moreland, *Philosophical Foundations*, 592. In fact, the challenge in such a case is not how to generate the plurality of persons, but how to unite them in one being!

3. The Son is not the Father.

4. There is exactly one God.

But if (1) and (2) are not identity statements but predications meaning *The Father is divine* and *The Son is divine*, then any appearance of inconsistency evaporates. To his credit, Branson acknowledges the adequacy of this solution, though he characterizes it uncharitably, saying, "there are ultimately *only* two ways to solve any version of 3G within classical logic: either equivocate on 'God' in exactly the way Craig does . . . , or count by a relation other than identity" (149n4). Since equivocation is typically regarded as an informal logical fallacy, it is prejudicial to label my solution the "Equivocation Solution." It is better called the "Ambiguity Solution" or even better the "Predicative Solution." As we have seen, it is precisely the failure to see this solution that causes Tuggy to stumble: Unitarianism draws its life from its anachronistic construal of (1) and (2) as identity statements. For my part, I find the Predicative Solution to be far more plausible than the weird relation of numerical sameness without identity to which Branson appeals. It would be at least imprudent to hang the doctrine of the Trinity upon so strange and widely rejected a relation.

Branson identifies three further difficulties related to Tritheism. First, *unclarity*: "Do the persons have a nature at all? If so, is it divine or non-divine? If they have no nature, or only a non-divine nature, how could Christ have two natures, one divine? If they have *a* divine nature, are there two qualitatively different divine natures—one for the persons, and one for the Trinity?" (149) This seems to me to be a reprise of the question whether there is more than one way to be divine.[12] It seems to me that there is. One way is by being an instance of the divine nature, in which case there is only one such instance, namely, the triune God. But the persons can be fully divine in some other way, such as sharing in the concrete divine nature. Maybe they are metaphysically inseparable and overlapping parts of God,[13]

---

12. See Craig and Moreland, *Philosophical Foundations*, 589–90.

13. The ancient doctrine of *perichoresis* seems to anticipate such a conception. In fact, just as the persons are metaphysically inseparable from God, God is also metaphysically inseparable from the persons. Such a position is compatible with my suggestion that any one person is not the whole Trinity. It is simply to say that the Father, for example, is not the whole Godhead. Tertullian, while denying that the Son and Spirit are parts (*pars*) of God, was happy to speak of each as being a portion (*portio*) of God and so sharing in God (Tertullian, *Against Praxeus* 9.2). Perhaps we could say that just as there are portions of my body (say, a strip of my left side and big toe) which are not parts of my body but nonetheless belong to my body (see van Inwagen, "Doctrine of Arbitrary Undetached Parts") so the persons of the Trinity, though not mereological parts of the divine substance, nonetheless belong to it and so share in its divinity. The Latin church father Hilary seems to capture the idea nicely when he asserts, "Each divine person is in the Unity, yet no person is the one God" (*On the Trinity* 7.2; cf. 7.13, 32).

as I have suggested, or maybe they exemplify properties unique to God,[14] as Hasker has maintained. It is an open question. Second, *Biblical problems*: Colossians 2:9 says that the fullness of the divine nature dwells bodily in Christ, but my model denies that Christ has the divine nature. No, my model denies that Christ is *an instance* of the divine nature (lest we have three Gods), but he has the divine nature insofar as he shares in the concrete divine nature. Third, *problems of counting*: On the Predicative Solution there remains a sense in which there are three Gods (the persons). No, there is *no* sense in which there are three Gods, but there are, indeed, three persons.

Other Problems of Counting

As for Branson's problems concerning multiple Saviors, etc., I do not think I need to add anything to what I have already said about the changing referents of such singular terms. Branson in any case admits that the Predicative Solution resolves this problem just as well as it resolves the problem of Tritheism. I stick with Hasker on the question of separable operations *ad extra*. These are challenges only for Branson's complex doctrine of the Trinity, but there is no reason to adopt such doctrinal accretions.

The Problem of Divine Aseity

As for the problem of divine aseity, this is an open question for discussion which the model is not intended to settle. It is not clear to me that the Triune God's existing *a se* and the Trinitarian persons existing *a se* is problematic, especially if the persons are metaphysically inseparable parts of the divine

---

14. Edward Wierenga argues that the persons are divine because they exemplify certain properties unique to God, such as aseity, necessity, omnipotence, omniscience, eternity, and so on (Wierenga, "Trinity and Polytheism"). This answer might seem in danger of lapsing into affirming that each person instantiates the divine nature, which I have rejected. But given that it is an essential property of the divine nature that God is triune, there is no danger here. The persons do not instantiate the divine nature but simply an array of properties belonging to the divine nature that ensure the divinity of each person, since no one but God possesses such properties. This option will be welcomed by those who are reluctant to affirm that God has parts. Hasker suggests a sort of combination of the two approaches: "Suppose, however, we reformulate the answer in this way: *each Person is a proper part of the Trinity 'as a whole' that possesses powers of rationality, volition, and so forth such that the Person is omnipotent, omniscient, and morally perfect*" (*Metaphysics and the Tri-Personal God*, 144). That answer seems to me perfectly acceptable. In the end Hasker advises, "It is much better, I believe, to explain the Godhood of the Persons ... in terms of their possession of the divine attributes of omnipotence, omniscience, perfect goodness, and so on" (249).

substance and not themselves substances. If we divide in thought a physical object such that each half has a property of the whole, are there then three things that have the property? That seems to me ontologically inflationary. If a substance exists necessarily, so do all its metaphysically inseparable parts, but they are not additional things; so also with aseity.

Who Is God? Problem

The problem "Who Is God?" depends on taking "The Father is God" as an identity statement. The fact that the singular term "God" in the relevant context of use in the NT usually refers to the Father does not imply identity.

Theophanies Problem

The so-called theophanies problem seems to have morphed somewhat in Branson's reply. I thought that the problem was supposed to be that the Bible says that no one has ever seen God the Father, but there are numerous theophanies in the OT. The solution is to say that Christ, not the Father, was seen. But this solution is available to any Social Trinitarian. Now the question seems to be whether Christ is the visible image (*eikōn*) of the Trinity or of the Father? As I read the relevant passages, it seems to me that either interpretation is feasible. My model is not intended to answer questions of this sort, and I must confess that I just cannot get worked up about it.

Problem of Socialism

I never expected to be accused of socialism and to have the Iron Lady herself quoted against me! Even granting Branson a good deal of tongue-in-cheek, this charge is spurious. The question here concerns the divine processions. The misgiving that many of us have with subordinationism (in the ontological Trinity, that is, not in the economic Trinity!) is that it diminishes the greatness of Christ, not to mention the Holy Spirit. We want to exalt Christ just as we exalt God the Father. It seems to diminish Christ's divinity to have him depend upon someone else for his very existence. Christ would be greater were he, like the Father, self-existent.

Never mind Branson's attempt to defend the doctrine of divine processions. I wish him well. I really do! What is relevant here, rather, is whether omitting this feature from my model of the Trinity is a positive deficit in that model. I just do not see that it is. Branson thinks that just as socialists achieve equality among the people by reducing everyone to poverty, so my model achieves equality among the Trinitarian persons by reducing them all to a lower status, in particular robbing the Father of a personal great-making property. But if being unbegotten (*agennētos*) is a personal great-making property of the first person of the Trinity, then this property is plausibly great-making when ascribed to the second person of the Trinity. What one takes from the Father is the property of begetting the Son. But I do not see that so doing robs God of any power. Omnipotence requires that there is no state of affairs that God is unable to actualize due to a lack of power on his part.[15] The metaphysical impossibility of begetting a divine person does not diminish God's power in any way. Thus, ascribing the personal property of being *agennētos* to all the Trinitarian persons removes nothing from the Father but adds enormously to the greatness of each of the other two persons.

Conclusion

Branson's conclusion is half-right: Tuggy and I do begin in the same place, with the final authority of inspired Scripture.[16] That is why I took the approach I did in this volume, laying out a biblical doctrine of the Trinity that Tuggy cannot consistently deny. But to suggest that Tuggy and I end in the same place is absurd. Tuggy is a Socinian who thinks that Jesus Christ is a creature, a mere man, and that God commands us to worship this creature. I am a Trinitarian who believes that Jesus Christ is fully and unequivocally divine.

---

15. For discussion, see Leftow, "Omnipotence."

16. As do we all: Ben Witherington III explains that the doctrine of *sola scriptura* meant "that the Bible was the *final authority, and the one that was the litmus test on all other claims in the church about authority, even claims by popes and patriarchs or councils*" (*Sola Scriptura*, 109). The doctrine did not imply that no other sources of authority should be recognized, but merely that none of these "*should be seen as independent* authorities . . . that can *trump* what the Bible actually *teaches*" (121). As such, the doctrine was not a Protestant novelty.

A Defense of Creedal Trinitarianism

Beau Branson

Is what I describe as "a way of stating the doctrine of the Trinity" properly so described—or should it be called a way of *mis*stating the doctrine of the Trinity? Whether my attempt at apologetic in fact *distorts* Christian belief is a point on which I humbly (and sensibly) defer to trained theologians. In matters of speculative theology—and particularly when the question at issue is whether certain theological speculations are in accord with historical orthodoxy—theologians must sit in judgment over mere philosophers.

—Peter van Inwagen[1]

I thank my interlocutors. Space constraints require extreme brevity, so I can only address highlights.

Misunderstandings

Elsewhere I subdivide Trinitarian models based on answers to the "Who Is God?" problem (WIG).[2] Contra Craig (178), and Tuggy (183), Unitarianism isn't a form of Monarchical Trinitarianism (MT), because it isn't a form of Trinitarianism at all.

Solving the Theophanies Problem (TP) doesn't require the doctrine of the Trinity (DOT). Craig infers that solving TP *isn't even a desideratum* for one's theology. This confuses necessary with sufficient conditions. So does his claim that it's a "problem" that the same solution MT provides for

---

1. Van Inwagen, "Three Persons in One Being."
2. Branson, "One God, the Father."

TP works for Social Trinitarianism. Craig quotes me as saying TP was "the most central motivation for [Two Powers] theology" (176). My words were that TP was "*if not* the most central motivation . . . at least *one of the most prominent*" (58). Hurtado's points, etc., I don't deny. I say nothing like, "TP is . . . the one, central, most important reason for affirming the doctrine of the Trinity" as Hasker puts it (170).

Next, I say Trinitarians see the Son and Spirit as "creator" (not creature!), but fourth-century Trinitarians and Arians agreed that the Father is the sole *ultimate reality*, not, as Craig puts it, that "Trinitarians believe that the Father alone is uncreated and the Son and Spirit are creatures" (180), which would be a non-sequitur.

Finally, I owe Craig an apology. He previously claimed that God = the Trinity, while the divine *hypostases* "are not instances of the divine nature" and "are not divine in virtue of exemplifying the divine nature."[3] Apparently, he now believes that God = the divine nature, and the divine *hypostases* "have" and "share" the divine nature (181). Naturally, I consulted his previous publications, as he provided no details about his current view in his opening essay. At any rate, his new position is a step in the right direction, if not ultimately satisfactory.

My Argument

The most important desiderata for a view about the Trinity, I argue, are that it solves the Three God's problem (3G), the Three *F*'s problem (3*F*), TP, and WIG. I discuss several fathers in this connection, but for brevity, let's spotlight Gregory of Nyssa's triadology (GNT) as satisfying the desiderata. My argument is:

GD. GNT is a version of DOT.

GS. GNT solves 3G, 3*F*, WIG, and TP.

DS. Therefore, some version of DOT solves 3G, 3*F*, WIG, and TP.

That's valid. Opponents must deny GD or GS. Hence, attacking "Branson's account" of the Trinity—something I emphasized doesn't exist and plays no role in my argument—constitutes a straw man. Hasker asks: Why not call GNT "my" account? That's flattering. And fine, if one avoids the mistake all my interlocutors make. Tuggy: "Branson does not have any account" (183). Hasker: "[I]t leaves Branson with . . . insoluble difficulties" (172). Craig: "Branson's affirmation . . . smacks of Unitarianism" (182). Below, I'll

---

3. Craig and Moreland, *Philosophical Foundations*, 590.

substitute "Gregory" for "Branson." Otherwise, these wouldn't address my actual argument. Hasker suggests others assume an analogue of GD:

MD. "My model... is an acceptable interpretation of" DOT (169).

That some such premise is necessary is precisely my point.[4] So here we agree. Hasker also agrees that instances of MD "must be argued on a case-by-case basis" (169). But doing so would require ascertaining enough about the content of DOT to determine its coherence directly, with no need for models at all. Hasker hasn't challenged that. So the argument stands. Now let's consider the argument's premises.

GD. GNT Is a Version of DOT

Craig distinguishes the "biblical doctrine of the Trinity" (BDT) from the "creedal doctrine of the Trinity" (CDT) and thinks the source of doctrinal authority is a red herring (176). Similarly, Tuggy imagines my "main concern" is what's "orthodox" (183). But were I a Muslim, or an atheist, rejecting both biblical and ecclesiastical authority, I'd still find nothing wrong with my argument. GNT is still a form of DOT. And GNT still solves the stated desiderata. So, grant whatever you like about "authority." Now back to the question: What is DOT? Is it BDT? CDT? Something else? Suppose Tuggy converted me to Unitarianism. I'd say, "I now believe what the Bible says about the Trinity (BDT) doesn't entail there are three divine persons." I wouldn't say, "I now believe *the doctrine of the Trinity* (DOT) doesn't entail there are three divine persons." If you'd resist the second belief ascription, even when the first fit, you implicitly agree it isn't analytic that:

BDT = DOT

nor that:

BD. BDT is *a version of* DOT[5]

But inferring DOT's coherence from BDT's coherence presupposes BD. Inferring it from the coherence of one's model presupposes an instance of MD. Inferring it from the coherence of GNT presupposes GD. And inferring it from the coherence of CDT presupposes:

CD. CDT is a version of DOT

---

4. See my "Ahistoricity in Analytic Theology."
5. Since versions entail at least as much as what they're versions of.

But neither BD nor just any arbitrary instance of MD is analytic, nor *a priori*. Comparing the content of BDT, or one's model, to that of DOT could support BD or MD. But that requires some independent way of ascertaining the content of DOT. And that's true *whenever* it's not analytic, or *a priori*, that *x* is, or is a version of, DOT. Finally, we can't just *stipulate* the content of DOT. So how do we ascertain its content?

Well, does "the doctrine of the Trinity" mean CDT (or some subset thereof)? Is CD analytic (or in some sense *a priori*)? *Something* like this must be right. Certain creedal, conciliar, and patristic statements are at least partly constitutive of the meaning of the phrase "the doctrine of the Trinity." Thus, I agree with the Hasker who wrote:

> The phrase "the doctrine of the Trinity" is not a neologism whose meaning is up for grabs. The phrase has a determinate denotation, and that denotation most certainly includes the assertions about the Father, the Son, and the Holy Spirit contained in the creed of the council of Constantinople in 381.[6]

Since Gregory, perhaps more than anyone, shaped the outcome of Constantinople I, we also know Gregory Constantinople:

GC. GNT is a version of CDT

Together, GC and CD entail GD. Notice this is simply a question about *semantics*. Authority is, once again, a red herring.

GS. GNT Solves 3G, 3F, WIG, and TP

Denying GS requires denying either my interpretation of GNT or that GNT (so interpreted) solves the desiderata. Nobody seriously challenged my interpretation.[7] And nobody argued GNT (so interpreted) fails to solve TP, WIG, or 3F. Rather, objections targeted 3G. The defense of GNT against 3G can be summarized as:

(1_{3G}) Scripture affirms that there's only one $god_{ULTIMATE-SOURCE}$, not that there's only one god in other senses (such as $god_{POWER/ACTION}$ or god_{NATURE}).

(2_{3G}) A view that endorses the Monarchy of the Father (MoF) has only one $god_{ULTIMATE-SOURCE}$.

---

6. Hasker, "God's Only Begotten Son," 218–19.

7. Though see Hasker's interpretation of Gregory as having the Father delegate operations to the Son.

(3_{3G}) Therefore, a view that endorses MoF has only one god, in the scriptural sense.

(4_{3G}) GNT endorses MoF.

(5_{3G}) Therefore, GNT has only one god, in the scriptural sense.

But (3_{3G}) and (5_{3G}) are valid inferences. And nobody denied (4_{3G}), or (1_{3G}). Finally, (2_{3G}) is true whether we count by identity *or* division. So the objections about counting were also red herrings. Really, that's the end. But I'll address some loose ends.

Tuggy's Definitions

Tuggy dislikes my definitions (184). So let's use Tuggy's definitions.[8] Tuggy says a "god" is an ultimate deity, and that something is "ultimate" if and only if it exists without its existence depending on, or being explained by, anything else, and the existence of everything else depends on, or is explained by, it. With these, we can argue:

(1) On GNT, there's only one thing such that it exists without its existence depending on, or being explained by, anything else, and such that the existence of everything else depends on, or is explained by, it—the Father.

(2) On GNT, the Father is a deity.

(3) Therefore, on GNT, there's only one ultimate deity—the Father.

(4) Therefore, on GNT, there's only one god—the Father.

Tuggy admits (1) and (2). And (3) and (4) are valid inferences. Hence, on Tuggy's own definitions, GNT has only one god—the Father. Tuggy could agree, but argue GNT *also* (inconsistently) entails there are *other* gods, or classify GNT as non-Trinitarian, i.e., reject GD. Tuggy dubs the first option "Basil's Bane" (138). I'll dub the second option "the Hail Mary."

Basil's Bane

Basil's Bane never gets off the ground. It begins with "Regarding the sort of divinity which implies being a god..." (138). But on Tuggy's definitions, having divinity *doesn't* imply being a god. Tuggy later asserts that "something is a god if and only if it is a thing with the divine nature" (188). But as I noted

[8]. From Tuggy, "On Counting Gods."

in my response to Haskser (128ff), a nature is a source of activity intrinsic to its bearer and (following Aristotle) identified with *substance*. So, a Tuggian god is defined partly in terms of *relations*. Nature, essence, or substance isn't. So, there'll be no logical entailment from having the divine nature to being a Tuggian god. Here's an (imperfect, but useful) analogy: the Emperor-Beyond-the-Sea is the supreme ruler ... and a talking lion. "Supreme ruler" tells us what he is in relation to others. "Lion" tells us what he is in himself. So his nature is leoninity, not rulerhood. His son, Aslan, has the same leonine nature. So, that doesn't make him another *supreme ruler*; it makes him another *lion*. Similarly, on Tuggy's definitions: God is the ultimate ... and a deity (i.e., a divine person). "Ultimate" tells us what God is in relation to others. "Deity" (or "divine person") tells us what God is in himself. So God's nature is divinity, not ultimacy. His Son, Jesus Christ, has the same divine nature. So, that doesn't make him another ultimate (another Tuggian god); it makes him another Tuggian deity (i.e., another divine person).

One might dislike these results of Tuggy's definitions. But we're simply asking whether Tuggy's argument works granting his own definitions. It doesn't. On different definitions, the claim that "something is a god if and only if it is a thing with the divine nature" might be analytic. But on Tuggy's definitions it's a substantive metaphysical claim: that certain non-relational features (a nature and its associated causal powers) must always be paired with a certain relational feature (ultimacy). Now, Tuggy could admit that this isn't analytic, and simply assert it as a synthetic *a priori* premise—one Gregory doesn't grant. But first, that would be begging the question. Worse, the metaphysics seems absurd anyway. Natures are individuated by the (aggregates of) causal powers they bestow upon their bearers.[9] Why think the Son couldn't *both* have whatever causal powers characterize the Father's nature, *and* be such that his existence and character somehow derive from the Father?[10] Indeed, why couldn't the Son be an exact intrinsic duplicate of the Father, but differ from the Father only with respect to relations? Furthermore, even if one accepted this metaphysical claim, the conclusion would not be that this version of DOT is *unbiblical* (as Tuggy likes to present things) but simply that it conflicts with one's metaphysics, and a dubious metaphysics at that.

---

9. See my *Logical Problem*, 184–89.

10. Non-causally, if one prefers. See Sijuwade, "Building the Monarchy of the Father."

The Hail Mary

Now consider Tuggy's Hail Mary option, implied when he says "In Branson's [read: Gregory's] view the one true God is *not* the Trinity, but the Father alone; I say that makes him a Unitarian . . . similar to . . . Samuel Clark, John Biddle, and Thomas Emlyn" (183). But Gregory attributes the divine nature to the Son and Spirit. These Unitarians don't. I think the claim that Gregory of Nyssa's triadology is non-Trinitarian is its own *reductio*. But even if it weren't, notice how much Tuggy gives away. My central argument would fail. But, would it matter?

Suppose you take tradition seriously. Tuggy thinks St. Basil's theology was Unitarian, not Trinitarian.[11] I don't know about other traditions, but if a resurrected St. Basil came to an Orthodox church and said, "A few corrections about the Trinity, folks . . . ," most people would sign off on it just given who said it. *Not one person* would say, "Sorry sir. Dale Tuggy says that's not 'properly Trinitarian.'" It's not the label; it's the pedigree.

On the other hand, suppose you're a (pretty extreme) *sola scriptura* Protestant, like Tuggy. You want to be biblical *and that's all*. Now suppose you agreed with Tuggy that, in the NT, God = the Father. But suppose you also agreed with Craig that, in the NT, the Son and Spirit are divine. Suppose further MT made sense of that for you. Then Tuggy says MT isn't "properly Trinitarian." Or, MT isn't really what Gregory of Nyssa believed. Why would you care? It's not unbiblical. Nor incoherent. So what if it's not part of the tradition? You aren't beholden to that tradition. So what if it's not "properly Trinitarian"? By your lights (and Tuggy's!) that doesn't matter. Ironically, right here, at this critical moment, when the ammo is spent, the arguments have all run dry, and Tuggy makes one final, last-ditch effort, it is precisely his fellow *sola scriptura* Protestants—the audience to whom Tuggy most wants to appeal—who have the least reason to care.

Quantity

Though there's much to say about quantity, with limited space I can only address points my interlocutors actually made. Recall, *my* discussion of quantity concerned a potential objection to my interpretation of Gregory, an objection that nobody made. *Gregory* addressed certain objections my interlocutors didn't make, and sometimes couldn't. So, the responses were mostly red herrings.

---

11. This is not a straw man. He literally thinks this. See Tuggy, "When and How?," 36; Tuggy, "Hasker's Tri-Personal God," 154.

Scripture-focused though they be, Tuggy and Craig overlook the source of warrant for the claim "there's only one god": Scripture! How we (today) do or should count isn't the issue. They'd need to show that the relevant scriptural "one god" passages were intended as employing the relatively recent (Fregean) idea that counting works by the relation of identity, rather than the standard view in antiquity that it worked by the relation of division. But no NT author mentions counting differently from other educated people in the Greco-Roman world. And in the Hebrew Bible, some of the very words used for counting have roots involving division. For example, 'מָנָה,' in Genesis 13:16, which Gesenius defines as "prop. to be divided, to be divided out, to divide."[12] My interlocutors made no attempt to show the biblical authors conceptualized number differently from other ancient people. But to pursue $3G_{POWER/ACTION}$ and/or $3G_{NATURE}$, they would've needed to show both

SCI. Scripture counts by identity (or something with similar results)

and, contrary to (1_{3G}), above, at least one of

$1G_{POWER/ACTION}$. Scripture affirms that there's only one god$_{POWER/ACTION}$

$1G_{NATURE}$. Scripture affirms that there's only one god$_{NATURE}$.

But even if they had argued for SCI, nobody argued for $1G_{POWER/ACTION}$. And Hasker and (now) Craig affirm the persons have the divine nature. So they *can't* affirm both SCI and $1G_{NATURE}$, or their own models would fail $3G_{NATURE}$ too. The only attempt to press $3G_{NATURE}$ came from Tuggy (Basil's Bane), who didn't assert $1G_{NATURE}$, but mistakenly thought being a god$_{NATURE}$ *entailed* being a god$_{ULTIMATE-SOURCE}$. Finally, $3F$ would only require showing SCI. But $3F$ affects all my interlocutors, too. So, if they affirm SCI, they owe us clear responses to $3F$.

Hasker's Challenges

So, all challenges to GD and GS have failed. But Hasker challenges GNT on other desiderata, specifically his "What Is a Divine Person?" problem (WIDP), to which he claims to have a "clear and concise answer" (171), and to which he supposes Gregory does not. But is his answer clear? Hasker says the Son "must have (or must be) a distinct center of consciousness" (172). Well, which? First, suppose a Haskerian person *is* a cognitive faculty, *had by* an underlying subject. Then, either I am some metaphysical item had by

---

12. Gesenius and Tregelles, *Gesenius's Hebrew*, 485.

an underlying subject (if I'm the person), or I am not a person, but I "have" a person (if I'm the underlying subject). Neither seems right. Surely I *am* a person and *have* a cognitive faculty.

Alternatively, suppose a Haskerian person *is* an underlying subject that *has* a cognitive faculty. This would be Gregory's answer to WIDP, and the more sensible one.[13] But it ruins one of Hasker's (and Craig's) criticisms,[14] namely that inseparable operations yield "a single person" (171), (181–182). Craig himself cites Hughes (181n12), who argues that if all the *F*s are *G*s, there are at least as many *G*s as there are *F*s.[15] But that entails that the Father, Son, and Spirit must be three persons, regardless of how one defines "person," so long as they are three of *anything*.[16]

The root of this inconsistency is telling. Hasker and Craig see Gregory as having "a single person" for precisely the reason Gregory himself says he has only "one god"[17]—inseparable operations.[18] In other words, their own protests notwithstanding, they actually *agree* with Gregory about counting here. They simply disagree in basic theological assumptions and in terminology. Specifically, there's a certain sort of thing that Gregory, Hasker, and Craig all in fact count in precisely the same way and for precisely the same reason—inseparable operations. Hasker and Craig say there are three of these things. Gregory, only one. Hasker and Craig call these things "divine persons." Gregory calls them "gods."[19] And given that what they call a "being" or *ousia* seems to be what Gregory calls a *hypostasis* (traditionally translated as "person"), they have essentially just reversed the traditional

---

13. This is clear for several reasons. First, Gregory's discussions of "*hypostasis*" trace back to textbooks on grammar (Apollonius Dyscolus) and logic (Porphyry) that are discussing concrete particulars. See *Logical Problem*, 151–61. Second, he explicitly identifies *hypostasis* with ἄτομον (individual) in *Ad Graecos*, GNO III/1, 31, 2–3. Finally, his examples of *hypostases* are always concrete particulars, but don't always have cognitive faculties. E.g., gold coins (*Ad Ablabium*, GNO III/1, 53, 17–21), and stones (*Catechism*, 1.5).

14. The following also holds if persons are *composites* of subject and faculty.

15. Briefly, I think Hughes' claim is simply analytic when we are dealing with *discreet* (*non-overlapping*) items. On the other hand, it's clearly false for overlapping items. If a gallon of water A and a gallon of water B overlap on half a gallon, A and B aren't *two* gallons of water—they're a gallon and a half! But the "undivided Trinity" is *not* divided, i.e., discreet, i.e., non-overlapping. Hence, Hughes' principle doesn't apply.

16. Note another inconsistency. In his response to me, Craig argues we count by identity (181). But in his response to Tuggy, he claims ancient people lacked the very concept of identity (203).

17. In the sense of gods$_{POWER/ACTION}$.

18. And this gives the lie to Craig's claim that inseparable operations are a "superfluous add-on" (181).

19. In the sense of gods$_{POWER/ACTION}$.

definitions of "person" and "nature" so that what Craig calls "Tripersonal Monotheism," Gregory might have called "Tritheistic Modalism."

Next, Hasker says the doctrine of inseparable operations "leaves Branson [read: Gregory] with major, perhaps insoluble, difficulties" (172). Quoting Leftow, he asks "did the whole Trinity will, 'the Son shall become incarnate?' The Son could not learn from that that *he* would become incarnate" (172). But what's the argument? Is the problem that there's a truth the Son doesn't know? Hasker himself says no divine person can know both what the Son knows in knowing "I shall become incarnate" and what the Father knows in knowing "I shall not become incarnate" (172). So on Hasker's own account no divine person knows all true propositions. Or, is the idea only that every truth should be known by at least one divine person? If so, consider proposition p: "No divine person knows this proposition (p) is true." If p is false, some divine person knows p. But that's incoherent, since a false proposition can't be known. So p must be true. So no divine person knows p. Such puzzles affect theism generally, not only specific theologies. Perhaps God's thoughts have "alien structure" and do not fit into any of our usual ontological categories.[20] If not, Hasker needs to show there's a solution to such general problems with indexicals that isn't simultaneously a solution to the problems he is raising. But he's given no reason to think this.

Next, Hasker says "All patristic writers . . . understood [Jesus' speaking to the Father in the NT] as a *relationship between Father and Son within the Trinity*" (173). But merely glancing at commentaries on the very passages he cites reveals numerous fathers reading these precisely as statements stemming from Christ's human nature, and specifically *not* the divine.[21] Further, as Derek King notes, in *Contra Eunomium*, Gregory argues at length against the possibility of speech (or communication generally) within the immanent Trinity.[22]

Finally, when Gregory says (in *Ad Ablabium*) that the Father judges *through* the Son, Hasker interprets this (with no textual evidence) as the Father "delegating" judgment to the Son, arguing, "this delegation is an act of the Father alone" (172). But Gregory explicitly rejects this view. Eunomius claims that "to him [i.e., the Son] is delegated by the Father the design of all things." Gregory calls this "blasphemy . . . like venomous wasps. The design of all things, he says, was 'delegated' by the Father. If the discussion were about some craftsman fitting his product at the will of his employer, could

---

20. See Eklund, "Alien Structure."

21. For just two examples, Ambrose, *De Fide* II.VII.56; Cyril, *Commentary on John*, 14:16–17.

22. See King, "To Whom Can God Speak?"

we not have used the same language? . . . The term 'delegated' implies that the ability and authority to be Designer was something acquired."[23]

Conclusion

I've argued a version of DOT (namely, GNT) satisfies our desiderata. Every challenge to that argument failed. Challenges to GNT based on additional desiderata also failed. Until some other challenge is articulated, I know of no good arguments against DOT.

---

23. Gregory of Nyssa, *Contra Eunomium III*.9. To clarify my exchange with Hasker, I think the mere relation of agent to principal, considered in the abstract, could be fairly described as grounding an "inseparable operation." Hence, the Father (as principal) judging through the Son (as agent) needn't in itself violate inseparable operations. However, Hasker's point is to introduce a *separate operation* of "delegating," which by hypothesis is not shared with the Son. *That* would indeed contradict inseparable operations. But it's also a bad interpretation of Gregory, as this quotation shows.

Facts Are Facts

Dale Tuggy

My thanks to Branson, Craig, and Hasker for a vigorous and revealing series of arguments. I'll try to address their most important points in this brief conclusion.

Retreat, Not Defense

Many will be disturbed by the defenses of "the doctrine of the Trinity" in this book. An army of apologists and conservative systematic theologians assure us that some Trinity doctrine or other is "clearly implied by all that Scripture says,"[1] that "faithful exegesis of biblical texts necessitates a Trinitarian reading,"[2] or that "the doctrine of the Trinity is taught in the 'gutter' between Malachi and Matthew" so that "in the incarnation . . . and the outpouring of the Holy Spirit . . . we have the full doctrine of the Trinity revealed to us."[3] In contrast, none of this book's Trinity theory defenders agrees that any such doctrine is a part of the contents of the NT books, being obviously implied or assumed by such. They are correct; *obvious* implications or assumptions are understood right away by most competent readers, but we have no record of any tripersonal-god defenders before the second half of the 300s, well into the so-called "Arian" controversy.

---

1. Olson and Hall, *Trinity*, 2.
2. Crowe and Trueman, *Essential Trinity*, 20.
3. White, "Conversation," 97. See also Barrett, *Simply Trinity*, 108.

Replacing U with Something Better?

In my opening essay I displayed twenty facts which strongly confirm the hypothesis that the NT authors are Unitarian (U) over the hypothesis that they are Trinitarian (T).[4] In response, all three of my interlocutors disavow T. What, then, could explain those facts, if not U?

Hasker gestures at the work of Hurtado and Ayres; I've read them both, and I can assure the reader that they say nothing about early Christian beliefs that explains F1–F20 better than U. Branson offers a rival thesis, what he calls MT_{NT}, that these authors identify the only god with the Father and also assume the full deity of each of the Father, Son, and Spirit (211). As MT_{NT} abandons the triune God of T, F1–F3 and F8–F19 don't confirm U over MT_{NT}. But F4–F7 and F10–F20 do, and very strongly. Craig's threadbare "biblical Trinity" thesis (a.k.a. T*) can't be disconfirmed relative to U by F1–F20, but as I've pointed out, it's compatible with U, and so should not count as interestingly "Trinitarian"; it's a surrender of Trinitarian orthodoxy masquerading as a defense of it. And it's too thin to serve as an explanation for the cited facts. In sum, no better explanation for F1–F20 than U has been proposed.

The Trinity Theories on the Menu

Four Trinity theories are proposed above.[5] Each of my opponents has left some things unclear. Of Hasker's many claims, the reader wonders which exactly are essential to "the" doctrine? That is, how many could be denied or at least not affirmed while still being an orthodox Trinitarian?

Craig's position in this book is unclear. In past writings and sometimes in this book he appears to assume the numerical identity of the one god with the Trinity (the tripersonal God).[6] But he also concedes that the unique "God" mentioned in the Old Testament is the Father! (29, 179) If so, then like some of the ancient gnostics, Craig would be committed to the view that the unique "God" of the Old Testament *isn't* the one true God (since

---

4. For definitions of U and T, see p. 88.

5. Craig offers two, his minimalist "biblical" one and his more speculative soul-based one; I take it that in his view these can both be true. The reader should note that many recent Trinity theories go unmentioned in this book, on which see my "Trinity."

6. "'The Trinity is God' is an identity statement" (Moreland and Craig, *Philosophical Foundations*, 589). See also Craig, "Another Glance at Trinity Monotheism," 129–30. In this book, "the one God exists as or in three equally divine persons" (51). Further, this seems to be assumed by his model of the Trinity as one soul (=God) with three cognitive faculties.

in his view the Father is numerically distinct from the Trinity).[7] But on the other hand, in his reply to me Craig *denies* that a core claim of any Trinity theory is the identity of the one God with the Trinity, and he also *denies* the identity of the one God with the Trinity (203). But Trinitarian theologians typically say things that imply that the only god is numerically the same as the tripersonal god/Trinity.[8]

In order to undermine my strong case that the NT authors assume and assert the numerical identity of the unique god with the Father, Craig resorts to the desperate claim that most ancient people lacked the concept of identity, and even that most modern people do (203)! This is about as plausible as urging that most normal people lack the concept *existing*. Both concepts are fundamental to human thinking; human adults naturally have and regularly employ the concept of numerical sameness. Suppose you refer to something. Now again a moment later, you refer to something. Have you referred to the same thing twice, or to two things? The ability to ask that question presupposes the concept of numerical identity.[9] While ancients lacked a formal logic that treats numerical sameness as a unique relation,[10] they had the concept *being-the-same-thing-as*, just as ordinary folk now do. The use of this concept is how we as it were collapse together multiple things in our picture of reality and its inhabitants.[11] Abram *just is* Abraham (Gen 17:5); counting two things each of which is a man would be overcounting. To say that most ancients lacked this concept is to attribute an odd mental handicap to them. Thus when trying to express what the ancient Christians thought about God, Craig goes mushy, assuring us that they held the word "God" to be properly applied to three "persons" and that "there is exactly one God" (203). Really? *And who or what was* that unique god, in their view? Evidently in his view they asserted the reality of exactly one god while not identifying this one god with either the Father or with the Trinity or indeed with anything whatsoever, since they lacked the concept of numerical identity. But this is uncharitable in the extreme. Meanwhile John *does* have the concept, as in Craig's view he "identifies the Logos with the pre-incarnate

---

7. If there are such things, they must be numerically distinct, as they simultaneously differ, e.g., one is and the other isn't tripersonal.

8. E.g., "the Christian God is triune" (Reeves, *Delighting in the Trinity*, 16.); "the one and only true God is the Trinity itself" (Lombard, *Sentences*, 29 [1.4.2.2]); "The one God is the Trinity" (Emery, *Trinity*, 46); "to Christians God means the Trinity . . . God is . . . a Trinity of three persons" (Ware, *Orthodox Church*, 208–9).

9. Alston and Bennett, "Identity and Cardinality," 558.

10. Sider, *Logic for Philosophy*, 107–9.

11. Morris, *Understanding Identity Statements*.

Christ" (39).[12] And the anti-modalist portion of Trinitarian confessions is most naturally understood as a denial of the numerical identity of any two "persons" of the Trinity.[13]

I'm puzzled by Branson's two definitions of "Monarchical Trinitarianism" (MT). He first defines it as affirming that the Father is the source without source and that "God" applies to him particularly because he is that (65). In my reply I pointed out that this definition is very broad, including some triune-god theories but not others, and also Unitarian theologies. But in his reply to me Branson offers a competitor to T and U called MT_{NT}, that the NT authors assume MT, which is *now* "the numerical identity of the one God with the Father, and the full deity of [each of] the Father, Son, and Holy Spirit" (211). The earlier definition of MT allows some triune-God theorists into the club, but the second excludes them, since a god that is numerically the same as the Father can't also be numerically the same as the Trinity.[14] The first definition is silent on the full deity of each person, but the second asserts it. The first definition allows for the Hasker (and former Craig) position that only the Trinity is fully divine (divine in the way that implies being a god), but the second rules it out.

To interpret Branson charitably, perhaps the first definition was meant to include conformity to the 381 Constantinopolitan creed, on the grounds that any Trinity theory properly so-called must be ecumenical-creed-compliant. This would arguably make the first definition compatible with the second, since that creed implies the equal divinity of each person, given Branson's view that the 381 creed assumes the identity of the only god not with the Trinity but rather with the Father.[15] Of course, if this interpretation of Branson is correct, then his first, official definition of MT doesn't, as one might think, allow tripersonal god theorists to count as "Monarchical Trinitarians."

---

12. I take it that Craig means not only that John *closely associates together* the *Logos* and the man Christ, but rather (as orthodoxy arguably requires) the *Logos* and the man Jesus are one and the same thing, being one and the same self.

13. Thus, analyses of Trinitarian claims standardly include statements we can represent as $f \neq s$, $s \neq h$, and $h \neq f$. See Branson, "No New Solutions"; Cartwright, "Logical Problem."

14. The Trinity, if there is such a thing, is numerically distinct from the Father, as it simultaneously or timelessly qualitatively differs from the Father, e.g., only the former is tripersonal.

15. I disagree; in my view that creed assumes the identity of God with the Trinity. See my "When and How?"

Not Enough Christology?

Hasker and Craig complain that I only defend Unitarianism in general, not also defending my Christology which denies Jesus' literal pre-human existence (197, 203). But this is as it should be; this book is about whether God just is the Father himself, as Branson and I hold, or whether God just is the Trinity, as Hasker holds.[16] No author here has defended his full Christology. I've proven that for the authors of the NT, the one God is none other than the Father, and not anyone or anything else, including an imagined Trinity (tripersonal God) which they never mention. Triune-God speculations clash with this teaching. It's a further question how to understand the metaphysics of God's unique human Son.

Facts Are Facts

I based my opening argument on facts each of which would be surprising if the NT authors were Trinitarians (T), but which would be either expected or much less surprising if they were Unitarians (U). As best I can tell, Branson grants the truth of F1–F20, and Hasker grants all but F5 and F18 (more on these below), while Craig denies F2–F5, F8, F11–F13, F15, and F18–19. Craig affirms F1, F9, F14, F16, and withholds judgment on (neither affirming nor denying) F2. The others—F6, F7, F10, F17, and F20—Craig fails to engage, instead mentioning them and then jumping off to other talking points. Craig is mistaken about F2 according to the standard lexicon, which mentions no use of *theos* for the Trinity,[17] and those facts that Craig affirms together with those he ignores taken together strongly confirm U over T. He asserts that the handful of texts in which the Greek word *theos* is used of Jesus prove that he's fully divine according to these authors, refuting U. I have thoroughly rebutted this argument above. But also, as he points out, a set of facts taken in isolation may point in one direction (*by itself*, that they call Jesus *theos* may suggest that these authors think him to be fully divine), although considered as part of a broader set of facts, they may point in a different direction[18]—which is the point of F6. The wider pattern of the NT usage of *theos is* fairly surprising if the authors believe Jesus is fully

---

16. As just explained, it is unclear where Craig stands on this question, given what he's written here.

17. *BDAG*, 398–400.

18. This is the answer to Hasker's question (198) about what is wrong with sticking to traditional proof texts for the Trinity or the deity of Christ.

divine (as thesis T says), not expected, but it is less surprising given U.[19] And that pattern is *very* surprising given T. Thus, F6 somewhat confirms U over the supposition that these authors believe the deity of Christ and strongly confirms U over T. In sum, Craig's assaults on the facts leave a compelling argument for U intact.

About Hasker's two factual challenges, F5 survives scrutiny, as the Jews of John 5:18 should be understood as misunderstanding Jesus' claims, as happens frequently in the book.[20] At Jesus' trials even in this book no Jewish opponent even bothers to lob the charge that Jesus claimed to be either God or fully divine (John 18:12–14, 19–24, 28–40; 19:1–22). And that makes sense, since according to this book on another occasion Jesus *corrected* the misunderstanding that he was "making himself God" (John 10:22–39).[21] About F18, the NT authors' total lack of interest in the eternality of the Son or Spirit: no, neither existing before Abraham nor at the time the cosmos was created ("in the beginning") nor even before then implies having always existed.[22] This is why Origen concocted a speculative argument that the existence of the Father logically implies that of the Logos/Son, so that it is impossible for the first to exist without the second.[23]

Craig's Shortcuts

Craig starts and ends with the objection that "scholars" simply don't countenance any Unitarian understanding of the NT. A Protestant should be wary of such short-cuts; such a charge would have been easily lobbed at the sixteenth-century Reformers—but that would have been to ignore their then-unpopular insights. When one is a member of an intellectual guild, here the relevant ones being present-day broadly conservative systematic theologians and NT scholars, a danger is that one doesn't take seriously what the guild doesn't take seriously. Craig, being a member of the first and a fellow-traveler of the second, has never, so far as I can tell, in his long and distinguished career taken seriously any sort of Unitarian understanding of the NT. I take it the reason is that those guilds don't. They suffer from a blind-spot that earlier generations didn't have. From the Reformation until

19. Similar points apply about the worship of Jesus and F7.
20. Carter, *John*, 69–71, 114–16.
21. Tuggy, "Jesus's Argument in John 10."
22. What would satisfy me, Hasker asks (198). Any clear statement, implication, or assumption of Jesus' always having existed.
23. Origen, *On First Principles*, vol. 1, section 1.2; Widdicombe, *Fatherhood of God*, chapter 3.

American congregationalist Unitarianism flamed out as a Christian movement in the second half of the 1800s, and even beyond, many scholars took Unitarian interpretations seriously, and rightly so.[24] In the late 1990s and early 2000s I read a lot of that same early modern literature, and it opened my mind to the plausibility of interpretations of the Bible that don't support any Trinity theory. Happily, most of the laity nowadays do not suffer from Craig's (and Hasker's) blind-spot, and so too now some PhDs have seen the light, with more daily.[25]

Craig strives to find some methodological disqualification for my main argument. He asserts that the likelihood principle can't be applied to understanding a written source (201). To the contrary, my whole procedure is in the service of historical-critical interpretation, understanding these authors' thoughts in their own contexts. My argument is not offered as a substitute for "a close and careful reading of the texts" (201). As I explained, one reason for my approach here was that experience shows that Trinitarians are liable to cry "begging the question" when non-Trinitarian exegesis is done, leading to an argumentative stalemate. Thus, I adopted a style of argument that visibly does *not* assume the truth of Unitarianism. About my arguments from silence, Craig cites an excellent article that in fact raises no problems for the sorts of arguments from silence I employ.

More on target, Craig is correct in noting that even if a bunch of observations favor H_1 over H_2, it could be that *given additional evidence*, on the whole H_2 is more plausible than H_1. In Craig's view, my argument egregiously ignores evidence that refutes the hypothesis U; but by this he means mostly what he takes to be rock-solid evidence that the NT authors held Jesus to be fully divine, which I've answered above and at greater length elsewhere.[26] In my view, U explains the NT facts better than any of Craig's thoughts on "the Trinity," and his Christology clashes both with the facts and with itself.[27]

---

24. In 1943 Trinitarian theologian Leonard Hodgson wrote, "The impression which they [i.e., early modern Trinitarian-Unitarian controversies] leave on my mind is that on the basis of argument which both sides held in common, the Unitarians had the better case. They could counter their opponents' biblical exegesis with interpretations equally, if not more, convincing." See Hodgson, *Doctrine of the Trinity*, 223.

25. E.g., Gaston, *Dynamic Monarchianism*; Nemes, *Trinity and Incarnation*.

26. See Tuggy and Date, *Is Jesus Human and Not Divine?*

27. Tuggy, "Craig's Contradictory Christ."

A Paradigm Shift

No Unitarian bases their understanding of NT theology and Christology only on something like my argument from F1–F20. Many of us have reflected long and hard over all the traditional Trinity and deity-of-Christ proof-texts, eventually finding non-anachronistic, well-motivated, and plausible interpretations that fail to support any Trinity theory. And those of us who began as some sort of Trinitarian have after much study undergone what philosophers of science describe as a paradigm shift.[28] Whereas before, some Trinity theory or other seemed like the only or best explanation of what we'd observed in Scripture, now some Unitarian theory seems a better explanation, and we no longer see the sources as even motivating any Trinity theory. The point of arguments like the one in my opening chapter is to get the Trinitarian reader to start to see a cascading pile-up of anomalies—phenomena that ill-fit her preferred theory—so that she can start to wonder if she's thus far considered a wide enough array of interpretations. Only her own further study and God's grace can lead her through an enlightening paradigm shift.

Nomina Sacra, and Which New Testament?

About Branson's five challenges, I've answered the second and third above.[29] About Jesus' names and titles being written as *nomina sacra* in early manuscripts, this is expected given Branson's second definition of MT (or T) and it is somewhat surprising given U. But as we've seen, for the early Christians Jesus should be given religious worship or honor; those special abbreviations are just a written form of that, and so they should not trouble Unitarians. Given U together with F7 the practice is unsurprising, maybe even expected.

Has Craig, as Branson urges, shown other NT facts that refute U? No. And F3–F8 and F11–F18 *strongly* confirm that the NT authors assumed Jesus not to be fully divine over the hypothesis that they assumed him to be fully divine.

What if *other*, less widely used New Testament collections teach some triune-god theory, or Branson's Unitarian subordinationism (MT), or at least the full deity of Christ? Given the history of theology, we would expect these to include at least one writing that is, respectively, (roughly)

---

28. The classic source on this is Kuhn, *Structure of Scientific Revolutions*.
29. About his first challenge, see my "Jude 4."

post-370,[30] post-381, or post-325. Thus, any such collection will be controversial, as it has abandoned the ancient requirement that any such writings should be from the apostles and their circles—or at least their era. For the sake of argument here I've assumed the correctness of the traditional Protestant-Catholic-Orthodox NT collection. But for me such books are authoritative not because Mother Church says they are, but rather because they are non-pseudepigraphal works that correctly capture the teachings of the original apostles and their circles. I assume that if anything this collection includes too much, not too little; I doubt that the mainstream passed over any genuinely apostolic text. Could I be mistaken? Yes. But in my view it is acceptable if we are a bit unsure about the exact boundaries of this collection, as we are concerning our Old Testament,[31] and as the Jews were with their Bible until the end of the second or the early third century CE.[32]

Conclusion

The case for U over T has not been successfully rebutted, nor has anyone put forward a hypothesis that explains the facts better than U. Let the reader decide: is the one God of the New Testament the Father alone, or is he (or it?) this unmentioned tripersonal god, the Trinity of later catholic traditions? If the former, then reformation must go further than most assume. First, decide who the one true God is, according to Scripture. Then, decide exactly what to make of the metaphysics of his unique Son and of God's spirit/Spirit. Use the clearer and more numerous texts to illuminate the darker and less numerous; this is the way of humility and discipleship.

---

30. The second version of Branson's MT requires the full deity of the Holy Spirit, a thesis that became mainstream only towards the end of the "Arian" controversy, and which is arguably first assumed or implied by a major creed in 381.

31. Brettler, "Canonization of the Bible," 2076.

32. McDonald, *Biblical Canon*, 187, 383–84.

Bibliography

Allfree, Mark. "The Holy Spirit." In *One God the Father*, edited by Thomas E. Gaston, 107–19. Tyne and Wear, UK: Willow, 2013.

Alston, William, and Jonathan Bennett. "Identity and Cardinality: Geach and Frege." *The Philosophical Review* 93 (1984) 553–67.

Ambrose of Milan. *Nicene and Post-Nicene Fathers*. 2nd series, vol. 10. Edited by Philip Schaff and Henry Wace. Reprint, Peabody, MA: Hendrickson, 1995.

Arnobius. *The Case against the Pagans*. Translated by George E. McCracken. Vol. 1. Ancient Christian Writers 7. New York: Newman, 1949.

Athenagoras. *Embassy for the Christians; The Resurrection of the Dead*. Translated by Joseph Hugh Crehan. Ancient Christian Writers 23. Westminster, MD: Newman, 1956.

Augustine. *On the Trinity*. Translated by Edmund Hill. Hyde Park, NY: New City, 1991.

Averroes (ibn Rushd). *Averroes' Middle Commentaries on Aristotle's Categories and De Interpretatione*. Translated by Charles E. Butterworth. Princeton: Princeton University Press, 1983.

Ayres, Lewis. *Augustine and the Trinity*. Cambridge: Cambridge University Press, 2010.

———. *Nicaea and Its Legacy: An Approach to Fourth-Century Trinitarian Theology*. Oxford: Oxford University Press, 2004.

Baber, Harriet. "The Trinity." In *The Internet Encyclopedia of Philosophy*. https://iep.utm.edu/trinity/.

Baker, Kenneth. *Jesus Christ—True God and True Man: A Handbook on Christology for Non-Theologians*. South Bend, IN: St. Augustine's, 2013.

Baker, Lynn Rudder. *The Metaphysics of Everyday Life: An Essay in Practical Realism*. Cambridge: Cambridge University Press, 2007.

Barnes, Michel René. *The Power of God: Dunamis in Gregory of Nyssa's Trinitarian Theology*. Washington, DC: Catholic University of America Press, 2001.

———. "The Visible Christ and the Invisible Trinity: MT. 5:8 in Augustine's Trinitarian Theology of 400." *Modern Theology* 19 (2003) 329–55.

Barker, Margaret. *The Great Angel: A Study of Israel's Second God*. Louisville: Westminster/John Knox, 1992.

Barrett, C. K. *The Gospel according to St. John*. 2nd ed. Philadelphia: Westminster, 1978.

Barrett, Matthew. *Simply Trinity: The Unmanipulated Father, Son, and Spirit*. Grand Rapids: Baker, 2021.

Basil of Caesarea. *Against Eunomius*. Translated by Mark DelCogliano and Andrew Radde-Gallwitz. The Fathers of the Church 122. Washington, DC: Catholic University of America Press, 2011.

———. *Letters and Select Works*. Edited by Philip Schaff and Henry Wallace. Translated by Blomfield Jackson. Nicene and Post-Nicene Fathers, 2nd series, vol. 8. Edinburgh: T&T Clark, 1894.

———. *On Christian Doctrine and Practice*. Edited by Mark DelCogliano. Popular Patristics Series 47. Crestwood, NY: St. Vladimir's Seminary Press, 2012.

———. *On the Holy Spirit*. Translated by Stephen Hildebrand. Popular Patristics Series 42. Crestwood, NY: St. Vladimir's Seminary Press, 2011.

Bauckham, Richard. "Biblical Theology and the Problems of Monotheism." In *Out of Egypt: Biblical Theology and Biblical Interpretation*, edited by Craig Bartholomew et al., 187–232. Carlisle, UK: Paternoster, 2004.

———. *Jesus and the God of Israel*. Milton Keynes, UK: Paternoster, 2008.

———. "The Throne of God and the Worship of Jesus." In *The Jewish Roots of Christological Monotheism*, edited by Carey C. Newman et al., 43–69. Leiden: Brill, 1999.

Bauer, D. R. "Son of God." In *Dictionary of Jesus and the Gospels*, edited by Joel Green and Scot McKnight, 769–75. Downers Grove, IL: InterVarsity, 1992.

Beale, G. K., and D. A. Carson. *Commentary on the New Testament Use of the Old Testament*. Grand Rapids: Baker Academic, 2007.

Beckwith, Francis. *Return to Rome: Confessions of an Evangelical Catholic*. Grand Rapids: Brazos, 2009.

Beeley, Christopher. *Gregory of Nazianzus on the Trinity and the Knowledge of God*. New York: Oxford University Press, 2008.

Bertaina, David, et al., eds. *Heirs of the Apostles: Studies on Arabic Christianity in Honor of Sidney H. Griffith*. Leiden: Brill, 2019.

Biddle, John. *A Confession of Faith Touching the Holy Trinity; According to the Scripture, in The Faith of One God*. In *The Faith of One God*, edited by T. Firmin. London: Thomas, 1691.

———. *The Testimonies*. 1691. Reprint, Morrisville, NC: Lulu, 2008.

———. "XII Arguments Drawn Out of the Scripture: Wherein the Commonly Received Opinion Touching the Deity of the Holy Spirit, Is Clearly and Fully Refuted." In *The Faith of One God*. Reprint, no loc: Lulu.com, 2008.

Bird, Michael. *Evangelical Theology: A Biblical and Systematic Introduction*. 2nd ed. Grand Rapids: Zondervan Academic, 2020.

Bock, Darrell. "Blasphemy and the Jewish Examination of Jesus." *Bulletin for Biblical Research* 17 (2007) 53–114.

Boethius. *Boethian Number Theory: A Translation of the "De Institutione Arithmetica."* With introduction and notes by Michael Masi. Amsterdam: Rodopi, 1983.

Bowman, Robert. "The Biblical Basis of the Doctrine of the Trinity: An Outline Study." https://bib.irr.org/biblical-basis-of-doctrine-of-trinity.

———. "Triadic New Testament Passages and the Doctrine of the Trinity." *The Journal for Trinitarian Studies and Apologetics* 1 (2013) 7–54.

Bowman, Robert, and J. Ed Komoszewski. *Putting Jesus in His Place: The Case for the Deity of Christ*. 2nd ed. Grand Rapids: Kregal, forthcoming.

Boyarin, Daniel. *Border Lines: The Partition of Judaeo-Christianity*. Philadelphia: University of Pennsylvania Press, 2010.

———. "The Gospel of the Memra: Jewish Binitarianism and the Prologue to John." *Harvard Theological Review* 94 (2001) 243–84.
———. *The Jewish Gospels: The Story of the Jewish Christ*. New York: New, 2012.
———. "Logos, a Jewish Word: John's Prologue as Midrash." In *The Jewish Annotated New Testament*, edited by Amy-Jill Levine and Marc Zvi Brettler, 688–91. 2nd ed. New York: Oxford University Press, 2017.
Bradshaw, David. *Aristotle East and West: Metaphysics and the Division of Christendom*. Cambridge: Cambridge University Press, 2004.
Branson, Beau. "Ahistoricity in Analytic Theology." *American Catholic Philosophical Quarterly* 92 (2018) 195–224.
———. "Gregory of Nyssa on the Individuation of Actions and Events." In *Eastern Christian Approaches to Philosophy*, edited by James Siemans and Joshua Matthan Brown, 123–48. Basingstoke, UK: Palgrave Macmillan, 2022.
———. "The Logical Problem of the Trinity." PhD diss., University of Notre Dame, 2014.
———. "No New Solutions to the Logical Problem of the Trinity." *Journal of Applied Logics* 6 (2019) 1051–92.
———. "One God, the Father: The Neglected Doctrine of the Monarchy of the Father, and Its Implications for the Analytic Debate about the Trinity." *TheoLogica* 6 (2022) 1–53.
Brant, Jo-Ann A. *John*. Grand Rapids: Baker Academic, 2011.
Bratcher, Robert, and William Reyburn. *A Handbook on Psalms*. New York: United Bible Societies, 1991.
Brettler, Marc Zvi. "The Canonization of the Bible." In *The Jewish Study Bible*, edited by Adele Berlin and Marc Zvi Brettler, 2072–77. New York: Oxford University Press, 2004.
Bricker, Philip. "Identity." In *Encyclopedia of Philosophy*, edited by Donald Borchert, 567–72. 2nd ed. Detroit: Macmillan Reference USA, 1996.
Brower, Jeffrey. "The Problem with Social Trinitarianism: A Reply to Wierenga." *Faith and Philosophy* 21 (2004) 295–303.
Brower, Jeffrey, and Michael C. Rea. "Material Constitution and the Trinity." *Faith and Philosophy* 22 (2005) 57–76.
Brown, David. *The Divine Trinity*. London: Duckworth, 1985.
Brown, Raymond. *The Birth of the Messiah: A Commentary on the Infancy Narratives in the Gospels of Matthew and Luke*. New York: Doubleday, 1999.
———. *The Epistles of John*. Garden City, NY: Doubleday, 1982.
———. *The Gospel according to John (I–XII)*. New Haven: Yale University Press, 2008.
Bruce, F. F. *The Gospel of John*. Grand Rapids: Eerdmans, 1983.
Bucur, Bogdan. "Theophanies and Vision of God in Augustine's *De Trinitate*: An Eastern Orthodox Perspective." *St. Vladimir's Theological Quarterly* 52 (2008) 67–93.
Bultmann, Rudolf. *Essays: Philosophical and Theological*. London: SCM, 1955.
———. *The Gospel of John: A Commentary*. Translated by G. R. Beasley-Murray et al. Philadelphia: Westminster, 1971.
Calvin, John. *Institutes of the Christian Religion*. Translated by Henry Beveridge. Peabody, MA: Hendrickson, 2008.
Capes, David. *Old Testament Yahweh Texts in Paul's Christology*. Tübingen: Mohr-Siebeck, 1992.
Carraway, George. *Christ Is God over All*. London: T&T Clark, 2013.

Carson, D. A. *The Gospel according to John*. Grand Rapids: Eerdmans, 1991.
Carter, Warren. *John: Storyteller, Interpreter, Evangelist*. Peabody, MA: Hendrickson, 2006.
Cartwright, Richard. "On the Logical Problem of the Trinity." In *Philosophical Essays*, 187–200. Cambridge: MIT Press, 1987.
Catechism of the Catholic Church. Mahwah, NJ: Paulist, 1994.
Chandler, Kegan A. *The God of Jesus in Light of Christian Dogma: The Recovery of New Testament Theology*. McDonough, GA: Restoration Fellowship, 2016.
Channing, William Ellery. "Unitarian Christianity. Discourse at the Ordination of the Rev. Jared Sparks. Baltimore, 1819." In *The Complete Works of W. E. Channing, D.D*. New York: Routledge, 1884.
Christie, William. *Dissertations on the Unity of God*. Reprint, no loc: Lulu.com, 2008.
Clarke, Samuel. *The Scripture Doctrine of the Trinity*. In *The Scripture Doctrine of the Trinity and Related Writings*. In *The Works of Samuel Clarke, D.D., Late Rector of St. James's Westminster; in Four Volumes*, edited by J. Clarke. London: John and Paul Knapton, 1738.
Coakley, Sarah. *God, Sexuality, and the Self: An Essay "On the Trinity."* Cambridge: Cambridge University Press, 2013.
Collins, Kenneth L., and Jerry L. Walls. *Roman but Not Catholic: What Remains at Stake 500 Years after the Reformation*. Grand Rapids: Baker Academic, 2017.
Cook, Catherine. "I Rolled a One and I'm Dead: Person Reference across the Multiple Worlds of Table-Top Roleplaying Games." PhD diss., Monash University, 2017.
Craig, William Lane. "Another Glance at Trinity Monotheism." In *Philosophical and Theological Essays on the Trinity*, edited by Michael C. Rea and Thomas McCall, 126–30. New York: Oxford University Press, 2009.
———. *Atonement and the Death of Christ: An Exegetical, Historical, and Philosophical Exploration*. Waco, TX: Baylor University Press, 2020.
———. *God and Abstract Objects: The Coherence of Theism III: Aseity*. Berlin: Springer, 2017.
———. *God over All: Divine Aseity and the Challenge of Platonism*. New York: Oxford University Press, 2016.
———. "Is God the Son Begotten in His Divine Nature?" *TheoLogica* 3 (2019) 22–32.
Cross, Richard. "Gregory of Nyssa on Universals." *Vigiliae Christianae* 56 (2002) 372–410.
———. "Two Models of the Trinity? *Heythrop Journal* 43 (2002) 275–94.
Crowe, Brandon, and Carl Trueman, eds. *The Essential Trinity: New Testament Foundations and Practical Relevance*. Phillipsburg, NJ: P&R, 2017.
Cyril of Alexandria. *Commentary on John*. Vol. 2. Downers Grove, IL: InterVarsity, 2015.
Dahms, John V. "The Generation of the Son." *Journal of the Evangelical Theological Society* 32 (1989) 493–501.
Danker, Frederick William (BDAG). *A Greek-English Lexicon of the New Testament and Other Early Christian Literature*. 4th ed. Chicago: University of Chicago Press, 2021.
Danker, Frederick William, and Kathryn Krug. *The Concise Greek-English Lexicon of the New Testament*. Chicago: University of Chicago Press, 2009.
De Young, Stephen. *The Religion of the Apostles: Orthodox Christianity in the First Century*. Chesterton, IN: Ancient Faith, 2021.

Dodd, C. H. *The Interpretation of the Fourth Gospel.* Cambridge: Cambridge University Press, 1953.

Dunn, James D. G. *Christology in the Making: A New Testament Inquiry into the Origins of the Doctrine of the Incarnation.* 2nd ed. Grand Rapids: Eerdmans, 2011.

———. *Did the First Christians Worship Jesus? The New Testament Evidence.* Louisville: Westminster John Knox, 2010.

———. *Jesus and the Spirit: A Study of the Religious and Charismatic Experience of Jesus and the First Christians as Reflected in the New Testament.* London: SCM, 1975.

———. Review of *The Pre-Existent Son: Recovering the Christologies of Matthew, Mark, and Luke*, by Simon Gathercole. *Review of Biblical Literature* 4 (2007). https://www.sblcentral.org/home/bookDetails/5607.

Ehrman, Bart. *How Jesus Became God.* New York: HarperOne, 2014.

Eklund, Matti. "Alien Structure and Themes from Analytic Philosophy." *Giornale di Metafisica* 41 (2019) 195–208.

Elliott, James Keith, ed. *The Apocryphal New Testament: A Collection of Apocryphal Christian Literature in an English Translation.* New York: Oxford University Press, 1993.

Ellis, Brannon. *Calvin, Classical Trinitarianism, and the Aseity of the Son.* New York: Oxford University Press, 2012.

Emery, Gilles. *The Trinity: An Introduction to Catholic Doctrine on the Triune God.* Washington, DC: Catholic University of America Press, 2012.

Emlyn, Thomas. *An Humble Inquiry into the Scripture-Account of Jesus Christ: A Short Argument concerning His Deity and Glory, according to the Gospel.* Edited by Dale Tuggy and Kegan A. Chandler. Nashville: Theophilus, 2021.

Erickson, Millard. *Making Sense of the Trinity: Three Crucial Questions.* Grand Rapids: Baker, 2000.

Euclid. *Euclid's Elements of Geometry.* Translated by Richard Fitzpatrick with Greek text of J. L. Heiberg. Edited by Richard Fitzpatrick. Self-published, 2007.

Eunomius. *The Extant Works.* Translated by Vaggione and Richard Paul. Oxford: Clarendon, 1987.

Fee, Gordon. *Pauline Christology.* Peabody, MA: Hendrickson, 2007.

Finnegan, Sean. "A Unitarian View of the Holy Spirit." https://restitutio.org/2016/07/26/a-unitarian-view-of-the-holy-spirit/.

Forster, Malcolm, and Elliot Sober. "Why Likelihood?" In *The Nature of Scientific Evidence*, edited by M. Taper and S. Lee, 153–65. Chicago: University of Chicago Press, 2004.

Freeman, Charles. *A.D. 381: Heretics, Pagans, and the Dawn of the Monotheistic State.* Woodstock, NY: Overlook, 2009.

Gaston, Thomas. *Dynamic Monarchianism: The Earliest Christology?* 2nd ed. Nashville: Theophilus, 2023.

Gathercole, Simon. *The Preexistent Son: Recovering the Christologies of Matthew, Mark, and Luke.* Grand Rapids: Eerdmans, 2006.

Geach, Peter. *Reference and Generality.* Ithaca, NY: Cornell University Press, 1962.

Gesenius, Wilhelm, and Samuel Tregelles. *Gesenius's Hebrew and Chaldee Lexicon to the Old Testament Scriptures.* London: Bagster, 1859.

Gibbard, Alan. "Contingent Identity." *Journal of Philosophical Logic* 4 (1975) 187–221.

Golitzin, Alexander. "Theophaneia: Forum on the Jewish Roots of Orthodox Spirituality." In *The Theophaneia School: Jewish Roots of Eastern Christian Mysticism*, edited by B. Lourié and A. Orlov, xvii–xx. Piscataway, NJ: Gorgias, 2009.

Gregory of Nazianzus. *Cyril of Jerusalem, Gregory Nazianzen*. In *Nicene and Post-Nicene Fathers*, 2nd series, vol. 7, edited by Philip Schaff and Henry Wallace. Reprint, Peabody, MA: Hendrickson, 1995.

———. *Oration 31 [The Fifth Theological Oration]*. Translated by Lionel Wickham. In *On God and Christ: The Five Theological Orations and Two Letters to Cledonius*. Crestwood, NY: St. Vladimir's Seminary, 2002.

———. *Select Orations*. Translated by Martha Vinson. The Fathers of the Church 107. Washington, DC: Catholic University of America Press, 2003.

Gregory of Nyssa. *Contra Eunomium I: An English Translation with Supporting Studies*. Translated by Stuart Hall. Edited by Miguel Brugarolas. Leiden: Brill, 2018.

———. *Contra Eunomium II: An English Version with Supporting Studies*. Edited by Johannes Zachhuber et al. Translated by Stuart Hall. Leiden: Brill, 2007.

———. *Contra Eunomium III: An English Translation with Commentary and Supporting Studies*. Edited by Johan Leemans and Matthieu Cassin. Translated by Stuart Hall. Leiden: Brill, 2014.

———. *Gregorii Nysseni Opera*. Vol. 1. Edited by Werner Wilhelm Jaeger et al. Leipzig: Weidmannos, 1921.

———. "On Not Three Gods, to Ablabius." In *Nicene and Post-Nicene Fathers*, 2nd series, Vol. 5, edited by Philip Schaff and Henry Wallace. Reprint, Grand Rapids: Eerdmans, 1989.

———. *The Trinitarian Works of Gregory of Nyssa*. Translated by Brian Duvick. For use during the 11th International Colloquium on Gregory of Nyssa. Tübingen/Freiburg, September 17-20, 2008. All rights reserved. Used by permission of the translator.

Griffith, Sidney. *The Church in the Shadow of the Mosque: Christians and Muslims in the World of Islam*. Princeton: Princeton University Press, 2012.

Griffith, Terry. *Keep Yourselves from Idols: A New Look at 1 John*. London: T&T Clark, 2002.

Grillmeier, Aloys. *Christ in Christian Tradition*. Vol. 1, *From the Apostolic Age to Chalcedon (451)*. Translated by John Bowden. 2nd rev. ed. Atlanta: John Knox, 1975.

Hanson, R. P. C. *The Search for the Christian Doctrine of God*. Edinburgh: T&T Clark, 1988.

Harris, Murray J. *Jesus as God: The New Testament Use of* Theos *in Reference to Jesus*. Grand Rapids: Baker, 1992.

Hasker, William. "Can a Latin Trinity Be Social? A Reply to Scott M. Williams." *Faith and Philosophy* 35 (2018) 356–66.

———. "Constitution, Identity, and the Trinity: Rebuttal to Leftow." *Religious Studies* 59 (2023) 165–72.

———. "Constituting the Trinity." *Religious Studies* 57 (2021) 523–31.

———. "Deception and the Trinity: A Rejoinder to Tuggy." *Religious Studies* 471 (2011) 117–20.

———. "God's 'Only Begotten Son': A Reply to R. T. Mullins." *European Journal for the Philosophy of Religion* 9 (2017) 217–37.

———. "Has a Trinitarian God Deceived Us?" In *Philosophical and Theological Essays on the Trinity*, edited by Michael C. Rea and Thomas McCall, 38–51. New York: Oxford University Press, 2009.

———. "How to Think about the Trinity." In *Christian Philosophy of Religion: Essays in Honor of Stephen T. Davis*, edited by C. P. Ruloff, 105–27. Notre Dame: University of Notre Dame Press, 2015.

———. "In Defense of the Trinitarian Processions." *Roczniki Filozoficzne* 71 (2023) 59–71.

———. "Is the Latin Social Trinity Defensible?" *Faith and Philosophy* 38 (2021) 505–13.

———. "'Latin' or 'Conciliar,' but Still Incoherent." *Faith and Philosophy* 38 (2021) 540–45.

———. *Metaphysics and the Tri-Personal God*. Oxford: Oxford University Press, 2013.

———. "Objections to Social Trinitarianism." *Religious Studies* 46 (2010) 421–39.

———. "The One Divine Nature." *TheoLogica* 3 (2019) 69–74.

———. "The Trinity and the New Testament: A Counter-Challenge to Dale Tuggy." *European Journal for Philosophy of Religion* 13 (2021) 179–99.

———. "The Trinity as Social and Constitutional: A Rejoinder to Brian Leftow." *Religious Studies* 57 (2021) 553–62.

———. "Tri-Unity." *The Journal of Religion* 50 (1970) 1–32.

Hawthorne, John. "Identity." In *The Oxford Handbook of Metaphysics*, edited by Michael J. Loux and Dean Zimmerman, 99–130. New York: Oxford University Press, 2003.

Heiser, Michael. "The Divine Council in Late Canonical and Non-canonical Second Temple Jewish Literature." PhD diss., University of Wisconsin-Madison, 2004.

———. "The Jewish Trinity—Dr. Michael Heiser—A Walk through The Old Testament Concerning the Trinity." https://youtu.be/lS22MPVFngs.

Hengel, Martin. *Jesus and Paul*. London: SCM, 1983.

Hodgson, Leonard. *The Doctrine of the Trinity: Croall Lectures, 1942–1943*. London: Nisbet, 1943.

Hooker, M. D. "On Using the Wrong Tool." *Theology* 75 (1972) 562–70.

Horner, George William. *The Statutes of the Apostles*. London: Williams & Norgate, 1904.

Howard-Snyder, Daniel. "Trinity." In *Routledge Online Encyclopedia of Philosophy*. https://www.rep.routledge.com/articles/thematic/trinity/v-2.

———. Review of *Metaphysics and the Tri-Personal God*, by William Hasker. *Faith and Philosophy* 32 (2015) 106–15.

Hughes, Christopher. "Defending the Consistency of the Doctrine of the Trinity." In *Philosophical and Theological Essays on the Trinity*, edited by Thomas McCall and Michael Rea, 293–313. Oxford: Oxford University Press, 2009.

———. *On a Complex Theory of a Simple God: An Investigation in Aquinas' Philosophical Theology*. Ithaca, NY: Cornell University Press, 1989.

Hurtado, Larry. "The Binitarian Shape of Early Christian Worship." In *The Jewish Roots of Christological Monotheism*, edited by Carey C. Newman et al., 187–213. Leiden: Brill, 1999.

———. *God in New Testament Theology*. Nashville: Abingdon, 2010.

———. *Lord Jesus Christ: Devotion to Jesus in Earliest Christianity*. Grand Rapids: Eerdmans, 2003.

———. *One God, One Lord: Early Christian Devotion and Ancient Jewish Monotheism*. 3rd ed. London: Bloomsbury T&T Clark, 2015.

———. "The Origin of the *Nomina Sacra*: A Proposal." *Journal of Biblical Literature* 117 (1998) 655–73.

Irenaeus. *Against the Heresies: Book 1*. Translated by Dominic J. Unger and John J. Dillon. Ancient Christian Writers 55. New York: Newman, 1992.

———. *Against the Heresies: Book 2*. Translated by Dominic J. Unger and John J. Dillon. Ancient Christian Writers 65. New York: Newman, 2012.

———. *On the Apostolic Preaching*. Translated by John Behr. Popular Patristics Series 17. Crestwood, NY: St. Vladimir's Seminary Press, 1997.

Irons, Charles. "A Lexical Defense of the Johannine 'Only Begotten.'" In *Retrieving Eternal Generation*, edited by Fred Sanders and Scott Swain, 98–116. Grand Rapids: Zondervan Academic, 2007.

Irons, Charles, et al. *The Son of God: Three Views of the Identity of Jesus*. Eugene, OR: Wipf and Stock, 2015.

Jenson, Robert W. *Systematic Theology*. Vol. 1, *The Triune God*. New York: Oxford University Press, 1997.

John of Damascus. *On the Orthodox Faith*. Translated by N. Russell. Popular Patristics Series 62. Crestwood, NY: St. Vladimir's Seminary Press, 2022.

———. *Three Treatises on the Divine Images*. Translated by Andrew Louth. Popular Patristics Series 24. Crestwood, NY: St. Vladimir's Seminary Press, 2003.

———. *Writings*. Translated by Frederic Hathaway Chase. The Fathers of the Church 37. Washington, DC: Catholic University of America Press, 2010.

Justin Martyr. *First Apology; The Second Apology; Dialogue with Trypho; Exhortation to the Greeks; Discourse to the Greeks; The Monarchy or The Rule of God*. Translated by Thomas B. Falls. The Fathers of the Church 6. Washington, DC: Catholic University of America Press, 2010.

Kaiser, Walter C., et al. *Three Views on the New Testament Use of the Old Testament*. Grand Rapids: Zondervan, 2008.

Kelly, J. N. D. *Early Christian Doctrines*. Rev. ed. New York: HarperCollins, 1978.

King, Derek. "To Whom Can God Speak? Trinitarian Persons in Gregory of Nyssa and William Hasker." *TheoLogica* 6 (2022) 59–68.

Kirk, J. R. Daniel. *A Man Attested by God: The Human Jesus of the Synoptic Gospels*. Grand Rapids: Eerdmans, 2016.

Kleinknecht, Hermann, et al. "πνευμα, πνευματικος." In *Theological Dictionary of the New Testament*. Vol. VI, *Pe-R*, edited by Gerhard Friedrich, 332–450. Translated by Geoffrey Bromiley. Grand Rapids: Eerdmans, 1968.

Kuhn, Thomas S. *The Structure of Scientific Revolutions*. 4th ed. Chicago: University of Chicago Press, 2012.

Kuschel, Karl-Jospeh. *Born before All Time: The Dispute over Christ's Origin*. Translated by John Bowden. New York: Crossroad, 1992.

Lacugna, Catherine. *God for Us: The Trinity and Christian Life*. Rev. ed. New York: Harper Collins, 1993.

Lactantius. *The Divine Institutes*. In *Lactantius, Venantius, Asterius, Victorinus, Dionysius, Apostolic Teaching and Constitutions, Homily, and Liturgies*, edited by A. Cleveland Coxe et al. The Ante-Nicene Fathers 7. Grand Rapids: Eerdmanns, 1975.

Layman, C. Stephen. *Philosophical Approaches to Atonement, Incarnation, and the Trinity*. Basingstoke, UK: Palgrave Macmillan, 2016.

Liebesman, David. "We Do Not Count by Identity." *Australasian Journal of Philosophy* 93 (2015) 21–42.
Leftow, Brian. "Anti Social Arinitarianism." In *The Trinity: An Interdisciplinary Symposium on the Trinity*, edited by Stephen Davis et al., 203–50. New York: Oxford University Press, 1999.
———. "Can the Constitution be Saved?" *Religious Studies* 59 (2023) 156–64.
———. "Omnipotence." In *The Oxford Handbook of Philosophical Theology*, edited by Michael C. Rea and Thomas P. Flint, 183–86. New York: Oxford University Press, 2009.
———. "The Trinity Is Still Unconstitutional." *Religious Studies* 57 (2021) 532–52.
———. "The Trinity Is Unconstitutional." *Religious Studies* 54 (2018) 359–76.
Letham, Robert. *The Holy Trinity*. Phillipsburg, NJ: P&R, 2004.
Lewis, David. "Many, but Almost One." In *Ontology, Causality, and Mind: Essays on the Philosophy of D. M. Armstrong*, edited by Keith Campbell et al., 23–38. New York: Cambridge University Press, 1993.
———. "Survival and Identity." In *The Identities of Persons*, edited by Amelie Oksenberg Rorty, 17–40. Berkeley: University of California Press, 1976.
Liebesman, David. "We Do Not Count by Identity." *Australasian Journal of Philosophy* 93 (2015) 21–42.
Lloyd, A. C. "Neoplatonic Logic and Aristotelian Logic: I." *Phronesis* 1 (1955) 58–72.
———. "Neoplatonic Logic and Aristotelian Logic: II." *Phronesis* 1 (1956) 146–60.
Lombard, Peter. *The Sentences. Book 1, The Mystery of the Trinity*. Translated by Giulio Silano. Toronto: Pontifical Institute of Mediaeval Studies, 2007.
Loux, Michael, and Thomas Crisp. *Metaphysics: A Contemporary Introduction*. 4th ed. London: Taylor and Francis, 2017.
Martens, Peter. "Origen's Christology in the Context of the Second and Third Centuries." In *The Oxford Handbook of Origen*, edited by Ronald E. Heine and Karen Jo Torjesen, 355–72. Oxford: Oxford University Press, 2022.
Mathison, Keith. *The Shape of Sola Scriptura*. Moscow, ID: Canon, 2001.
Maurin, Anna-Sofia. "Tropes." In *The Stanford Encyclopedia of Philosophy*, edited by Edward N. Zalta. https://plato.stanford.edu/entries/tropes/.
Maximus the Confessor. *The Disputation with Pyrrhus of Our Father among the Saints Maximus the Confessor*. Translated by Joseph Farrell. South Canaan, PA: St. Tikhon's Seminary Press, 1990.
McCall, Thomas. "The Trinity." In *T&T Clark Handbook of Analytic Theology*, edited by James Arcadi and James T. Turner, 181–94. London: T&T Clark, 2022.
———. *Which Trinity? Whose Monotheism?* Grand Rapids: Eerdmans, 2010.
McDonald, Lee Martin. *The Biblical Canon: Its Origin, Transmission, and Authority*. 3rd ed. Peabody, MA: Hendrickson, 2007.
McGrew, Timothy. "The Argument from Silence." *Acta Analytica* 29 (2014) 215–28.
McIntosh, Chad. "The God of the Groups: Social Trinitarianism and Group Agency." *Religious Studies* 52 (2016) 167–86.
———. Review of *God over All* and *God and Abstract Objects*, by William Lane Craig. *Philosophy in Review* 39 (2019) 61–65.
———. Review of *Metaphysics and the Tri-Personal God*, by William Hasker. *Philosophy in Review* 34 (2014) 309–11.

Melito of Sardis. *On Pascha: With the Fragments of Melito and Other Material Related to the Quartodecimans*. Translated by Alistair Charles Stewart. Popular Patristics Series 55. Crestwood, NY. St. Vladimir's Seminary Press, 2020.

Moreland, J. P., and William Lane Craig. *Philosophical Foundations for a Christian Worldview*. Downers Grove, IL: InterVarsity, 2003.

Morgridge, Charles. *The True Believer's Defence, against Charges Preferred by Trinitarians, for Not Believing in the Divinity of Christ, the Deity of Christ, the Trinity, &c.* Reprint, no loca: Lulu.com, 2008.

Morris, Thomas V. *Understanding Identity Statements*. Atlantic Highlands, NJ: Humanities, 1984.

Mosser, Carl. "Fully Social Trinitarianism." In *Philosophical and Theological Essays on the Trinity*, edited by Thomas McCall and Michael C. Rea, 131–50. New York: Oxford University Press, 2009.

Mullins, R. T. *The End of the Timeless God*. New York: Oxford University Press, 2016.

———. "Hasker on the Divine Processions of the Trinitarian Persons." *European Journal for the Philosophy of Religion* 9 (2017) 181–216.

———. "The Trinitarian Processions." *Roczniki Filozoficzne* 71 (2023) 33–57.

Nemes, Steven. *Trinity and Incarnation: A Post-Catholic Theology*. Eugene, OR: Cascade, 2023.

Nersessian, Vrej. *The Bible in the Armenian Tradition*. Los Angeles: Getty, 2001.

Nicomachus of Gerasa. *Introduction to Arithmetic*. Translated by Martin Luther D'Ooge. Edited by D'Ooge et al. Reprint, London: Macmillan, 1926.

Noble, Samuel, and Alexander Treiger, eds. *The Orthodox Church in the Arab World, 700–1700: An Anthology of Sources*. DeKalb, IL: Northern Illinois University Press, 2014.

Novatian. *The Trinity; The Spectacles; Jewish Foods; In Praise of Purity; Letters*. Translated by Russell DeSimone. The Fathers of the Church 67. Washington, DC: The Catholic University of America Press, 1974.

Olson, Roger, and Christopher A. Hall. *The Trinity*. Grand Rapids: Eerdmans, 2002.

Olsson, Birger. "*Deus Semper Maior*? On God in the Johannine Writings." In *New Readings in John*, edited by Johannes Nissen and Sigfred Pedersen, 108–25. Sheffield, UK: Sheffield Academic Press, 1999.

Origen. *Commentary on the Gospel according to John, Books 1–10*. Translated by Ronald E. Heine. Washington, DC: The Catholic University of America Press, 1989.

———. *Contra Celsum*. Translated by Henry Chadwick. New York: Cambridge University Press, 1953.

———. *An Exhortation to Martyrdom, Prayer, First Principles: Book IV, Prologue to the Commentary on the Song of Songs, Homily XXVII on Numbers*. Translated by Rowan A. Greer. New York: Paulist, 1979.

———. *On First Principles*. In *Origen: On First Principles, Volume I*. Translated by John Behr. New York: Oxford University Press, 2017.

———. *Treatise on the Passover and Dialogue with Heraclides and His Fellow Bishops on the Father, the Son, and the Soul*. Translated by Robert J. Daly. New York: Paulist, 1992.

Orlov, Andrei. *The Glory of the Invisible God: Two Powers in Heaven Traditions and Early Christology*. London: Bloomsbury, 2019.

Palamas, Gregory. *Apodictic Treatises on the Procession of the Holy Spirit*. Translated by C. Moody and G. Heers. Jordanville, NY: Uncut Mountain, 2022.

Pawl, Timothy. "Conciliar Trinitarianism, Divine Identity Claims, and Subordination." *TheoLogica* 4 (2020) 1–27.
Pentiuc, Eugen J., ed. *The Oxford Handbook of the Bible in Orthodox Christianity*. New York: Oxford University Press, 2022.
Pharr, Clyde, ed. and trans. *The Theodosian Code and Novels and the Sirmondian Constitution*. Princeton: Princeton University Press, 1952.
Philo. *The Works of Philo: Complete and Unabridged*. Translated by Charles Duke Yonge. Peabody, MA: Hendrickson, 1993.
Pfizenmaier, Thomas C. *The Trinitarian Theology of Dr. Samuel Clarke (1675–1729): Context, Sources, and Controversy*. Leiden: Brill, 1997.
Plantinga, Cornelius. "Gregory of Nyssa and the Social Analogy of the Trinity." *The Thomist* 50 (1986) 325–52.
Plantinga, Alvin. *The Nature of Necessity*. Oxford: Clarendon, 1978.
Platt, Thomas Pell. *The Ethiopic Didascalia; or, the Ethiopic Version of the Apostolical Constitutions, Received in the Church of Abyssinia*. London: Richard Bentley, 1834.
Prestige, G. L. *Fathers and Heretics*. Minneapolis: Fortress, 1940.
———. *God in Patristic Thought*. Reprint, Eugene, OR: Wipf and Stock, 2008.
Pseudo-Dionysius the Areopagite. *Pseudo-Dionysius: The Complete Works*. Translated by Colm Luibhéid and Paul Rorem. Mahwah, NJ: Paulist, 1987.
Rahner, Karl. *The Trinity*. New York: Crossroad, 1997.
Rea, Michael C. "The Trinity." In *The Oxford Handbook of Philosophical Theology*, edited by Michael C. Rea and Thomas P. Flint, 403–29. New York: Oxford University Press, 2009.
Reeves, Michael. *Delighting in the Trinity: An Introduction to the Christian Faith*. Downers Grove, IL: InterVarsity, 2012.
Roberts, Colin H. "*Nomina Sacra*: Origins and Significance." In *Manuscript, Society, and Belief in Early Christian Egypt: The Schweich Lectures 1977*, 26–48. New York: Oxford University Press, 1979.
Russell, Bertrand. *Introduction to Mathematical Philosophy*. Eastford, CT: Martino Fine, 2017.
Salmon, Nathan. "Wholes, Parts, and Numbers." *Philosophical Perspectives* 11 (1997) 1–15.
Sanders, Fred. *The Triune God*. Grand Rapids: Zondervan, 2016.
Schäfer, Peter. *Two Gods in Heaven: Jewish Concepts of God in Antiquity*. Translated by Allison Brown. Princeton: Princeton University Press, 2020.
Schnackenburg, Rudolf. *The Johannine Epistles*. New York: Crossroad, 1992.
Segal, Alan. *Two Powers in Heaven: Early Rabbinic Reports about Christianity and Gnosticism*. Waco, TX: Baylor University Press, 2012.
Sider, Theodore. *Logic for Philosophy*. Oxford: Oxford University Press, 2010.
Sijuwade, Joshua. "Building the Monarchy of the Father." *Religious Studies* 58 (2022) 436–55.
Smith, Dustin. "The Plural of Majesty in the Hebrew Bible: Assessing the Extent of Its Pervasiveness and the Implications for Monotheism." Unitarian Christian Alliance Conference, 2022.
Stead, Christopher. "Why Not Three Gods?" In *Studien Zur Gregor Von Nyssa und Der Christlichen Spätantike*, edited by H. R. Drobner and C. Klock, 149–64. Leiden: Brill, 1990.

Stevenson, J., and W. H. C. Frend, eds. *Creeds, Councils, and Controversies: Documents Illustrating the History of the Church, AD 337–461*. Grand Rapids: Baker Academic, 2012.

Swinburne, Richard. "Could There Be More Than One God?" *Faith and Philosophy* 5 (1988) 225–41.

———. "The Social Theory of the Trinity." *Religious Studies* 54 (2018) 419–37.

———. "The Trinity." In *Philosophical and Theological Essays on the Trinity*, edited by Thomas McCall and Michael C. Rea, 19–37. Oxford: Oxford University Press, 2009.

Tanner, Norman, ed. *Decrees of the Ecumenical Councils*. 2 vols. Washington, DC: Georgetown University Press, 1990.

Tertullian. *Against Marcion*. In *The Ante-Nicene Fathers, Volume 3*, edited by Alexander Roberts et al., translated by Peter Holmes. Edinburgh: T&T Clark, 1885.

———. *Against Praxeas*. Translated A. Souter. London: SPCK, 1920.

———. *On Modesty* [*De Puticitia*]. In *The Ante-Nicene Fathers, Volume 4: Fathers of the Third Century*, edited by Alexander Roberts et al., translated by S. Thelwall, 74–101. Edinburgh: T&T Clark, 1885.

Theon of Smyrna. *Mathematics Useful for Understanding Plato*. Edited by Christos Toulis et al. Translated by Robert Lawlor and Deborah Lawlor. Mecosta, MI: Wizards Bookshelf, 1979.

Theophilus of Antioch. *To Autolycus*. In *Theophilus of Antioch: Ad Autolycum*. Translated by Robert M. Grant. Oxford: Clarendon, 1970.

Treiger, Samuel, and Alexander Treiger, eds. *The Orthodox Church in the Arab World, 700–1700: An Anthology of Sources*. DeKalb, IL: Northern Illinois University Press, 2014.

Tuggy, Dale. "Antiunitarian Arguments from Divine Perfection." *Journal of Analytic Theology* 9 (2021) 262–90.

———. "Constitution Trinitarianism: An Appraisal." *Philosophy and Theology* 25 (2013) 129–62.

———. "Craig's Contradictory Christ." *TheoLogica* 7 (2023) 1–28.

———. "Divine Deception, Identity, and Social Trinitarianism." *Religious Studies* 40 (2004) 269–87.

———. "Divine Deception and Monotheism." *Journal of Analytic Theology* 2 (2014) 186–209.

———. "Divine Deception and Monotheism: A Reply to Hasker." *Religious Studies* 47 (2011) 109–15.

———. "God and His Son: The Logic of the New Testament." *Trinities* (blog), June 4, 2012. https://trinities.org/blog/god-and-his-son-the-logic-of-the-new-testament/.

———. "Hasker's Quests for a Viable Social Theory." *Faith and Philosophy* 30 (2013) 171–87.

———. "Hasker's Tri-Personal God vs. New Testament Theology." *European Journal for Philosophy of Religion* 13 (2021) 153–77.

———. "Jesus as an Exemplar of Faith in the New Testament." *International Journal for Philosophy of Religion* 81 (2017) 171–91.

———. "Jesus's Argument in John 10." *Trinities* (blog), November 14, 2014. http://trinities.org/blog/jesuss-argument-in-john-10/.

———. "Jude 4, John 17:1–3, and 'Only' Arguments." *Trinities* (blog), July 23, 2023. https://trinities.org/blog/jude-4-john-171-3-and-only-arguments/
———. "Jude 5: Did Jesus Deliver the People out of Egypt?" *Trinities* (blog), May 29, 2023. https://trinities.org/blog/jude-5-did-jesus-deliver-the-people-out-of-egypt/.
———. "Metaphysics and Logic of the Trinity." In *The Oxford Handbook of Topics in Philosophy*, edited by Sandy Goldberg et al. New York: Oxford University Press, 2016. https://academic.oup.com/edited-volume/42642/chapter/358146326.
———. *Monotheism, History, and Heresy: Essays on Biblical Monotheism and the Gospel*. Nashville: Theophilus, 2023.
———. "On Bauckham's Bargain." *Theology Today* 70 (2013) 128–43.
———. "On Counting Gods." *TheoLogica* 1 (2017) 188–213.
———. "Podcast 258—Who Is the One Creator?—Part 1." *Trinities* (blog), April 8, 2019. https://trinities.org/blog/podcast-258-who-is-the-one-creator-part-1/.
———. "Podcast 259—Who Is the One Creator?—Part 2." *Trinities* (blog), April 15, 2019. https://trinities.org/blog/podcast-259-who-is-the-one-creator-part-2/.
———. "Tertullian the Unitarian." *European Journal for Philosophy of Religion* 8 (2016) 179–99.
———. "Trinity." In *The Stanford Encyclopedia of Philosophy*, edited by Edward N. Zalta. https://plato.stanford.edu/archives/win2021/entries/trinity/.
———. "The Unfinished Business of the Reformation." In *Herausforderungen und Modifikationen des Klassischen Theismus, Band 1: Trinität*, edited by Thomas Marschler and Thomas Schärtl, 199–227. Münster: Aschendorff, 2019.
———. *What Is the Trinity? Thinking about the Father, Son, and Holy Spirit*. Createspace, 2017.
———. "What John 1 Meant." Unitarian Christian Alliance Conference, 2021.
———. "When and How in the History of Theology Did the Triune God Replace the Father as the Only True God?" *TheoLogica* 4 (2020) 27–51.
Tuggy, Dale, and Chris Date. *Is Jesus Human and Not Divine? A Debate*. Apollo, PA: Aeropagus, 2020.
Unger, Peter. "The Problem of the Many." *Midwest Studies in Philosophy* 5 (1980) 411–68.
van Inwagen, Peter. "The Doctrine of Arbitrary Undetached Parts." *Pacific Philosophical Quarterly* 62 (1981) 123–37.
———. "Three Persons in One Being: On Attempts to Show that the Doctrine of the Trinity Is Self-Contradictory." In *The Trinity: Studies in Philosophy and Religion*, edited by Melville Stewart, 83–97. Dordrecht: Springer, 2003.
Wainwright, Arthur. *The Trinity in the New Testament*. London: SPCK, 1962.
Waldron, Sam. "The Scriptural Support for the Historical Doctrine of the Eternal Generation of the Son in Light of Current Evangelical Objections." Unpublished manuscript.
Wallace, Daniel. *Granville Sharp's Canon and Its Kin*. Bern: Peter Lang, 2008.
Wallace, Robert. *A Plain Statement and Scriptural Defence of the Leading Doctrines of Unitarianism*. Chesterfield, UK: Woodhead et al., 1819.
Walton, John H. *Old Testament Theology for Christians: From Ancient Context to Enduring Belief*. Downers Grove, IL: InterVarsity, 2017.
Ware, Timothy. *The Orthodox Church*. New ed. London: Penguin, 1997.
Warfield, B. B. "Trinity." In *International Standard Bible Encyclopedia*, edited by James Orr, 5:3012–22. Chicago: Howard-Severance, 1915.

Wasserman, Tommy. *The Epistle of Jude: Its Text and Transmission*. Stockholm: Almqvist and Wiksell International, 2006.

White, James. "Conversation: James R. White." *Faith and Practice* 1 (2016) 97–98.

Widdicombe, Peter. *The Fatherhood of God from Origen to Athanasius*. Oxford: Clarendon, 1994.

Wierenga, Edward. "Trinity and Polytheism." *Faith and Philosophy* 21 (2004) 281–94.

Williams, C. F. J. "Neither Confounding the Persons nor Dividing the Substance." In *Reason and the Christian Religion: Essays in Honour of Richard Swinburne*, edited by Alan G. Padgett, 227–43. Oxford: Clarendon, 1994.

Williams, George Huntston. *The Radical Reformation*. 3rd ed. Kirksville, MO: Truman State University Press, 1995.

Williams, Rowan. *Arius: Heresy and Tradition*. Rev. ed. Grand Rapids: Eerdmans, 2001.

Williams, Scott. "In Defence of a Latin Social Trinity." *Faith and Philosophy* 31 (2020) 96–117.

———. "Discovery of the Sixth Ecumenical Council's Trinitarian Theology: Historical, Ecclesial, and Theological Implications." *Journal of Analytic Theology* 10 (2022) 332–62.

———. "Gregory of Nyssa, Conciliar Trinitarianism, and the Latin (or Conciliar) Social Trinity: A Reply to William Hasker." *Faith and Philosophy* 38 (2021) 356–66.

———. "Indexicals and the Trinity: Two Non-Social Models." *Journal of Analytic Theology* 1 (2013) 74–94.

———. "Unity of Action in a Latin Social Model of the Trinity." *Faith and Philosophy* 34 (2017) 321–46.

Wilson, John. *Scripture Proofs and Scriptural Illustrations of Unitarianism*. 3rd ed. Reprint. Lulu.com, 2007.

———. *Unitarian Principles Confirmed by Trinitarian Testimonies; Being Selections from the Works of Eminent Theologians Belonging to Orthodox Churches. With Introductory and Occasional Remarks*. 13th ed. Boston: American Unitarian Association, 1890.

Witherington, Ben, III. *Sola Scriptura: The Story of the Final Authority*. Waco, TX: Baylor University Press, 2023.

Wright, Clair Louise. "On Whether or How Far We Can Know God: A Reflection on Epistemology, Language, and Trinity in the *Five Theological Orations* of Gregory of Nazianzus." In *Essays on the Trinity*, edited by Lincoln Harvey, 108–24. Eugene, OR: Cascade, 2018.

Wykstra, Stephen J. "Rowe's Noseeum Arguments from Evil." In *The Evidential Argument from Evil*, edited by Daniel Howard-Snyder, 126–50. Bloomington, IN: Indiana University Press, 1996.

General Index

Agennētos (unbegotten), 20, 67, 119–20, 181, 246
Al-Ghazali, 76
Ambrose of Milan, 256n21
Analogy, 16, 24, 69, 79n77, 118n6, 120n13, 121n16, 122, 149, 155, 160, 177, 202, 233, 242, 252
Analogical predication, 60n15, 149n6, 155, 156n25, 180n11
Angel(s), 8, 28n2, 31, 34–36, 47, 58, 68n42, 70n51, 93, 106, 162, 164, 170n1, 176–77, 185–86, 189, 216, 235, 237
Arabic formula, 79n76, 82
Aristotle, 63, 75–77, 81n82, 128, 252
Arianism (Arian), 11, 17, 20, 56–57, 58n9, 70, 78n72, 84, 88n6, 115–16, 119, 123, 130, 151, 155–56, 180, 183, 187, 190, 196–97, 203, 216, 220n25, 230, 231, 258, 266n30
Arius, 104, 116, 230
Arnobius, 187n27
Aseity, 83, 120, 134, 140n36, 140n37, 150ff, 181, 187, 244–45
Atonement, 203n5
Aquinas, 21, 65n31, 77, 79, 121, 131n26
Athanasius, 65n31, 120n10, 197, 230
Athenagoras, 187n27
Augustine, 12n14, 16, 18, 21, 23, 65n31, 67, 70, 79, 125, 170, 185, 230

Basil of Caesarea, 56, 65, 68–70, 74, 120, 138, 154n23, 161, 183n1, 186–87, 197, 230, 251, 253, 254
Biddle, John, 106n69, 183, 253
Binitarianism, 7, 9, 16, 28, 58, 71–72, 74, 84–85, 176, 180, 204n7, 205n9
See also Two Powers in Heaven
Boethius, 76, 79

Calvin, John, 65n31, 67
Cappadocian Fathers, 56, 57, 65n31, 73, 75n61, 79, 82n86, 84, 180, 187
Channing, William, 88n6, 92
Christie, William, 88n6
Clarke, Samuel, 11, 106n66, 110, 183
Confirmation (probability), 88–89, 195ff, 200–203, 211–12
Confession(s)
  Baptist Confession of Faith, 65n31
  Thomas's confession, 39, 42, 45, 240n8
  Westminster Confession of Faith, 65n31
Council(s)
  of Constantinople (381), 3, 13, 56, 87, 97, 104, 109, 139, 140, 187, 190, 220n28, 230, 250
  of Chalcedon, 13, 186n20

281

GENERAL INDEX

Council(s) (*continued*)
  Ecumenical, 52, 56–57, 65n31, 112, 129, 176, 183, 261
  of Nicea (325), 139–40, 266
  Fifth Ecumenical, 129n19
  Sixth Ecumenical, 129n19
  Seventh Ecumenical, 70
Creed(s)
  Apostle's, 67, 74
  Athanasian, 52, 65n31, 139n34
  Conciliar, 52, 147, 153, 250
  Nicene (325), 11, 18n18, 66, 139–40, 175, 230, 266
  Nicene-Constantinopolitan (381), 3, 11, 18n18, 56, 65n31, 66, 74, 97n32, 104, 136, 139, 156–57, 175, 187, 199, 230, 231, 250, 261, 266n30
Cyril of Alexandria, 256

Emlyn, Thomas, 102n49, 183, 185n11, 253
Eternal generation (and procession), 15, 19ff, 41, 65n31, 66, 67n38, 81, 84, 107, 110, 116, 118ff, 123, 125n10, 127n15, 129–32, 134, 136–37, 146, 153, 159, 171, 175, 177–78, 180, 182, 184, 185n17, 187, 191, 225ff, 241, 245
Euclid, 76
Eunomius, 20, 116, 119, 130n21, 155–56, 187, 216, 230, 256

Father, God the, 29,
  as alone God, 17–18, 30n3, 43–45, 61, 65ff, 74, 84, 88, 90–92, 95, 103, 108, 110–12, 115, 123, 134–36, 139, 151–52, 155–56, 158, 161, 166, 170–71, 178ff, 183ff, 196, 203ff, 211, 212n5, 229, 251, 253, 259ff
  monarchy of, 10, 18, 20, 55, 62, 65ff, 74–75, 80, 83–84, 101n47, 115, 121n16, 123, 151–52, 155, 158n1, 170–71, 176–78, 180, 184, 211, 247, 250, 261
Filioque, 19n23, 125n10, 130ff

Gregoras, Nicephorus, 62n19
Gregory of Nyssa, 12n14, 16, 19, 21, 56, 63, 66, 68, 78n70, 81n84, 85n93, 124–25, 154n23, 172, 183, 216, 227–28, 230, 248, 253ff, 257n23
Gregory of Nazianzus, 18, 62n21, 66–67, 79–80, 81n84, 106, 130n21, 171, 183n1, 219n18, 230

Hilary of Poitiers, 243n13
Holy Spirit,
  as (non)person, 13ff, 47ff, 86, 97, 105–6, 109, 117, 165, 208n12
Homoousios, 11, 20, 65, 78n72, 119, 129, 181, 187
Hypostasis (hypostatic) 35, 47, 59, 73, 75, 79–80, 81n82, 83n91, 84–85, 117, 123ff, 154n22, 154n23, 181, 189, 215, 248, 255

Ibn Rushd (Averroes), 76
Identity
  concept of, 23–25, 52–53, 121n14, 121n15, 136n12, 188, 203, 255n16, 260
  counting by identity vs. counting by division, 75ff, 149n4, 151–52, 181, 188–89, 251, 254, 255n16, 260
  'is' of identity vs. 'is' of predication, 45, 61, 148, 179–80, 238, 243
  relative identity, 103n51, 190
  sameness without identity, 121n16, 181, 190, 243
Idolatry, 4–5, 7, 207, 236, 241
Ignatius, 119n9
Indexicals, 47–48, 117, 126, 141, 234, 256

GENERAL INDEX 283

Inseparable operations, 80ff, 118, 123ff, 152n13, 171–72, 181–82, 227, 241, 255–57
Irenaeus, 68, 187n27

Jehovah's Witnesses, 11, 231
Jesus
   As God's son, 30, 99–100
   as *kyrios*, 5–6, 9, 30ff, 42, 98–99, 162–63, 206, 217–18, 238ff
   as *Logos* (see *Logos*)
   as messiah (the Christ), 5, 9, 30n4, 72, 83, 93, 98–101, 107, 191, 205–6, 216–18
   as mere man (see also Socinianism), 10, 99, 100ff, 116, 163, 165, 196–97, 203n5, 206–7, 220n25, 229–31, 236–37, 241, 246
   as only begotten (see *Monogenēs*)
   prayer to, 7, 28n2
   as *theos*, 9, 32ff, 69, 90, 93, 119, 158, 159n4, 163, 165, 204n6, 205, 236ff, 262
   as the theophany figure (see Theophanies)
   pre-existence of, 6, 9, 10, 12–13, 26, 28n2, 38n22, 39, 41, 83, 88n6, 104, 115, 117, 164–65, 177, 186, 203, 207, 208n11, 229, 238, 240, 260, 262
   worship of (see Worship)
   as Yahweh, 6, 9, 31, 36, 41–42, 69–70, 98–99, 162, 206, 217–18, 238–39
John of Damascus, 55–56, 65n31, 66–68, 73, 76, 79, 82, 84, 123–24, 171, 229
John Philoponus, 79
Justin Martyr, 68, 104, 139, 186, 187n27

Lactantius, 187n27
Latin trinitarianism, xiii, 14
Logos, 21, 39–40, 55, 101n47, 104–5, 116, 118, 158n1, 165–66, 180, 186–87, 197, 207n11, 226, 237, 238n5, 260, 261n12, 263
Lombard, Peter, 260n8
Love, inter-Trinitarian, 14–15, 20, 118n6, 119
Luther, Martin, 65n31, 219n17, 220

Manuscript(s), 40, 72n55, 153n18, 217ff, 239n7, 265
Masoretic text, 153n18
Material constitution, 23ff, 118, 121–22, 127, 135, 140, 146, 190, 232–33
Maximus the Confessor, 65n31, 130n19
Melito of Sardis, 68
Modalism, 57, 73, 74n60, 110, 115–16, 139, 149n3, 158–59, 165, 189, 236, 256, 261
Monarchianism, 115–16, 177–78 (see also Father, Monarchy of)
Monogenēs (only begotten), 19, 21, 40–42, 67, 72, 119, 125n10, 137, 156, 172, 175, 178n9, 207, 214, 240n8
Monolatry, 205, 235n1, 236, 240
Monotheism, 7, 16–17, 34, 46, 62, 74, 83, 92–93, 117–18, 123–24, 138, 140, 159n4, 165, 174, 177, 180, 184, 186–87, 191, 198, 204–6, 229, 231–32, 235n1, 240
Morgridge, Charles, 105n62, 106n64
Mormon scripture, 213–14

Nature (*ousia*), 73, 77, 128ff, 138, 154–55, 159, 255
   divine nature as abstract, 21–22, 120
   divine nature as concrete, 21ff, 26, 53–54, 117, 120ff, 128, 134, 146, 180–81, 228, 243–44, 252
Newton, Isaac, 11
New Testament canon, 87, 198, 219–20, 265–66
Nicomachus of Gerasa, 76

Noetus, 116
Novatian, 139, 185n10, 186n26, 187n27
Nomina sacra, 217ff, 265

Origen, 11, 110, 133, 136, 139, 158–59, 185n10, 186, 187n27, 197, 236, 263
Overdetermination, 160, 241–42

Palamas, Gregory, 62n19, 62n21
Parts (mereology), 22, 25, 27, 76–77, 84, 134, 135, 140–41, 149, 150ff, 180n11, 182, 188, 232, 241, 243–45
Paul of Samosota, 10
Perichoresis, 18–19, 26, 118–19, 134, 243n13
Persons, nature of, 3n1, 14–16, 24–26, 53, 75n61, 117, 130n19, 133, 160, 171–73, 181–82, 228, 242, 254–55
   divine persons as modes, 15, 110, 158
   divine persons as life-streams, 26–27, 54, 120, 122, 135
   divine persons as a group, 14, 17, 30n3, 117–18, 133–34
Personification, 27, 96–97, 105, 116, 151, 165, 176, 237–38
Philo, 62n18, 207n11, 237
Plato, Platonism, 39, 63, 165, 237
Polytheism, 62, 83, 93, 140, 186–87, 191, 198, 232
Praxeas, 116
Processions, divine (see Eternal generation)
Proto-Trinitarianism, 11, 58n9, 84, 116, 133, 176, 178
Pseudo-Dionysius, 65n31, 130n22

Richard of St. Victor, 20
Röell, Alexander, 65n31

Sabellius, 116
Second Temple Judaism, 58–59, 70–71, 74, 85, 159n2, 177, 180, 216

Septuagint (LXX), 31, 34, 39, 41n26, 42, 63n24, 153
Severus of Antioch, 79
Sharp's Rule, 36ff, 44, 46
Simplicity, divine, 23–25, 45, 121, 127n14, 131n26, 241
Sirach, 165n25, 237n4
Social trinitarianism, 15–16, 20, 24, 75n61, 81, 83, 177, 119, 120n13, 122, 130n19, 131n26, 137, 146, 155ff, 160, 170–72, 177, 242, 245, 248
Socinius, Socianism, 88n6, 116, 200, 203, 207–8, 230, 236, 241, 246
Sola scriptura, 157, 220, 246n16, 253
Soul (immaterial substance), 24, 26, 30n3, 47, 53, 54n50, 117–18, 120–21, 128, 135, 146, 159–60, 233, 241, 242n10, 243n13, 245, 259n5, 259n6
Subordination, subordinationism, 7n5, 11, 17, 20, 35–36, 48, 84, 110, 116, 120, 123, 133–34, 139, 153, 155, 158, 159n3, 171, 178, 184, 196–97, 206, 230–31, 236, 245, 265

Tertullian, 11, 90n9, 104–5, 133, 139, 185n10, 186n26, 187n27, 197, 243n13
Theon of Smyrna, 76
Theophanies, 58–59, 64, 68ff, 83–84, 151, 170, 176–78, 185, 212ff, 245, 247–48
Theophilus of Antioch, 90n9
Triadic passages, 14, 18, 39, 48, 50–51, 106ff, 117, 208
Tritheism, 59, 75, 78, 80, 93, 120, 125, 137–38, 140, 148ff, 161, 170, 179–80, 182, 184, 187–88, 198, 210, 232, 242ff
Trope(s), 26, 54n50, 77ff, 84, 120, 126ff, 228
Two Powers in Heaven (see also Binitarianism), 58, 176–77, 248

Unity, divine, 16, 18–19, 22–23, 26, 62n20, 67, 118n6, 234, 241, 243n13
Unitarianism, 10–11, 29, 46, 57, 59–60, 63n25, 83, 86ff, 115–16, 133–34, 151, 158, 161, 178, 182ff, 195ff, 209, 211–12, 216ff, 229ff, 236, 243, 247ff, 253, 259ff
Universals, 76ff, 189–90

Warfield, B. B., 65n31, 110n79
Wilson, John, 91n14, 102n49, 106n69, 109n77
Wisdom (see Personification)
Worship, 4–10, 13, 16, 28n2, 31, 36, 80, 92, 94, 105, 141, 176–77, 204n7, 205–7, 212, 234, 236–37, 240–41, 246, 263n19, 265

Scripture Index

OLD TESTAMENT

Genesis

1:1	39, 208n11
1:26	220n25
1:27	185n16
2:24	76n64
13:16	254
16:7–14	58n7
17:5	260
22:11–12	58n7
24:12	218n15
31:11–13	58n7
31:19	184n9
48:16	108n73

Exodus

3:14	68n42
7:1	73, 184n9
15:11	184n9
23:13	108n73
24:9–11	212
33:11	58
33:18–23	58, 212–13

Numbers

25:2	184n9

Deuteronomy

4:35	74
6:4	92
10:17	184n9
18:20	108n73
32:6	29

Judges

13:21–23	58n7

1 Samuel

7:14	29

1 Chronicles

17:8	108n73

Job

33:4	59, 105n59

Psalms

2:7	29
24:1	6
33:6–9	59, 185n16
34:23	42
35:23	42
44:7	34
45:6–7	34, 162n13, 164, 184n9, 237
68:5	29
77:13	62
82:6–7	74, 184n9
89:26	29
95:5	63n24

96:5	63n24
97:7	31
102:16	70n48
102:25–27	31
104:30	59
109:1	218n15
109:3	153
110:1	7n5, 92, 98, 218n15
110:3	153
110:5–6	210

Proverbs

8	237
22:28	157

Isaiah

4:18	47
6:1	41, 212
7:14	162n13
8:8, 10	162n13
29:16	96
41:21–24	48
43–45	31, 59n11, 84, 182
43:11	59, 212
44:24	185n16
45:12	185n16
45:18	103
45:21	59, 212
45:23	6, 31
46:9	103
61:1	47, 105n59
63:16	29
64:6–8	29

Jeremiah

3:19–20	29
9:23–24	6
Jer 10:11	74
23:16–18, 22	55

Ezekiel

28:9	61–62
37:16–17	76n64

Hosea

4:15	96
11:1	162n13

Joel

2:32	6, 31, 239

Malachi

2:10	29

∽

NEW TESTAMENT

Matthew

1:1	101n42, 104
1:1–17	137, 163
1:18	105
1:18–25	104, 137
1:21–23	119, 137, 162n13
1:25	101, 137
2:15	98, 162n13
3:11	105n59
3:16	105n59
3:17	105
4:2–3	102n49
4:7	98
5:45, 48	108
6:6	108
6:8–15	108
6:9	29
6:24	98
7:29	5
6:30–33	108
8:8	98
8:25	98
8:27	100n38
9:8	102n48, 162n12
10:40–41	101n39
11:27	106n67, 214
12:18	101n40
12:28	102n48
15:13	108
15:31	108

Matthew (continued)

15:34	101
16:15–17	99, 105, 108
18:21	98
19:5	76n64
21:46	101n39
22:36–40	14
22:42–44	98n34
24:36	102n49, 106
26:64	98n34
27:46	103n52, 173
27:54	105
27:50	101, 102n49
27:60	101
27:63	98
28:6	101
28:18	102n48, 108
28:19	14, 50, 90, 107, 108

Mark

1:11	173
1:35	101
4:38	101
5:9	101
5:30–32	102n49
6:2	100n38
6:4	101n39
6:15	101
6:46	101
8:27	101
8:29	99
9:7	173
9:21	102n49
10:6	185n16
10:8	76n64
10:18	102n49
10:37–40	102n49
12:28–34	92
12:37	102n49
13:19	185n16
13:32	163, 102n49
14:32	101
14:36	163
14:62–64	93n22
14:67	100n38
15:34	103n52, 173

Luke

1:26–38	104
1:30–37	105n62, 119, 137
1:31	101
1:42	101
1:32–34	47, 98, 102n48, 163
1:47	59, 212
2:7	101
2:11	59, 212
2:21	101
2:41–52	101
3:21	47, 101
4:1–13	163
4:18	47
4:18–21	162n12
4:24	101n39
5:16	101
6:12	101
6:22	108n73
8:42–48	101
6:35–36	92
9:18	101
9:20	99
10:16	102n48
10:21–22	92, 214
16:6	101n43
20:42–44	98n34
22:8	101
23:2–6	100n38
23:13	100n38
23:41	100n38
23:47	100n38
23:38	98
23:46	102n49
24:19	101n39, 101n43
24:34	98

John

1:1ff	9, 21, 32, 38ff, 41, 44, 59, 104, 119, 150, 165–166, 198, 204n6, 207, 207n11, 226, 229, 237
1:4	44
1:9	44

SCRIPTURE INDEX

1:10–11	39	10:22–39	263
1:14	39, 41, 119, 198, 238	10:29	102n49
		10:30	240n8
1:15–18	112	10:30–39	93n24
1:17	39	10:33	205, 240n8
1:18	9, 32, 40ff, 44, 72, 119, 205, 207, 214	10:35	184n9
		10:34–36	159n2, 159n4, 163
1:30	100n38	12:41	41, 206, 239
1:34	119	12:44–45	214
1:45	101n45	14–16	173
3:2	102n48	14:7–9	72, 215
3:6	41	14:10	102n48
3:8	105n59	14:10–12	162n12
3:16	21	14:15–31	105n58
3:18	41	14:16–17	48, 105n60, 173
3:35	102n48	14:21	173
4:19	101n39	14:28	48, 102n49, 119, 207
4:29	100n38		
4:34	101	14:31	101
4:44	101n39	15:1	44
5:11–12	100n38	15:10	101, 173
5:18	102n48, 198, 205, 240, 263	15:16–17	14
		15:26	48, 173
5:19–29	102n49, 137, 163	16:4–7	48
5:20	102n48	16:8	48
5:22	210	16:13–15	12, 48, 173, 231
5:22–23	102n48	16:23	173
5:23	240n8	16:27	173
5:21–27	162n12	16:30	102n48
5:26	21, 119, 136, 226	17	101, 173
5:30	102n49	17:1–3	91, 106
5:36	162n12	17:3	12, 44, 45n32, 52, 117, 229, 238
5:37	214		
5:43–44	91	17:5	26, 104, 225, 238
6:32	44	17:6	198
6:38	101	17:8	102n48
6:42	101n45	17:10	173
6:44–46	58, 95, 214	17:14	102n48
6:52	100n38	17:15	173
7:16	102n48	17:21	173
7:25, 27	100n38	17:24	208n11, 238
7:35	100n38	17:25	173
7:37–39	105n59	18:5, 7	101n43
8:28	102n48	18	263
8:40	100n38	19:1–22	263
8:54	92	19:7	205, 240n8
8:58	198, 240n8,	19:21	100n38
9:17	101n39	19:30	102n49

John (*continued*)

20:17	103n52, 163
20:24	44
20:28	9, 32, 38n22, 39, 42ff, 45, 204n6
20:30–31	99, 206

Acts

1:2	106n66
1:5	106n66
1:16	47
1:21	98
2:4	106n66
2:17–18	106n66
2:22–36	100n38, 101, 102n48
2:30	101n42
2:32–35	92, 95, 98n34, 105n60, 107, 162n12
2:36	98, 162n12
3:13	91, 92n21, 101n40
3:22–23	101n39
4:8	106n66
4:11	96
4:24–27	92n21, 98, 101n40, 185n16
5:2–4	13, 48, 94, 106n66
5:9	48
5:28	92n21, 100n38
5:30	102n49
5:32	48
6:5	106n66
6:10	48
7:37	101n39
7:51	48
7:53	185
7:55–56	92, 105n65
8:2	106n66
8:29	47
9:27	98
10:19	47
10:37–38	101n43, 102n48
10:45	105n60
11:12	47
13:2	47
13:4	48
13:38	100n38
14:15	185n16
15:8	48
16:6–7	48, 106n66
17:24–31	185n16
17:31	100n38, 102n48, 162n12
18:25	98
20:23	48
20:28	32n7, 48
24:14–15	92n21
28:25	47

Romans

1:3	101n42, 104
1:20	185n16
1:25	33
5:6–10	102n49, 163
5:12–19	100n38, 186
6:3	108
8:14	48
8:9–11	49–50, 105n60
8:26–27	13, 49, 208n12
8:34	98n34
9:5	9, 32ff, 204n6, 207
10:9	31, 218n15, 238
10:11–13	6, 31, 33
11:34–36	33
14:9	33
15:6	103n52
15:30	50–51

1 Corinthians

1:3	102n48
1:31	6
2:10–11	49, 208n12
3:16	94
8:6	91, 152
10:2	108
10:4	186n21
10:21	5
10:26	6
11:3	163
12:3	218n15
12:4–6	50
15:20	100n38

15:24–28	98n34, 102n48, 163	Colossians	
15:47	100n38	1:15	70, 73, 151, 178, 215, 226
16:22	7	1:16–17	33, 59, 104, 229, 237
		1:19	240
2 Corinthians		2:9	149–150, 240, 244
1:21–22	50	3:1	98n34
1:3	33, 103n52, 162	3:16–17	94
4:4	72, 151, 159n4, 184n9, 215		
6:18	103n50	**1 Thessalonians**	
10:17	6	3:7	38
11:31	103n52		
13:13	107n72	**2 Thessalonians**	
13:14	50	2:13	50
Galatians		**1 Timothy**	
2:20	50	1:17	215
3:13	93	2:5	100n38
3:19	185	4:1	106n66
4:4	119	4:3–4	185n16
4:6	48, 51	5:21	106, 108
		6:15–16	215
Ephesians		**2 Timothy**	
1:3	33, 103n52		
1:4	208n11	1:2–3	92
1:13	105n59	1:9	207n11
1:17	103n52, 162	2:8	102n42
1:20–23	33, 98n34, 101		
2:18	51	**Titus**	
2:20	96	1:2–3	208n11
3:5	38	1:3	59, 212
3:9	185n16	1:4	59, 212
4:1–6	107	2:13	9, 32, 36ff, 204n6
4:30	106n66		
5:20	94	**Hebrews**	
5:31	76n64	1	163, 206
		2	206
Philippians		1:2	9, 12, 17, 21, 35, 36, 102n48, 164, 186, 225, 229
2:5–11	6, 31, 33, 35, 94, 102n49, 162n12, 206, 218n15, 229, 239–40	1:1–3	21, 35, 73, 92n21, 98n34, 104, 164, 215, 226, 229
3:19	159n4		

Hebrews (continued)

1:4-7	31, 35, 36, 119, 164
1:5-14	34, 186
1:8-9	32, 34ff, 69, 70n48, 103n52, 162n13, 164, 184n9, 204n6, 206, 237
1:10-12	31ff, 69-70, 237
1:13	98n34
2:2	185
2:4	102n48
2:9	35
2:10-18	101
2:17	164
2:18	102n49
2:14	35
3:2	36
3:7-11	36
3:15	36
4:15	102n49
5:5	36
5:8	102n49
5:10	36
9:14	208
10:5	36
10:12-13	98n34
10:29	14
11:3	185n16
12:2	36, 98n34, 164
13:8	104
13:15	94
13:20	36

James

1:13	102n49
3:8-9	95

1 Peter

1:2	51
1:3	33, 103n52
1:11	105n60
1:20	208n11
2:6	96

2 Peter

1:1	9, 32, 37ff, 204n6
1:10-11	38
2:20	38
3:2	38
3:18	38

1 John

1:1-3	44, 106
2:3	44
2:8	44
2:22	43
4:8	14
4:9	41
4:12	215
4:20	215
5:5-6	43
5:11-12	44
5:13	44
5:20	32n6, 32n7, 42ff, 52-53, 206, 238, 241
5:21	45, 241

2 John

1:7	43
1:9	95

Jude

3	112, 135, 191
4	265n29
5	186n21, 206, 239
20-21	51
25	207n11

Revelation

1:1	102n48
1:5-6	103n52
1:8	103n50
1:9	38
1:18	102n49
2:10	7
2:26-27	102n48
3:2	103n52
3:6	106n66

3:12	103n52	11:17	103n50
3:14	44	13:4	8
4	105n63	14:7	185n16
4:8	103n50	14:9–11	8
4:11	185n16	15:3	103n50
5	105n63, 162n12	16:7	103n50
5:6	102n49	16:14	103n50
5:9	94	19:6	103n50
5:9–14	159n4	19:10	8
5:10	103n52	20:6	106
5:11–13	8	21:22	103n50
9:2–21	8	21:23	106
9:13	119	22:8–9	8
10:6	185n16	22:16	101n42, 163

www.ingramcontent.com/pod-product-compliance
Lightning Source LLC
Chambersburg PA
CBHW032051220426
43664CB00008B/960